H
O
Wh, ECONOMISTS DISAGREE

W9-AUB-265

DATE DUE	
OCT 1 3 1998	

GAYLORD   PRINTED IN U.S.A.

THE RICHARD STOCKTON COLLEGE
OF NEW JERSEY LIBRARY
POMONA, NEW JERSEY 08240

WHY ECONOMISTS DISAGREE

THE RICHARD STOCKTON COLLEGE
OF NEW JERSEY LIBRARY
POMONA, NEW JERSEY 08240

SUNY Series, Diversity in Contemporary Economics

David L. Prychitko, Editor

WHY ECONOMISTS DISAGREE

AN INTRODUCTION TO THE ALTERNATIVE SCHOOLS OF THOUGHT

∞

EDITED BY
DAVID L. PRYCHITKO

STATE UNIVERSITY OF NEW YORK PRESS

THE RICHARD STOCKTON COLLEGE
OF NEW JERSEY LIBRARY
POMONA, NEW JERSEY 08240

Published by
State University of New York Press, Albany

© 1998 State University of New York

All rights reserved

Printed in the United States of America

No part of this book may be used or reproduced in any manner whatsoever
without written permission.
No part of this book may be stored in a retrieval system or transmitted in any
form or by any means including electronic, electrostatic, magnetic tape,
mechanical, photocoying, recording, or otherwise without the prior
permission in writing of the publisher.

For information, address State University of New York Press,
State University Plaza, Albany, N.Y. 12246

Production by M. R. Mulholland
Marketing by Nancy Farrell

Library of Congress Cataloging-in-Publication Data

Why economists disagree : an introduction to the alternative schools
   of thought / edited by David L. Prychitko.
        p.   cm. — (SUNY series, diversity in contemporary economics)
     Includes bibliographical references and index.
     ISBN 0-7914-3569-5 (alk. paper). — ISBN 0-7914-3570-9 (pbk. :
alk. paper)
     1. Economics.   2. Economics—History.   3. Economics—Philosophy.
I. Prychitko, David L.   II. Series.
HB171.W578   1997
330—dc20   97-1725
                                                                 CIP

10 9 8 7 6 5 4 3 2 1

To my professors, colleagues, and students

❦

CONTENTS

ACKNOWLEDGMENTS

This book is the first in the SUNY series, Diversity in Contemporary Economics, and it fits quite well. The series seeks to publish books that explore theoretical and empirical alternatives to mainstream neoclassical economics, from a broad array of schools of economic thought (and even from scholars outside economics). *Why Economists Disagree*, I hope, will help introduce readers to the heterodox traditions in contemporary economics. I thank Christine E. Worden, the former acquisitions editor at SUNY Press, for helping me establish the series and I thank my current editor, Zina Lawrence, for her steadfast and timely committment to this book as well. My initial proposal has evolved into a more manageable and tightly woven book, thanks to the comments and concerns of four anonymous readers.

My interest in the theoretical and methodological diversity in economics has been shaped, no doubt, by my past professors: from the solid neoclassicism of Michael Alexeev, James Buchanan, Tom Holmstrom, Phil May, and Howard Swaine, to the radical Austrianism of Jack High and Don Lavoie and the cheerful eclecticism of both Kenneth Boulding and Jaroslav Vanek. I owe them all a debt of gratitude. I thank SUNY-Oswego's Scholarly and Creative Activity Committee and the Provost's Office for awarding me a summer grant to work on this project, which began a few years before my move to NMU.

I'd also like to thank my former students, especially those who participated in my Seminar on Contemporary Schools of Thought, Seminar on Austrian Economics, and my courses in the History of Economic Thought and on Economic and Social Institutions. At a time when it is hard enough to absorb the standard material, my students remained enthusiastic while I discussed many of the heterodox issues that are part of this book. Little do they know that I learned more than they did in the classroom.

As for my wife Julie, and our girls Sonja and Emily, suffice it to say that dedicating to them something called *Why Economists Disagree* isn't the best thing I could do. (They don't agree with me that it's a fascinating subject.) So, instead, I truly thank them for their patience, love, and just plain fun.

Finally, I thank the authors whose papers are reprinted here (with minor editorial changes), and the following journals, books, editors, publishers, and associations who kindly allowed me to reprint:

To the editor and to Louisiana State University Press for Roger W. Garrison, "Time and Money: The Universals of Macroeconomic Theorizing," *Journal of Macroeconomics*, vol. 6, no. 2 (Spring 1982) (reprinted here as chapter 1). Special thanks to Marybeth Theriot and Cheri Marquette.

To Ronald L. Trowbridge of Hillsdale College Press and to Richard M. Ebeling for Israel M. Kirzner, "The Driving Force of the Market: The Idea of 'Competition' in Contemporary Economic Theory and in the Austrian Theory of the Market Process," which originally appeared in chapter 3 of Richard M. Ebeling, ed., *Austrian Economics: Perspectives on the Past and Prospects for the Future* (Hillsdale, MI: Hillsdale College Press, 1991) (reprinted here as chapter 2).

To the American Economics Association for the following three articles: Ludwig M. Lachmann, "From Mises to Shackle: An Essay on Austrian Economics and the Kaleidic Society," *Journal of Economic Literature*, vol. 15 (1976) (reprinted here as chapter 3); for Alfred S. Eichner and J. A. Kregel, "An Essay on Post-Keynesian Theory: A New Paradigm in Economics," *Journal of Economic Literature*, vol. 14 (1975) (reprinted here as chapter 5); and for Albert O. Hirschman, "Against Parsimony: Three Ways of Complicating Some Categories of Economic Discourse," *American Economic Association Papers and Proceedings*, vol. 74, no. 2 (May 1984) (reprinted here as chapter 13). Special thanks to Dana Ragan.

To Paul Davidson, editor of the *Journal of Post Keynesian Economics*, for Paul Davidson, "Reviving Keynes's Resolution," *Journal of Post Keynesian Economics*, vol. 6, no. 4 (Summer 1984) (reprinted here as chapter 4); and for Tony Lawson, "The Nature of Post Keynesianism and Its Links to Other Traditions," *Journal of Post Keynesian Economics*, vol. 16, no. 4 (Summer 1994) (reprinted here as chapter 6). Special thanks to G. Chandoha.

To Carfax Publishing Company (P.O. Box 25, Abingdon, Oxfordshire OX143NB, United Kingdom) for Geoffrey M. Hodgson, "Institutionalism and Economic Theory: The Old versus the New," *Review of Political Economy*, vol. 1, no. 3 (1989) (reprinted here as chapter 7). Special thanks to Mrs. Margaret Hutchinson, and to Gary Mongiovi, co-editor of *Review of Political Economy*.

To John B. Davis, editor of *Review of Social Economy*, for William R. Waters, "Social Economics: A Solidarist Perspective," *Review of Social Economy*, vol. 46, no. 2 (October 1988) (reprinted here as chapter 8); and for Warren Samuels, "The Methodology of Economics and the Case for Policy Diffidence and Restraint," *Review of Social Economy*, vol. 47, no. 2 (Summer 1989) (reprinted here as chapter 14). William M. Dugger and Howard J. Sherman, "Comparison of Marxism and Institutionalism," *Journal of Economic Issues*, Vol. XXVIII, no. 1 (March 1994) (reprinted here as chapter 9) is reprinted from the *Journal of Economic Issues* by special permission of the copyright holder, the Association for Evolutionary Economics. Special thanks to Ann Mari May.

To Jack Amariglio, editor of *Rethinking Marxism*, for Jack Amariglio and David F. Ruccio, "Postmodernism, Marxism, and the Critique of Modern Economic Thought," *Rethinking Marxism*, vol. 7, no. 3 (Fall 1994) (reprinted here as chapter 10); and for Arjo Klamer and Donald McCloskey, "The Rhetoric of Disagreement," *Rethinking Marxism*, vol. 2, no. 3 (Fall 1989) (reprinted here as chapter 15, with Donald's name changed to Deirdre).

To Blackwell Publishers for Thomas E. Wiesskopf, "Toward a Socialism for the Future in the Wake of the Demise of the Socialism of the Past," *Review of Radical Political Economics*, vol. 24, no. 3 & 4 (Fall & Winter 1992) (reprinted here as chapter 11). A very special thanks to Jennifer Good.

To Francis R. Woolley and to Ann Newton, Managing Editor of *Cambridge Journal of Economics*, for Francis R. Woolley, "The Feminist Challenge to Neoclassical Economics," *Cambridge Journal of Economics*, vol. 17, no. 4 (December 1993) (reprinted here as chapter 12).

David L. Prychitko

Every surmise and vaticination of the mind is entitled to a certain respect, and we learn to prefer imperfect theories, and sentences which contain glimpses of truth, to digested systems which have no one valuable suggestion.

—Ralph Waldo Emerson

Introduction:
Why Economists Disagree: The Role of the Alternative Schools of Thought

David L. Prychitko

If All Economists Were Placed End to End,
They Still Wouldn't Reach a Conclusion

Economists disagree. We disagree over policy, prediction, and matters of pure theory. We even disagree over why we disagree.

We've disagreed for so long that the jokes have become legion. Even the Internet has snagged us. Search the World Wide Web under "Resources for Economists," for example, and you'll find a page containing jokes such as the one above.

To some, our growing disagreement suggests that economics has finally reached a state of crisis; to others, it is perhaps a long overdue sign of diversity and healthy heterodoxy.

Not to Worry: The Views of Milton Friedman and Fritz Machlup

And yet to others our disagreements mean neither. Milton Friedman said so in his "Methodology of Positive Economics," and later in an especially readable version titled, simply, "Why Economists Disagree." So did Fritz Machlup in his own essay titled "Why Economists Disagree."[1]

Friedman and Machlup both argued that most of the disagreement among economists is only apparent. We generally agree on theoretical fundamentals—the basic models. As Machlup stated, "no outsider . . . appreciates the broad agreement of the analysts about the theoretical system that constitutes their discipline" (pp. 388–89). We economists disagree over applications, and that's what the public (Machlup's "outsiders") hears on the evening news and reads in the financial pages.

Friedman asks us to consider minimum wage policies, for example. Friedman claims that "reputable" economists on either end of the political spectrum believe that higher minimum wages increases unemployment among the unskilled (p. 2). But on the evening news, two economists may nevertheless express very different judgments as to what *should* be done with the minimum wage. For Friedman, their difference is over politics, not economic theory. The conflation of solid economic theory with political (and moral) judgments helps explain a good deal of the apparent disagreement among economists—on television, in the papers, in the policy reports of think tanks.

Personal values shape and color policy choices in many ways. Consider the meaning of the "free society," for instance. A libertarian economist suggests laissez-faire as the foundation for freedom, while a radical economist views extreme income inequalities of capitalism as an obstacle to freedom, properly understood. "Each will place the burden of proof differently," Friedman claims, "one on the proponent of governmental intervention, the other, on the proponent of laissez-faire" (p. 7). Personal and political values also shape one's time perspective: Shall we pursue long run targets? Or is it true that, because we're all dead in the long run, we can help the living (we owe it to ourselves) by favoring short-run consequences of economic policy?

Nevertheless, Friedman argues that these value judgments (differences in which, unfortunately, "men can only fight") don't explain all, or perhaps not even the bulk of, disagreements among economists. Friedman holds back from concluding that our differences are ultimately differences in value judgments alone: "The major reasons for differences of opinion among economists on inflation, monetary policy, and the balance of payments," for example, "are not differences in values but differences in scientific judgements about both economic and non-economic effects" (p. 10).

This is curious.

To appreciate Friedman's claim, let's consider the historical context of this statement. Written in the late 1960s, the so-called neoclassical synthesis was at its peak. The macroeconomics of John Maynard Keynes's *General Theory* was shaped into the aggregate supply-and-demand frameworks of Paul Samuelson and then the IS-LM models of Hicks and Hansen: macroeconomics had become wedded—synthesized—with the neo-Walrasian general equilibrium framework. A single agreed-on model could be used to explain and predict the behavior of macroeconomic aggregates—GNP, employment, prices, and interest rates. Keynesians could use the model to justify interventionist fiscal and monetary policies to rationally correct the deficiencies of the capitalist system. But monetarists such as Friedman would apply the *same* framework to justify laissez-faire policies, namely a monetary rule rather than discretionary monetary policy, and balanced fiscal budgets. True, there was some difference in time perspectives (Keynesians apparently favoring the short run more heavily than the monetarist's long run), but both groups held the same *basic* values of a dynamic, growing, efficient capitalist economy. After all, Keynes considered himself a realist in the classical liberal tradition.

Both groups employed the core model of the neoclassical synthesis. The great Keynesian-Monetarist debates of the 1960s and 1870s were not so great after all, in terms of economic theory: the debates really boiled down to the slopes of the curves, as it were. As Friedman put it in an oft-quoted statement, "We are all Keynesians now." Meaning: "We all use the Keynesian language and apparatus; none of us any longer accepts the initial Keynesian conclusions" (p. 15). The differences, in other words, were mostly differences in *scientific* judgments. Being so, these differences could be discussed rationally, they could be empirically tested.

Like Machlup, Friedman concluded that there is a great deal of misunderstanding concerning economists' disagreements. Economic theory is solidly intact. Economists fundamentally agree on the core of economic theory. They simply have to iron out the differences in their interpretations of applied, empirical work. Sure, personal and political differences will remain (although they, too, may diminish with advances in economic science), but these differences of opinion should not be construed as a weakness of mainstream economic theory.

Thurow Agrees

That was the argument of the 1960s and 1970s. Lester Thurow would essentially reiterate the Friedman-Machlup position much later, in his own essay, "Why Do Economists Disagree?"[2] "Economists disagree much less about economics than the general public thinks," he states. "Most of the disagreements are about noneconomic aspects of economic problems" (p. 176). And he, too, considers the minimum wage exemplary: "The minimum wage dispute is not a dispute about economics, but a political dispute as to whether government should or should not intervene in the labor market to alter market incomes" (p. 177).

Although Thurow admits that our ability to predict is not as great as we once hoped (and, at any rate, "To judge economics in terms of its predictive record is to judge it in a way that no other science is judged" [p. 182]), economic theory is still essentially a sound enterprise. (Is Thurow aware of the joke that economics was invented to make astrologers look like good predictors?)

But Not So Fast . . .

Reading both Friedman's and Thurow's widely disseminated articles, one would hardly be aware of the rapidly growing methodological and theoretical diversity in contemporary economics. Today we witness a near-explosion of heterodox thought.

Milton Friedman's optimism about the beneath-the-surface agreement within the economics profession is not hard to understand. Again, he wrote during the height of the neoclassical synthesis. In the 1950s and 1960s "everybody" seemed to be part of a mainstream view. Lester Thurow's reaffirmation—written in the 1980s—is a bit harder to understand, however, for the period of the 1970s witnessed a near-unraveling of neoclassicism, with the Phillips curve controversy, the great period of stagflation, and the burst of energies in search of the microfoundations of macroeconomics, particularly in regard to finding an adequate framework that offers a full account of expectations. True, the mainstream would become reinvigorated with the rational expectations axiom, in the model proposed by the New Classical economists (students of Friedman himself), and with the New Keynesian rebuttal. But during the same time several schools of thought, many of which were lying dormant for decades, have reemerged to challenge and offer alternative approaches to the neoclassical mainstream, both in its traditional Keynesian-Monetarist form and in the current New Classical–New Keynesian form.

Today unfolds a rapidly growing diversity within the economics profession. New methodological and theoretical alternatives are being discussed, debated, and published in an astonishing array of scholarly outlets. The disagreements have grown stronger, the debates more grand. Economists no longer argue simply over the slopes of curves; neither do they only focus on the relationship between rational expectations and the (ad hoc) assumptions regarding price stickiness or wage rigidities. The entire equilibrium-based model is open to serious reexamination and criticism. Indeed, the status of economics as a *science* itself, and its potential as an a priori, value-free theory, is in dispute.

This book is about those alternatives to the mainstream.

A Growing Diversity in Contemporary Economics:
The Alternative Schools

We begin in Part I with the Austrian School, for onlookers (and many practitioners within the school) believe it to be the "closest" or perhaps most sympathetic to the neoclassical mainstream. We shall then move "further" from the mainstream by turning to the Post Keynesian

(Part II), Institutionalist (Part III), and Radical Political Economy or Marxist (Part IV) traditions. We will conclude in Part V by considering issues in the contemporary philosophy of economics. A final bibliographic essay is added to suggest further readings.

The Austrian School

Austrian economics began with Carl Menger's 1871 text, *Principles of Economics*. Menger, who helped forge the "marginal" revolution in economic theory (along with France's Leon Walras and Britain's William Stanley Jevons), founded perhaps the most strongly "subjectivist" branch of modern economics. Menger was also a key player in the great *Methodenstreit*, the classic debate over methods. Menger defended the role of a priori, deductive theory against the antitheoretical stance of the burgeoning German Historical School. His fellow Austrian students, Eugen von Boehm-Bawerk and Friedrich von Wieser, and especially their students, Ludwig von Mises and F. A. Hayek, would later create what has come to be called, for the lack of a better name, "Austrian" economics.

Contemporary Austrian economics is characterized by its commitment to *methodological individualism*. For Austrians, economic theory is ultimately about people's choices and both the intended and unintended consequences of their choices. Economics, in other words, is a general science of human action.

Their individualist methodology is further buttressed by a profound, if not radical, *subjectivism*. Choice, or action in general, occurs through *time* (i.e., historical time, rather than logical or mathematical time denoted by the *t* subscript used in the formulae of physicists and neoclassical economists), and under conditions of *uncertainty* (as opposed to measurable risk). Austrians argue that the standard rational choice model has nothing in common with action in the real world; indeed, one would neither act nor choose if their future was known with perfect certainty and their maximizing problems could be solved instantaneously. Allowing for an uncertain world means that individuals are guided, at best, by their subjective *expectations* of the world.

A world riddled with uncertainty, less-than-rational expectations, and historical time is necessarily a world outside of general economic equilibrium. Austrians—indeed, all the alternative schools of thought in this book—see neoclassical theory as being too preoccupied with the general equilibrium model, an abstract picture of how the world would look like *only if* it were peopled with rational maximizers who face none of the above conditions. Opposed to neoclassicism, Austrians consider the goal of their theory to explain the market system as an evolving and dynamic *process* that may perhaps tend toward equilibrium, but will never reach it.

Roger W. Garrison's "Time and Money: The Universals of Macro-economic Theorizing" (chapter 1) juxtaposes this Austrian position against both mainstream neoclassicism and the Keynes–Post Keynesian approaches. Garrison argues that Austrian economics lies on a stable middle ground between the neoclassical "equilibrium always" assumption and the Post Keynesian "equilibrium never" counterargument. For Garrison, as for most Austrians, the market process notion supplies a sensible theory that avoids the pitfalls of either of the others. Also implicit here is the notion of an Austrian microfoundation for macroeconomics. As Garrison states, "Time is the medium of action, money is the medium of exchange. Together these two media can serve to define macroeconomics." In other words, Austrian economics need not be separated into "distinct" branches called micro or macro. The macro or economywide consequences of individual human actions is logically deduced from the micro.

Israel M. Kirzner further describes the market process concept in his "The Driving Force of the Market: The Idea of 'Competition' in Contemporary Economic Theory and in the Austrian Theory of the Market Process" (chapter 2). Here Kirzner pits the process theory against the mainstream model of perfect competition. Austrians would agree with Frank Knight's early views that there really is no competition—as we all know it in the real world—within the economist's fiction of perfect competition. For Austrians, competition is not necessarily about the size of markets, the number of competitors, the amount of information, and so on—and it certainly has nothing to do with equilibrium price-taking behavior. Rather, competition is a rivalrous *discovery process*, which, to Kirzner, "is driven by the entrepreneurial element in each human being, by the propensity to notice the implications of earlier errors (which propensity is the essence of entrepreneurship)." For Kirzner, as for most Austrians, the equilibrium fiction depicts a world of perfect knowledge, while a theory of entrepreneurship explains how knowledge is discovered and conveyed in the first place, and thus how entrepreneurship operates as the equilibrating vehicle in a free-market system. Moreover, viewed from this perspective, the neoclassical model of monopoly (and, implicitly, imperfect competition) is open to Austrian criticisms. The reader will also find in this chapter, however, that not all Austrians agree on the monopoly question.

Furthermore, not all Austrians agree that the market process is a *fundamentally equilibrating* process. Ludwig M. Lachmann's "From Mises to Shackle: An Essay on Austrian Economics and the Kaleidic Society" (chapter 3) offers an immanent theoretical challenge to contemporary Austrian economists. An Austrian himself (a student of Hayek, and enormously influenced by G. L. S. Shackle), Lachmann suggests that if Austrians take time, uncertainty, and expectations seriously—which is what their much-touted *radical subjectivism* is all about—then it is unclear, a priori, that market participants' expectations will converge. In other words, each step in a dynamic, entrepreneurial market process does not necessarily improve economic coordination; expectations, and thus individual plans, may diverge. Rather than equilibrate the system, the decisions of households, consumers, and entrepreneurs may create a "kaleidic" (though not necessarily *chaotic*) economy. Lachmann is well aware that he raises a thorny issue among his Austrian colleagues: "The kaleidic society is thus not the natural habitat of Austrian economics," but nevertheless he was optimistic because "it is quite possible that a bastion of extended subjectivism, enhanced by the inclusion of divergent expectations, will offer us an excellent vantage point from which to watch the happenings of such a society in a dispassionate perspective, a perspective superior to what we have had before."

While Austrians currently debate this crucial issue, it offers us a good jumping-off point, and leads us to a central thesis of our next alternative.

The Post Keynesian School

Post-Keynesian economists take their inspiration from the work of J. M. Keynes, especially that of his *General Theory*, as opposed to the later Keynesians such as John Hicks and Paul Samuelson, who fit Keynesian macroeconomics onto a neoclassical foundation. The Post Keynesians such as Michael Kalecki, Roy Harrod, Joan Robinson in England; and Sidney Weintraub, Alfred S. Eichner, and Paul Davidson in the United States, reject the *neoclassical synthesis* (in fact, Joan Robinson went so far as to call the neoclassical synthesis "Bastard Keynesianism," an illegitimate interpretation of what Keynes really meant). They instead argue that mainstream equilibrium theory is ultimately irrelevant in the real world of time, uncertainty, and change.

Post Keynesians (notably Paul Davidson, Alfred S. Eichner, and Hyman Minsky) argue that Keynes tried to develop a theory that focuses on problems of real existing economies. In particular, he studied money, money-wages, contracts, expectations, time, unemployment, and their relations to output. These phenomena simply do not exist under general equilibrium. Because general equilibrium assumes that all activities take place in a single instant, every commodity or service is signed for and paid for in advance through a set of futures contracts that spell out every possible contingency and accords a measurable probability to it, under given prices, production functions, utility functions, and so forth. Time as we know it does not exist in the neoclassical model. Nor, then, does *uncertainty*.

The Post Keynesian disagreement with standard theory seems to share some common ground with the Austrian School noted above. But there's more to consider.

Paul Davidson's "Reviving Keynes's Revolution" (chapter 4) suggests that the mere existence of a general medium of exchange—*money*—should lead us to cast a profound skepticism on the validity of general equilibrium modeling. People hold money because they live in *time*, in a truly uncertain world. Money contracts—including money wages—suggest that a Walrasian general equilibrium *cannot* be described—let alone attained—in the real world of high finance capitalism (or anyplace else, for that matter). "The existence of money contracts—a characteristic of the world in which Keynes lived and which we still do," Davidson observes, "implies there need never exist, in the long run or the short run, any rational expectations equilibrium or general equilibrium market clearing vector." Davidson takes both classical and neoclassical economics to task, including the Neo-Keynesianism of Clower and Leijonhufvud (and one might add, now, the currently popular New Keynesian theories of Stiglitz and others) for suggesting that somehow, somewhere in the long run there is a general equilibrium solution to society's coordination problems. Davidson argues that, in a *nonergodic* world plagued with uncertainty and error, and thus *disequilibrium*, money must affect both nominal *and* real variables; money is not neutral. (And the upshot of this, in light of the previously mentioned Austrian theory of a fundamentally equilibrating market process, is that the Austrian argument, too, is jeopardized.)

Although most contemporary Post Keynesians would retain the role of formal axiomatic theory, they reject the methodological individualism associated with all facets of neoclassicism, and would consider (non-Lachmann-inspired) Austrian economics a variant of neoclassicism. Austrians still swim in the mainstream, as it were. Post Keynesians display no qualms of using more holistic analysis, and further developing the *aggregative* framework deployed in Keynes's *General Theory*.

Post Keynesian theory focuses on the *rate of investment* and in particular its relationship to *economic growth* and *income distribution*. The rate of investment reflects, in large part, the confidence entrepreneurs have about the future. The more confident, the more likely they will invest in the present. If their expectations are correct, entrepreneurs will become financially successful, they will enjoy higher profits, and thus a larger share of National Income. But if their expectations err, a huge waste of resources could result, cascading into economic losses and a pessimistic view of the future. A fall in aggregate demand could occur, sending the economy into mass unemployment (an "unemployment equilibrium"). While Davidson's chapter focuses on the issue of money and uncertainty (the nonergodic hypothesis), Alfred S. Eichner's and Jan Kregel's "An Essay on Post-Keynesian Theory: A New Paradigm in Economics" (chapter 5) provides a more formal survey of the development of Post Keynesian thought on the issues of investment, distribution, and growth, and nicely compares Post Keynesians and neoclassicals.

But the Post Keynesian "paradigm" may not be as homogeneous or internally coherent as Eichner and Kregel suggest. In his "The Nature of Post Keynesianism and Its Links to Other Traditions" (chapter 6), Tony Lawson argues that Post Keynesian theory can move beyond its negative critique of mainstream orthodoxy—and offer a more coherent theoretical *alternative*—by adopting a more self-conscious critical-realist methodology. "If coherency is desirable " states Lawson, and "if Post Keynesians do believe there is a consistent basis to their contributions, it would seem to follow that something very much like the explanation here being provided [i.e., of a critical realist philosophy] has to be accepted." Of course, it remains to be seen whether Lawson's position provides the best route to coherence, and if it will be accepted within the Post Keynesian tradition.

Institutional and Social Economics

Institutionalism developed as a uniquely American variant of economics, particularly with the writings of Thorstein Veblen, John Commons, and Wesley C. Mitchell through the early part of this century. Institutionalists criticized the emerging trend in neoclassical economic theory—especially its deeply *reductionist* methodological individualism. Veblen went so far as to charge Carl Menger as offering an exemplary hedonistic caricature of "economic man," one reduced to a "lightning calculator of pleasure and pain," and the consumer as nothing but an "isolated, definitive human datum." Now whether that really fits Menger is still open to debate. But as a loose description, it does capture a core feature of mainstream economic theory.

The real problem, according to the institutionalists, is the neoclassical concern with equilibrium. Neither individuals—properly understood as social actors—nor institutions matter in general equilibrium. For a century now, institutionalists argue that economics must become an *evolutionary science*. Thorstein Veblen called for an evolutionary science back in 1898, in his "Why Is Economics Not an Evolutionary Science?"

Walter Hamilton followed suit in his "The Institutional Approach to Economic Theory" (1919). Veblen argues that economics had dragged years behind the natural sciences, because the natural sciences had already become evolutionary (most particularly, the biological sciences). Economics, however, was (and still is) concerned with developing a model based on equilibrium. Instead (and not unlike the others discussed above), institutionalists focus on the *processes* of change rather than an abstract equilibrium state. At best, standard economics assumes certain institutions are simply *given* in the theory. If economics is to be a science, it must explain the process by which institutions appear, persist, and fade away. For example, private property rights—an apparent "foundation" of the market system—are given by neither economics nor natural law. Instead, they are more like human artifacts that are explained through the interplay of profits, politics, and power. To understand the complex chains through which economic processes occur, institutionalists call for a sophisticated *methodological holism* that accounts for the behaviors of both individuals *and* groups.

Moreover, (and here's where institutionalists would differ from Austrians and some aspects of Post Keynesian theory), institutionalists argue that the concept of *the* market (or *the* economy) is a chimera. Market institutions are *embedded* within a panoply of social, cultural, and political institutions, and markets shape, and are shaped by, institutions. To isolate and analyze something called the market (examples: the mainstream perfectly competitive model, the sectoral, aggregative models of Keynesian economics, the Austrian theory of the market as a purely entrepreneurial process or the dialectical materialism of orthodox Marxism) is a highly, misleading scientific abstraction, and an ideological confusion. The market, in the institutionalist view, is neither a coherent, self-regulating system in itself nor the primary vehicle that allocates scarce goods and resources. *Power structures* (such as the always evolving distribution of wealth, property rights, technology) play an even greater role in the allocation of resources.

Which leads us to another feature of institutionalism. Institutionalists generally agree that the method and concepts of economic theory are neither *universal* nor *ahistorical*. Nor are they *value free*.

This cuts to the bone of mainstream theory.

This is not to say that all institutionalists reject a deductive methodology, or are blind empiricists seeking to describe the facts of the real world without the aid of theory (although some institutionalists have leaned in that direction). Some institutionalists, such as Commons and his students, interpret their efforts as offering an empirical complement to mainstream theory. Others such as Veblen, Ayres, and their descendants, see institutionalism as a radical alternative to main-stream preoccupations. As a group, institutionalists take a more *pragmatic*, problem-centered approach to economics, and do not shy away from equating institutional economics with a body of knowledge spearheaded toward social and political change.

Of course, this says nothing of the so-called New Institutionalism that has come to the fore in recent years, whose roots are found in the neoclassical property-rights literature, and in Oliver Williamson's work on the organization of firms, and, to a lesser extent, on Hayek's notion of spontaneous order. Geoffrey M. Hodgson offers a readable comparison of the New Institutionalism against the "old" American tradition in his "Institutional Economic Theory: The Old Versus the New" (chapter 7). Hodgson argues that the New Institutionalism still clings to the main-stream's overly reductionistic and naive individualism, and therefore it is tainted with the ideology of classical liberalism. It offers no significant *alternative* to neoclassicism: the bulk of the New Institutionalism still carries "the enduring hegemony of Walrasian and Marshallian ideas in economic theory," while the lesser-developed Hayekian branch, although emphasizing the market as a discovery process, is nevertheless still anchored in the "fundamental assumptions of neoclassical liberalism." Hodgson argues that the New Institutionalism has failed to answer Veblen's critique of the assumptions of mainstream theory.

Hodgson's chapter nicely juxtaposes old, or American, institu-tionalism with the new neoclassical interest in property rights. But there's more to consider. Institutionalism is a multifaceted, century-old tradition, which shades into other research agendas, including those of social economics and radical political economy.

William R. Waters's "Social Economics: A Solidarist Perspective" (chapter 8) provides a clear discussion of the concerns of social econo-mists, backed with a solidarist social philosophy and institutionalist theory. (Social economics itself can be traced back to two rather different sources: Friedrich von Wieser's 1914 book of the same title, *Social Economics*, and much more so to Pope Leo XIII's 1894 encyclical, *Rerum Novarum*, which inspired the founding of the Catholic Economic Association, later merged into the Association for Social Economics.) Today, social economics draws scholars from several schools of thought, generally united by the earthly goal of improving material comfort and human dignity. While economists in the Social Economics tradition are united more by social-political purpose than by an underlying theoretical perspective, Waters's chapter nevertheless offers a highly readable application of institutionalism's focus on innovation, tech-nology, and financial and legal institutions. He is especially instructive in his discussion of the ever-changing face of property rights, using the Mondragon experiment in economic democracy as a case in point.

But institutionalism also carries a radical bite, as attested by William M. Dugger's and Howard J. Sherman's "Comparison of Marxism and Institutionalism" (chapter 9). Dugger, a leading proponent of radical institutionalism (as compared to, say, the more liberal institutionalism associated with the writings of John Commons, Wendell Gordon, and others, including Waters's chapter above), and Sherman, a Marxist, compare and contrast the radical institutionalist project with that of contemporary Marxism, each addressing their School's approach to structural relationships in society, the role of individuals and class, technology and ideology, the nature of sociohistorical evolution, and the status of social scientific theory. The authors find that there is some agreement on studying society as an evolutionary process, equipped with a methodological holism, but they disagree over the nature (or relative weight of) *power* and *class*.

This chapter offers a fine introduction to both radical institutionalism and Marxian political economy.

Radical Political Economy

But, considering the recent collapse of one socialist regime after another, isn't Marxism dead?

Not according to our next group of contributors.

Jack Amariglio and David F. Ruccio, in their "Postmodernism, Marxism, and the Critique of Modern Economic Thought" (chapter 10), argue that *modernism* is crippled and dying, not Marxism per se. Amariglio and Ruccio criticize neoclassical economics for its modernist impulse, one which prefers scientific modeling based on order, a centered subject, and certainty, and they propose a *postmodernist* approach which emphasizes the possibilities of *disorder, decentering,* and *uncertainty.* Amariglio and Ruccio write that, "while modern economic thought may not entirely discard—and may even relish the challenge of theorizing disorder, decentering, and uncertainty—it does so in the conceit that these elements are, in the end, superseded by the discursive ordering and analysis that are presumed to make up modern scientific activity." This is true of mainstream theory, and of some elements of Post-Keynesian theory (which the authors also take to task). One could add that the Austrian School might be open to their charge as well.

But the real purpose of the chapter is to reinvigorate Marxism and free it from the constraints of its *own* modernist presuppositions—a terribly difficult task! The authors state that they "do not think that modernism has done Marxism proud since, to our mind, it has built up a theoretical edifice with political consequences that are questionable." Moreover, the modernist features of Marxist political economy "has overemphasized both the existence of disorder in capitalism and the negative consequences of the types of disorder that arise there," while "it has exaggerated the orderly nature of socialism, and especially of planning, and has viewed as unduly positive the consequences of such order." Instead, the postmodern Marxism proposed by Amariglio and Ruccio embraces radical uncertainty so much that the "teleological laws of motion" of capitalism, the inevitability of emancipatory revolution, and the superiority of central planning (compared to markets) is all open to serious questioning. They conclude that "the totalizing promise of rational centralized planning is a modernist one. The declared partiality, relativism, and uncertainty of planning is, in contrast, postmodern."

This chapter is, admittedly, challenging to read, but it is well worth the effort.

Postmodern or not, the Marxist critique of capitalism still depends in part on some vision of an *attainable* alternative. Thomas E. Weisskopf's chapter, "Toward a Socialism for the Future, in the Wake of the Demise of the Socialism of the Past" (chapter 11) offers a readable account of the practical project of radical political economy in light of the unprecedented collapse of socialist governments in 1989. Weisskopf explores market socialism and participatory socialism as potential alternatives, which, in itself, serves as a good introduction to these models. Weisskopf ultimately favors a market-based socialism, one which emphasizes democratic, self-managed political and economic institutions.

New Philosophical Issues

Most economists follow George Stigler's professional advice: Don't think about methodological or philosophical issues until you retire. Mainstream economists are taught to do economics *first* and philosophize *last*, if at all.

Like that Nike add, we're told to *just do it*.

But there's no such thing as doing economics without philosophy. (And, alas, even Nike sells a philosophy.) With the growing disenchantment of mainstream positivism—emphasis on operational, "as if" assumptions such as *homo economicus*, its attempt to predict rather than understand, and so on—there's now an astonishing dialogue over the philosophy and methodology of economics. Part V therefore turns from particular schools of economic thought to some general philosophical issues.

For example, Frances R. Woolley's "The Feminist Challenge to Neoclassical Economics" (chapter 12) questions the simple rational choice model embodied in the *homo economicus* assumption. Her chapter offers a readable introductory survey of the feminist critique of neoclassicism. Although less than a decade old, feminist economics attempts to document the difference between the welfare of men and women, promote policies to reduce gender-based inequities in income and leisure time (for example), and offer a theory free from androcentric biases. A feminist methodology, Woolley concludes in her survey, is "first and foremost, a focus on economic justice between men and women, which unifies an otherwise disparate literature, and gives a compelling motivation for continuing to challenge traditional economic thinking."

But doesn't this unnecessarily complicate mainstream modelling? Despite the cries of the less-than-mathematically-adept, neoclassical economics is heralded as being theoretically simple and straightforward. The standard rational choice model isn't championed for its descriptive *realism*, but rather its *predictive* power, and with that, its committment to the law of parsimony. Hence, the title alone of Albert O. Hirschman's "Against Parsimony: Three Ways of Complicating Economic Discourse" (chapter 13) is sacrilegious. Influenced in part by Amartya Sen's work on metapreferences, and reconsidering his own illuminating notions of "voice" and "exit" options within the workplace, Hirschman's paper undergirds a theme of Woolley's previous chapter: economics can become more powerful, if more complicated, by incorporating endogenous (rather than "given") preferences, and especially a richer, truer concept of *self* (something far beyond a set of indifference curves). According to Hirschman, the profession's focus on formalism and prediction carries a high cost: greater realism and better *understanding*.

According to Warren J. Samuels, the role of economic theory for social control and prediction is all too often shrouded in ideology, particularly at the level of policy advocacy. While the two previous chapters provide a radical criticism of the traditional rational choice model, and its corresponding welfare standard based on Pareto optimality conditions, Samuels' "The Methodology of Economics and the Case for Policy Diffidence and Restraint" (chapter 14) carries the critique all the way to the level of policy espousal, one of the primary occupations of economists (and of course the focus of much heated disagreement in the media). "The supreme irony resident within economics," Samuels writes, "is that we tend to adopt an official posi-tivist methodology which presumes that the economy is independent and transcendental to man, as is in part the case with the physical and chemical world, while at the same time we seek policy implications and recommendations—to make or to influence policy—which presume that the economy is not independent and transcendental to man and which have the effect of contributing to the (re)production of the economy." Samuels challenges the mainstream claim that economic policy can be conducted in an objective, value-free, and optimal manner. Instead, Samuels concludes, "True scientific and scholarly spirit requires considerable diffidence and restraint by economists."

The final chapter of Part V, Arjo Klamer's and Deirdre (previously Donald) McCloskey's "The Rhetoric of Disagreement" (chapter 15) provides, in effect, a postscript to the book's previous chapters. Written as a fictional dialogue between the two authors, it offers an example of the rhetoric of modern economics, and, especially, a plea for openness and respect.

A Final Word

This book borrows, without apology, the title *Why Economists Disagree* from Friedman, Machlup, and Thurow. Although I share their concerns, I also believe that the Friedman-Machlup-Thurow answer, trickled down to today's textbooks, is based more on faith than economists care to admit. I hope this book serves as both an introduction to the alternative schools of thought *and* as a challenge to that prevailing faith.

In the chapters that follow, our authors criticize mainstream economics while they attempt to construct theoretical alternatives, and thereby offer views of mainstream economics from unique angles and interpretive spectacles. If you're already a dyed-in-the-wool neoclassical economist and you've come *this far* in the book, the following chapters may expose you to previously unreflected or taken-for-granted features of neoclassical theory, and on that basis alone it may make you a better neoclassicist. You may find, for instance, that the traditional interpretation of why economists disagree is more problematic than you first thought. At the very least, you'll find out what all the commotion is about.

If you're already a student of one of the alternative schools of thought, you'll perhaps find some common concerns, criticisms, and grounds for dialogue among the other heterodox schools. And if you're fairly new to economics, having successfully passed your core micro and macroeconomics courses, well . . . get ready for yet another ride.

Notes

1. Milton Friedman, "The Methodology of Positive Economics," in his *Essays in Positive Economics* (Chicago: University of Chicago Press, 1953) and *idem.*, "Why Economists Disagree," in his *Dollars and Deficits: Living with America's Economic Problems* (Englewood Cliffs, NJ: Prentice-Hall, 1968), pp. 1–16. Fritz Machlup's "Why Economists Disagree," *Proceedings of the American Philosophical Society*, vol. 109 (February 1965) makes essentially the same argument as Friedman. The interested reader can find it reprinted in Machlup's *Methodology of Economics and Other Social Sciences* (New York: Academic Press, 1978), pp. 375–89. Because Friedman's argument covers much the same ground as Machlup's, and was more widely disseminated, I shall focus more on Friedman's.

2. Lester Thurow "Why Do Economists Disagree?," *Dissent* 29 (Spring 1982), pp. 176–82.

PART I

AUSTRIAN ECONOMICS AND THE MARKET PROCESS

※

Economics is not about goods and services, it is about the actions of living men. Its goal is not to dwell upon imaginary constructions such as equilibrium. These constructions are only tools of reasoning. The sole task of economics is analysis of the actions of men, is the analysis of processes.

Both the logical and the mathematical economists assert that human action ultimately aims at the establishment of such a state of equilibrium and would reach it if all further changes in data were to cease. But the logical economist knows more than that. He shows how the activities of enterprising men, the promoters and speculators, eager to profit from discrepencies in the price structure, tend toward eradicating such discrepencies and thereby also toward blotting out the sources of entrepreneurial profit and loss. He shows how this process would finally result in the establishment of the evenly rotating economy. This is the task of economic theory. The mathematical description of various states of equilibrium is mere play. The problem is the analysis of the market process.

—Ludwig von Mises, *Human Action: A Treatise on Economics*, rev. ed.

1

TIME AND MONEY: THE UNIVERSALS OF MACROECONOMIC THEORIZING

ROGER W. GARRISON

Introduction

This paper suggests that macroeconomic propositions should be anchored in economizing behavior related to time and money, and that macromaladies stem from the special ways in which time and money interact in a market economy. Section 2 makes the case for according special status to the "market for time" and the "market for money" in macroeconomic theorizing. Section 3 argues that markets for capital goods, which serve as the focus for Austrian macroeconomics,[1] are the most direct and concrete manifestation of intertemporal markets. Section 4 introduces money as a "loose joint" in the market mechanism. This Hayekian imagery allows for a fruitful comparison of Keynesians and Monetarists. Section 5 shows that these two mainstream views represent polar positions and that the Hayekian view, because of its particular treatment of time and money, represents the middle ground. Section 6 provides an elaboration of the Hayekian, or Austrian, view and identifies its theoretical advantages. Section 7 considers related developments in the mainstreams, and Section 8 offers a summary and conclusion.

The Universals of Macroeconomic Theorizing

Much has been written about the need for a microeconomic foundation for macroeconomic theorizing.[2] There has been little effort, though, to identify just what it is that sits on this foundation. Interpreting the prefix "macro-" to mean "economywide" suggests the need to identify economizing behavior whose effects are economywide in some special sense. The Walrasian insight that everything depends upon and influences everything else is a reminder of how encompassing the notion of economy-wide can be. But the attempt of market participants to economize on *time* and on *money* and the economywide consequences of this economizing behavior have a special claim on our attention. It is argued below that the "market for time" and that "market for money," both in their conceptual isolation and in their actual interaction, give rise to all the phenomena that are conventionally regarded as macroeconomic in nature.

The most explicit recognition of the universal nature of time in economic theory is found in the writings of the Austrian School.[3] All choices are made with an eye to the future, and all actions take place in time. While there is no market for time as such, the time element is inextricably wedded to every market that does exist. The analysis of a market economy consists of identifying actions of individuals that give rise to various market phenomena, and time, literally, is the medium through which these actions transpire.

The common practice in microeconomics, particularly in Walrasian general-equilibrium theory, of limiting the subject matter to the case of a pure exchange economy is an attempt to abstract from the time element. The simple act of exchange can be conceptually collapsed into a single instant of time without any serious distortion. But the (timeless) models which consist of nothing but various constellations of such exchanges bear little resemblance to the economy being modeled.[4] In modern market economies the more relevant, and more troublesome, considerations of time are associated not with pure exchange but with production. Acts of production, though, cannot be conceptually collapsed into a single instant of time without negating an essential aspect of all production processes.

Explicit attention to the time element associated with production decisions and production processes can serve to distinguish macroeconomic theory from conventional general-equilibrium theory and to give the theory its distinct macroeconomic flavor. Considerations of time may enter the theory by way of the cost of information about an uncertain future (as in the Chicago-UCLA tradition), the sluggishness of money wages or prices (as in the Keynesian approach), or the capital structure (as emphasized by the Austrian school). In any case the intertemporal relationships among individual choices in a production economy is the stuff of which macroeconomic theory is made. Alternative macroeconomic theories, whatever their particulars, consist of different explanations of the behavior of individuals in their attempt to "defeat the dark forces of time and ignorance which envelop our future."[5] But further inquiry into the particulars of intertemporal markets must await a brief discussion of the second universal of macroeconomic theorizing.

Though it may be thought unnecessary to argue the centrality of money in macroeconomic theory, it is worthwhile to consider the special sense in which money is a marketwide phenomenon. Monetary theorists have long recognized that "money has no market of its own."[6] It is the obverse of this truth that highlights the macroeconomic character of money. With trivial exceptions *every* market is a market for money. In a modern economy every exchange involves some specific quantity of money. That this fact should be the focus of our attention has been recognized by economists both new and old.[7] There is no denying, of course, that money serves several functions, as listed in any principles text, but the presence of money on one side of each exchange in every market is the special sense in which money is an economywide phenomenon.

The particular reason that money is singled out for special attention is not just a matter for idle reflection. It has important implications about the particular way that money is to enter into a satisfactory macroeconomic theory. As with the treatment of the time element, the way that money is introduced—that is, as a noninterest-bearing asset, as a hedge against rising interest rates, or as the medium of exchange— accounts for many of the major differences between competing theories. And the role that money plays in a given macroeconomic model provides clues about the model's ability to explain macroeconomic phenomena.

Time is the medium of action; money is the medium of exchange. Together these two media can serve to define macroeconomics. If the intertemporal exchanges and the interpersonal exchanges in a market economy could be isolated one from the other, conventional macroeconomics would be largely redundant. Cambridge capital theory (which abstracts from interpersonal exchanges) coupled with Walrasian general-equilibrium theory (which abstracts from intertemporal exchanges) would adequately cover the field. The fact that these two categories of economic theory, taken together, shed no light whatever on the conventional macroeconomic issues is evidence of the extent to which intertemporal exchanges and interpersonal exchanges are in fact intertwined. And it is precisely the "intersection" of the "market for time" and the "market for money" that constitutes macroeconomics' unique subject matter.

Capital and Time

Economics in general is concerned with the allocation of resources. Thus, the most general and direct way of dealing with the time element is to focus on those resources that bear a distinct intertemporal relationship with one another in the minds of market participants. We have it from William Stanley Jevons [(1970), p. 226] that "the single and all-important function of capital is to enable the laborer to await the result of any long-lasting work—to put an interval between the beginning and the end of an enterprise." Jevons is suggesting that one way of concretizing the notion of the "market for time" is to recognize the essential temporal aspect of the market for capital goods broadly conceived. Again, the most explicit effort to intertemporalize economic theory by focusing on capital goods and to build a macroeconomic theory on a foundation of capital theory is found in the Austrian school. Menger [(1970), pp. 149–74] introduced the idea of "goods of various orders" where order denotes a temporal relationship between a capital good and the eventual consumer good that this piece of capital helps to produce. Böhm-Bawerk [(1959), 2:102–18] provided a description of what goes on during the interval of time referred to by Jevons and how the assortment of capital goods must be restructured if that interval is to be shortened or lengthened. This early work on capital theory provided a foundation for later developments by Mises [(1953), pp. 339–66; (1966), pp. 538–86], Hayek [(1967), pp. 69–100; (1979), pp. 139–92], and others writing in the Austrian tradition.

In the 1930s this direct and general approach to dealing with the problem of intertemporal coordination had to compete with the Keynesian revolution. It would be constructive if the Austrian formulation of capital theory could be compared to an alternative formulation offered by Keynes. But this is not possible. Keynes [(1964), pp. 213–17] dismissed the contribution of Böhm-Bawerk out of hand, but offered no alternative of his own.[8] The objective, instead, was to press on with macroeconomic theory in the absence of any underlying theory of capital. The effect of Keynes's contribution is neatly summarized by Axel Leijonhufvud [(1968), p. 212].

> The theory of capital and interest was the subject of great debate in the early thirties . . . [But the] issues were not resolved. Keynes' *General Theory* had the effect of cutting the debate short. The capital-theoretic controversies were buried under the avalanche of pro-, anti-, and (soon enough) post-Keynesian writings, and the issues were to remain in abeyance for some twenty years.

Thus, Keynesianism represents an emancipation of macroeconomic thought from the thorny issues of capital theory but it also represents the abandonment of the most direct approach for dealing with the element of time. It is not argued here that Keynes eliminated the time element from his theory. To the contrary, considerations of time loom large throughout the entire book. But to account for the particular ways in which time is taken into consideration would embroil us in controversies that are yet to be resolved forty-odd years after the book's publication. Most significant is the very lack of any such resolution. In the relevant passages discussions of capital goods or the capital structure seem to be replaced by allusions to "casinos" and "musical chairs" [(1964), pp. 156 and 159]. Some kind of speculation about the future is necessitated by his theory, but when the "animal spirits" [(1964), p. 161] of Keynesian investors are pitted against the "dark forces of time and ignorance," the dark forces seem always to win out. This characteristic of Keynesian theory follows directly from the rejection of the capital theory that had served in pre-Keynesian formulations as the embodiment of the "market for time."

Money as a "Loose Joint"

Intertemporal market forces find their most direct and concrete expression in the market for capital goods. If capital goods were traded directly for consumer goods or other capital goods, the nature of macroeconomics would be substantially different from what it is. The fact that capital goods and the corresponding consumer goods are traded indirectly via the medium of exchange adds the other essential dimension. Macroeconomic theory, then, should highlight the implications of indirect exchange in the context of a capital-using economy.

In the closing pages of *The Pure Theory of Capital* [(1941), pp. 408–10], Hayek provides a piece of imagery that hints about how the "pure theory" might be qualified with monetary considerations. Money is conceived as the "loose joint" in the self-equilibrating market system. The fact that money is a *joint* linking the ability to demand with the willingness to supply gives meaning to Say's Law correctly understood. The fact that the joint is a *loose* one keeps Say's law from being true in the vulgar sense. The play in the system associated with the use of money allows for deviations between the quantities of nonmonetary goods supplied and the quantities demanded. Recognizing money as the loose joint in the context of a capital-using economy focuses attention on the looseness between the supply of an assortment of capital goods and the subsequent demand for the corresponding consumer goods. It is this looseness that gives rise to the most common macromaladies—such as "overinvestment," or what the Austrian writers call "malinvestment." (More on these phenomena later.)

Many macroeconomic theories accord money a central role. Hayek's imagery provides an acid test of the adequacy of these theories. The conception of money as a loose joint suggests that there are two extreme theoretical constructs to be avoided. To introduce money as a "tight joint" would be to deny the special problem of intertemporal coordination. Macroeconomic models with tight-jointed money serve to collapse all exchanges, whether intertemporal or atemporal, into a timeless general equilibrium framework. At the other extreme, to introduce money as a "broken joint" would be to deny even the possibility of a market solution to the problem of intertemporal coordination. In a world of broken-jointed money, prices could not conceivably transmit information about the desired allocation of resources over time or provide the correct incentives for such a desired allocation to he actualized. In short, the concepts of tight-jointed money and broken-jointed money serve to deny, respectively, the central macroeconomic problem and its solution. It will be argued below that the mainstreams of macroeconomic thought, Monetarism and Keynesianism, have tended to adopt one of the two polar positions with the result that, as a first approximation, macroeconomic problems are seen to be either trivial or insoluble. Between these extreme conceptions is Hayek's notion of loose-jointed money, which serves to recognize the problem while leaving the possibility of a market solution to it an open question.[9]

The Mainstreams of Macroeconomics

That the monetary mechanism is an essentially loose one is precisely the fact that is ignored in one of the two mainstream views. It may be instructive to consider the writings of Knut Wicksell [(1936), pp. 122–56] as an early example of tight-jointed macroeconomic models. Wicksell's formulation is singled out because of its praiseworthiness on other counts. It incorporates a modified version of Böhm-Bawerk's capital theory and thus takes due account of the time dimension of economic activities. And his formulation squares with the ultimate truth of the quantity theory. But while Wicksell is generally credited with having integrated monetary theory and value theory, this is precisely what he did *not* do.[10] His model was so constructed that, in the simplest case, all prices, driven by the real-cash-balance effect, moved up and down together. In instances when it was recognized that some prices may (temporarily) increase more than others, no corresponding quantity changes were allowed. The result was that the Wicksellian model obscured all the ways in which the "market for money" and markets for capital goods interact and focused instead on the relationship between the total quantity of money and the general level of prices.[11] But, of course, a theory that truly integrated monetary theory and value theory would have to focus on those very interactions that Wicksell's formulation assumed away.

Modern developers of Wicksell's formulation have recognized that the real-cash-balance effect is the *only* link in that formulation between the real and the monetary factors. Even though the equilibrating forces were originally described in the context of a quasi–Böhm-Bawerkian capital structure, the monetary forces were never allowed to impinge on the intertemporal relationships reflected in the existing structure of capital goods. Monetary considerations and value considerations were kept *segregated* by the assumption—sometimes explicit, sometimes implicit—of tight-jointed money. And it is precisely this segregation of monetary and value theory that allows modern theorists, such as Don Patinkin [(1965), pp. 199–213], to replace the complex intertemporal structure of production and its output with a single aggregate labeled "commodities." Simplifying the formulation in this way transforms the assumption of tight-jointed money into the equivalent assumption that nothing of relevance to macroeconomics is taking place *within* the commodities sector. Clearly, those who see loose-jointed money as the ultimate source of all the troublesome macroeconomic phenomena will see that Patinkin's analysis is trivial in this context.[12]

While the notion of tight-jointed money trivializes macroeconomic problems, the opposing notion of money as a broken joint renders them insoluble. This opposing polar assumption, however, lies at the root of the second mainstream. Keynes denied the applicability of Say's Law to a monetary economy and chided his contemporaries for "fallaciously supposing that there is a nexus which unites decisions to abstain from present consumption with decisions to provide for future consumption . . ." [(1964), p. 21]. Keynes saw the money rate of interest, which his contemporaries took to be a loose intertemporal link, as a *"current phenomenon"* [(1964), p. 146]. The perceived absence of any mechanism in a monetary economy which could conceivably achieve intertemporal coordination of economic activities explains how Keynes could summarily dismiss the theory of capital devised by Böhm-Bawerk without seeing the need to replace it with some other comprehensive view of capital. The relationships between the various elements of the capital structure were simply no part of his theory. Instead, it was only by "accident or design" [(1964), p. 28]—as opposed to the outcome of an undesigned order—that the economy achieved macroeconomic coordination. That is, with the assumption that money constitutes a broken joint, a market solution to macroeconomic problems is beyond the pale.

Viewed from this perspective the macroeconomic theory offered by Hayek and other members of the Austrian school represents a middle-ground position.[13] At the same time it constitutes a radical position—radical in the sense of going to the root of the matter. The following section provides a broad outline of the Austrian view and the penultimate section evaluates some modern advancements in mainstream views in the light of this outline.

Austrian Macroeconomics

As was noted earlier, indirect exchange in a pure exchange economy allows for some discrepancies—some looseness—between the supply of goods and the demand for goods. But excess supplies and demands in such an economy are simple in nature and can be eliminated in a relatively painless way through simple price changes that alter relative prices and possibly the general price level as well. Apart from adjustments in real cash balances, the market process in a pure exchange economy is of very little interest to macrotheorists.

The implications of a loose monetary joint grow in complexity when the setting is generalized to allow for goods of various orders—to use the Mengerian terminology. The constellation of capital goods that facilitate production is the embodiment of the time element in the production process. In this setting the availability of the goods that characterized the pure exchange economy is preceeded by a *sequence* of exchanges of goods of "higher order"—plant and equipment, raw materials, goods in process. This sequence of exchanges gives leverage to the looseness of the monetary joint. For example, an excess of higher-order goods that are several steps removed from the emergence of consumer goods (e.g., lumber destined for use in the construction industry) may not be seen immediately as an excess at all. Such a perception depends critically on entrepreneurial forecasts of future consumer demand. An erroneous forecast may not be revealed before the creation of corresponding excesses in the subsequent stages of the production process. But in accordance with Say's Law, the excess will eventually reveal itself. Although the revelation could take any of a number of forms, in the Austrian literature it usually takes the form of a (relative) shortfall of the capital goods needed to complete the production process.[14] This particular scenario emphasizes the notion of intertemporal complementarity among different kinds (orders) of capital goods. The significant point is that the excess supplies and demands, once revealed, are not remedied in any simple manner. The necessary adjustments may involve a fundamental restructuring of the economy's production processes. The looseness of the monetary joint, in effect, has allowed for a certain amount of intertemporal *dis*coordination to go unperceived for a period of time. The resulting "malinvestment" consists of an overinvestment of some kinds of capital (typically, long-term capital goods) and an underinvestment of other kinds (typically, short-term capital goods). Not surprisingly, the market process that corrects for this economywide malinvestment can be a long and painful one. The looseness of the monetary joint that allows discoordination to arise in the first place precludes a quick and painless remedy.

The Hayekian theory contains an implicit criticism of practically all mainstream theories. It warns against making a stipulative distinction between structural unemployment and cyclical unemployment. The mainstream approach is to abstract from the structural component of unemployment in order to focus more clearly on the cyclical component; the Austrian approach recognizes that cyclical unemployment can arise from a discoordinated capital structure.[15]

Further, the Austrian view has clear implications about the broadly conceived goals of macroeconomic policy. Policymakers should recognize the inherent looseness in the system and should abstain from any actions that would further weaken the loose joint or render the inherent looseness more difficult to deal with. Space does not permit a full consideration of alternative policy schemes, but there is room for a broad generalization. The conceptualization of money as a loose joint strengthens our intuition that discretionary policy is likely to exacerbate the problems that stem from the loose jointedness of the system. Hayek [(1941), p. 408)] issued an early warning against such policies.

> [M]oney by its very nature constitutes a kind of loose joint in the self-equilibrating apparatus of the price mechanism which is bound to impede its working—the more so the greater the play in the loose joint. But the existence of such a loose joint is no justification for concentrating attention on that loose joint and disregarding the rest of the mechanism, and still less for making the greatest possible use of the short-lived freedom from economic necessity which the existence of this loose joint permits.

This passage captures the flavor of modern writings within the Austrian tradition and anticipates in a significant way the essential aspect of many modern developments. The Hayekian view is consistent with the Public-

Choice view of policy decisions, the notion of the political business cycle, and the Chicago-originated analysis that hinges on the distinction between the short-run and the long-run Phillips curve.[16]

Related Developments in the Mainstreams

In the interest of contrasting the mainstream views with those offered here, the former were presented in their polar forms. Apart from matters of style and attention to the real-cash-balance effect, Patinkin's macroeconomics is a specimen of Ricardian long-run analysis. The objective is to compare the characteristics of successive states of equilibrium which are separated by a period of time sufficiently long for the economy fully to adjust to all parametric changes. Changes in the relative prices and quantities of different kinds of capital goods or other productive factors during the equilibrating process are never brought into view.[17]

At the other end of the spectrum is the extreme Keynesian view. With no effective intertemporal link (money is a broken joint) the analysis focuses exclusively on the short run. The long run, in this view, is nothing more than an unending sequence of short runs each with its own equilibrium (or disequilibrium) solution. Long-run truths, such as those implied by the quantity theory, do not "fall out of" Keynesian models but rather have to be "forced into" them. Analyses based on these models are wholly inadequate for showing how the market adjusts over time to parametric or policy changes.

Clearly, the frontiers of macroeconomics lie somewhere between the two extreme views. Somewhere between the short run and the long run is the relevant run, the run in which all the macromaladies manifest themselves, and hence the run in which these phenomena must be analyzed. Modern attempts to get at the relevant run, that is, to take both short-run and long-run considerations into account, differ in terms of which of the two polar positions is adopted as the starting point and what particular device is introduced to allow some movement toward the other pole. While any number of individual contributions illustrating this general approach could be cited, it will be convenient to focus attention on two articles, one by David Laidler (1975), the other by Paul Davidson (1980). These particular articles deserve to be singled out in part because each of the two authors is clearly identified with one of the mainstream views, and in part because both of the articles explicitly recognize the centrality of time and money in macroeconomic analysis. This facilitates a comparison between the mainstream approaches and the Austrian approach as outlined above.

Quoting selectively from the Laidler article can establish that Laidler correctly perceives the fundamental importance of time and money. On time: "Once they are committed to a certain course of behavior, economic agents may not instantaneously and costlessly change that commitment; thus the passage of time and its irreversibility are matters of paramount importance in understanding economic activity" [(1975), p. 5]. On money: "There is no unique market for money, and its 'price' emerges as a result of economic agents each setting the price of a particular good he is supplying in terms of money" [(1975), p. 7]. But Laidler is working within the quantity-theory tradition—the tradition that adopts as its starting point (and sometimes its ending point) the assumption that enough *time* is allowed to elapse so that the unique effects of *money* are fully dissipated. Some analytical device is needed that will transform his long-run analytical framework into a framework that can deal with the interplay between time and money. He needs to shorten the long run, to loosen the tight joint of money. The device Laidler employs is the one whose development is associated with that same tradition—the market for information. By taking into account the simple fact that information about the uncertain future is not costlessly available, Laidler is able to deal with the phenomena that characterize the relevant run. The time dimension, in effect, is captured, at least in part, by the market for information. The interaction between this market for information and the market for money constitutes what Laidler refers to as "the new micro-economics." And he clearly recognizes the payoff of this approach. "It is the peculiar contribution of the new micro-economics to macroeconomics that it explains the time path of prices and their potential incompatibility with full employment as a result of rational behavior in the face of imperfect and costly information that is inherent in a market economy" [(1975), p. 74].

In the above capsulization of the approach that Laidler outlines, the market for information is somewhat contentiously referred to as a "device." This characterization is intended to suggest that the "new micro-economics" does not deal with the relevant run in the most fundamental or direct way. The actual "market for information"—even when conceived broadly to include education, consulting services, advertising, and all printed matter—consists of a circumscribed set of activities. Though important, the analysis of this market (or these markets) belongs to the realm of the "old microeconomics." In order to transform the notion of the "market for information" into a macro-economic concept the term has to be taken in a metaphorical sense. In any transaction involving any good the buyer is also "buying information" about the price at which the seller is *actually* willing to sell, and "selling information" about the price he is *actually* willing to pay.[18] Transactions involving particular goods may imply the "buying" and "selling" of other kinds of information as well. For instance, in buying a tiller the buyer "sells" information about the future demand for reapers.

Identifying the metaphoric character of Laidler's "market for information" facilitates a comparison between this particular approach and the one adopted by the Austrian school. It suggests that the Austrian approach is the more fundamental and direct. Markets that actually exist are markets for goods and services. Money is taken into account by recognizing that each of the goods and services is exchanged for money. The two approaches are equivalent in this respect. Time is taken into account in the Austrian tradition by recognizing the intertemporal relationship among the different goods and services. This approach requires a theory of capital and an understanding of the economy's structure of production. It is true that the passage of time implies the existence of uncertainty which gives rise to a "market for information," but it does not follow that incorporating the market for information into macroeconomics takes full account of the time dimension. The fundamental intertemporal relationship between tillers and reapers, for instance, is not captured by this approach. Uncertainty is a weak proxy for time. The "market for information" is best viewed as a *device* for venturing into the relevant run without having to grapple with capital theory and hence with the more fundamental intertemporal relationships among the various objects of exchange.

Paul Davidson's article is, in an important sense, the Keynesian counterpart to Laidler's. In a section entitled "The importance of money" [(1980). p. 164], Davidson discusses indirect exchange in the context of the passage of time. He is clearly attempting to get at the macroeconomics of the relevant run. The subject matter is the same as in the Laidler article. But Davidson is working in the tradition of the other mainstream. Where Laidler needed to loosen a tight monetary joint, Davidson needs to create a joint where none existed; where Laidler needed to shorten the long run, Davidson needs to lengthen the short run. The device that Davidson employs is the money-wage contract [(1980), pp. 164–67]. It is primarily this particular intertemporal exchange that keeps the passage of time from being nothing more than a sequence of unrelated short runs. In Davidson's own words: "In a decentralized market economy . . . moving irresistibly through historical time into the uncertain future, forward contracting for production inputs is essential to efficient production planning. And the most ubiquitous forward contract of all in such an economy so long as slavery and peonage are illegal, is the money-wage contract" [(1980), pp. 165–66]. Where Laidler attempted to capture the time dimension in the market for information, Davidson attempts to capture it in the forward market for labor.

The term "device" is as appropriate in describing Davidson's formulation as it was in describing Laidler's. Although labor markets span the entire economy, the forward dealings in these markets is only one of many ways that intertemporal exchange takes place. Contrary to Davidson's suggestion, there is no reason that this particular type of intertemporal transaction should be singled out for special treatment. Goods and services in general are related to one another over time. The general theory of the nature of these intertemporal relationships and of how these relationships may be acted by parametric or policy changes is what constitutes capital theory. But capital theory is precisely what is lacking in both mainstreams. The "money-wage contract" is best viewed as Davidson's *device* for venturing into the relevant run (venturing in to meet Laidler, who has ventured in from the other direction) without having to deal in any general way with the basic issues of capital theory.

Summary and Conclusion

To recognize time and money as the universals of macroeconomic theorizing is to define the domain of macroeconomics as the interaction of the "market for time" and the "market for money." This conception of macroeconomics, which has merit in its own right, allows for a fruitful comparison of mainstream views. It points to the indirectness with which the mainstream theories deal with the time element. The practice of using weak surrogates for the time dimension, such as the market for information or the forward market for labor, causes the more fundamental intertemporal relationships, as spelled out in Austrian capital theory, to be overlooked.

The inadequacies of the two mainstreams are identified in a way that suggests the appropriate remedy. Since the Keynesian revolution the development of macroeconomics (by both Keynesians and Monetarists) has proceeded in the absence of any coherent theory of capital. The present paper suggests that the reincorporation of capital theory into macroeconomics would pave the way toward a more fundamental treatment of the time element and a reconciliation of the two mainstream views.

Notes

The author gratefully acknowledges helpful comments from Don Bellante; Don Boudreaux; Gerald P. O'Driscoll, Jr.; Mario J. Rizzo; Leland B. Yeager; and two anonymous referees.

1. See Hayek (1967), Garrison (1978), and O'Driscoll and Rizzo (1985).

2. Major contributors to this literature include Clower (1967) and Leijonhufvud (1974). For recent Austrian-oriented contributions, see O'Driscoll (1979) and Lewin (1982).

3. See, for instance, Böhm-Bawerk [(1959), 2: 259–89, and Mises [(1966), pp. 99–104, 479–537, and *passim*].

4. Efforts to reintroduce the time dimension in some artificial way—such as by defining the different goods of a general-equilibrium model partly in terms of the time they are available for consumption—have served to obscure rather than resolve the difficulties associated with the time element. For a candid recognition of this and other limitations of general equilibrium theory, see Hahn (1980).

5. This imagery, of course, is from Keynes (1964)

6. For early attention to this aspect of a monetary economy, see Mises (1953). More recently, this aspect has received due attention from Yeager (1968) and Birch, Rabin, and Yeager (1982).

7. In laying the "foundations of monetary theory," Clower [(1967), pp. 208–08] offers the idea in the form of an aphorism. "*Money buys goods and goods buy money, goods do not buy goods.* This restriction is—or ought to be—the central theme of the theory of a money economy" (emphasis in the original). To recognize the validity and importance of Clower's aphorism is to endorse the assessment that Whilhelm Roscher, founder of the early historical school, made over a century ago. All *false* theories of money fall into one of two categories: those that take money to be something more than the most saleable of all commodities, and those that take it to be something less. See Schumpeter [(19540, p. 699].

8. Keynes's "Sundry Observations on the Nature of Capital" [(1964), pp. 210–11] do not add up to a coherent theory of capital.

9. It might be noted that the assumption of tight-jointed money is not to be condemned in all contexts. This assumption gives meaning to the notion that "money is a veil." It allows us to identify the underlying general-equilibrium relationships with which any theory macroeconomic or otherwise, must ultimately be reconciled. The assumption of tight-jointed money also allows us to defend the kernel of truth in the quantity theory of money. At the same time

the need to make this assumption warns us of the limited applicability of the simple quantity theory. But all the interesting macroeconomic phenomena, which manifest themselves as economywide coordination failures, depend critically on the fact that real-world money is not of the tight-jointed variety.

10. For a corroborating assessment of the "post-Wicksellians," see Hutt [(1979), p. 117].

11. Hayek [(1975), pp. 109–16] was critical of Wicksell for his undue attention to the general price level.

12. See, for instance, the criticisms of Lutz [(1969), pp. 115–16].

13. For a general view of Austrian economics as a middle-ground position, see Garrison [(1982), pp. 131–38].

14. See Hayek [(1967), pp. 54–60].

15. For development of this contrast between the mainstream and Austrian views, see Bellante (1983).

16. Although Milton Friedman made the short-run/long-run distinction in terms of the Phillips curve in his 1967 AEA presidential address, the distinction itself and its relevance to monetary policy are prominent in the early works of Mises (1953) and Hayek (1967, 1975). I am indebted to an anonymous referee for making this point.

17. In its polar form, Patinkin-type macroeconomics comes complete with a modern analog of the Ricardian vice: In effect, the analysis that is only applied after the dust has settled is used to suggest that there is no problem with dust.

18. This is the sense in which prices are "signals" and the market is a "communications network." See Hayek (1945).

References

Ballante, D. "A Subjectivist Essay on Modern Labor Economics." *Managerial and Decision Economics.* 4 (December 1983): 234–43.

Birch, D. E., A. A. Rabin, and L. B. Yeager. "Inflation, Output, and Employment: Some Clarifications." *Economic Inquiry* 20 (April 1982): 209–21.

Böhm-Bawerk, E. *Capital and Interest.* 3 vols. South Holland, IL: Libertarian Press, 1959.

Clower. R. W. "A Reconsideration of the Microfoundations of Monetary Theory." *Western Economic Journal* 6 (December 1967): 1–9.

Davidson, P. "Post Keynesian Economics." *Public Interest* (Special Issue, 1980): 151–73.

Garrison, R. W. "Austrian Economics as the Middle Ground: Comment on Loasby." In *Method, Process, and Austrian Economics: Essays in Honor of Ludwig von Mises*. I. M. Kirzner, ed. Lexington, MA: Lexington Books, 1982, 131–38.

————. Austrian Macroeconomics: A Diagrammatical Exposition." In *New Directions in Austrian Economics*. L. M. Spadaro, ed. Kansas City: Sheed, Andrews, and McMeel. 1978, 167–204.

Hahn, F. "General Equilibrium Theory." *Public Interest* (Special Issue, 1980): 123–38.

Hayek. F. A. *Monetary Theory and the Trade Cycle*. New York: Augustus M. Kelley, 1975.

————. *Prices and Production*, 2nd ed. New York: Augustus M. Kelley, 1967.

————. *The Pure Theory of Capital*. Chicago: University of Chicago Press, 1941.

————. "The Use of Knowledge in Society." *American Economic Review* 35 (September 1945): 519–30.

Hutt, W. H. *The Keynesian Episode*. Indianapolis: Liberty Press, 1979.

Jevons, W. S. *The Theory of Political Economy*. Middlesex: Penguin Books, 1970.

Keynes, J. M. *The General Theory of Employment, Interest, and Money*. New York: Harcourt, Brace, and World, 1964.

Laidler, D. E. W. "Information, Money and the Macro-Economics of Inflation." In his *Essays on Money and Inflation*. Chicago: University of Chicago Press, 1975.

Leijonhufvud, A. *On Keynesian Economics and the Economics of Keynes*. New York: Oxford University Press, 1968.

————. "The Varieties of Price Theory: What Microfoundations for Macro Theory?" UCLA Discussion Paper, No. 44, 1974.

Lewin, P. "Perspectives on the Cost of Inflation." *Southern Economic Journal* 48 (January 1982): 627–41.

Lutz, F. A. "On Neutral Money." In *Roads to Freedom: Essays in Honor of Friedrich A. von Hayek*. E. Streissler, G. Haberler, F. A. Lutz, and F. Machlup, eds. London: Routledge and Kegan Paul, 1969.

Menger, C. *Principles of Economics*. New York: Free Market Press, 1950.

Mises, L. *Human Action: A Treatise on Economics*, 3rd rev. ed. Chicago: Henry Regnery, 1966.

————. *The Theory of Money and Credit*. New Haven: Yale University Press, 1953.

O'Driscoll, G. P., Jr. "Rational Expectations, Politics, and Stagflation." *In Time, Uncertainty, and Disequilibrium*. M. J. Rizzo, ed. Lexington, MA: Lexington Books, 1979.

———— and M. J. Rizzo with R. W. Garrison. *The Economics of Time and Ignorance*. Oxford: Basil Blackwell, 1985.

Patinkin, D. *Money, Interest, and Prices*, 2nd ed. New York: Harper and Row, 1965.

Schumpeter, J. A. *History of Economic Analysis*. New York: Oxford University Press. 1954.

Wicksell, K. *Interest and Prices*. London. Macmillan, 1936.

Yeager, L. B. "Essential Properties of the Medium of Exchange." *Kyklos* 21 (January/March 1968): 45-68.

2

THE DRIVING FORCE OF THE MARKET: THE IDEA OF "COMPETITION" IN CONTEMPORARY ECONOMIC THEORY AND IN THE AUSTRIAN THEORY OF THE MARKET PROCESS

ISRAEL M. KIRZNER

The crucial role played by the notion of dynamic competition in Austrian economics is by now well known. It is widely appreciated that perhaps the critical respect in which the modern Austrian paradigm differs from the mainstream approach consists in the Austrian rejection of the centrality in the latter of the perfectly competitive model, and its replacement by the idea of the entrepreneurial-competitive market *process*. In this process the essential element is the steadily expanding field of mutual awareness on the part of potential market participants. Whereas the perfectly competitive model expresses the equilibrium pattern of decisions expressing already attained, complete mutual knowledge, the competitive market process expresses the course of mutual discovery through which an equilibrium may possibly be approached.[1]

Although this fundamental difference has been articulated by the Austrians now for several decades,[2] there has been disappointingly little impact upon mainstream contemporary theory. Precisely during a period in which mainstream theorists have come to recognize the limitations of their models in explaining the equilibrating process,[3] and have come to appreciate the importance of changing knowledge in determining market outcomes[4]—the textbook paramountcy of the perfectly competitive model appears to be as solidly ensconced as ever. Despite the "uprising" of contestable market theory,[5] the perfectly competitive model appears not to have been dislodged. More to the point, perhaps, there is little in this uprising itself which reflects the insights of the theory of the dynamic competitive process.

I shall not attempt yet another Austrian assault on mainstream perfect competition orthodoxy. Instead I shall briefly review the principal insights embodied in the Austrian approach to understanding competition, in order to place emphasis upon certain insufficiently noticed features of this approach. Beyond these points of emphasis (and an attempt to illustrate the significance of this emphasis by reference to certain recent disagreements among Austrians), there will be very little new here.

The point upon which I wish to place emphasis can be stated simply: Economists contrast monopolistic markets with competitive markets. But while this contrast is appropriate within the equilibrium understanding of the meaning of competition, this is not the case for a theory concentrating on the competitive market *process*. In the context of the theory of market process, *competition should be recognized as universal*—even for the market process which operates to bring about monopoly prices. To speak of the *competitive* market process is in fact to engage in periphrasis. There *is* no market process other than the competitive one. Competitive activity is the activity which constitutes the market process. So it is misleading to inquire, for example, into the conditions required to render the market process competitive. To understand the dynamic motion of competition is at the same time to grasp the nature of the market process—with or without monopoly. Although this insight is certainly not new,[6] it appears not to have been sufficiently emphasized. I will suggest in this paper that this insight offers a useful vantage point from which to appraise certain issues debated in modern Austrian literature.

The Model of Perfect Competition

The equilibrium character of the perfectly competitive market model is now widely understood. The model presumes satisfaction of a series of conditions which together assure a pattern of decisions by market participants insulated from the possibility of disappointment or regret. No decision to buy or to sell can fail to be accepted in this model. Nor can hindsight ever reveal to any buyer or seller that a more attractive market opportunity has been missed. Each potential buyer (seller) correctly anticipates the lowest (highest) price available in the market, and, moreover, correctly expects to be able to buy (sell) as much as he wishes to buy (sell) at this price. The price which all market participants correctly anticipate is that price which, when indeed anticipated by all, inspires the decisions to buy and sell which dovetail completely. It is not merely that the buying and selling decisions so made do indeed mesh perfectly; it is, in addition to such "pre-reconciliation of plans,"[7] that the sets of expectations underlying and inspiring each of these plans have somehow come to correctly and mutually anticipate what each of the other plans will in fact bring about. In fact, the perfection of knowledge underlying the model is, ultimately, more than simply the correct anticipation by each participant of the actions of others; it involves, in the final analysis, the correct and self-fulfilling anticipation by each of the (correct and self-fulfilling) anticipations by each of the others, of the (correct and self-fulfilling) anticipations, et cetera, et cetera, ad infinitum.

To put the matter concisely, the perfectly competitive model portrays (as does each and every equilibrium model of a market) a pattern of mutual anticipations and executed decisions which, if somehow attained, would lead no participant to wish that he had acted differently. It was this equilibrium character of the model to which Hayek was referring when, over forty years ago, he criticized it as blandly assuming that "situation to exist which a true explanation ought to account for as the effect of the competitive process."[8] *If* such a perfectly competitive situation in fact exists, Hayek was exclaiming, the scientific challenge is surely to account for the chain of events which has led to the quite remarkable fulfillment of the extraordinarily demanding set of relevant conditions. Of course no such account can be expected from the model itself.

Unless one adopts a methodology in which the truthfulness of the assumptions of models is of no concern, all this must render the model of perfect competition far less useful than the standard microeconomics textbooks appear to believe. The model can*not* be used to "explain" market prices; the model *presumes* that everyone has, somehow, correctly and self-fulfillingly guessed what the market price is going to be. The circumstance that (quite apart from the assumed correctness of the anticipated price) the model treats each market participant as a price-taker further underscores the uselessness of the model as an explanation for the manner in which prices are adjusted. No one in the model ever does change his price bids or offers.

These limitations of the model have not altogether escaped mainstream acknowledgment. One recent writer on the perfectly competitive model pointed out that "the competitive model is inherently unable to contemplate economic activity out of equilibrium."[9] An entire issue of the *Journal of Economic Theory* was devoted, several years ago, to exploring the rationale for the perfectly competitive model.[10] Yet the centrality of the model in mainstream microeconomics seems to continue virtually unchallenged. Even more disturbing, perhaps, is the circumstance that, where attention is paid to the need for a theory of the equilibrating process, and even where it is recognized that such a theory must involve systematic processes of knowledge and expectations modification, it is somehow not perceived that the notion of dynamic competition is precisely the analytical device needed for the required theoretical task.

Competition as an Entrepreneurial/Discovery Procedure

The emphasis by Austrians in recent decades upon dynamic competition has been part of their comprehensive attack on the dominance, in modern economics, of equilibrium analysis. Following Ludwig von Mises in his conception of the market as a dynamic entrepreneurial *process*, rather than as an array of mutually sustaining optimal exchange decisions, Austrians have drawn the attention of economists back to an earlier classical notion of competition as a rivalrous process.[11] This notion, so congenial to the experience of the businessman, underscores competition not in the sense of individual powerlessness in the face of the presence of competitors, but in the sense of a procedure inspired by the incentive of outstripping one's competitors in order to achieve market success. As Austrians came to appreciate, the essence of this rivalrous process lies in the pressure it applies, and the incentives it offers, to competing market participants to recognize the opportunities created by earlier decisions (which failed to offer the best possible conditions to other market participants), and the disappointments to be avoided in repeating earlier decisions (which erroneously insisted on unattainable exchange terms). To put it concisely, Austrians came to understand *competition as a process of discovery*. Both over-optimism and undue pessimism, as expressed in earlier rejected bids and offers and in earlier regrets (at attained, but less than optimal, exchange transactions) may come to be replaced in this process by more realistic assessments of market opportunities.

In other words, the changing patterns of bids and offers made in the course of the market process reflect, in the perspective of this Austrian approach, the lessons learned, rightly or wrongly, during that process. If the course of this competitive market process turns out to be equilibrating, this is seen, from this dynamic perspective, as the result of the systematic improvement in mutual knowledge (among market participants) generated by the competitive pressures. The possibility of systematic equilibrating tendencies is underscored by recognition of the *entrepreneurial* character of the competitive process.

Initial errors by market participants generate a disequilibrium pattern of market bids and offers. Some bids and offers are rejected as hopelessly unattractive. Prospective buyers may have been prepared to offer better terms, but had erroneously overestimated the eagerness of the potential sellers. And so on. Market experience may teach more realistic estimates in this regard. Again, bids and offers may be accepted, but may generate regret as market experience demonstrates that even more advantageous market opportunities might have been grasped. The changes in bids and offers stimulated by these market experiences represent *entrepreneurial discovery* of the true dimensions of market opportunities. Without deliberate search (by prospective buyers and sellers) for the best terms consistent with the attitudes of other market participants, decision makers come to learn how to avoid disappointment and elude regret. Their alertness to earlier disappointments and to regrettably overlooked opportunities teaches them, during an equilibrating process, to adopt more accurate attitudes in anticipating the reactions of others.

The net result is that, to the extent that entrepreneurial alertness indeed induces steadily more realistic estimates of the attitudes of others, the course of market transactions becomes steadily closer to a pattern avoiding both disappointments and regrets. The competitive-entrepreneurial process then becomes an equilibrating process leading, possibly, close to that very state of affairs assumed from the very beginning by the modelists of perfect competition. To the extent that economic history ever does display market conditions roughly consistent with the perfectly competitive model, this can then be accounted for by reference to the achievements of the dynamic process of competition. To the extent that economic history (as it invariably does) displays features which are thoroughly inconsistent with the perfectly competitive model, this may be accounted for by understanding how the dynamic process of competition has, as yet, not fully run its equilibrating course. Features of real world markets will typically reflect the errors which it is the function of the competitive process to identify and correct.

What drives this competitive process is the alertness of market participants to the profit possibilities created by past errors, and to the unfortunate frustrations that would be the result of repeating past errors. This entrepreneurial process is competitive in the sense that it relies upon the freedom of alert entrepreneurs to enter markets and exploit these possibilities. It is the possibility of such entry which not only provides an incentive for alert potential entrants, but also, through acting as a threat, inspires parallel alertness on the part of incumbent market participants, spurring them to anticipate potential entrants through their own entrepreneurial decisions. Constantly looking over their shoulders, market participants are inspired alertly to notice and implement opportunities for offering superior options to the market. The competitive process is driven by the entrepreneurial element in each human being, by the propensity to notice the implications of earlier errors (which propensity is the essence of entrepreneurship). The competitive process itself consists of the systematic series of revised decisions on the part of market participants, generated by their entrepreneurial discoveries. I am now in a position to spell out more fully the point in this approach to competition which I wish to emphasize in this paper.

Competition and Monopoly

It is ordinarily assumed that competition and monopoly are at opposite poles of a single continuum. Along this spectrum, being "more monopolistic" means being correspondingly "less competitive." At the one extreme one has the perfectly competitive market, at the other a market characterized by pure monopoly. (Theories of imperfect or monopolistic competition were designed to avoid confining economic theory strictly to these polar cases.) Each type of market is, in this perspective, characterized by a series of defining criteria. The criteria defining the polar cases are mutually exclusive; those governing intermediate cases partly overlap with those defining one or both of the polar models.

My claim here is that this way of looking at competition and monopoly might be appropriate for the classification of alternative static equilibrium models. To the extent, for example, that the demand curve confronting a firm is less than perfectly elastic, this may be interpreted as reflecting a degree of "market power" possessed by the firm. With perfect competition defined in terms of total absence of such power, a degree of power expressed in a downward-sloping demand curve may plausibly come to be labelled a degree of monopoly. This was indeed the approach expressed in Abba Lerner's classic attempt to conceive of a measure of monopoly power.[12]

But, I wish to point out, for an approach which puts the emphasis on competition as a dynamic process, the idea of competition and monopoly being at opposite poles of a single spectrum is confused and almost incoherent. For this approach, competition is the essential defining characteristic of the market process itself. No matter what the institutional contours of the market may be, no matter what the economic power possessed by market participants may be, the market process (if such a process does exist and occur) is itself necessarily competitive. It is a process during which entrepreneurial, competitive-minded market participants, whether incumbent participants or merely potential participants, discover the true shape of market possibilities and constraints. The only situation in which competition can be said to be absent is one in which markets do not operate. Such a situation presumes, as in the centrally planned economy, the existence of institutional prohibitions on market exchanges. In any *market* situation, however, no matter what the degree of monopoly may be (and regardless of how monopoly is to be defined), the market process itself must be a competitive one. There simply is no market process other than that consisting of competitively inspired discoveries of opportunities for gain through exchange.

If, for example, a firm is the monopolist in an industry (whether as the result of unique control over some essential input or as the result of governmental grant of exclusive privilege), the manner in which the monopolist's price and quantity of sales is determined in the market is one that emerges from the competitive interplay of the decisions of potential buyers (of the monopolized commodity) as well as of those of participants in related markets. There is no other procedure governing the sequence of prices and quantities as determined in a world of open-ended uncertainty. Textbooks present, of course, the monopolized market as one in which the monopolist is confronted by a given and known demand curve, from which he at once selects his profit-maximizing price-quantity combination. But in fact no monopolist knows his demand curve in advance. It is the market process that reveals what the contours of the market possibilities really are, so that for the monopolized market it is the competitive process that tends to ensure that the monopoly equilibrium is in fact approached.

It is reasonable to try to formulate the conditions defining a monopolized market, but it is almost incoherent to ask for the conditions that must be satisfied in order for a market process to be described as being competitive. A market process *is* competitive by the very nature of being a market process. Sometimes I try to characterize the competitive nature of the market process by drawing attention to "freedom of entry" (or its correlate, "absence of privilege"), but it would be confusing to state that a market process is competitive according to the extent to which it permits free entry. A market process *consists* of the decisions of those who enter or who might enter. At most one can say that the extent to which a social process can be described as a market process depends on the extent to which freedom of entry to buy and sell are permitted. Freedom of entry is indeed a defining characteristic of competition, but only because the market process is, by definition, a competitive one.

Admittedly all this does create a certain difficulty for economic terminology. A market may be monopolized or it may not be monopolized. How *am* I to describe a market in which exclusive monopolistic privilege is absent? Surely the adjective "competitive" has a reasonable claim, in economic history and in the history of economic theory, to be the label describing the absence of exclusive privilege? The terminological difficulty is a real one, and is, probably, responsible in part for the extraordinary confusion which has surrounded the concepts of monopoly and competition during the twentieth century. It is, therefore, useful to examine one recent example of the problem, an example taken from an internal disagreement within Austrian economics.

The Misesian Theory of Monopoly

Standard theory defines competition in terms of the degree of elasticity of demand facing the firm. In the case of perfect competition this elasticity is infinite; there are so many firms in the industry, and knowledge is so perfect, that no one of them can sell anything above the going market price. The polar opposite case is then that of a single firm selling in a well-defined market. With outside entry somehow absent, this monopolist then confronts the market demand curve, and chooses his profit-maximizing position accordingly. Clearly, if this monopoly position does indeed yield pure profit, the question arises as to why outside entry is indeed absent. Why *don't* others enter in an attempt to grasp some of this profit? It was this insight which inspired Mises to recognize that, *within the market system itself*, the only possible source for monopoly was sole ownership of some scarce essential input. (Of course Mises made it clear that government intervention in a market system can—and has historically very frequently indeed—generated monopolized markets.) If government forbids others to compete with a licensed producer, this certainly places him in a monopoly position, able to earn a supernormal return (which competition will be unable to "compete away").

Without government blocking of competitive entry, the number of firms in an industry, no matter how small, does not insulate them from the cold winds of potential competition; they are subject to the threat of the process of competitive entry. With the possibility, however, of a single owner of a scarce essential resource, Mises argued, we must recognize the possibility that this owner may be able to obtain greater revenue out of his resource by withholding part of it from the market. Whether he uses the resource in production himself or whether he sells it to other producers, his revenues may turn out to be greater as a result of his refusing to sell all that he, in his capacity as resource owner, might be prepared to sell were he to be only one of a number of such resource owners. Mises did *not* consider this possibility to be of much practical importance. Certainly he was convinced that most situations usually described as monopolistic are either not monopolistic at all or are likely to be the result of government obstacles against entry, rather than being the result of unique resource ownership. Yet, from the theoretical perspective, the possibility of a true monopoly occurring within a market is an interesting one and Mises pursued it for the sake of theoretical completeness.

With exclusive resource ownership, the extra monopoly revenue (that results from withholding some of the available supply from the market) is clearly not in the nature of any pure entrepreneurial profit. Rather it is an extra rent obtainable from the scarce resource as a result of the economic power created out of the peculiar pattern of ownership coupled with the absence of close substitute resources. "Entrepreneurial profit has nothing to do with monopoly. If an entrepreneur is in a position to sell at monopoly prices, he owes this advantage to his monopoly with regard to a monopolized factor m. He earns the specific monopoly gain from his ownership of m, not from his specific entrepreneurial activities."[13] There is, therefore, no problem of explaining why entrepreneurial entry does not compete away this surplus revenue; this surplus revenue is not an entrepreneurial profit, it can be obtained only by virtue of ownership of the resource.

Just as in the case of other markets, price in the monopolized market emerges through the rough and tumble of competing entrants. Of course, with exclusive resource ownership the entrants are (apart from the competing potential buyers) the owners of (possibly distant) substitute resources, or producers of competing products. It is the process of such competition that guides the monopoly resource owner to his best obtainable position. Mises points out that the "monopolist does not know the shape of the curve of demand" for his resource.[14] Clearly Mises is relying on the competitive market process to guide the monopolist to the profit-maximizing position obtainable by withholding some of the resource.

Mises: A Neoclassical

I shall not deal comprehensively with the various criticisms from within Austrian economics which the Misesian theory has drawn.[15] I shall concern myself here only with one line of criticism which I believe can be traced to the terminological ambiguities cited earlier.

Several years ago, Gerald O'Driscoll argued that the theory of monopoly presented by Mises is "a variant of the neoclassical theory."[16]

By the neoclassical theory of monopoly, O'Driscoll means the approach which (a) ignores the case of monopolies created by the state, and (b) ignores, in effect, the problem of why monopoly profits do not attract competitive entry (or, at any rate, provide untenable solutions to this problem). "[Neoclassical] theory lacks any defensible, coherent answer to the entry question. Monopoly is postulated without being explained."[17] O'Driscoll contrasts the neoclassical theory of monopoly with the "property-rights" approach. In the property-rights approach, entry will indeed occur. "A profitable open-market monopoly is not a stable situation and hence is not one to concern either the economist or the policymaker. The property-rights tradition is to concentrate on the many varied ways in which governments create, foster, and maintain monopoly."[18] Although O'Driscoll exonerates Mises from the charge of ignoring the cases of state-created monopoly,[19] he charges him with having a neoclassical monopoly theory in two senses. First, resource monopoly is one source of neoclassical monopoly. Second, Mises's theory "is no more successful at answering the entry question than is neoclassical theory."[20] In what follows I shall not deal directly with the unimportant issue of the neoclassical label which O'Driscoll has polemically pinned on to the Misesian theory. Instead I will attempt to address the substance of O'Driscoll's quite astonishing charge that Mises has ignored the problem of competitive entry.[21]

O'Driscoll's charge is astonishing primarily because in any reading of Mises's vehement disagreements with the standard theories of perfect competition, pure monopoly and monopolistic competition, the *absolutely* central role must surely be assigned to his insistence on the driving force of competitive entry (actual and potential) into profitable markets. It was precisely the Misesian insistence on the power of dynamic competitive entry that has inspired the revival of interest, within contemporary Austrian economics, in the market as a process, rather than as an equilibrium configuration. It was undoubtedly precisely because of this concern with competitive entry that Mises offered his drastic idea (as it must be judged by the standards of neoclassical equilibrium theory) of restricting the notion of monopoly (and its "welfare" consequences) to the level of resource ownership.

And this brings us to a second sense in which O'Driscoll's charge against Mises (that he ignored the problem of competitive entry) appears astonishing. Mises avoided the entry problem entirely by deliberately restricting the notion of monopoly, in its primary sense, to the resource owner. The entrepreneur-producer is never a monopolist *qua entrepreneur*. If he is a monopolist it is only due to the circumstance that earlier (possibly entrepreneurial) transactions may have made him, at a given point in time, the sole owner of a scarce essential resource. (In this case he is a monopolist *qua* resource owner, *not qua* entrepreneur.) To ask why competitive entry does not compete away a monopoly resource owner's monopoly gain, is, one suspects, to misunderstand that gain as a sub-species of pure entrepreneurial profit.

O'Driscoll states the central theoretical issue to be solved by a monopoly theory as being that of explaining why, if "monopoly yields a net revenue or surplus . . . does entry of new firms not occur? The profitability of monopoly should ensure its own demise."[22] The answer which Mises's theory of resource monopoly offers to the question of why competition does not wipe out the monopolist's special gain (attributable to his monopoly position) is that this special gain is, "admittedly" (if that is the appropriate adverb) by hypothesis, a result of his exclusive ownership of this (apparently essential) resource.[23] One presumes that O'Driscoll would argue that, if we accepted this interpretation of Mises, this will mean that (as O'Driscoll remarks on Ricardo) Mises has then "trivialized the central question" which O'Driscoll believes must be dealt with by any monopoly theory. Our point here is that for Mises (perhaps even more than for the writers whom O'Driscoll labels the "property-rights theorists"), the entry problem in fact erases the monopoly case completely from the agenda of the theorist *insofar as concerns the entrepreneur.* "A profitable open-market monopoly," at the entrepreneurial level, "is not a stable situation and hence is not one to concern either the economist or the policymaker."[24] Even more to the point, for our purposes, a "profitable open-market monopoly" at the entrepreneurial level is simply, for Mises, an unfortunate misnomer. When a single entrepreneur in an open market engages in a profitable venture he has, *in Misesian terminology, engaged in it competitively, not monopolistically.* Others could have entered into this line of activity. Their not having done so, so far from rendering the profit-making entrepreneur a monopolist, simply means that they have been out-competed by him. His activity is part of the entrepreneurial competitive process.

The only sense in which the idea of a monopoly retains any meaning for Mises is in the context of resource ownership. As explained in the preceding section, the monopoly gain that may, under appropriate conditions, be made by the monopoly resource owner, has nothing to do with entrepreneurial gain. It is a gain, obtainable by virtue of ownership of his resource, which would not have been forthcoming were the resource supply to be owned by more than one independent owner. There simply is no ignored "entry problem" that needs to be addressed by the Misesian theory of monopoly.

The Source of the Misunderstanding

That so perceptive and so Austrian an economist as O'Driscoll came to misunderstand Mises in this regard seems to illustrate the terminological difficulties and confusions referred to earlier. It seems evident that O'Driscoll, recognizing the Austrian emphasis on the competitive process, has thought of monopoly as a case to be contrasted with that process. It is in this context that O'Driscoll raises the entry problem. "No one would seek a monopoly position . . . unless he expected to earn returns in excess of revenues foregone. Why then do others not follow suit or imitate the first rent seeker, thus breaking down the monopoly and competing away that monopoly rent?"[25] Clearly O'Driscoll is thinking of an entrepreneur who has successfully sought a monopoly position. But this was not Mises's approach at all. He thought of a monopoly position somehow *already* existing (as a result of historical patterns of resource ownership, or whatever).[26]

In regard to the competitive-entrepreneurial process itself, it is utterly vain to search for any monopoly case. There can be none, such as we have seen, not merely because any monopoly gains so won in an open market must tend to be competed away, but also because in an open market *every* action is taken competitively (i.e., with full awareness of the need to anticipate the actions of others, actual or potential competitors). And here we have a source of misunderstanding. Mises contrasted the special case of "monopoly price" with the more general case of "competitive price."[27] This use of terminology is readily understandable but may, I fear, easily lead to a degree of confusion. It might be understood that, by using the contrasting terms, "competitive price" and "monopoly price," Mises was implying that monopoly is the opposite of competition in the sense of the competitive entrepreneurial process. Perhaps, as we have seen, O'Driscoll was led so to assume. But we have seen how this would be incorrect. The Austrian process of entrepreneurial competition has no contrast *within the market*. So long as there is a market at all, or to any degree to which a market is able to proceed, it proceeds through the sequence of transactions generated by dynamic competition.

Monopoly, for Mises, has been reduced to a particular, not-very-important case, of a resource-owner who, by virtue of history and market conditions, happens to be the sole owner of a scarce essential ingredient in the production of a good. Market outcomes in this context are, as always, determined through the course of the competitive market process. Monopoly resource ownership does not compromise the competitive character of the market process; it merely *diverts* it from the particular pattern which that process might have taken in the absence of monopoly resource ownership. Had this resource not been exclusively owned, the driving forces of competition among entrepreneurs seeking to buy the resource from competing sellers of the resource, would have tended to make it desirable for resource owners to sell all of their resource supplies (beyond what they might retain for their own consumer purposes or for speculation). With all supplies of the scarce essential resource concentrated in the hands of one owner, the forces of market competition may not tend to induce him to sell all of his supply; they may teach him how to enhance his sales revenue from the resource by throwing some of it into the sea. Such a possibility, Mises argued, would, if ever realized, pit the interests of the consuming public against those of the exclusive resource owner. It was this theoretical possibility that Mises recognized (without considering it to be of much practical significance).

Competition as the Fundamental Principle in Market Theory

In his doctoral dissertation, Frank Machovec documented the thesis that the dynamic notion of competition pervaded the bulk of economics in the neoclassical period up until the 1920s.[28] It was only during the twenties and thirties that equilibrium thinking, and thus the static model of perfect competition, assumed its current dominance in mainstream economic thought. It was presumably this prevalence of the dynamic notion of competition which led Mises into believing, as late as 1932, that the various schools of twentieth-century economic thought shared a common basic understanding of the workings of the market economy.[29]

Whatever the degree of shared understanding may have been, and whatever the diverse directions toward which these schools were respectively pointing,[30] the prevalence of the dynamic notion of competition at this time may lend support to a thesis I recently suggested. Our emphasis here has been upon the *universality* in market processes in all contexts, of the dynamically competitive element. Recently I suggested that it is the character of the discoveries which make up this dynamically competitive process to which the central economist's assumption of universal self-interest in fact pertains.[31] The self-interest assumption in economics, this suggestion argues, does not so much identify a particular pattern of choices among given available options, as it illuminates the discovery process through which market participants identify the options available to them. The self-interest assumption sees market participants as purposeful human beings alert to changing conditions and to the new opportunities these may create. The alertness which inspires the discoveries made by market participants in the course of the market process, is an alertness fueled, not necessarily by selfish or materialistic goals, but by concern to further one's goals, whatever these may be. What is being suggested, then, is that the critical place filled by the self-interest assumption is not in the theory of the consumer decision, or the theory of the producer's decision, but in the entrepreneurial decision. Because all market participants are, to some degree, entrepreneurial, the self-interest assumption has universal relevance. From this perspective it turns out that the competitive character of market processes, and the self-interested character of market behavior, are simply two sides of the same coin.

Something of this seems to have been present in the thinking on competition of major economists at the turn of the century. "Broadly defined," Herbert J. Davenport observed, "economic competition is a struggle for maximum economic rewards (minimum sacrifice)."[32] The rivalrous character of dynamic competition and the self-interested purposefulness of individual market behavior "fold into" each other. The ubiquity in markets of self-interest, and the universality in markets of dynamic competition turn out to be one and the same.

Notes

1. W. Duncan Reekie, *Markets, Entrepreneurs and Liberty: An Austrian View of Capitalism* (New York: St. Martin's Press, 1984), pp. 37ff; Gerald P. O'Driscoll, Jr. and Mario J. Rizzo, *The Economics of Time and Ignorance* (Oxford: Basil Blackwell, 1985), chap. 6; Stephen C. Littlechild, "Misleading Calculation of the Social Costs of Monopoly Power," *Economic Journal*, 1981; Alexander H. Shand, *The Capitalist Alternative: An Introduction to Neo-Austrian Economics* (New York: New York University Press, 1984), pp. 65–71.

2. See especially Ludwig von Mises, *Human Action*, 3rd rev. ed. (Chicago: Henry Regnery, 1966), chaps. XV, XVI; Friedrich von Hayek, "The Meaning of Competition," in *Individualism and Economic Order* (Chicago: University of Chicago Press, 1948); "Competition as a Discovery Procedure," in *New Studies in Philosophy, Politics, Economics and the History of Ideas* (Chicago: University of Chicago Press, 1978); Israel M. Kirzner, *Competition and Entrepreneurship* (Chicago: University of Chicago Press, 1973).

3. See, for example, Franklin M. Fisher, *Disequilibrium Foundations of Equilibrium Economics* (Cambridge: Cambridge University Press, 1983).

4. See, for example, Roman Frydman, "Towards an Understanding of Market Processes: Individual Expectations, Learning and Convergence to Rational Expectations Equilibrium," *American Economic Review* 72 (1982).

5. See William J. Baumol, "Contestable Markets: An Uprising in the Theory of Industry Structure," *American Economic Review* March 1982.

6. See, for example, Kirzner, *Competition and Entrepreneurship* (op. cit.), pp. 19ff.

7. See George L. S. Shackle, *Epistemics and Economics: A Critique of Economic Doctrines* (Cambridge: Cambridge University Press, 1972), pp. 54, 124, 137, etc.

8. Friedrich von Hayek, *Individualism and Economic Order*, op. cit., p. 94.

9. Joachim Silvestre, "The Elements of Fixprice Microeconomics" in Larry Samuelson, ed., *Microeconomic Theory* (Boston: Kluwer-Nijhoff, 1986), p. 197. Earlier references include Kenneth Arrow, "Toward a Theory of Price Adjustment," in *The Allocation of Economic Resources*, ed. Abramowitz et al. (Stanford, CA: Stanford University Press, 1959); G. B. Richardson, *Information and Investment* (London: Oxford University Press, 1960): J. M. Clark, *Competition as a Dynamic Process* (Washington: Brookings Institution, 1961).

10. *Journal of Economic Theory* 22(2) (April 1980).

11. On this see P. J. McNulty, "A Note on the History of Perfect Competition," *Journal of Political Economy* 75 (August 1967).

12. Abba P. Lerner, "The Concept of Monopoly and the Measurement of Monopoly Power," *Review of Economic Studies* (June 1934).

13. Mises, *Human Action*, op. cit., p. 360.

14. Mises, ibid., p. 378.

15. See, for example, Dominick T. Armentano, "A Critique of Neoclassical and Austrian Monopoly Theory," in Louis M. Spadaro, ed., *New Directions in Austrian Economics* (Kansas City: Sheed Andrews and McMeel, 1978).

16. Gerald P. O'Driscoll, Jr. "Monopoly in Theory and Practice" in Israel M. Kirzner, ed., *Method, Process, and Austrian Economics, Essays in Honor of Ludwig von Mises* (Lexington, MA: D. C. Heath, 1982), p. 190. O'Driscoll's sentence reads: "Some [modern Austrians], such as Ludwig von Mises and Israel Kirzner, present a variant of the neoclassical theory." Certain of O'Driscoll's criticisms (pp. 205–6) do relate especially to this writer's presentation of the Misesian theory (in *Competition and Entrepreneurship*). However, the remarks in the text relate strictly to the sense in which O'Driscoll finds Mises's own theory to be neoclassical. Accordingly no further references will be made to O'Driscoll's specific criticisms of this writer's presentation.

17. Ibid., p. 199.

18. Ibid.

19. Ibid., p. 205.

20. Ibid.

21. O'Driscoll's charge is all the more surprising in that he uses, as the epigraph introducing his paper, a quotation from Mises explicitly emphasizing that in dealing with cases of monopoly price "one must first of all raise the question of what obstacles restrain people from challenging the monopolist." (Ibid., p. 189)

22. Ibid., p. 189.

23. It must certainly be recognized that, in the Misesian theory of resource monopoly, this monopoly is, to use O'Driscoll's language, "postulated without being explained" (Ibid., p. 199). The theory deals with the implications of a particular possible situation. That is all.

24. Ibid., p. 199.

25. Ibid., p. 189.

26. For a discussion of the forces that might lead entrepreneurs to attempt to win the position of a Misesian resource monopolist, see the writer's *Competition and Entrepreneurship*, pp. 199ff.

27. See, for example, Mises, *Human Action*, p. 357.

28. Frank Machovec, "The Destruction of Competition Theory: The Perfectly Competitive Model and Beyond," unpublished doctoral dissertation, New York University, 1986.

29. Ludwig Mises, *Epistemological Problems of Economics* [1933] (Princeton, NJ: Van Nostrand, 1960), p. 214.

30. See Israel M. Kirzner, "The Economic Calculation Debate: Lessons for Austrians" in *The Review of Austrian Economics*, vol. 2, pp. 2ff.

31. Israel M. Kirzner, "Self-Interest and the New Bashing of Economics: A Fresh Opportunity in the Perennial Debate?" in *Critical Review* 8(3) (Summer 1994).

32. Herbert J. Davenport, *Outlines of Economic Theory* (New York: Macmillan, 1905), p. 201.

3

FROM MISES TO SHACKLE: AN ESSAY ON AUSTRIAN ECONOMICS AND THE KALEIDIC SOCIETY

LUDWIG M. LACHMANN

I

A delicate task faces the historian of thought whenever an established doctrine, what in the language of current fashion is called a paradigm or, more recently, a "research program," is challenged. He has to trace the genealogy of the challengers. To this end he must pick up threads covered by the sands of time, dust them, and try to connect them with the new skein of thought.

His task is all the more difficult, but also the more urgent and rewarding, since history of thought is almost invariably written from the point of view of the reigning orthodoxy. For Schumpeter, Walras's system is the crowning achievement, hence every earlier economist is either a predecessor or belongs to a lost tribe. From such a perspective most unorthodox strands of thought appear as blind alleys if they are mentioned at all. By the same token the challengers must seem "rootless" iconoclasts. Nevertheless, the historian cannot rest or claim to have completed his task until he has unearthed at least some of the historical roots of the ideas of the challengers of his day.

Professor Shackle's *Epistemics and Economics* is a case in point [1972]. His bold challenge to neoclassical orthodoxy, with its determinism borrowed from the natural sciences and with its bland assumption of a world sufficiently tranquil and restful to provide us with a set of supposedly constant "data," is bound to have far-reaching repercussions. Although neoclassical orthodoxy is the main target of his attack, the subtitle of his book *A Critique of Economic Doctrines* (we may note the plural) indicates a wider scope. Some economic doctrines of our time, we may surmise, invite more trenchant criticism than do others.

In what follows we attempt to show that the body of economic thought that has come to be known as "Austrian," and in particular that part of it which found expression in the seminal work of Ludwig von Mises [1949], is not only less vulnerable to Shackle's attack than the main body of current orthodoxy, but that to a striking extent Mises and Shackle share a common outlook on the foundations of our discipline. In the light of this circumstance, we then examine the position of Austrian economics with regard to Shackle's *kaleidic society*, a society in which sooner or later unexpected change is bound to upset existing patterns, a society "interspersing its moments or intervals of order, assurance and beauty with sudden disintegration and a cascade into a new pattern" [Shackle, 1972, p. 76].

II

Shackle has attacked the neoclassical citadel just where it is most vulnerable. The assumptions made by general equilibrium theory about nature and scope of the knowledge possessed by economic actors have never been stated with much precision. All economic action is of course concerned with the future, the more or less distant future. But the future is to all of us unknowable, though not unimaginable. Shackle strongly contends that our ignorance of the future invalidates any theory attributing knowledge of the future to economic actors engaged in providing for it. To defend a theory against this criticism, we evidently have to know exactly what assumptions are made about knowledge. With the modern neoclassical model this move is anything but easy.

We are often told that knowledge is to be included among the equilibrium "data" along with tastes and resources, so that changing knowledge entails changing prices and output quantities. But "data" must be measurable and knowledge is not. How do we determine that change of knowledge that would be required just to offset any given change of tastes or resources in such a way as to maintain an existing vector of prices?

Moreover, how can tastes and resources be of any economic relevance without being known? The independent datum "knowledge" evidently cannot refer to them. Perhaps we should take it to refer to technological knowledge only, knowledge about how to turn input into output, about feasible "coefficients of production" in Walras's terminology. If so, what do we have to assume about market knowledge, the knowledge of tastes and resources without which nobody can operate in a market? Do we assume that all market actors know all the tastes and resources in all markets in which they, actually or potentially, do or might operate? But if so, equilibrium should at once be attained in all markets. If we were to make this assumption, there could be no disequilibrium, no dealings at "false prices." Walras's "auctioneer" would become superfluous. If, on the other hand, we do not make it, how do we delimit the extent of each actor's knowledge at each point of time, and how do we deal with the flow of knowledge between actors over time?

It is perhaps only another aspect of this dilemma that it has never, to our knowledge, been made clear whether a "state of knowledge" means a state of affairs in which everybody shares the knowledge everyone else has, or whether it merely denotes an existing "pattern of knowledge" that permits differences in knowledge between individuals. If the former, we should be told how it could come about and how, in a world of change, it could ever be maintained. If the latter, and knowledge as a datum means just any existing pattern of knowledge, evidently not a day can pass without some change in this interindividual pattern of knowledge. As it seems to be widely agreed that some constancy of the data is necessary for general equilibrium theory to be of much relevance, daily changes in the pattern of knowledge, quite inevitable in a world of change, must be fatal to it. Whatever assumptions about knowledge we may attribute to it, general equilibrium does not seem to stand up well to a critical inquiry into them.

In modern Austrian economics, by contrast, we find the problem of knowledge to be a matter of fundamental concern. In 1937 Professor Hayek divided the subject matter of economics into the pure logic of choice and the enquiry into the dissemination of knowledge.[1] In 1946, in criticizing most modern theories of market forms, he pointed out that competition is a process, not a state of affairs, and that it reflects continous changes in the pattern of knowledge.[2] In Mises's *Human Action*, the market process kept in motion by the flow of events is a major theme [1949].

New knowledge may originate "exogenously," by technical progress, or discovery of new resources or markets by alert minds. Some new knowledge, however, is generated "endogenously," within the market, every day by equally alert minds observing and exploiting profitable changes in the pattern of relative prices. Old knowledge may unexpectedly became obsolete in similar ways.

The world of the market economy is thus a kaleidic world, a world of flux in which the ceaseless flow of news daily impinges on human choice and the making of decisions. We shall trace some consequences of this important insight in the work of Mises and Professor Shackle. But we can hardly expect to find more congruence between the thought of two such highly individualistic minds than the kaleidic nature of our world permits. It may be worth our while to ask to what extent, and in regard to what, Shackle in his latest work "made progress" beyond the common ground he shares with Mises.

III

It might sound rash to say that in Mises's work on praxeology in the opening chapters of *Human Action*, in which he gathers and examines the elements of a logic of successful action to serve as the basis of a methodology of the social sciences, Austrian economics attained a level of methodological self-awareness it had never previously enjoyed. But those who will be most reluctant to agree with this statement are likely to be identical with those who object strenuously to the principle of *a priorism* Mises expounds in the same pages, and there may be several Austrians among them. Such objections, to be sure, are largely due to a misunderstanding, a confusion between form of thought and its empirical content, which Mises attempted to clarify (e.g., [1949, pp. 38, 66]). But whatever our attitude to this particular controversy, it seems to us that a good deal remains to be said for our statement about methodological self-awareness.

Before Mises, Austrians, by and large, took little interest in methodology. Carl Menger in 1883, to be sure, published his *Untersuchungen* [1883]. However, what he defended in it against the attacks of the German Historical School was the Ricardian method rather than any kind of subjectivism. Moreover, this defense occurred in 1883, before the age of Poincaré and Mach. When, in 1908, Schumpeter applied Mach's positivistic methodology to economics, most Austrians felt shock and revulsion, but they lacked the firm methodological basis from which they could have attacked him (see Schumpeter [1908]).

Mises drew his inspiration from a different source, the Neo-Kantian philosophy that dominated academic Germany in the first decade of this century. Max Weber can hardly be called an Austrian economist, but he made a contribution of fundamental significance to what in the hands of Mises became Austrian methodology. In 1909 Weber wrote: "The rational theory of price formation not only has nothing to do with the concepts of experimental psychology, but has nothing to do with a psychology of any kind, which desires to be a 'science' going beyond everyday experience. . . . The theory of marginal utility, and every other subjective value theory, are not psychologically, but, if one wants a methodological term, 'pragmatically' based, i.e. they involve the use of the categories 'ends' and 'means.'"[3] Here, then, we have the origin of the Misesian *praxeology*, the Hayekian "pure logic of choice." As Mises put it, "If Weber had known the term 'praxeology', he probably would have preferred it" [1949, p. 126, fn. 5].

In all essentials the views on the nature of human action, the character of the world in which it takes place and the methods appropriate to its study, which we find in the work of Mises and Shackle are virtually identical. Action is thought. For Mises "economics is not about things and tangible material objects; it is about men, their meanings and actions. Goods, commodities, and wealth and all the other notions of conduct are not elements of nature; they are elements of human meaning and conduct" [1949, p. 92]. For Shackle "[e]conomics, concerned with thoughts and only secondarily with things, the objects of those thoughts, must be as protean as thought itself" [1972, p. 246]. Action is guided by plans, i.e., by thought, and all action has to be interpreted as the outward manifestation of such plans, which must be coherent if they are to have a chance of success. In fact all economic phenomena are intelligible only as the outcome of planned action.

For both our authors the world in which thinkers and actors have to move is one of ceaseless change. Shackle describes it as a kaleidic world. For Mises "[t]here is in the course of human events no stability and consequently no safety" [1949, p. 113]. He points out that consistency of plans does not entail constancy of observable action in a world of change. "Constancy and rationality are entirely different notions. . . . Only in one respect can acting be constant: in preferring the more valuable to the less valuable. If the valuations change, acting must change also" [1949, p. 103].

In each plan means and ends are riveted by choice. In a world of change plans have to be revised, but such revision is also always a matter of choice of ends and means. Both our authors thus regard choice as the "pure" type of action and reject determinism along with the other paraphernalia of positivism. Two of Shackle's statements make that quite clear. "[I]f the world is determinist, then it seems idle to speak of choice" [1972, p. 122], but "[c]hoice is always amongst thoughts, for it is always too late to choose amongst facts" [1972, p. 280]. According to Mises, "What counts for praxeology is only the fact that acting man chooses between alternatives. That man is placed at crossroads, that he must and does choose is . . . due to the fact that he lives in a quantitative world and not in a world without quantity" [1949, pp. 126–27].

Both our authors emphasize that the mathematical notion of time as a continuum, a dimension in which events take place, does not fit the requirements of a science of human action. According to Mises, "Time as we measure it by various mechanical devices is always past, and time as the philosophers use this concept is always either past or future. The present is, from these aspects, nothing but an ideal boundary line separating the past from the future. But from the praxeological aspect there is between the past and the future a real extended present. Action is as such in the real present because it utilizes the instant and thus embodies its reality" [1949, p. 100]. He quotes from Henri Bergson, "What I call my present is really my attitude to the immediate future, that is to say, my imminent action."[4]

Shackle refrains from stressing the Bergsonian affiliation of his thought, but makes the same point. "We cannot have experience of actuality at two distinct 'moments'. The moment of actuality, the moment in being, 'the present,' is *solitary*. Extended time, beyond 'the moment', appears in this light as a figment, a product of thought" [1972, p. 245].

Both authors emphatically reject the calculus of probability as a tool for dealing with human conduct in a world of uncertainty. Shackle devotes his chapter 34 ("Languages for Expectation") to this matter. He sums up his view in the heading of section 34.40: "Probability concerns groups of events, not single critical choices" [1972, p. 400]. Mises makes the same point by distinguishing between class and case probability. "Case probability has nothing in common with class probability but the incompleteness of our knowledge. In every other regard the two are entirely different. . . . Case probability is a peculiar feature of our dealing with problems of human action. Here any reference to frequency is inappropriate, as our statements always deal with unique events which as such—i.e., with regard to the problem in question—are not members of any class. . . . Case probability is not open to any kind of numerical evaluation" [1949, pp. 110–13].

To sum up, then, in their emphasis on the spontaneous, and thus unpredictable nature of human action, in their rejection of mechanistic notions of time and probability, our two authors are completely at one. They also agree that a science of human action requires a methodology *sui generis*.

IV

One is not surprised to find differences alongside similarities between two such original minds. With such striking identity of outlook and methodological approach, however, as we have just encountered, any differences in conclusions must be due to differences in what Schumpeter called "vision," in the interpretation and evaluation of facts in the world around us. In theoretical argument these are then reflected in the form of "subsidiary assumptions," which have to be elucidated and weighed for the degree of insight into the social world they afford us. Once we have done this, we may say that the more comprehensive vision, if it affords us a deeper insight into the world and does not merely encompass more facts, has advanced our understanding of the phenomena in question.

It is in this sense that we now have to ask how far Shackle may be said to have widened the scope of the enquiry beyond the common ground of praxeology we outlined above. In what ways, then, does his recent work differ from that of Hayek and Mises? In this regard three aspects of it call for our particular attention.

In the first place, Shackle has extended the scope of subjectivism from tastes to expectations. It is a curious fact that, when around 1930 (in Keynes's *Treatise on Money*), expectations made their appearance in the economic thought of the Anglo-Saxon world, the Austrians failed to grasp with both hands this golden opportunity to enlarge the basis of their approach and, by and large, treated the subject rather gingerly. Professor Hayek, to be sure, dealt with expectations in 1933 in his Copenhagen lecture on "Price Expectations, Monetary Disturbances and Malinvestments" [1939] and in "Economics and Knowledge" [1948], but not with the causes and consequences of their divergence. In fact, expectations were here regarded as being of analytical interest only to the extent to which they converge.[5] They were, on the whole, treated as a mode of foresight, a rather unfortunate but inevitable consequence of imperfect knowledge. Mises hardly ever mentions expectations, though entrepreneurs and speculators often enough turn up in his pages. Thus from 1939 onwards Shackle had to take on expectations more or less single-handedly without much benefit of support from the Austrian side.[6]

Secondly, there is a sense in which Shackle's emphasis on action without knowledge poses an even stronger challenge to Austrians than to neoclassical equilibrium theory. In the work of Hayek, I. M. Kirzner [1973], and Mises the market as process, not as a state of rest, is of fundamental importance. Its main economic function here is to coordinate existing knowledge scattered over many parts of the economic system and to disseminate the market knowledge thus gained. Nobody can profitably exploit his knowledge without conveying hints to others. But can the market process diffuse expectations in the same way as it diffuses knowledge where this exists? This is by no means obvious. The dissemination of superior knowledge is entailed by the fact that men can judge it by success. But how successful an expectation is we can know only when it is too late for others to embrace it. Moreover, in a kaleidic society in which there is always some hope that better knowledge will be available tomorrow if only we wait, and nobody can tell how soon today's successful knowledge will become obsolete, the diffusion of knowledge may be held up and the market process thus impeded. Can the market process "digest" expectations? If it can, what is its *modus operandi*? If it cannot, is not the image of the market economy as presented to us in the Austrian writings impaired, or at least shown to be incomplete? To answer these questions we have, first of all, to ask what expectations are and how they fit into the perspective of praxeology.

The future is unknowable, though not unimaginable. Future knowledge cannot be had now, but it can cast its shadow ahead. In each mind, however, the shadow assumes a different shape, hence the divergence of expectations. The formation of expectations is an act of our mind by means of which we try to catch a glimpse of the unknown. Each one of us catches a different glimpse. The wider the range of divergence the greater the possibility that somebody's expectation will turn out to be right.

In this way new knowledge, paradoxically, can have an economic impact before it is actually "here." Divergent expectations are nothing but the individual images, rather blurred, in which new knowledge is reflected, before its actual arrival, in a thousand different mirrors of various shapes. In the same way existing knowledge may become problematical even though nothing better is in existence at the moment. An expectation that it will soon be superseded by superior knowledge may suffice to stop its diffusion. In such cases, it might appear, the market process will stop for lack of digestible knowledge without anything really digestible taking its place. Must expectations, then, be fatal to the market process?

The market, of course, cannot diffuse "superior expectations" in the sense in which it diffuses superior knowledge because *ex ante* no criterion of success can exist. It cannot make bulls and bears change their expectations, but it nevertheless can coordinate these. To coordinate bullish and bearish expectations is, as Keynes showed, the economic function of the Stock Exchange and of asset markets in general. This is achieved because in such markets the price will move until the whole market is divided into equal halves of bulls and bears. In this way divergent expectations are cast into a coherent pattern and a measure of coordination is accomplished. This is a topic Shackle has very much made his own, which has a bearing on Austrian economics that we now have to examine.

Divergent expectations give rise to a third aspect of Shackle's model that has no counterpart in Mises's work and thus invites our attention. In studying the relevance of expectations to the market process, we come to learn that they play a different part in different markets, and these differences of their *modus operandi* will have to be explored. The relationship of the third aspect to the second is thus that of a particular instance to a general type of problem. In an ordinary product market in which an output flow is sold, most participants are either producers or consumers. Fluctuations of limited size may originate on either side. When we add stock-holding merchants, the range of possible fluctuations increases as these merchants may be buyers today and sellers tomorrow or *vice versa*. But in an asset market in which the whole stock always is potentially on sale and in which everybody can easily choose or change sides, we find an element of volatility that is absent from product markets. Such asset markets are inherently "restless," and equilibrium prices established in them reflect nothing but the daily balance of expectations. In the cotton market, for example, it is likely that expectations about the probable price in July 1976 will tend to converge as this date draws nearer. But this cannot happen in the Stock Exchange, since what is being traded there are titles to (in principle) permanent income streams, which have no "date" that could "move nearer." All we get is a succession of market-day equilibria determined by a balance of expectations tilting from one day to the next as the flow of the news turns bulls into bears and *vice versa*. There is here no question of a gradual approach towards long-run equilibrium. It is not surprising that this conception of a sequence of market-day equilibria in asset markets has incurred the disdain of prominent neoclassical thinkers. "A truncated theory of temporary equilibrium in which markets for future goods are replaced by some form of expectations, themselves functions of current prices and quantities, has indeed been developed, though its empirical content is necessarily meager if the formation of expectations is left unanalyzed. But the true neoclassical spirit is being denied in such a model" [Arrow, 1974, p. 7].

It may be felt that the failure of the true neoclassical spirit to find adequate reflection in the list of Wall Street closing prices need cause little concern to Austrians most of whom, from Menger onwards, have been skeptical about the general equilibrium model since the days of the school of Lausanne. We may even be inclined to retort: The worse for the neoclassical spirit! But the issue, "Restless asset markets versus long-run equilibrium," is one we cannot ignore, partly owing to the prominent part asset markets play in the market economy as a whole and partly because not all Austrians have scorned the neoclassical model. In volatile asset markets new capital gains and losses are made every day that change the distribution of resources. It is hard to see how the system can attain long-run equilibrium while these changes are taking place.

Professor Hayek and Mises both espouse the market process, but do not ignore equilibrium as its final stage. The former, whose early work was clearly under the influence of the general equilibrium model, at one time appeared to regard a strong tendency towards general equilibrium as a real phenomenon of the market economy. Mises, calling the Austrians "logical" and neoclassicals "mathematical" economists, wrote: "Both the logical and the mathematical economists assert that human action ultimately aims at the establishment of such a state of equilibrium and would reach it if all further changes in data were to cease" [1949, p. 352].

It is this view of the market process as at least potentially terminating in a state of long-run general equilibrium that now appears to require revision.

V

In a kaleidic society the equilibrating forces, operating slowly, especially where much of the capital equipment is durable and specific, are always overtaken by unexpected change before they have done their work, and the results of their operation disrupted before they can bear fruit. Restless asset markets, redistributing wealth every day by engendering capital gains and losses, are just one instance, though in a market economy an important one, of the forces of change thwarting the equilibrating forces. Equilibrium of the economic system as a whole will thus never be reached.[7] Marshallian markets for individual goods may for a time find their respective equilibria. The economic system never does. What emerges from our reflections is an image of the market as a particular kind of process, a continuous process without beginning or end, propelled by the interaction between the forces of equilibrium and the forces of change. General equilibrium theory only knows interaction between the former.

For Shackle long-run equilibrium theory is of course an expression of the Victorian world view, a vision of a world shaped mainly by the forces of slow but orderly progress. The older Austrians, non–Anglo-Saxon Victorians like Menger and Boehm-Bawerk, certainly shared this world view, though not the expression it found in the Walrasian model. Boehm-Bawerk's capital theory embodies a vision of a world of steady progress through capital accumulation without technical progress or malinvestment. One of Menger's interests was the increasing range of variety of products in economic progress.

The kaleidic society is thus not the natural habitat of Austrian economics, but the alien soil may prove nourishing. A model in which individual plans, each consistent in itself, never have time to become consistent with each other before new change supervenes has its uses for elucidating some striking features of our world. It may even be that Austrian economics will come into its own in our society in which the apparently irreconcilable nature of economic and political forces at large finds its expression in our permanent inflation, and in which "public policy decisions" are largely a euphemism for incoherent sequences of desperate expedients. It is quite possible that a bastion of extended subjectivism, enhanced by the inclusion of divergent expectations, will offer us an excellent vantage point from which to watch the happenings of such a society in a dispassionate perspective, a perspective superior to what we have had before.

Notes

1. In "Economics and Knowledge," reprinted in Hayek [1948, pp. 33–56].

2. In "The Meaning of Competition," reprinted in Hayek [1948, pp. 92–106].

3. Our translation. A reprint of Max Weber's 1909 essay, "Die Grenznutzlehre und das psychophysische Grundgesetz," may be found in a collection of his writings, [1929, p. 372].

4. Our translation. Mises quotes from the French text Matière et mémoire [1911, pp. 205].

5. For in the general equilibrium perspective Hayek adopted in the 1930's, it is convergence, and the nature of the economic processes promoting or impeding it, that must be of primary interest. The divergence of expectations appears in this perspective mainly as an obstacle to equilibrium, if not as a reflection of a temporarily distorted view of the world.

6. See, however, Lachmann [1943].

7. As Shackle pointedly puts it: "But if the rational equilibrium is an illusion, basically at odds with the human condition, the Scheme of Things, if it neglects the fact and meaning of time, that prescript of the Rational Calculus is itself an illusion" [1972, pp. 228].

References

Arrow, Kenneth J. "Limited Knowledge and Economic Analysis," *Amer. Econ. Rev.*, March 1974, 54(1), pp. 1–10.

64 *Ludwig M. Lachmann*

Bergson, Henri. *Matière et mémoire*, 7th ed. Paris, 1911.

Hayek, F. A. *Profits, Interest and Investment*. London: Routledge and Sons, 1939.

————. *Individualism and Economic order*. Chicago: University of Chicago Press, 1948; London: Routledge and Kegan Paul, 1949.

Kirzner, I. M. *Competition and Entrepreneurship*. Chicago: University of Chicago Press, 1973.

Lachmann, L. M. "The Rôle of Expectations in Economics as a Social Science," *Economica, N.S.*, Feb. 1943, 10, pp. 12–23.

Menger, Carl. *Untersuchungen über die Methode der Socialwissenschaften und der Politischen Oekonomie insbesondere*. Leipzig: Verlag von Duncker and Humblot, 1883. Translated as *Problems of economics and sociology*, by Frank J. Nock. Edited by Louis Schneider. Urbana: University of Illinois Press, 1963.

von Mises, Ludwig. *Human action: A treatise on economics*. New Haven: Yale University Press, 1949.

Schumpeter, Joseph A. *Das Wesen und der Hauptinhalt der theoretischen Nationalökonomie*, Leipzig: 1908.

Shackle, L. S. *Epistemics and economics: A critique of economic doctrines*. Cambridge: Cambridge University Press, 1972.

Weber, Max. *Gesammelte Aufsätze zur Wissenschaftslehre*. Tübingen: J. C. B. Mohr [1922] 1929.

PART II

POST KEYNESIAN ECONOMICS FOR AN UNCERTAIN WORLD

In [the] neoclassical view Keynes's enduring contribution lies mainly in the arena of public policy: his arguments made it intellectually respectable to advocate activist intervention to guide the economy. It is also held that once the fact that some adjustment processes are sluggish is taken into account, intervention of an aggregate nature, i.e., monetary and fiscal policy, was implicit in the presumably laissez-faire-oriented classical economics.

. . . The alternative interpretation emphasizes that Keynes constructed a theory to explain the behavior of a capitalist economy which is sophisticated in its financial institutions. Such an economy is inherently flawed, because it is intractably cyclical—that is, such a capitalist economy cannot by its own processes sustain full employment, and each of the succession of cyclical states is transitory in the sense that relations are built up which transform the way in which the economy will behave.

. . .To understand Keynes it is necessary to understand his sophisticated view about uncertainty, and the importance of uncertainty in his vision of the economic process. Keynes without uncertainty is something like Hamlet without the Prince.

—Hyman P. Minsky, *John Maynard Keynes*

4

REVIVING KEYNES'S REVOLUTION

PAUL DAVIDSON

Addressing *The General Theory* chiefly to his "fellow economists" (1936, p. v), Keynes insisted that

> the postulates of the classical theory are applicable to a special case only and not to the general case. . . . Moreover, the characteristics of the special case assumed by the classical theory happen not to be those of the economic society in which we actually live, with the result that its teaching is misleading and disastrous if we attempt to apply it to the facts of experience. (1936, p. 3)

Keynes (1936, p. 26) believed that he could *logically* demonstrate why "Say's Law . . . is not the true law relating the aggregate demand and supply functions" when we model an economy possessing real world characteristics; and until we get our theory to accurately mirror and apply to the "facts of experience," there is little hope of getting our policies right. That message is just as relevant today.

Keynes compared those economists whose theoretical logic was grounded in Say's Law to Euclidean geometers living in a non-Euclidean world,

> who discovering that in experience straight lines apparently parallel often meet, rebuke the lines for not keeping straight—as the only remedy for the unfortunate collisions which are taking place. Yet, in truth, there is no remedy except to throw over the axiom of parallels and to work out a non-Euclidean geometry. Something similar is required today in economics. (1936, p. 16)

To throw over an axiom is to reject what the faithful believe are "universal truths." The Keynesian revolution in economic theory was therefore truly a revolt since it aimed at rejecting basic mainstream tenets and substituting postulates which provide a logical foundation for a non–Say's Law model more closely related to the real world in which we happen to live. Unfortunately, since Keynes, mainstream macro-theorists, seduced by a technical methodology which promised precision and unique results at the expense of applicability and accuracy, have reintroduced more sophisticated forms of the very axioms Keynes rejected almost a half century ago. Consequently the Keynesian revolution was almost immediately shunted onto a wrong track as more obtuse versions of the axioms underlying a Say's Law world became the keystone of modern mainstream theory. Monetarists and the New Classical Economists, as well as Neoclassical Synthesis Keynesians, have reconstructed macrotheory by reintroducing the "universal truths" that Keynes struggled to overthrow.

The major neoclassical axioms rejected by Keynes in his revolutionary logical analysis were (1) *the axiom of gross substitution*, (2) *the axiom of reals*, and (3) *the axiom of an ergodic economic world*. The characteristics of the real world which Keynes believed could be modeled only by overthrowing these axioms are: (1) Money matters in the long and short run; that is, money is not neutral—it affects real decision making.[1] (2) The economic system is moving through calendar time from an irrevocable past to an uncertain future. Important monetary time series realizations will be generated by nonergodic circumstances; hence decision making agents know that the future need not be predictable in any probability sense (see Davidson, 1982–83). (3) Forward contracts in money terms are a human institution developed to efficiently organize time consuming production and exchange processes (Davidson, 1980, p. 299). The money-wage contract is the most ubiquitous of these efficiency oriented contracts. Modern production economies are therefore on a money-wage contract based system. (4) Unemployment, rather than full employment, is a common *laissez-faire* situation in a market oriented, monetary production economy.

Only the Monetarists and the New Classical Theorists (like Ricardo)

> offer us the supreme intellectual achievement, unattainable by weaker spirits, of adopting a hypothetical world remote from experience as though it was the world of experience and then living in it consistently. With most of . . . [the Keynesians?] common sense cannot help breaking in—with injury to their logical consistency (Keynes, 1936, pp. 192–193)

Spending, Constrained Demand, Say's Law, and Gross Substitution

Keynes's *General Theory* is developed via an aggregate supply-aggregate demand function analysis which can be used to illustrate the difference between Say's Law and Keynes's analytical structure (Keynes, 1936, pp. 25–26).

The aggregate supply function (Z) relates entrepreneurs' expected sales proceeds with the level of employment (N) entrepreneurs will hire for any volume of expected sales receipts. In Figure 4.1a this aggregate supply (Z) function is drawn as upward sloping, indicating that the higher entrepreneurs' sales expectations, the more workers they will hire. The aggregate demand function relates buyers' desired expenditure flows for any given level of employment. In Figure 4.1b. the aggregate demand (D) function is drawn as upward sloping indicating that, the greater the level of employment hire, the more buyers will spend on goods and services.

The aggregate supply and demand functions can be brought together in a single quadrant to provide the equilibrium employment solution. In Figure 4.2a the aggregate supply (Z) and aggregate demand (D) functions are drawn as they would be developed in a Say's Law world where supply creates its own demand. In a Say's Law world (as explained below and as shown in Figure 4.2a), the aggregate supply and demand functions are coincident throughout their entire length. Thus if at any point of time the actual employment level is N^a_1, actual demand is constrained to point G. Any coordinated expansion in hiring by entrepreneurs to provide additional output (say to point H in Figure 4.2a) will increase actual demand concomitantly to point H and full employment (N^a_f) could be established. In a Say's Law world there is no obstacle to full employment.

In Figure 4.2b, on the other hand, the aggregate demand and supply functions are distinguishable functions which intersect at a single point, the point of *effective demand* (E); and in a manner consistent with Keynes's theory (1936, p. 25) the equilibrium level of employment is N^b_1. At the full employment level (N^b_f in Figure 4.2b) there is a deficiency in effective demand equal to the vertical distance JK, and hence all of the full employment output cannot be profitably sold.

As defined by Keynes, Say's Law required that the aggregate supply curve be coincident with the aggregate demand curve over its entire length so that supply could create its own demand. Accordingly, *effective demand* "instead of having a unique equilibrium value, is an infinite range of values, all equally admissible" (Keynes, 1936, p. 26). If, therefore, Say's Law prevails, then the economy is in neutral equilibrium

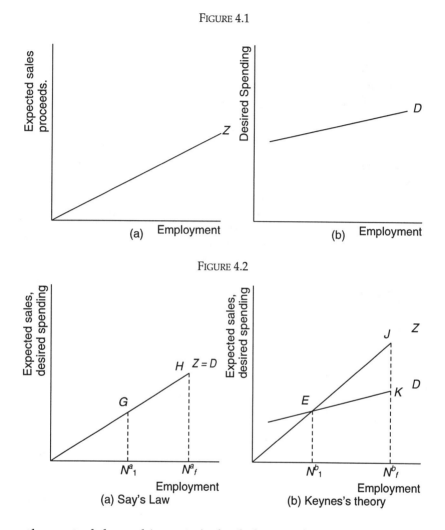

FIGURE 4.1

(a)   Employment

(b)   Employment

FIGURE 4.2

N^a_1 N^a_f

Employment
(a) Say's Law

N^b_1 N^b_f

Employment
(b) Keynes's theory

where actual demand is *constrained* only by actual income (supply). In other words, Say's law requires that aggregate demand is a *constrained demand function* (in the terminology of Clower, 1965, or Barro and Grossman, 1976), and a "short-side of the market rationing" rule limits employment opportunities. This short-side rule is specifically adopted by Malinvaud (1977, pp. 12–35) to "explain" Keynesian unemployment. It has also been used by most of the "Keynesians" who have manned the Council of Economic Advisers under Democratic administrations to explain what their logical unconstrained model cannot.[2]

In the Clower-Leijonhufvud neoclassical synthesis version of the Keynesian system, which has been labeled the dual decision hypothesis with a coordination failure, purchasing decisions are always equal to, and constrained by, *actual* income (Clower, 1965). The economy is in neutral equilibrium at any level of actual income. There is no obstacle to full employment except that entrepreneurs do not receive a market signal that they would be able to profitably sell the full employment output if only they would coordinate and march together to the full employment hiring level. Unemployment is solely due to a "coordination failure" of the market system to signal entrepreneurs that, if they would only hire the full employment level of workers, actual income would equal *notional* (full employment) *income* and the spending decisions by income earners would be equal to, and constrained by, the full employment budget line and all markets would clear.[3] Hence, in contrast to Keynes (1936, pp. 30–31), these "Keynesians" argue that if only entrepreneurs would hire all workers there would never be an insufficiency of aggregate demand.

Those who believe a short-side rule or constrained demand function limits employment opportunities should, if they follow their logic and not their common sense, support President Reagan's proposal for solving the unemployment problem. In the Spring of 1983 Reagan suggested that unemployment could be ended if each business firm in the nation immediately hired one more worker. Since there are more firms than unemployed workers, the solution is obviously statistically accurate—but unless the employment by each of these additional workers created a demand for the additional output at a profitable price (additional supply creating *pari passu* additional demand), it would not be profitable for entrepreneurs to hire additional workers.

Neoclassical Keynesians should applaud Reagan's clarion call for firms to coordinate increased hiring. If each firm does hire an additional worker so that full employment is (at least momentarily) achieved, then actual income flows earned would be equal to notional income and therefore aggregate demand would not be constrained short of full employment. There is no coordination failure—and no short-side rule limits job opportunities.

In a Keynes world, on the other hand, involuntary unemployment is due to an insufficiency or lack of effective demand (at full employment) as shown by the vertical distance JK in Figure 4.2b. The sales of the additional output produced by private sector entrepreneurs hiring workers above the N^b_1 level in Figure 4.2b cannot be profitable.

Keynes would never have endorsed Reagan's Say's Law solution to the unemployment problem. In a closed economy context, Keynes held that neither of the two private sector components of the aggregate demand function (D_1 and D_2 or aggregate consumption and investment spending) are constrained by actual income, although D_1 may be related to income earned! To put it bluntly and in its most irritating—thought provoking—form, the underlying axioms of Keynes's revolutionary theory of effective demand require that *the demand for goods produced by labor need never be constrained by income; spending is constrained only by liquidity and/or timidity considerations.* Thus the budget constraint, in a Keynes model, need never limit individual spending—or aggregate spending at less than full employment.

In the real world, planned spending need never be equal to, or constrained by, actual income as long as (a) agents who earn income by selling their labor (or goods produced by labor in the private sector) are not required to spend all of their earned income on goods produced by labor, and/or (b) agents who plan to spend on currently producible goods are not required to earn income (previously or concurrently) with their exercise of this demand (where by "demand" we mean "want" *plus the ability to pay*).

Hahn (1977, p. 31) has put point (a) as meaning that Say's Law is done away with and involuntary unemployment can occur whenever there are "resting places for savings in other than reproducible assets" so that all income earned by engaging in the production of goods is not, in the short or long run, spent on assets producible by labor. For savings to find such ultimate resting places, the axiom of gross substitution must be thrown over (see Davidson, 1980, pp. 303–305).

This axiom is the backbone of mainstream economics; it is the assumption that any good is a substitute for any other good. If the demand for good x goes up, its price will rise inducing demand to spill over to the now relatively cheaper substitute good y. For an economist to deny this "universal truth" is revolutionary heresy—and as in the days of the Inquisition, the modern day College of Cardinals of mainstream economics destroys all nonbelievers—if not by burning them at the stake, then by banishment from the mainstream professional journals. Yet in Keynes's analysis (1936, Ch. 17) "The Essential Properties of Interest and Money" requires that the elasticity of substitution between all liquid assets including money (which are not reproducible by labor in the private sector) and producible (in the private sector) assets is zero or negligible. These properties which Keynes (1936, p. 241, n. 1) believed are *essential* to the concepts of money and liquidity necessitate that a basic axiom of Keynes's logical framework is that nonproducible assets that can be used to store savings are not gross substitutes for producible assets in savers' portfolios.

Instead, if the gross substitution axiom is true,[4] then even if savers attempt to use nonreproducible assets for storing their increments of wealth, this increase in demand will increase the price of nonproducibles. This relative price rise in nonproducibles will, under the gross substitution axiom, induce savers to substitute reproducible durables for nonproducibles in their wealth holdings and therefore nonproducibles will not be ultimate resting places for savings (cf. Davidson, 1972, 1977, 1980). The gross substitution axiom therefore restores Say's Law and denies the logical possibility of involuntary unemployment.

In *Debate with His Critics*, Friedman could correctly attack Tobin and other Neoclassical Keynesians for logical inconsistencies involving "differences in the range of assets considered" as possible gross substitutes in savings portfolios. For Friedman the total spectrum of assets including "houses, automobiles, let alone furniture, household appliances, clothes and so on" (1974, p. 29) is eligible for savings. (After all in his *permanent income hypothesis*, Friedman deliberately defines savings to include the purchase of producible durable goods.) Thus, Friedman, in his logical world, remote from reality, can "prove" that savings does not create unemployment; for the Samuelsons, Tobins, and Solows of the world their common sense if not their logic tells them better.

To overthrow the axiom of gross substitution in an intertemporal context is truly heretical. It changes the entire perspective as to what is meant by "rational" or "optimal" savings, as to why people save or what they save. Recently Sir John Hicks noted that all Keynes needed to say was that income was divided between current consumption and a vague provision for the uncertain future. The mathematical assumption that "planned expenditures at specified different dates in the future have independent utilities [and are gross substitutes] . . . this assumption I find quite unacceptable. . . . the normal condition is that there is strong complementarity between them [consumption plans in successive periods]" (Hicks, 1979, pp. 76–77, n. 7). Indeed Danziger et al. (1982–83) have shown that the facts regarding consumption spending by the elderly are incompatible with the notion of intertemporal gross substitution of consumption plans which underlie both life cycle models and overlapping generation models currently so popular in mainstream macroeconomic theory.

In the absence of the axiom of gross substitution, income effects (e.g., the Keynesian multiplier) predominate and can swamp any hypothetical neoclassical substitution effects. Consequently, relative price changes via a flexible pricing mechanism will not be the cure-all "snake-oil" medicine usually recommended by many neoclassical doctors for the unfortunate economic maladies that are occurring in the real world.

Investment Spending, Liquidity, and the Axiom of Reals

Point (b) *supra* is that agents who planned to spend in the current period are not required to earn income currently or previously to their exercise of demand in the market. This implies that spending for D_2, the demand for fixed and working capital goods (or even consumer durables) reproducible by labor in the private sector, is constrained by neither actual income nor endowments. For Keynes, given animal spirits and not timidity on the part of entrepreneurs, D_2 is constrained solely by the *monetary*, and not the real, *expected return on liquid assets* (Keynes, Ch. 17). The rate of interest, which is strictly a monetary phenomenon in Keynes, rules the roost.

Keynes (1936, p. 142) believed that the "real rate of interest" concept of Irving Fisher was a logical confusion. In a monetary economy moving through calendar time towards an uncertain (statistically unpredictable) future there is no such thing as a forward looking real rate of interest. Moreover, money has an impact on the real sector in both the short and long run. Thus, money is a real phenomenon, while the rate of interest is a monetary phenomenon (cf. Kregel, 1983).

This is just the reverse of what classical theory and modern mainstream theory teaches us. In orthodox macrotheory the rate of interest is a real (technologically determined) factor while money (at least in the long run for both Friedman and Tobin) does not affect the real output flow. This reversal of the importance or the significance of money and interest rates for real and monetary phenomena between orthodox and Keynes's theory is the result of Keynes's rejection of a second neoclassical universal truth—the axiom of reals.

For the D_2 component of aggregate demand not to be constrained by actual income, agents must have the ability to finance investment by borrowing from a banking system which can create money. Such money creation is therefore inevitably tied to the creation of money (debt) contracts. This financing mechanism involves the heresy of overthrowing what Frank Hahn calls the "axiom of reals" (cf. Minsky, 1984). Hahn describes this axiom as one where:

> The objectives of agents that determine their actions and plans do not depend on any nominal magnitudes. Agents care only about "real" things such as goods . . . leisure and effort. We know this as the axiom of the absence of money illusion, which it seems impossible to abandon in any sensible sense. (Hahn, 1983, p. 44)

The axiom of reals implies that money is a veil so that all economic decisions are made on the basis of real phenomena and relative prices alone. Money does not matter!

To reject the axiom of reals does not require assuming that agents suffer from a money illusion. It only means that "money is not neutral" (Keynes, 1973, p. 411); money matters in both the short run and the long run, or as Keynes put it:

> The theory which I desiderate would deal . . . with an economy in which money plays a part of its own and affects motives and decisions, and is, in short, one of the operative factors in the situation, so that the course of events cannot be predicted in either the long period or in the short, without a knowledge of the behavior of money between the first state and the last. And it is this which we ought to mean when we speak of a *monetary economy*. (Keynes, 1973, pp. 408–409)

Can anything be more revolutionary? In this passage from an article entitled "The *Monetary* Theory of Production" (and I emphasize the word *Monetary*) Keynes specifically rejects the axiom of reals! The only objective for a firm is to end the production process (which takes time) by liquidating its working capital in order to end up with more money than it started with (Keynes, 1979, p. 82).

Let me illustrate: suppose during the next great depression a firm has a production process gestation period of one year. At the beginning of the year it hires workers, buys materials, and so on, on forward money contracts for the entire production process and thereby has, except for acts of God, controlled its costs of production. Suppose that during the year, the CPI falls by 10 percent but the price at which the firm expected to sell its product at the end of the gestation period falls by only 5 percent. In relative real terms the firm is better off; but in the real world the firm is really worse off. Now change the numbers to say 50 percent and 45 percent respectively. The firm still has a 5 percent improvement in real terms, but in all likelihood if this continues the firm will soon have to file for bankruptcy. (Of course a good neoclassical economist would respond the firm will not go bankrupt if it can recontract without penalty—but such recontracts without penalties are not a characteristic of the world we live in.)

If on the other hand we had assumed the CPI goes up by 10 percent (or 50 percent) while the firm's product price went up by 5 percent (or percent), although the firm's real position has deteriorated its real world position is better. As long as money contracts are used to efficiently plan the production process, production decisions will be affected by nominal values and money is a real phenomenon![5]

Once we admit that money is a real phenomenon, that money matters, then the traditional axiom of reals must be rejected. Hahn should realize this, since Arrow and Hahn have demonstrated that:

> The terms in which contracts are made matter. In particular, if money is the goods in terms of which contracts are made, then the prices of goods in terms of money are of special significance. This is not the case if we consider an economy without a past or future. . . . *If a serious monetary theory* comes to be written, the fact that contracts are made in terms of money will be of considerable importance. (1971, pp. 356–357 italics added)

Moreover Arrow and Hahn demonstrate (p. 361) that, if contracts are made in terms of money (so that money affects real decisions) in an economy moving along in calendar time with a past and a future, then *all existence theorems are jeopardized.* The existence of money contracts—a characteristic of the world in which Keynes lived and which we still do—implies that there need never exist, in the long run or the short run, any rational expectations equilibrium or general equilibrium market clearing price vector.

The Pervasive Ergodic Axiom—Precision versus Accuracy

Most neoclassical and New Classical economists suffer from the pervasive form of envy which we may call the " Economist's Disease"; that is, these economists want to be considered as first class scientists dealing with a "hard science" rather than be seen as "second class" citizens of the scientific community who deal with the non-precise "social" and "political" sciences. These economists, mistaking precision (rather than accuracy) as the hallmark of "true" science, prefer to be precise rather than accurate.

Precision conveys the meaning of "sharpness to minute detail." Accuracy, on the other hand, means "care to obtain conformity with fact or truth." For example, if you phone the plumber to come fix an emergency breakdown in your plumbing system, and he responds by indicating he will be there in exactly 12 minutes, he is being precise, but not exercising care to obtain conformity with fact or truth. If he says he will be there before the day is over, he is being accurate, if not necessarily precise.

Most economists, unfortunately, prefer to be precisely wrong rather than roughly right or accurate. The axiom of ergodicity permits economists to act "as if" they were dealing with a "hard" science where data are homogeneous with respect to time. In an ergodic world, observations of a time series realization (i.e., historical data) are useful information regarding the probability distribution of the stochastic process which generated that realization. The same observations also provide information about the probability distribution over a universe of realizations which exist at any point of time such as today, and the data are also useful information regarding the future probability distribution of events. Hence by scientifically studying the past as generated by an ergodic situation, present and future events can be forecasted in terms of statistical probabilities(cf. Davidson, 1982–83).

Keynes (1936, Ch. 12) rejected this view that past information from economic time series realizations provides reliable, useful data which permit stochastic predictions of the economic future. In a world with important nonergodic circumstances—our economic world—liquidity matters, money is never neutral, and neither Say's Law nor Walras's Law is relevant (cf. Davidson, 1982–83). In such a world, Keynes's revolutionary logical analysis is relevant.

Conclusions

Mainstream economic theory has not followed Keynes's revolutionary logical analysis to develop what Arrow and Hahn have called a "serious monetary theory" in which contracts are made in terms of money in an economy moving from an irrevocable past to an uncertain, non ergodic future (cf. Davidson, 1982–83). At the very beginning of his *Treatise on Money*, Keynes (1930. p. 3) reminded the reader that, in a modern economy, money exists only because there are contracts and therefore money is intimately related to the existence of contracts.

In his writings Keynes explicitly assumed things which are incompatible with (a) the gross substitution axiom, (b) the axiom of reals, and (c) ergodicity. Unfortunately, many of the popularizers and professional interpreters of Keynes's analysis either did not read what he wrote, or did not comprehend his revolutionary logic requiring the overthrow of these fundamental neoclassical axioms. Nevertheless, Keynes's policy prescriptions made a great deal of common sense. Hence Keynes won the policy battles of the first three decades after the publication of *The General Theory*, even though "Keynesians" had erected a "neoclassical synthesis" microfoundation to Keynes's macroeconomics which could not logically support Keynes's general case.

From a logical standpoint the neoclassical synthesis Keynesians had created a Keynesian Cheshire Cat—a grin without a body. Thus, Friedman and the rational expectations—New Classical—theorists were able to destroy the rickety neoclassical Keynesian scaffolding and replace it with a technologically advanced, logically consistent, but irrelevant and inaccurate theory.

In this one-hundred-first year after Keynes's birth, it is surprising how few in the economics profession are willing or able to defend the logical basis of Keynes's analysis. It is almost as if many believed that, as Clower (1965, p. 120) indicated, "the *General Theory* is theoretical nonsense" unless Keynes believed in the constrained demand function, dual decision hypothesis. Yet, we have shown *supra* that this constrained demand function analysis implies Say's Law. Hence, if Clower is correct in his claim that Keynes had the dual decision hypothesis at the back of his mind, then Keynes was a theoretical charlatan in claiming his analysis eliminated Say's Law. Of course, it is Clower and the other neoclassical Keynesians who maintain axioms rejected by Keynes who are in error in trying to apply Keynes's label to their logical system.

At the Royal Economic Society's Centennial Celebration of Keynes's birth in July 1983 the detractors of Keynes on the program far exceeded those who were attempting to honor Keynes's accomplishments and build on the legacy he left. Some such as Professors Samuelson and Solow proudly labeled themselves as "reconstructed Keynesians" to differentiate their theory from the "unreconstructed" Keynesians of Cambridge, England. As Samuelson put it—a reconstructed Keynesian was one who found the Keynesian structure imperfect and had therefore to reconstruct it.

This "reconstructed Keynesian" appellation is, however, a misnomer when applied to the Neoclassical Synthesis Keynesian approach of Samuelson and Solow. These mainstream American "Keynesian" models never began with the same logical foundations and axioms as Keynes's model. Hence these Keynesians cannot, and will not, reconstruct Keynes until they throw over the neoclassical axioms rejected by Keynes.

The "unreconstructed" Keynesians—or Post Keynesians as I would call them—recognize that there may be many flaws in the Keynes superstructure and that the times have brought forth new and different pressing problems. Post Keynesians may not have worked out all the answers but at least they recognize that Keynes started with a logically different theoretical system—a system which accurately reflects the characteristics of the real economic world—those of Wall Street and the Corporate Board room, rather than those of Robinson Crusoe or the Medieval Fair.

Post Keynesians recognize that their logical model is neither fully developed, nor as neat and precise as the neoclassical one—after all, the number of person-hours put into developing the orthodox model exceeds those invested in the Post Keynesian analysis several million fold. Nevertheless, Post Keynesians believe it is better to develop a model which emphasizes the special characteristics of the economic world in which we live than to continually refine and polish a beautifully precise, but irrelevant, model. Moreover, when one is dealing with human activity and institutions, one may be, in the nature of things, outside of the realm of the formally precise. For Keynes as for Post Keynesians the guiding motto is "it is better to be roughly right than precisely wrong!"

After the revolution comes evolution. Post Keynesians are trying to build on the logical foundations of Keynes's real world analysis to resolve modern day economic problems. They invite all who possess open minds to undertake the further evolution of Keynes's logical heresy and to explore a Keynesian (non-Euclidean) world where the axioms of ergodicity, of gross substitution, and of reals are not universal truths applicable to all economic decision making processes.

Unlike Samuelson's "reconstructed Keynesians," Post Keynesians do not believe that a regression to pre-Keynesian (Euclidean) axioms represents progress no matter how much technological garb these postulates are wrapped in. Only in the world of 1984 and Doublespeak can a regressive analytical structure be considered an advance!

Notes

1. Despite Friedman's use of the motto "money matters," he remains faithful to the axiom of reals (see below) and does not permit money to affect the long run real outcome of his system. In his own description of his logical framework, Friedman states:

> that changes in the quantity of money as such *in the long run* have a negligible effect on real income so that nonmonetary forces are "all that matter" for changes in real income over decades and money "does not matter." . . . I regard the description of our position as "money is all that matters for changes in *nominal income* and for *short-run* changes in real income" as an exaggeration but one that gives the right flavor to our conclusions. (Friedman, 1974, p. 27)

2. These liberal Democratic Economic Advisers, however, have the difficulty that their logic is based on Say's Law, but their common sense tells

them that unemployment is a problem which the system cannot solve without direct government interference. Thus they turned to *ad hoc* modifications of their neoclassical model—a short-side rule or a constrained demand function—to abrogate Say's Law and achieve a non-Walrasian equilibrium, at least in the short run.

3. Since in this neoclassical world, engaging in a production process is assumed distasteful it would seem axiomatic that no agents would contribute to production unless they planned to spend all their income on producible goods. Consequently, full employment hiring decisions should always bring forth sufficient demand to buy all the products of industry.

This belief also underlies the rational expectations hypothesis via Lucas's aggregate supply analysis. Lucas believes there is not way of explaining real world unemployment patterns except via an analysis of intertemporal substitutability of labor by optimizing households (Lucas, 1983, p. 4). In order for households to achieve utility maximization solely in terms of the four arguments of Lucas's utility function—(1) today's consumption, (2) today's labor supply, (3) tomorrow's consumption, (4) tomorrow's labor supply—Lucas must assume that the intertemporal marginal propensity to spend on producible goods is unity. Say's Law therefore prevails by assumption. Unemployed workers are optimizing by preferring leisure today with rational expectations that they will get more real income per unit of effort tomorrow when they go back to work. Hence today's unemployed are not suffering any loss in permanent real welfare; that is, the colliding lines that we observe are not really colliding—it is all apparently an optical illusion.

If, on the other hand, you believe, as Keynes did and Post Keynesians do, that today's unemployed know they are suffering a permanent loss in real well-being then you must throw off the classical axioms of gross substitution *and* the axiom of reals and enter the world of Keynes's non-Euclidean economics! In such a world, the desire to possess liquidity—liquid assets not producible by labor—is also an argument in any labor (factor owner) supply function.

4. Recent empirical work by Benjamin Friedman (1983) has demonstrated that the facts do not justify assuming gross substitutability among all assets in savers' portfolios.

5. It should be noted that Minsky (1982) has explicitly demonstrated the inapplicability of the axiom of reals for at least one major sector of the economy. In his work Minsky has emphasized that there are at least some entrepreneurs, we call them bankers, who are guided solely by money-cash flows and maintaining increasing nominal values of net worth in balance sheets even if this means lower real values. Thus at least for this very important sector of the economy, the axiom of reals cannot be applicable.

References

Arrow, K. S., and Hahn, F. H. *General Competitive Analysis*. San Francisco: Holden Day, 1971.

Barro, J. R. and Grossman, H. I. *Money, Employment, and Inflation*. Cambridge: Cambridge University Press, 1976.

Clower, R. W. "The Keynesian Revolution: A Theoretical Appraisal." In *The Theory of Interest Rates*. Ed. by F. H. Hahn and F. P. R. Brechling. London: Macmillan, 1965.

Danziger, S., van der Gaag, J., Smolensky, E., and Taussig, M. K. "The Life-Cycle Hypothesis and Consumption Behavior of the Elderly." *Journal of Post Keynesian Economics*, Winter 1982–83, 5(2), 208–227.

Davidson, P. *Money and the Real World*. London: Macmillan, 1972.

———. "Money and General Equilibrium." *Economie Appliquée*, 1977, 30.

———. "The Dual-faceted Nature of the Keynesian Revolution." *Journal of Post Keynesian Economics*, Spring 1980, 2(3) 291–307.

———. "Rational Expectations: A Fallacious Foundation for Studying Crucial Decision-making Processes." *Journal of Post Keynesian Economics*, Winter 1982–83, 5(2), 182–198.

Friedman, B. "The Substitutability of Debt and Equity Securities." National Bureau of Economic Research Working Paper 1130, May 1982.

Friedman, M. "A Theoretical Framework for Monetary Analysis." In *Milton Friedman's Monetary Framework: A Debate with his Critics*. Ed. by R. J. Gordon. Chicago: University of Chicago Press, 1974.

Hahn, F. H. "Keynesian Economics and General Equilibrium Theory." In *Microfoundations of Macroeconomics*. Ed. By G. C. Harcourt. London: Macmillan, 1977.

———. *Money and Inflation*. Cambridge: MIT Press, 1983.

Hicks, J. R. *Causality in Economics*. New York: Basic Books, 1979.

Keynes, J. M. *A Treatise on Money*. London: Macmillan, 1930.

———. *The General Theory of Employment, Interest and Money*. New York: Harcourt, 1936.

———. *The Collected Writings of John Maynard Keynes*, Vol. 13, Ed. by D. Moggridge. London: Macmillan, 1973.

————. *The Collected Writings of John Maynard Keynes*, Vol. 29. Ed. by D. Moggridge. London: Macmillan, 1979.

Kregel, J. A. "The Multiplier and Liquidity Preference: Two Sides of the theory of Effective Demand." (Mimeo), 1983.

Lucas, R. E. *Studies in Business Cycle Theory*. Cambridge: MIT Press, 1983.

Malinvaud, E. *The Theory of Unemployment Reconsidered*. Oxford: Blackwell, 1977.

Minsky, H. P. *Can It Happen Again?* Armonk, N.Y.: M. E. Sharpe, Inc., 1982.

————. "Frank Hahn's *Money and Inflation*: A Review Article." *Journal of Post Keynesian Economics*, Spring 1984, 6(3), 449–457.

5

An Essay on Post-Keynesian Theory:
A New Paradigm in Economics

Alfred S. Eichner and J. A. Kregel

The impact of Keynes's work in the 1930's has been viewed by some economists as a "revolution" in economic thinking (see Lawrence R. Klein [1947]). Yet, to those who were most closely associated with Keynes at Cambridge during that period, the revolution proved largely abortive. Over the past 30 years, many of Keynes's critical insights into the workings of a modern, technologically advanced economy seem to have been ignored, with the result that there has been little fundamental change in the way economists perceive the world. Those one-time associates of Keynes, joined by a small number of the younger generation at Cambridge and elsewhere, have consistently tried to highlight the incompatibility of Keynes's views with orthodox theory even as they worked to develop more fully a "generalization of *The general theory*" (see Joan Robinson [1952]).

This generalization may be said to represent, in Thomas Kuhn's sense [1962], a new paradigm; and since it extends the analysis set forth in Keynes's *Treatise on Money* (1930) and *The General Theory*, it can be termed post-Keynesian.[1] Few American economists seem aware of the major works that have contributed to the development of this new paradigm[2] and fewer still, even among those likely to be sympathetic, seem to be aware of the possible significance of the new approach.[3]

Part of the problem has been the diversion created by the "Cambridge controversy" over the theory of capital (see Geoffrey C. Harcourt [1972]). While it is true that some of the elements of post-Keynesian theory became better known through the criticisms by Cambridge, England, of the treatment of capital in the neoclassical growth models favored by Cambridge, Mass., the debate has nonetheless left the misleading impression that the adversaries from across the Atlantic had only a negative critique to offer, one which applied only to highly abstract capital theory and which only persons skilled in mathematics could understand.

The purpose of this review article is to provide a guide to the post-Keynesian literature, not only noting the basic works but also bringing out the salient features of the new approach. The paper divides into four parts, each dealing with a separate distinguishing characteristic of the post-Keynesian approach, plus a brief concluding section. The four distinguishing characteristics emphasized are (1) growth dynamics, (2) distributional effects, (3) the Keynesian constraints, and (4) the micro-economic base. No attempt is made to provide a substitute for all the various aspects of the orthodox viewpoint in economics; nor indeed is the new theoretical structure meant to displace all of the old. None-theless, implicit in the paper is the view that post-Keynesian theory has the potential for becoming a comprehensive, positive alternative to the prevailing neoclassical paradigm. Trying to grasp this potential from the arguments about capital reversal and double-switching,[4] however, is likely to be just as treacherous as trying to understand the marginalist revolution of the late 19th century from the debate over the "wages fund" doctrine.

Growth and Dynamics: History and Time

Post-Keynesian theory, in contrast to other types of economic analysis, is concerned primarily with the depiction of an economic system expanding over *time* in the context of *history*. This point means that not only must time rates of change be included in the analysis but also the basis for change—the impact of both past history and expec-tations about the future on the current decisions that are bringing about the change—must be taken into account. It is through invest-ment and savings behavior that this influence of past history and expectations about the future is felt. To incorporate this influence into the analysis, one must therefore make explicit allowance for the role of investment and savings, not only at the macroeconomic level but at the micro level as well. This first distinguishing characteristic of post-Keynesian theory—its being rooted in a dynamic process—is sufficient by itself to set the new approach apart from the neoclassical model, especially that variant found in most textbooks, the one which begins with the analysis of the individual household and the individual firm in static equilibrium.

The dynamic element in post-Keynesian theory can be traced to the influence of Roy Harrod,[5] in particular his fundamental equation. The equation is better known to Americans as the Harrod-Domar formula,[6] and in the form, $G = \frac{s}{v}$, with G as the rate of growth of national income, s as the average propensity to save and v as the capital/output ratio. This equation provides the starting point not only for the post-Keynesians but for the various neoclassical growth theorists as well. (See R. M. Solow [1956; 1970], T. W. Swan [1956], and J. E. Meade [1962]; all of whom have sought to make the neoclassical model more relevant to a world known to be experiencing continuous economic expansion, but with the analysis carried out at the macroeconomic level only.) Where the two approaches diverge is in how the fundamental equation is elaborated. The neoclassical growth model modifies the Harrod-Domar formula by insisting that at least two factors of production—homogeneous aggregate capital[7] and labor—be taken explicitly into account, with changes in their relative scarcities and prices in a long-period context the main explanatory variables.

The post-Keynesian approach modifies the assumption that the average propensity to save—s in the equation—is constant by allowing changes in the distribution of income and differences in the propensity to save out of different incomes to affect aggregate savings ratios.[8] This line of inquiry has been pursued by Mrs. Robinson [1956; 1962; 1971], N. Kaldor [1956; 1959; 1961], N. Kaldor and J. Mirrlees [1962], and L. L. Pasinetti [1962; 1966]; and their work constitutes the main body of post-Keynesian literature. Professor Joan Robinson's *The Accumulation of Capital* is typical of this literature, making clear its concern with the problems of an economy expanding over time [1956]. In order to emphasize the influence of clock-time and history on the process of growth, the argument is carried out through the method of comparing economies that have digested any short-period changes that might momentarily disturb their expansion path. By then showing how the expansion of one economy is affected over time relative to the other by differences in specific variables, Mrs. Robinson is able to isolate the most critical determinants of the long-run growth of a developed, market-oriented economy. These determinants are (1) the initial endowment of capital equipment, (2) the real wage rate (and thus, given the assumptions employed, the real savings rate), (3) the rate of growth of the labor force, and (4) the rate of technical progress [1956, Book II].

More important than the specific conclusions reached, however, is the method of analysis employed: the comparison of alternative growth paths based on a difference in one of the underlying variables in one but not the other economy. The purpose behind this approach is to replace what Mrs. Robinson refers to as "pseudo-causal" models predicated on "logical" time with historical models that are empirically testable predicated on real time [1962, pp. 23–29]. The key point is that causation is not the same as simultaneity of determination; one cannot infer the one from the other as the usual static equilibrium analysis, based on the neoclassical model, attempts to do.[9]

The purpose of the exercise in comparative dynamics is not to show how some hypothetical economy can expand indefinitely over time given certain underlying conditions. It is rather to explain why, as the historical record bears such strong witness, the expansion path of a free enterprise economy is likely to be so erratic. Post-Keynesians are thus ultimately concerned with the analysis of the economy in disequilibrium, but this presents methodological problems not encountered when the concern is simply with what conditions would be consistent with the system being in a steady state of rest.[10]

To handle these problems, post-Keynesians first consider explicitly the conditions required for a steady rate of expansion, based on the warranted growth rate given by the Harrod-Domar formula. Once this has been done, the actual observed rate of growth can be analyzed in terms of (1) a change in the warranted growth rate due to a change in one of its underlying determinants and (2) the forces operating in the short run to divert the economy from its warranted growth path. Approaching the problem of disequilibrium in this manner gives rise to the distinction found in the post-Keynesian literature between long-period analysis, focusing on the determinants of the warranted growth rate; and the short-period analysis, focusing on cyclical deviations in the actual rate relative to the warranted rate. The methodological point is that the deviations cannot be understood except with respect to some reference growth path. The mistake that is all too frequently made is not just in confusing the long- and the short-period adjustments for the difference between closed, equilibrium and open, causal models) but in leaving out the short-period altogether, thereby fusing the actual and warranted rates into one through the belief that technical substitutability is sufficient to establish the validity of Say's Law.

Distributional Effects

A second distinguishing characteristic of post-Keynesian theory is that the distribution of income is considered integral to the explanation of economic activity. Rather than ignoring this factor altogether or assuming that it can be derived from the technological nature of the production process, post-Keynesian theory treats the distribution of income as a variable directly linked to the rate of economic expansion— one which, moreover, may well be subject to political manipulation.

Indeed, the simple versions of the post-Keynesian model have been set up to show how control over the rate of investment implies control over the distribution of income and the rate of profit (see Pasinetti [1974, p. 113]).[11]

In these simple versions of the model, which can be traced back to Keynes's *Treatise* as well as Kalecki's work in the 1930's, but which were first fully elaborated by Mrs. Robinson and Kaldor independently of one another in 1956, the national income is divided into total wage income and total profits. This recalls the world of classical economics, with its twofold class structure: (1) workers, whose income consists solely of the wages and salaries they receive for their labor services and which are entirely spent on personal consumption, and (2) capitalists, whose income consists solely of the profits obtained through their ownership of the means of production. It is because profits are the only source of finance for capital expenditures that the capitalist class, in this model, controls the rate of investment. In other words, the workers consume all their income (their marginal propensity to save, s_w, is zero) and the capitalists carry out and finance all investment (their marginal propensity to save, s_p, is unity).[12] If this nineteenth century terminology seems inappropriate to the twentieth century, one can just as easily substitute the term nonworker for capitalist and the term nonwage income for profits. The essential point is that one group receives a wage determined by market forces, collective bargaining, or custom while the other receives the residual income of all the producing units in the system. This makes the argument considerably more general.

From the "classical" assumption that the workers do all the consuming and that the capitalists do all the investing and saving, it follows that the amount of wages and salary on the income side of the national income and product accounts must be equal to the amount of consumption goods enumerated on the product side as having been produced. Similarly, the amount of profits received as income will be equal to the amount of investment goods produced. A higher growth rate, given the same production techniques and money wage rate, will therefore, because of the implied increase in the rate of investment, imply a different distribution of income, with a higher ratio of profit (nonwage income) to wages. On the other hand, a lower growth rate, everything else unchanged, will mean a lower ratio of profits to wages.

The point can be further elaborated with the aid of an algebraic formula based on that given by Kaldor [1956] (see also Kregel [1971, chaps. 9–10]). With s_w and s_p, as defined above, total savings in the system can be written as $S = s_w Y + (s_p - s_w)P$. That is, total savings at any point in time are equal to the savings rate of workers applied to the total national income plus the difference between the savings rate of capitalists and workers applied to that portion of the national income received as profit. Substituting the above relation for S into the Keynesian $S = I$ condition yields the following equation:

$$I = s_w Y + (s_p - s_w)P \qquad (1)$$

Dividing through by Y and rearranging terms,

$$\frac{P}{Y} = \frac{1}{(s_p - s_w)} \frac{I}{Y} - \frac{s_w}{(s_p - s_w)} \qquad (2)$$

When the classical assumptions hold (i.e., $s_w = 0$, $s_p = 1$), the equation collapses to

$$\frac{P}{Y} = \frac{I}{Y} \qquad (3)$$

This brings out most sharply the relationship between the share of investment in total output and the share of profit in total income. The greater the rate of economic expansion as a result of a higher level of investment, the greater will be the share of national income going to the capitalists (non-wage earners) in the form of profits (nonwage income) and the lower the share going to workers.

Relaxing the assumption that $s_p = 1$ means that some income from profits is spent on consumption goods. The equation then becomes

$$\frac{P}{Y} = \frac{1}{s_p} \cdot \frac{I}{Y} \qquad (4)$$

Under these circumstances the profit (nonwage) share of national income for a given ratio of investment to total output will be higher by a factor equal to the reciprocal of the marginal propensity to save out of profits. Thus, if the capitalist class uses half of its income to purchase consumption goods, its share of the national income would be twice as high as it would be with $s_p = 1$. If the propensity to consume by capitalists (non-wage earners) is greater than 0.5, the share of profits (nonwage income) will be correspondingly higher. There are, then, two basic factors determining the relative shares of national income: (a) the ratio of investment to total output and (b) the propensity to consume out of profits.

It should be pointed out that what is being discussed here is the distribution of income, not the level of income. The two are not necessarily the same, and one of the insights that can be derived from the post-Keynesian theory is that it is possible for the level of income going to workers to be increasing at the same time that their share of the national income is declining. The determination of the level of income will be taken up in the next section.

Finally, if savings from wages are positive, that is, if $s_w > 0$, the correspondence with the classical categories of workers and capitalists is lost and, as Pasinetti emphasized [1962], equation (2) above will not be an adequate representation of the distributional relationships of a system where $s_w > 0$ and $s_p < 1$. The relative shares of workers and capitalists (non-wage recipients) must be considered separately from that of wages and profits (non-wage income).

If workers save and are allowed a return on the investment of their savings, they will have both wage and nonwage income. It is then obvious that the distribution of income between wages and profits will not be the same as the distribution between workers and capitalists, since some of the profits must be paid to workers as a return on their savings. Pasinetti, however, has shown that when workers become entitled to a share of the profits as a result of their contributing to the financing of investment through their own direct savings (with the rate of return paid them equal to or less than the rate of profit), it makes no difference insofar as the distribution between wages and profits is concerned. The ratio of wages to total income is still determined by the share of investment in total output and the marginal propensity to consume by the capitalist (non-wage-earning) class. Only the distribution between workers as a social class and other income recipients will be affected, with the share going to workers increasing with their marginal propensity to save, s_w. As Pasinetti has noted, "These conclusions . . . shed new light on the old Classical idea . . . of a relation between the savings of that group of individuals who are in a position to carry on the process of production and the process of capital accumulation" [1974, p. 113].

Thus the relationship given in equation (4) above can be considered adequate as a description of the distribution of income between wages and profits (nonwage income) if sp is defined as the propensity to save by non-wage earners. Most importantly, it holds independently of the value assigned to s_w.[13] This goes back to another earlier point, namely, that what lies behind the post-Keynesian delineation of income shares is not so much a distinction between social classes as a distinction between quasi-contractual and residual forms of income (see Kregel [1973, chap. 11]). The point becomes clearer when, in addition to dropping the classical assumptions, the analysis is removed from the nineteenth century context of small, family-held business enterprises and brought into the world of the modern industrial corporation.

While there were early hints that the post-Keynesian arguments about income distribution applied just as well to an economy dominated by large industrial corporations,[14] systematic efforts to develop the theory along these lines are of relatively recent date (e.g., Kregel [1971]). In this type of formulation (found in Kregel [1973] and Eichner [1973]), the saving propensity of the capitalist class becomes the savings propensity of the corporate sector. With just this one change in nomenclature, all the conclusions that seem to apply only to an economic system in which the participants are divided into capitalists and workers applies to an economic system dominated by large corporations as well. The higher the level of investment that the corporate sector as a whole undertakes, the higher will be its share of the national income. And if there is consumption out of the profits earned by these corporations, whether it be as a result of distributing dividends to the rentier remnants of the earlier entrepreneurial group or as a result of expenditures by the corporations themselves on such non-capital-augmenting items as advertising, their relative share will be even higher. Savings by workers, especially if turned back over to the corporations for reinvestment, will improve the relative position of that group *vis à vis* the corporate sector but it will not change the functional distribution of income between quasi-contractual payments (wages, fixed interest, and rent) and residual earnings (corporate profits). Indeed, these conclusions apply to any economic system in which some one group, private or public, receives a residual share depending on the level of economic activity—and it is hard to conceive of an economic system without that characteristic.[15]

With the focus on the savings behavior of a type of economic institution rather than a class of individuals or type of income, there is reason to inquire as to what, besides some undiscoverable indifference map, lies behind savings behavior. For Kregel, at least in this 1971 work, the explanation lies in the rate at which corporations decide to pay out dividends. The higher the dividend rate, and thus the lower the retention (of profits) rate, r the lower will be the marginal propensity to save—s_p in the notation used up to now—of the group receiving nonwage income.[16] For Eichner, the key to the savings behavior of large corporations is their pricing policy. To generate a higher rate of savings, the large corporation—or megacorp, as he terms it—need only increase the margin above costs which it establishes as part of its price. While Kregel focuses on the retention rate, r, holding the price level constant, Eichner focuses on the price level, holding r constant. The two explanations are therefore complementary rather than antithetical to one another.[17]

Even though considerable work still remains to be done in refining the above arguments, what the post-Keynesian paradigm has to say about the distribution of income is already far more easily verified empirically (see National Bureau of Economic Research [1964] than what can be gleaned from the marginal productivity analysis that lies at the heart of the prevailing neoclassical model. Still, as has been pointed out, explaining the distribution of income is not the same as explaining how much there is to be distributed. It is to the latter point that we now turn.

The Keynesian Constraints

The third distinguishing characteristic of post-Keynesian theory is that it retains the fundamental approach to a monetized production economy outlined by Keynes in his *Treatise* and *The General Theory*. This implies more than just the use of a certain set of aggregate classifications and accompanying vocabulary—words like consumption function, multiplier, etc. It implies as well the following:

1. *The need to recognize that real commodity and labor flows are expressed in the system as monetary flows, the real aspect being reflected on the product side of the national accounts and the monetary flows on the income side.* Post-Keynesian theory is thus a theory of a monetized production economy, one in which commodities and labor exchange for something which, because of its unique characteristics—a zero, or negligible, cost of production together with a zero, or negligible, elasticity of substitution with respect to anything else able to serve as a store of value and/or a medium of exchange—can be called money.[18] While this would seem to set post-Keynesian theory apart only from the basic Walrasian variant of the neoclassical model,[19] it actually involves a considerably greater degree of differentiation, as can be seen once all the implications of a monetized economy are fully spelled out. Among these corollary features are a full panoply of financial institutions ranging from commercial banks to investment brokers; the ability of these financial institutions, acting together, to sterilize or activate the available monetary stocks and thereby provide a cushion against exogenous shocks to the system; and the possibility that, as a result of these monetary adjustments to the real commodity and labor flows, the money wage rate will vary independently of the real wage rate.[20]

2. *The division of the national product and of the national income into discretionary and nondiscretionary components.* On the product side, the relevant distinction is between discretionary expenditures and

nondiscretionary expenditures. (Keynes himself used the terms "non-available" and "available" goods in the *Treatise* and the terms "investment" and "consumption" in *The General Theory*. The three sets of terms are broadly interchangeable.) Nondiscretionary expenditures represent the flow of goods and services required to keep economic units functioning at a given level of output, whether they be the material and labor inputs used by business firms in the production process or the food and other items consumed on a daily basis by households. Even in a monetized economy, these expenditures are so closely linked to the corresponding monetary flows that there is no need to distinguish between the two. Those making the purchases are the same as those with the currently earned and disposable income. The situation is somewhat different, however, in the case of discretionary expenditures. One of the most important of Keynes's insights was that those with the power to determine the level of discretionary expenditures, or investment, were not the same as, nor need they be limited by what they can obtain from, those with the discretionary income, or savings. Thus the level of discretionary expenditures can deviate from the level of discretionary income—at least in an *ex ante*, anticipatory or planned sense.

3. *An ex post equality between discretionary expenditures (investment) and discretionary income (savings) as the sole condition for aggregate equilibrium.* This gives greater freedom to the analysis because, with only one set of flows that must be brought into balance before the chain of causal explanation can be considered complete, many other things—like the flow of those who would like to obtain employment or the desired portfolios of wealth holders—can remain out of balance. It should be stressed that in setting up an *ex post* equality between discretionary expenditures (investment) and discretionary income (savings) as the one condition which must be met before the analysis can be considered complete, no causal relationship is implied by what is essentially an accounting identity. The causal relationship follows from the next, quite separate point.

4. *Discretionary expenditures (investment) as the primary factor determining the level of economic activity.* This means that if the level of economic activity or—shifting into a post-Keynesian framework—the rate of economic expansion is to be increased, it can only be accomplished by increasing the rate at which discretionary expenditures are being undertaken. A corollary proposition is that when, as a result of any such change in the rate of discretionary spending, there develops an *ex ante* imbalance between the two flows, it is the discretionary income (savings) that will necessarily have to adjust to the level of

discretionary expenditures (investment), and not *vice versa*. This decisive role played by discretionary expenditures needs to be kept firmly in mind when considering the distributional effects pointed out in the preceding section.[21] The capitalist class (or, if you prefer, the non-wage-earning group, the corporate sector, the state or whoever else is viewed as receiving the residual income) in effect determines its own relative share of the national product in the process of deciding what the rate of discretionary expenditures will be. The more it invests (and consumes), the greater will be the share it obtains of the total output.[22]

Because of the importance placed on it in their analysis, post-Keynesians have, quite naturally, been concerned with what determines the rate of discretionary expenditures. Most of the attention has been given to discretionary expenditures (investment) in the narrow sense of spending by business firms on capital equipment. Here the starting point has usually been Keynes's own emphasis on the "animal spirits" of entrepreneurs and the volatility of their expectations. To the extent that any formal model of investment behavior can be said to be favored, it is Kalecki's in which the level of spending on new capital equipment is a function of past profits.[23] Together with a macrodynamic model in which the level of profits is a function of the rate of investment, it makes for an economy which is cyclically unstable. However, this type of explanation for investment behavior is not intrinsic to post-Keynesian theory; and indeed, almost from the beginning, Kaldor has given at least equal place to the endogenous factors emphasized in the alternative "accelerator" model.[24] Eichner [1976] has shown how Robert Eisner's [1963; 1967] lagged-sales accelerator model can be made consistent with Kaldor's approach to investment determination. The point is that post-Keynesian theory is compatible with a number of different models of investment behavior, the main exception being the so-called "neo-classical" model developed by Dale W. Jorgenson [1963].[25] The latter makes the rate of spending on new capital equipment a function of the change in the returns to capital relative to wages, and thus it reverses what, according to post-Keynesian theory, are cause and effect.[26]

Just as there is nothing inherent in post-Keynesian theory that would limit the determinants of investment, narrowly defined as expenditures on new capital equipment, to past profits as a proxy variable for entrepreneurial expectations or "animal spirits," so, too, there is nothing inherent in the theory that would limit investment itself to spending by business enterprises on capital equipment. Eichner has shown how the argument can be generalized, so that not just the business sector but the household and government sectors as well are capable of discretionary spending [1975]. Besides leading to a multi-sector analysis of investment-savings equilibrium, with deficits in one sector being offset by surpluses in others, this extension of post-Keynesian theory opens up the question of what are the separate, and perhaps quite distinct, determinants of discretionary expenditures in the several sectors. Part of the answer can be found in the quite substantial work which has been done by economists over the past 20 years on the determinants of spending by households on consumer durables[27] and by government on public and quasi-public goods[28]—work that has clearly been inspired by *The General Theory* and which can now be incorporated back into the mainstream of post-Keynesian developments in economic theory. Clearly, however, much still remains to be done in synthesizing these disparate elements before a fully satisfactory explanation of what determines the overall rate of discretionary spending will have been produced.

The rate of growth of discretionary expenditures is but one of three rate-of-change variables required for the analysis of macrodynamic disequilibrium. Another is the warranted growth rate given by the Harrod-Domar formula. Should the rate of growth of discretionary expenditures, $\overset{*}{I}$, not be equal to the warranted growth rate, G_{w}, the economy will move off its secular growth path and begin tracing out a cyclical pattern around that trend line. Thus, the post-Keynesian analysis of macrodynamic disequilibrium begins by looking at the current or actual growth rate, whether it be of the economy as a whole, G_{a}, or of some component thereof, say investment, $\overset{*}{I}$, relative to the warranted growth rate. Whenever there is a difference between the two, that is, $\overset{*}{G}_{a}$ or $\overset{*}{I} \neq G_{w}$, the analysis ceases to be that of long-run steady-state expansion and instead becomes that of a shorter-period cyclical movement.

Pasinetti has provided an algebraic framework [1974, chap. 3] and Eichner [1976, chap. 6] a geometric one for considering the possible dynamic growth paths that may be traced out once an economy has been dislodged from its warranted growth path. The Eichner diagram measures the rate of growth of discretionary expenditures, $\overset{*}{I}$, and the rate of growth of discretionary income, $\overset{*}{S}$, on the same vertical axis. Separate curves can then be drawn showing how each of these two rate-of-change variables will respond as the aggregate growth rate, $\overset{*}{G}$, itself varies. The curves can be drawn so as to depict either the type of cyclically unstable situation that ensues when a Kalecki-type investment demand model is postulated or, alternatively, the type of economy that, when pushed off its steady-state expansion path by some exogenous factor, is subject to forces from within that will cause it to return to the

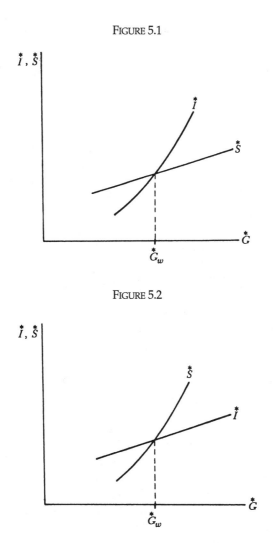

FIGURE 5.1

FIGURE 5.2

warranted growth rate. It all depends, as can be seen from the accompanying diagrams, on the slope of the savings curve, $\overset{*}{S}$, relative to that of the investment demand curve, $\overset{*}{I}$.[29] Figure 5.1 depicts an unstable situation and Figure 5.2 a stable one. What, in fact, are the slopes of the two curves, as well as what are their respective parameters, is therefore of crucial importance, but these are questions which need to be dealt with empirically, not a priori. The answers will depend on the values of the savings propensities, the composition of discretionary expenditures, etc.

While this type of analysis may at first seem unfamiliar, it is actually implicit in the large-scale econometric models that have been developed for the American and other economies based on the pioneering work of Jan Tinbergen and Lawrence R. Klein.[30] One need only reduce the equations in these models to two: one attempting to explain or predict discretionary expenditures and the other attempting to explain or predict discretionary income.

The third rate-of-change variable required for the analysis of macrodynamic disequilibrium is what is usually referred to, following Harrod [1948], as the "natural" growth rate but which, following Mrs. Robinson [1956, p. 405], is perhaps better thought of as the "potential" growth rate. Both the actual growth rate, G_a^*, and the warranted growth rate, G_w^*, reflect the constraints on the growth process that derive from the endogenous forces at work within the economic system itself. On the other hand, the potential growth rate, G_p^*, reflects the constraints imposed by the availability of resources from without, as well as by technological possibilities. While these limiting, exogenously supplied resources could just as well be natural ones, in line with the recently revived Malthusian sensitivity to what are the true limits on economic growth, the emphasis within the post-Keynesian literature has been almost entirely on human resources, together with changes in technology. In the simplest formulation, then, the potential growth rate, G_p^*, is identified with the growth of the work force, N. Compounding this variable by the rate of growth of output *per* worker as most post-Keynesians would do or substituting for it the skill matrix of the work force as suggested by Eichner [1975] makes the analysis somewhat more refined but does not change the essential point. This is that comparing the actual growth rate, G_a^*, with the warranted growth rate, G_w^*, to determine whether a steady-state rate of expansion can be maintained on the basis of the endogenous forces at work within the system is not enough. In addition, the warranted growth rate, G_w^*, must be compared with the potential growth rate, G_p^*, to determine whether the availability of exogenously supplied resources—*vis.*, manpower—makes that steady-state rate of expansion either feasible or desirable.

Within this framework, there if no fixed point of "full employment." All that one can say, based on the model, is whether the amount of unemployed human resources is decreasing or increasing, depending on whether G_w^* is greater or less than G_p^*. It is on this basis that Mrs. Robinson [1962] has defined the several possible variants to the Golden Age whose existence neoclassical growth theorists are so fond of demonstrating. There is, of course, the true Golden Age in which not only is the warranted growth rate, $\overset{*}{G}_w$, the desired growth rate but, even more important, $\overset{*}{G}_a = \overset{*}{G}_w = \overset{*}{G}_p$. In addition, however, there is the "limping" Golden Age in which, although $\overset{*}{G}_a = \overset{*}{G}_w$ and this is the desired growth rate, it turns out that $\overset{*}{G}_w < \overset{*}{G}_p$. This implies a growing class of unemployed workers. The obverse of the limping Golden Age is the restrained Golden Age. Here $\overset{*}{G}_w > \overset{*}{G}_p$, implying an eventual slowing down of the growth process as the economy bumps against the upward limit on the rate of expansion set by the availability of manpower and technological progress. Finally, there is the "bastard" Golden Age. This occurs when, even though $\overset{*}{G}_a = \overset{*}{G}_w = \overset{*}{G}_p$ and this is the desired growth rate, the real wage dictated by the rate of economic expansion is less than what workers are willing to accept. The result, as workers seek to push up their money wage rates, is the now all too familiar wage-price inflationary spiral, with its resulting effect on $\overset{*}{G}_w$ as well as on the share of wages in national income. This brings us to the last of the four points to be taken up.

The Microeconomic Base

The fourth distinguishing characteristic of post-Keynesian theory is its microeconomic base. It is necessary to assume neither that the individual firms are price takers equating marginal cost with marginal revenue nor that wages reflect the "marginal productivity" of labor. Indeed, post-Keynesians view both prices and wages as being determined by a quite different set of considerations.

The real wage is, of course, set in the manner already indicated—by the rate of discretionary expenditures that has been opted for by the society and the relative distribution of income between residual and nonresidual income recipients which that rate of expansion requires. There is, however, still the nominal wage to be explained, the difference between the two being crucial to the macro adjustment process. Post-Keynesian theory accepts Keynes's view that the nominal wage is for the most part exogenously determined. It may depend on the type of Malthusian population dynamic, which in the classical model keeps wages at the subsistence level. Or it may depend, as Keynes himself emphasized, on the bargaining strength of the trade union movement.[31] In either case what is being put forward is something other than a strictly economic explanation for the nominal wage rate. A corollary proposition is that the major role played by the level of money wages is in the determination of the level of money prices. While some economists may be uncomfortable with an exogenously determined money wage rate, this approach has two advantages. First, it seems to agree with the situation that is observable in most countries. Second, it introduces another instrumental variable for influencing the aggregate price level. To understand what is implied by that, one must turn to the post-Keynesian pricing model.

The competitive conditions assumed in post-Keynesian theory are far less stringent that those postulated in the conventional neoclassical analysis. There is no need to stipulate that the individual firm is a price taker, with little or no ability to affect the price prevailing at the industry level. All that is required is that there be sufficient rivalry among firms, whether in the same industry or not, so that no potentially profitable investment opportunity is eschewed. In other words, the rivalry among firms need only be sufficient to assure that the expected rate of return on investment will tend to be equalized for all firms. This means that competition is focused around investment, or discretionary expenditures, rather than around the price variable.

Post-Keynesian theory also employs far less stringent assumptions about the technical conditions of production in the short run. Kaldor early raised the question of why the firm should be thought of as encountering diseconomies, or increasing costs, over the range of output at which it tends to find itself producing [1934].[32] Today the accepted view among post-Keynesian economists, based both on the empirical evidence available on the subject and on the theoretical implications of assuming fixed technical coefficients in the short run, is that the firm actually faces constant prime or direct costs over the relevant range of output, with the zone of increasing costs lying to the right of that (*cf.* Robinson and Eatwell [1974, p. 168], Kregel [1973, p. 139], Davidson [1972, pp. 37–40], and Eichner [1976, chap. 2]. This gives rise to the set of cost curves depicted in Figure 5.3, rather that the U-shaped cost curves of the conventional neoclassical analysis. Two significant propositions follow from this formulation. The first is that the firm is not subject to any pressure on the cost side to raise its price solely as a result of an increase in the demand for its product. This lends support to the argument that it is the firm's supply curve—and not its demand curve as assumed in Walrasian-type models—that is perfectly elastic in the short run. The other significant proposition that follows from cost curves as drawn above is that the profits, or residual income, of the firm will be an increasing function of the rate of capacity utilization or—what is essentially the same thing—the level of demand. This is because, while prime or direct costs remain constant as output expands, the *per* unit overhead costs are continuously falling, leaving a growing gap between a fixed price and average total costs, even when the latter include a certain "normal" or anticipated profit. This disproportionate increase in

FIGURE 5.3

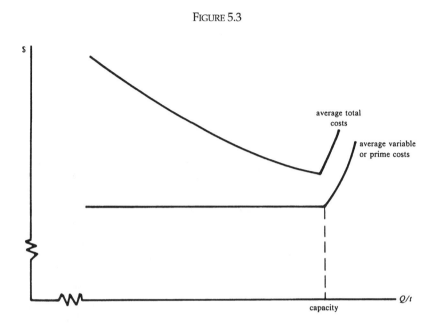

the firm's residual income as the level of demand rises produces at the micro level the same redistributive effects already described at the macro level. It thus demonstrates the consistency of the theory at the two levels.

Putting these various elements together leads inexorably to the formulation of a pricing model based on a certain mark-up or margin above costs. This type of "cost-plus" pricing model goes back to Kalecki's writings in the 1930's,[33] although the empirical work being carried out contemporaneously by Andrews at Oxford pointed in the same direction.[34] While the connection between the mark-up above costs in Kalecki's model and the savings out of which investment is financed was pointed out by Steindl as early as 1952,[35] it is only recently that post-Keynesians have turned their attention to what actually determines the size of the mark-up, and hence the savings rate, in the business sector.

Donald J. Harris [1974] has pointed to two factors—besides the "monopoly power" stressed by Kalecki—upon which the margin above costs may depend. One is the "normal" or expected rate capacity utilization. In the resulting model, which Harris attributes to Mrs. Robinson [1969, p. 260], the expected rate of capacity utilization becomes the basis for estimating the average total casts upon which the margin is figured. The model has the important short-run property, already mentioned, that above average levels of aggregate demand lead to above average profits and/or business savings, and *vice versa*. The other factor pinpointed by Harris is the planned level of investment. In the alternative model based on this second factor, a model attributed to Harcourt [1972, p. 211], the planned level of investment serves as a measure of business confidence, including confidence in the ability to maintain a given margin above costs. Thus the higher the planned level of investment, the higher will be the margin that prevails.

While Harris sets up these two models as alternatives to one another, there is no reason why they need be treated as such. Eichner has combined the two models into one, at the same time offering a somewhat different interpretation of the relationship between planned investment and the margin above costs [1973; 1976]. He has also given a more specific meaning to Kalecki's "degree of monopoly" by positing three separate constraints on the individual firm's pricing discretion. One of these is the substitution effect, reflecting the influence exerted by the elasticity of industry demand, the same factor emphasized in the conventional pricing models except that greater weight is placed on the impact of that variable over time. A second constraint is what is termed the entry factor, this being the probability of new firms entering the industry as the margin above costs is increased. Inclusion of this factor serves to make much of the work that has been done over the years in industrial organization a central part of microeconomic theory rather than the *corpus* of anomalies it is viewed as being from the perspective of orthodox price theory.[36] The third constraint is the fear of government intervention in all its possible forms. This incorporates an exogenous political factor into the analysis.[37] The three constraints each impose a certain long-run cost on the firm if it should decide to exercise its pricing power to increase the margin above costs, m. Together, the three constraints give rise to a supply curve for internally generated funds—S'_I in quadrant I of the accompanying diagram—which is positively sloped, indicating that the higher the mark-up above costs, the greater will be the cost to the firm—transformed into an implicit interest rate, R—of obtaining additional investment funds, F, internally. This supply curve, after taking into account the possibility of obtaining additional investment funds at a market rate of interest, i, can be compared with the firm's marginal efficiency of investment schedule, D_I,[38] to indicate what is the optimal change in mark-up. (Quadrant II shows how the implicit interest rate, R, increases as the mark-up, m, is increased, while quadrant IV shows how the additional funds being generated internally, F, increases simultaneously as a result of a change in the same factor.)

The essential point here is that the mark-up above costs depends on the demand for investment ends relative to the cost of obtaining those

FIGURE 5.4

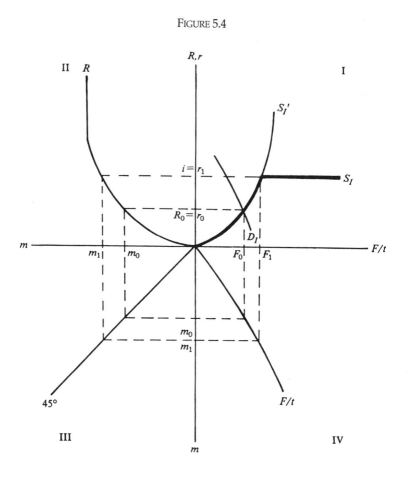

funds internally rather than externally. Thus, while the conventional theory of the firm emphasizes the importance of external funds—the availability of internal funds except to replace worn-out capital equipment being viewed as necessarily the result of some disequilibrium situation—the post-Keynesian microeconomic model takes internal fund generation as the rule and external financing as the exception.

From this microeconomic base—a nominal wage rate that is exogenously determined and a mark-up above costs that reflects the rate of growth of investment—post-Keynesian theory has little trouble interpreting what has been unfathomable to the alternative, neoclassical paradigm. The recent inflationary experience in the United States and other Western nations can be simply described as the bastard Golden

Age outlined by Mrs. Robinson. At the heart of the inflationary process is the question of relative income distribution; and because the neoclassical model is not able to take this aspect into account, it is not able to offer any viable solution to the problem of inflation. Just as Keynes had pointed out how difficult it was for a market-oriented economy to avoid unemployment, so now the post-Keynesians are bringing out how difficult it is for such an economy to escape an inflation-prone bastard Golden Age. Indeed, the tendency, given the reluctance of the economists who advise governments to abandon the neoclassical model, is to convert the bastard Golden Age into a limping one.

A Concluding Thought

In this brief review of post-Keynesian theory, a number of aspects—such as money,[39] technological change—have been touched on only tangentially. Others such as value,[40] international trade[41]—have not been dealt with at all. Still, enough should have been said to indicate the scope of post-Keynesian theory as well as its most essential features. For some readers, the important question will be how this body of theory differs, if at all, from the prevailing neoclassical model. It is a question that can readily be answered—indeed has already been dealt with obliquely—but which needs to be approached, if confronted directly, with care lest the issues become muddled. It must first be pointed out that there is no single neoclassical model with which post-Keynesian theory can be compared. The Arrow-Debreu elaboration of the basic Walrasian model is different from the Marshallian partial equilibrium model emphasized in intermediate price theory courses, and the latter is different from the Swan-Solow aggregate growth model. All of these neoclassical models share certain features in common. Indeed, it is these common features that make a comparison with post-Keynesian theory possible. Still, not all the different versions display every one of the common features, just as not all post-Keynesian models have every one of the characteristics outlined above. This means that only a rough comparison can be made between the post-Keynesian group of models and the neoclassical, or orthodox, group; and even then the comparison runs the risk of misrepresenting some particular variant. None the less, Table 5.1 may serve at least a heuristic purpose:

All but the last of the several aspects in Table 5.1 have already been touched on in the earlier discussion, and there is no need to dwell on them further. The last point, however, has not previously been brought out. It reflects the distinction made by Kornai between theory as that term is understood by the natural sciences, meaning some general

TABLE 5.1

Aspect	Post-Keynesian Theory	Neoclassical Theory
Dynamic Properties	Assumes pronounced cyclical pattern on top of a clearly discernible secular growth rate	Either no growth, or steady-state expansion with market mechanisms assumed to preclude any but a temporary deviation from that growth path
Explanation of how income is distributed	Institutional factors determine a historical division of income between residual and non-residual shareholders, with changes in that distribution depending on changes in the growth rate	The distribution of income explained solely by variable factor inputs and the marginal productivity of those variable factor inputs
Amount of information assumed to be available	Only the past is known, the future is uncertain	Complete foresight exists as to all possible events
Conditions that must be met before the analysis is considered complete	Discretionary income must be equal to discretionary expenditures	All markets cleared with supply equal to demand in each of those markets
Microeconomic base	Imperfect markets with significant monopolistic elements	Perfect markets with all micro units operating as price takers
Purpose of the theory	To explain the real world as observed empirically	To demonstrate the social optimality if the real world were to resemble the model

statement about the empirically observable world, and theory as the basis for an optimal decision rule [1971]. The distinction is an important one for understanding why those who use the one type of model often seem to be talking past—that is, failing to communicate with—those who use the other type. The problem of communication is, of course, compounded when the neoclassical theory is used for a purpose for which it is not suited, that of explaining the real world.[42]

Once the quite different purposes which post-Keynesian and neoclassical theory are meant to serve are clearly understood, certain other differences between the two theories begin to fall into place. For example, the willingness to make assumptions so at variance with the available evidence is less clearly a fault when the objective is to define an optimal decision rule rather than to explain the world as it is. At the same time, however, the quite different purposes that post-Keynesian and neoclassical theory are meant to serve makes even more problematical the already difficult task of determining which of these two models is the better one for analyzing a modern, market-oriented economy. As Kuhn's work brings out, it is difficult to choose between alternative paradigms—especially when the newer one is still in an inchoate state—even if there is agreement that the purpose of a theory is to explain the empirically observable world. When there are two alternative paradigms, each designed to serve a quite different purpose, the task of choosing between them is further complicated.

Notes

We wish to acknowledge the helpful comments made on earlier drafts of this paper by Joan Robinson, Luigi Pasinetti, Geoffrey Harcourt, and Paul Davidson.

1. The term neo-Keynesian has also been used. It should be added that Keynes's is only one of the contributions upon which the new approach is based. Certainly the work of Michal Kalecki has been no less important than that of Keynes; and to the extent that the new approach rests on the theory of value which grows out of the work of John von Neuman and Piero Sraffa, those names need to be mentioned as well. Indeed, to Marxists the work of Sraffa is seen as being the most fundamental of all, and they are likely, as a result, to refer to the new approach as neo-Ricardian.

2. The American tradition is more representative of Keynesianism than of Keynes's own work. See, for example, the distinction set out by Axel Leijonhufvud [1968]. Even he now admits that his own interpretation is based on Walrasian rather than Marshallian principles and, thus, not a valid representation of Keynes's work [Leijonhufvud, 1974]. The distinction he draws, however, still holds true.

3. However, one should point out the work of Sidney Weintraub as one of the few American economists to appreciate the extent of Keynes' contribution towards over-throwing the neoclassical orthodoxy. (See Weintraub [1959; 1966].)

4. Many critics have mistakenly focused on these issues as being the central ones of post-Keynesian economics. (*Cf.* Mark Blaug [1974] and Joseph Stiglitz [1974].)

5. See his *Economica* discussion [1934; 1934] with D. H. Robertson as well as the hints laid in his *Trade Cycle* [1936] and the final paragraph of his review [1939] of Keynes's *General Theory*. The publication of Keynes's correspondence with Harrod suggests that Harrod's dynamic theory grew out of discussions between Harrod and Keynes about the dynamic aspects of Harrod's book as applied to *The General Theory*. (See Keynes [1973, XIV, pp. 150–79, 298, 321–50].)

6. See Harrod [1939; 1948; 1973]. Pasinetti [1974, pp. 93–95] makes clear the independent contribution of Domar.

7. One of the first important questions raised by the post-Keynesians about neoclassical theory was whether it was possible to define any homogeneous set of goods as "capital," and this was before the appearance of the neoclassical models of growth which became the focal point of the capital controversy. (See Robinson [1954] and Sraffa [1960].) The first use of aggregate capital in a neoclassical production function as a basis for a model of growth is in Solow [1956] and Swan [1956], building on the earlier static use of aggregate capital found in Clark [1899] and Wicksell [1934].

8. The effect on the savings ratio of the distribution of income and the association of a higher propensity to save out of profits than out of wages are both found in Keynes's *Treatise* and *The General Theory*. Keynes, however, did not countenance the constancy of these values over time.

9. See L. L. Pasinetti [1974, pp. 45–48]; F. H. Hahn [1973, p. 15].

10. See Robinson [1962, pp. 6–7]. Thus Blaug [1974, p. 82], in arguing that post-Keynesian theory is concerned only with long-run steady-state growth, has missed the essential point.

11. Within the context of Keynes's own model, this requires that two of the three independent variables (liquidity preference and the propensity to consume) be taken as given, leaving the marginal efficiency of capital or the rate of aggregate investment as the one exogenously determined variable.

12. This seems to be the kind of model Keynes had in mind when he gave his interpretation of the pre–World War I economic history. (See Keynes, [1920, p. 16].)

13. It should be stressed that Pasinetti strictly confines his analysis to the long period; and that the main thrust of his argument, notwithstanding the response from critics (e.g., Meade [1963]; Meade and Hahn [1965]; Samuelson and Modigliani [1966]), was to show that the distribution of income between wages and profits as well as the rate of profit is "determined by the natural rate of growth divided by the capitalists' propensity to save, independently of any

'productivity' of capital (no matter how it may be defined), and indeed independently of anything else" [Pasinetti, 1974, p. 144]. Further analysis of the points at issue are dealt with by Harcourt [1972] and Kregel [1971]. Pasinetti, besides reprinting the earlier article, has now made a further clarified assessment [1974, chaps. 5, 6] in which he says, "The most surprising outcome of all is that the long-run rate of profit is even independent of 'capital'! In the long run, capital itself becomes a variable; and it is capital that has to be adapted to an exogenously determined rate of profit, not the other way round" [1974, p. 144].

14. See Robinson [1956, pp. 404–06]; Kaldor [1956]; Pasinetti [1974, p. 112, n. 2]. Kaldor went further in an appendix to his response [1966] to Samuelson and Modigliani's critique [1966] of Pasinetti [1962]. To deal with one of the issues that had been raised, Kaldor explicitly introduced corporate share finance and the concept of the "valuation ratio" (cf. Marris [1964]) and Kahn [1972] for further uses of this concept), but the intention was more to remove an anomaly from the analysis than to fully analyze the effect of a change in institutions on the performance of the model.

15. Kregel entitles the appendix in which the corporate model is first laid out, "The Classless, Non-Income Differentiated Model," thereby hinting at its universal applicability.

16. This linking of s_p to r establishes a direct relationship between post-Keynesian theory and the managerial theory of the firm developed by Marris [1964; 1973; Marris and Wood, 1971].

17. The difference in approaches taken by Kregel and Eichner can be attributed to the different national contexts in which they were writing. U.S. corporations have much less to fear from international competition if they should raise their prices than do U.K. companies. When Kregel considers the possibility of the price being varied, he introduces international considerations into the analysis [1973].

18. Cf. Keynes [1936, chaps. 16, 17]. The necessity of these requirements is explained by P. Davidson [1972] and Kregel [1974].

19. See Bent Hansen [1970, chaps. 5–7.]

20. The essential features of the type of monetized economy that is the subject of post-Keynesian theory have been perhaps best described by Paul Davidson [1972]. See also Kregel [1973, chap. 11]. The influence of financial institutions is stressed in the work of Hyman Minsky [1972; 1975].

21. See Kregel [1971, pp. 148–49].

22. This is what lies behind Kalecki's pithy observation so often quoted by post-Keynesians, that "the workers spend what they get and the capitalists get what they spend." The phrase is not to be found in any of Kalecki's English works, but the essence of the argument is to be found in Kalecki [1939, p. 76].

Another of Kalecki's epigrams is that "the capitalists cannot decide to earn more; they can only decide to invest more" [1971].

23. The model first appeared in Polish [Kalecki, 1933] but has since been reprinted in English [1966; 1971]. See also Kalecki [1939; 1954].

24. See Kaldor [1957; 1961] and Kaldor and Mirrlees [1962].

25. See also Jorgenson [1971, especially pp. 1116–1117, 1126–1127], and the sources cited therein.

26. It is on this point, of course, that the post-Keynesian argument about double-switching and capital reversal apply.

27. See Michael Evans [1969, chaps. 6–7].

28. Since government expenditures are usually considered to be an exogenous variable entirely subject to political control, less empirical work has been done on that component of discretionary spending. But see the various econometric models, Duesenberry [1965], Evans and Klein [1967], and Hickman [1972]. The progress in developing a theory of public goods has been more impressive. See Head [1962], Schultze [1968], Eatwell [1971], Asimakopulos and Burbidge [1974], and Kregel [1973, Italian ed., Latarza, Rome.]

29. The fact that the investment demand curve, $\overset{*}{I}$, has any slope at all reflects a point brought out by Asimakopulos [1971]—namely, that current economic conditions are likely to cause some revision in planned investment. In Pasinetti's algebraic analysis, the slopes of the two curves are identified as the marginal propensity to save and the marginal propensity to invest. Pasinetti's use of algebra makes his analysis more general [1974, pp. 59–61].

30. In addition to the sources cited in fn. 28 above, see Tinbergen [1939] and Klein and Goldberger [1955].

31. There is a third possibility pointed out by post-Keynesians, this being that the nominal wage may actually reflect the degree of tightening in the labor market. But this does not alter the main point.

32. He has by no means dropped the point. See Kaldor [1972].

33. See Kalecki [1966; 1971]. It is only recently that these earlier writings by Kalecki have been translated into English. For the first source in English, see Kalecki [1954]. For a full explication of Kalecki's contributions, see Feiwel [1975] and Asimakopulos [1974].

34. See Andrews [1949] and Wilson and Andrews [1951].

35. Steindl's work, in relation to post-Keynesian theory, is surveyed in Kregel [1972]. For an early Post-Keynesian model based on this point, see Harcourt [1965].

36. See Bhagwati and the sources cited therein [1970]. See also Scherer [1970].

37. A fourth constraint would be the fear of market inroads by foreign-produced goods. *Cf.* Glyn and Sutcliffe [1973] and Kregel [1973, chap. 12]. Although Eichner encompasses this factor as part of the substitution effect, it perhaps deserves separate treatment, especially when examining open types of economies [1976].

38. It is important to distinguish the *ex ante* demand curve for investment from the *ex post* demand curve (*cf.*, Asimakopulos [1971]).

39. On the view presented here, that post-Keynesian theory deals with a monetized production economy in Keynes's sense, there can be no analysis of money separate from the analysis of the overall actions of the system.

40. Here one would need to trace a line of development going back to Sraffa [1926; 1960].

41. In some ways, this has been the least developed areas in post-Keynesian theory. But see Steedman [1971], Steedman and Metcalfe [1973] and Kregel [1973, chap. 12].

42. The best example of this is the use of the Swan-Solow growth model to "measure" the importance of technological change in economic growth. Actually, all that is measured is what the relative importance of technological change would be if the marginal productivity theory were empirically valid. But since the empirical validity of the marginal productivity theory has never been rigorously tested—indeed, considered simply as the basis for an optimal decision rule for the distribution of income there is no need to test its "realism"—it is not clear what meaning is to be attached to the estimates derived from plugging data into a Swan-Solow growth model.

References

Andrews, P. W. S. *Manufacturing Business*. London: Macmillan, 1949.

Asimakopulos, A. "The Determination of Investment in Keynes's Model," *Can. J. Econ.*, August 1971, 4(3), pp. 382–88.

———. "A Kaleckian Theory of Income Distribution," *Can. J. Econ.*, August 1975, 8(3), pp. 313–33.

——— and Burbidge, J. B. "The Short-Period Incidence of Taxation," *Econ. J.*, June 1974, 84(133), pp. 267–88.

Baran, P. A. and Sweezy, P. M. *Monopoly Capital*. New York: Monthly Review Press, 1966.

Bhagwati, J. N. "Oligopoly Theory, Entry-prevention and Growth," *Oxford Econ. Pap.*, Nov. 1970, 22(3), pp. 297–310.

Blaug, M. *The Cambridge Revolution: Success or Failure?* London: Institute of Economic Affairs, 1974.

Clark, J. B. *The Distribution of Wealth*. New York: Macmillan,1899.

Davidson, P. *Money and the Real World*. London: Macmillan, 1972.

Duesenberry, J. S., et al., eds. *The Brookings Quarterly Econometric Model of the United States*. Chicago: Rand McNally, 1965.

Eatwell, J. L. "A New Approach to the Problem of Public Goods," unpublished paper, Cambridge, England, 1971.

Eichner, A. S. "A Theory of the Determination of the Mark-up Under Oligopoly," *Econ. J.*, Dec. 1973, 83(332), pp. 1184–1200.

————. *The Megacorp and Oligopoly: Micro Foundations of Macro Dynamics*. New York: Cambridge University Press, 1976.

Eisner, R. "Investment: Fact and Fancy," *Amer. Econ. Rev.*, May 1963, 53(2), pp. 237–46.

————. "A Permanent Income Theory for Investment: Some Empirical Explorations," *Amer. Econ. Rev.*, June 1967, 57(3), pp. 363–90.

Evans, M. K. *Macroeconomic Activity: Theory, Forecasting, and Control, an Econometric Approach*. New York: Harper & Row, 1969.

———— and Klein, L. R. *The Wharton Econometric Forecasting Model*. Philadelphia: Economics Research Unit, Wharton School of Finance and Commerce, University of Pennsylvania, 1967.

Feiwel, G. R. *The Intellectual Capital of Michal Kalecki*. Knoxville: University of Tennessee Press, 1975.

Glyn, A. and Sutcliffe, R. *Capitalism in Crises*. New York: Pantheon, 1973.

Hahn, F. H. *On the Notion of Equilibrium in Economics*. London: Cambridge University Press, 1973.

Hansen, F. *A Survey of General Equilibrium Systems*, New York: McGraw-Hill, 1970.

Harcourt, G. C. "A Two-Sector Model of the Distribution of Income and the Level of Employment in the Short Run," *Econ. Rec.*, March 1965, 41, pp. 103–17.

————. *Some Cambridge Controversies in the Theory of Capital*. Cambridge University Press, 1972.

Harris, D. J. "The Price Policy of Firms, the Level of Employment and Distribution of Income in the Short Run," *Australian Econ. Pap.*, June 1974, *13*(22), pp. 114–57.

Harrod, R. "The Expansion of Credit in an Advancing Economy," *Economica*, N.S., August 1934, *1*, pp. 287–99.

————. "Rejoinder to Mr. Robertson," *Economica, N.S.*, Nov. 1934, *1*, pp. 476–78.

————. *The Trade Cycle: An Essay*. Oxford: Clarendon Press, 1936.

————. "An Essay in Dynamic Theory," *Econ. J.*, March 1939, *49*, pp. 14–33.

————. *Towards a Dynamic Economics*. London: Macmillan, 1948.

————. *Economic Dynamics*. London: Macmillan, 1973.

Head, J. G. "Public Goods and Public Policy," *Public Finance*, 1962, *17*(3), pp. 197–219.

Hickman, B. G., ed. *Econometric Models of Cyclical Behavior*. New York: National Bureau of Economic Research; distributed by Columbia University Press, 1972.

Hicks, J. R. "Capital Controversies: Ancient and Modern," *Amer. Econ. Rev.*, May 1974, *64*(2), pp. 307–16.

Jorgenson, D. W. "Capital Theory and Investment Behavior," *Amer. Econ. Rev.*, May 1963, *53*(2), pp. 247–59.

————. "Econometric Studies of Investment Behavior: A Survey," *J. Econ. Lit.*, Dec. 1971, *9*(4), pp. 111–47.

Kahn, R. F. *Selected Essays on Employment and Growth*. London: Cambridge University Press, 1972.

Kaldor, N. "The Equilibrium of the Firm," *Econ. J.*, March 1934, *44*, pp. 60–76. Reprinted in Kaldor [1960].

————. "Alternative Theories of Distribution," *Rev. Econ. Stud.*, 1956, *23*(2), pp. 83–100. Reprinted in Kaldor [1960].

————. "A Model of Economic Growth," *Econ. J.* Dec.1957, *67*, pp. 591–624. Reprinted in Kaldor [1960].

————. "Economic Growth and the Problem of Inflation." Parts I and II. *Economica*, August and Nov. 1959, *26*, pp. 212–26; 287-98.

————. *Essays on Value and Distribution*. London: Duckworth, 1960.

————. *Essays on Economic Stability and Growth.* Glencoe, Ill.: Free Press, 1960.

————. "Capital Accumulation and Economic Growth," in *The Theory of Capital.* Edited by F. A. Lutz and D. C. Hague. London: Macmillan, 1961.

————. "Marginal Productivity and the Macro-Economic Theories of Distribution," *Rev. Econ. Stud.*, Oct. 1966, *33*, pp. 309–19.

————. "The Irrelevance of Equilibrium Economics," *Econ. J.*, Dec. 1972, *82*(328), pp. 1237–55.

———— and Mirrlees, J. "A New Model of Economic Growth," *Rev. Econ. Stud.*, June 1962, *29*, pp. 174–92.

Kalecki, M. *Probe Teorii Koniunktury.* Warsaw: 1933.

————. *Essays in the Theory of Economic Fluctuations.* London: Allen and Unwin, 1939.

————. *Theory of Economic Dynamics: An Essay on Cyclical and Long-Run Ranges in Capitalist Economy.* New York: Rinehart; London: Allen and Unwin, 1954.

————. *Studies in the Theory of Business Cycles, 1933–1939.* New York: Kelley, 1966.

————. *Selected Essays on the Dynamics of the Capitalist Economy, 1933–1970.* London: Cambridge University Press, 1971.

Keynes, J. M. *The Economic Consequences of the Peace.* London: Macmillan; New York: Harcourt, Brace & Howe, 1920.

————. *Treatise on Money.* 2 vols. London: Macmillan; New York: Harcourt, Brace, 1930.

————. *The General Theory of Employment, Interest and Money.* London: Macmillan, 1936.

————. *The Collected Writings of John Maynard Keynes.* 24 vols. Edited by E. Johnson and D. Moggridge. London: Macmillan, 1971–73.

Klein, L. R. *The Keynesian Revolution.* New York: Macmillan, 1947.

————and Goldberger, A. S. *An Econometric Model of the United States, 1923–1952.* Amsterdam: North-Holland, 1955.

Kornai, J. *Anti-equilibrium: On Economic Systems Theory and the Tasks of Research.* New York: American Elsevier; Amsterdam and London: North Holland, 1971.

Kregel, J. A. *Rate of Profit Distribution and Growth: Two Views.* Chicago: Aldine, 1971.

————. "Post-Keynesian Theory and the Theory of Capitalist Crisis," Conference of Socialist Economists, *Bulletin*, Winter 1972.

————. *The Reconstruction of Political Economy: An Introduction to Post-Keynesian Economics*. New York: Wiley, Halsted Press, 1973.

————. "Radical Keynesianism and Monetary Theory," Conference of Socialist Economists, *Bulletin*, Autumn and Summer 1974.

Kuhn, T. S. *The Structure of Scientific Revolutions*. Chicago: University of Chicago Press, 1962

Leijonhufvud, A. *On Keynesian Economics and the Economics of Keynes*. New York: Oxford University Press, 1968.

————. "Keynes' Employment Function: Comment," *Hist. Polit. Econ.*, Summer 1974, 6(2), pp. 164–70.

Marris, R. *The Economic Theory of Managerial Capitalism*. New York: Free Press, 1964.

————. "Why Economics Needs a Theory of the Firm," *Econ. J.*, supplement 1973, 83, pp. 321–52.

————. and Wood, A., eds. *The Corporate Economy, Growth, Competition and Innovative Potential*. Cambridge, Mass.: Harvard University Press; London: Macmillan, 1971.

Meade, J. E. *A Neo-classical Theory of Economic Growth*, 2nd ed. Oxford: Oxford University Press, [1962] 1963.

————. "The Rate of Profit in a Growing Economy," Econ. J., Dec. 1963, 73, pp. 665–74.

———— and Hahn, F. H. "The Rate of Profit in a Growing Economy," *Econ. J.*, June 1965, 75, pp. 445–48.

Minsky, H. "Financial Instability Revisited: The Economics of Disaster," in *Reappraisal of the Federal Reserve Discount Mechanism*. Vol. 3. New York: Board of Governors of the Federal Reserve System, 1972.

————. *John Maynard Keynes*. New York: Columbia University Press, 1975.

Moore, A. M. "A Reformulation of the Kaldor Effect," *Econ. J.*, March 1967, 77, pp. 84–99.

National Bureau of Economic Research. *The Behavior of Income Shares: Selected Theoretical and Empirical Issues*. Princeton, N.J.: Princeton University Press, 1964.

Pasinetti, L. L. "Rate of Profit and Income Distribution in Relation to the Rate of Economic Growth," *Rev. Econ. Stud.*, Oct. 1962, *29*, pp. 267–79. Reprinted in Pasinetti [1974].

———. "New Results in an Old Framework: Comment on Samuelson and Modigliani," *Rev. Econ. Stud.*, Oct. 1966, *33*, pp. 303–06. Reprinted in Pasinetti [1974].

———. *Growth and Income Distribution: Essays in Economic Theory.* London: Cambridge University Press, 1974.

Robinson, J. *The Rate of Interest, and Other Essays.* London: Macmillan, 1952.

———. "The Production Function and the Theory of Capital," *Rev. Econ. Stud.*, 1954, *21*(2), pp. 81–106. Reprinted in Robinson [1964].

———. *The Accumulation of Capital.* London: Macmillan, 1956.

———. *Essays in the Theory of Economic Growth.* London: Macmillan, 1962.

———. *Collected Economic Papers.* Vol. 2. Oxford: Basil Blackwell, 1964.

———. "A Further Note," *Rev. Econ. Stud.*, April 1969, *36*(106), pp. 260–62.

———. "Harrod after Twenty-one Years," *Econ. J.*, Sept. 1970, *80*(319), pp. 731–37.

———. *Economic Heresies: Some Old-Fashioned Questions in Economic Theory.* New York: Basic Books, 1971.

——— and Eatwell, J. *An Introduction to Economics.* London: McGraw-Hill, 1974.

Samuelson, P. A. and Modigliani, F. "The Pasinetti Paradox in Neoclassical and More General Models," *Rev. Econ. Stud.*, Oct. 1966, *33*, pp. 269–301.

Scherer, F. M. *Industrial Market Structure and Economic Performance.* Chicago: Rand McNally, 1970.

Schultze, C. L. *The Politics and Economics of Public Spending.* Washington, D.C.: The Brookings Institution, 1968.

Schumpeter, J. A. *Business Cycles, a Theoretical, Historical and Statistical Analysis of the Capitalist Process.* New York: McGraw-Hill, 1939.

———. *Capitalism, Socialism and Democracy.* New York: Harper & Row, 1950.

Solow, R. M. "The Production Function and the Theory of Capital," *Rev. Econ. Stud.*, 1956, *23*(2), pp. 106–08.

———. *Growth Theory: An Exposition,* Oxford and New York: Oxford University Press, 1970.

Sraffa, P "The Laws of Return under Competitive Conditions," *Econ. J.*, Dec. 1926, *36*, pp. 535–50.

———. *Production of Commodities by Means of Commodities*, Cambridge: Cambridge University Press, 1960.

Steedman, I. "On Foreign Trade." Unpublished paper, Manchester, England, 1971.

——— and Metcalfe, J. S. "On Foreign Trade," *Econ. Int.*, Aug.–Nov. 1973, *26*(3–4), pp. 516–28.

Steindl, J. *Maturity and Stagnation in American Capitalism*. Oxford: Basil Blackwell, 1952.

Stiglitz, J. E. "The Cambridge-Cambridge Controversy in the Theory of Capital; A View from New Haven: A Review Article," *J. Polit. Econ.*, July/August 1974, *82*(4), pp. 893–903.

Swan, T W. "Economic Growth and Capital Accumulation," *Econ. Rec.*, Nov. 1956, *32*, pp. 334–61.

Tinbergen, J. *Statistical Testing of Business Cycle Theories*. 2nd ed. New York: Agathon Press, [1939] 1968.

Weintraub, S. *A General Theory of the Price Level, Output, Income Distribution, and Economic Growth*. Philadelphia: Chilton, 1959.

———. *A Keynesian Theory of Employment, Growth and Income Distribution*. Philadelphia: Chilton, 1966.

Wicksell, K. *Lectures on Political Economy*. London: Routledge, 1934.

Wilson T. and Andrews, P. W. S. *Oxford Studies in the Price Mechanism*. Oxford: Clarendon Press, 1951.

6

THE NATURE OF POST KEYNESIANISM AND ITS LINKS TO OTHER TRADITIONS

TONY LAWSON

Introduction

A browse through prominent assessments and internalist statements of Post Keynesian contributions reveals or suggests (at least to this browser) the following seemingly diverse features:

i. The most common or unifying theme of Post Keynesianism is a generalized dissatisfaction with, or opposition to, something called neoclassical, mainstream, or orthodox economics.[1]

ii. There is a significant emphasis upon methodological questions and reasoning.[2]

iii. At a very abstract or general level various substantive themes or emphases do appear with a high degree of frequency. Specifically, it is not uncommon to find claims or requirements that the economy be viewed as a dynamic historical process; that uncertainty be recognized as a significant feature of all economic life; that questions of distribution are as fundamental as any other; that human choice be acknowledged as real; that economic and political institutions (especially money and structures of power) be acknowledged as shaping economic events; that human emancipation be included amongst the goals of policy.[3]

iv. At the level of more concrete substantive issues, Post Keynesianism gives the impression of being little more than a collection of largely unrelated questions, aims, theories, and arguments united only in their claimed status as constituting alternatives to contemporary orthodoxy.[4]

v. Post Keynesians perceive their roots as lying in some or other feature of the writings of Keynes, some classical economists, and (sometimes) Marx.[5]

Now the obvious question that arises here—one that in some form or other has often been posed before—is, can such apparently disparate features as these[6] be interpreted as mutually supportive/consistent and central characteristics of some coherent whole or perspective? Unlike most previous commentators, I shall answer in the affirmative.[7] The achieving of this coherence, however, not only necessitates an emphasis upon philosophical reasoning in line with feature (ii) noted above, but relies upon it to a degree that some Post Keynesians may regard as disturbing. Specifically, I shall argue that (a) contemporary economic orthodoxy is a project founded upon erroneous philosophical results, and in particular upon results that are rooted in an unsustainable Humean version of positivism; (b) the transcendence of these errors requires an elaboration of an alternative philosophical perspective to positivism—one that will be systematized here as transcendental realism or, with respect to the social realm specifically, as critical realism; and (c) it is the philosophical system stylized here as critical realism that provides the coherence to the noted nominal features of Post Keynesian contributions.[8] It will be seen, however, that a cost of the coherence achieved by such reasoning, the consequence that some may regard as unfortunate, is that Post Keynesianism may have to jettison (or at least moderate) any claim to being a body of specific substantive economic doctrine at all. Let us examine how this all works out.

Contemporary Economics and the Results of Positivism

What, first of all, are these results upon which contemporary economics is founded, and how do they derive from the philosophical system of positivism? As I have indicated elsewhere (Lawson, 1989a, 1989b, 1992, 1994a, 1994b, 1994d), the result that, in my view, is the most significant in its influence on contemporary economics relates to a particular conception of science. Specifically, the essential feature (and primary error) of contemporary orthodox economics, or so I shall argue, is a commitment to the formula "whenever event (type) X then event (type) Y" as a generalized condition, image or goal of, or ideal for, science.[9]

Now it is not, I think, contentious to suggest that this general formulation of the condition or goal of science is fundamental to ortho-dox reasoning. As Allais (1992), a recent winner of the Nobel Memorial

Prize in Economic Science, puts it in his assessment of "the economic science of today":

> The essential condition of any science is the existence of regularities which can be analysed and forecast. This is the case in celestial mechanics. But it is also true of many economic phenomena. Indeed their thorough analysis displays the existence of regularities which are just as striking as those found in the physical sciences. This is why economics is a science, and why this science rests on the same general principles and methods as physics. [P. 25]

Perhaps not all orthodox economists would put things quite like this. Nevertheless, the fundamental conception in question is clearly presupposed by most econometric time-series analyses just as it is underlies the axiomatic-deductive reasoning of orthodox pure theory. Quite simply, the supposed generalized relevance of both streams of orthodoxy rests upon the supposed universal validity of this particular image, or condition, of science. What is particularly noteworthy here is the manner in which such orthodox methods as econometrics or axiomatic-deductive reasoning, and so implicitly the "whenever this then that" view of science, are considered by their proponents as being so obviously universal in their legitimacy or scope that their automatic adoption, in any context, is in effect, considered to be beyond reproach. Frank Hahn's dismissal of criticisms of the axiomatic-deductive approach provides a recent case in point. He writes (1985, p. 9)[10]:

> Opponents of [economic] theory often argue that it is tautologous because it consist of logical deductions from axioms and assumptions. If one is kind to such critics one interprets them as signalling that they do not care for these axioms or these assumptions. In any case all theory in all subjects proceeds in this manner.

A second conception that is more or less universally embraced in contemporary orthodox economics, one that we shall see below is once more a result rooted in positivist philosophy, is that of the human agent as an essentially passive responder to external knowledge stimuli. Usually the agent of contemporary economic theory responds merely to market price "signals" or some such. In this fashion, if amongst other things, knowledge is analyzed in a purely individualistic way.

One further characteristic of contemporary economic orthodoxy that ought also to be mentioned here—one that, as we shall see below, is again rooted in positivist thinking—is a reluctance (to say the least) to indulge in questions of methodology. Manifestations abound. In the latest U.K. Economic and Social Research Council *Guidelines for Post Graduate Training*, for example, only the disciplines of economics and town planning, out of twenty subject areas listed, fail to require or encourage any methodological/philosophical training. On the occasion of his retirement from Cambridge, Frank Hahn chose to mark the event with an inclusion in the Royal Economic Society *Newsletter* (April 1992) advising young economists to "give no thought at all to methodology." His view (also restated in a subsequent *Newsletter* [July 1992]) is that methodological reasoning is inconsequential, merely an avoidable distraction. In addition, of course, there is the jibe, often heard, that "those who can—do orthodox economics, while those who cannot do methodology," and so on.

There are other nominal features of contemporary economic orthodoxy that abound. But I think that these three results, the conceptions of science, of human beings, and of the limited usefulness of methodology, capture the most enduring and fundamental. With a bit of reflection (and as I have argued explicitly elsewhere [see Lawson 1994d]), it can be seen that most of orthodoxy's standpoints—its individualist orientation including its stress on rationality, concern for equilibrium, assumptions about knowledge and foresight, significant emphasis upon exchange activities rather than those of production and distribution, and the like—can be shown to be rooted in one or more of these three results or conceptions.[11] The question then is what do these conceptions have in common? Or rather, given that I have already asserted that they all are results that stem from a particular (Humean) version of the philosophical position of positivism, the question is how do they come about? What exactly does this assertion entail and how can it be established?

The Foundations of Contemporary Economic Orthodoxy in a Humean Version of Positivism

What, then, is to be understood here under the heading of positivism, and how do the results already discussed arise? Before addressing this question, let me briefly introduce explicitly some philosophical terminology that facilitates the discussion that follows. Two terms that require some clarification immediately are *realism* and *ontology*. Any position can be designated a (philosophical) *realism* which asserts the existence of some disputed (kind of) entity (such as black holes, causal laws, economic equilibria, or utility functions). The concept of realism is thus clearly associated with that of *ontology*—that is, the study of, or theories or claims about, the *nature* of being, the nature of objects of study.

Now positivism, at least in its Humean guise under consideration here,[12] is first of all a theory of knowledge, its nature, and its limits. Specifically, it is a claim that human knowledge takes the form of sense-experience or impression. Hume[13] encouraged this viewpoint with his attempted critique of any philosophical account of being, with his denial of the possibility of establishing the independent existence of things, of the operation of natural necessity. Of course, it is never possible to dissolve completely any conception of being, of the object of study. Any theory of knowledge, Hume's included, must assume, even if only implicitly, that the nature of reality is such that it could be the object of knowledge of the required or specified sort. Humean analysis, then, implicitly entails an account of reality, or an *ontology*, of experiences or impressions constituting atomistic events. Humean theory, in other words, entails implicitly an *empiricist ontology*-that is, one that restricts reality to the objects of direct experience. Thus, because reality, on this conception, is effectively constituted in experience I shall follow Bhaskar and others in referring to the perspective entailed as *empirical realism*. Now the point to note is that if particular knowledge is of atomistic events sensed in experience, then any general, including scientific, knowledge must be of patterns that such events reveal in space and over time. From the Humean perspective these are the only sort of generalizations conceivable. In other words, science, if it is to be possible at all, must take the form of elaborating the constant conjunctions of events—that is, regularities of the form "whenever event (type) X then event (type) Y"—that provide the basis for contemporary orthodox economics. These event regularities, of course, constitute the Humean or positivist account of "causal laws." The recognition that science not only exists, but that its successes are pervasive, encourages, in turn, a belief in the ubiquity of such constant event conjunctions.

Any theory of knowledge, to repeat, presupposes an ontology, an account of the nature of reality, and in the case of positivism, as noted, this comprises atomistic events and their constant conjunctions. It is a conception that gives rise to the image of science noted above, and which is entailed by just about all branches of contemporary economic orthodoxy. Now, in addition to an ontology, any theory of knowledge also presupposes a social theory, that is, some account of human agency and institutions. Clearly these must be of the form that enables knowledge of the specified type to be produced. Positivism, then, supports a conception of human agents as passive sensors of atomistic events and recorders of their constant conjunctions. It is this conception, of course, that encourages the behaviorist theories of contemporary economic orthodoxy. It is this that underpins the orthodox conception of agents as,

in effect, mindless (albeit frequently programmed to be endlessly opti-
mising) atomistic automata, perpetually rebounding under the influence
of external market signals and the like.

Finally, it is also the case that any theory of knowledge presupposes, in addition to an ontology and a social theory, some account
of how its characteristic results are achieved. Positivism presupposes
some theory of methodology just like any other theory of knowledge. In
fact, in positivism, whatever is experienced is an event, while experience,
because in effect constitutive of the world, is in consequence held to be
certain. The impression, the viewpoint, sustained, then, is that science is
monistic, the accumulation of incorrigible facts. In consequence, clearly
the certainty of facts, the incorrigibility of knowledge in positivism,
serves ultimately, if implicitly, to undermine the possibility of substantive scientific criticism. The result is a conservative ideology that
serves always to rationalize contemporary orthodox practice; a perspective notoriously expressed within positivism itself precisely as a
denial of the usefulness of methodology/philosophy.

No wonder, then, the often found orthodox economic dismissal of
methodology as inconsequential. It is not inconsequential, of course,
even as understood within positivism. Specifically, as just observed, it is
crucial to sustaining the status quo. The truth of the assessment that
methodology is inconsequential is that the *specific* theory or conception
of methodology that is supported by positivism is *useless for science*
including economics. The upshot, then, the real import of all this, is that
the jibe that "those who can—do orthodox economics, while those who
cannot—do methodology" is better reformulated as "those who do
orthodox economics—cannot (fruitfully)[14] do methodology."

Now, while it is doubtful that many economists would wish to
accept the Humean analysis upon which these results rest, it is (a) clear,
as noted above, that the results themselves have been accepted in
economics quite pervasively(if often selectively), while (b) difficult to
imagine how else results such as these could have been generated. In
short, positivism, whether or not explicitly acknowledged or understood, functions as an ideology for economics, encouraging by injunction
or by resonance conceptions of the nature of science, nature, society.
economy, people, and their interconnections. The point, then, is that *if*
the characteristic forms of contemporary orthodox economics are to be
rejected, as Post Keynesians amongst others suggest, then, at the very
least, their positivist foundations need to be transcended. In other words,
a philosophical perspective on the nature of society, science, and people,
and the like is required that provides an acceptable set of alternatives to
the noted results of positivism and that can be shown simultaneously to

be a more sustainable, more adequate, philosophical position. The elaboration of such a perspective is the issue that I turn to next.

The Transcendental Realist Alternative

The alternative perspective that I want to maintain here can be gathered under the general heading of *transcendental realism*.[15] According to this perspective, and in contrast to the claims of empirical realism, reality is constituted not only by events, and our experience or perception of these events, but also by (irreducible) structures, mechanisms, powers, and tendencies that, although perhaps not directly observable, nevertheless underlie actual events and govern or produce them. Thus, not only does the autumn leaf pass to the ground, and not only do we experience it as falling, but, according to this perspective, underlying such movement and governing it are real mechanisms such as gravity. Similarly, the world is composed not only of such "surface phenomena" as skin spots, puppies turning into dogs, and relatively slow productivity growth in the United Kingdom, but also of underlying and governing structures or mechanisms such as, respectively, viruses, genetic codes, and the British system of industrial relations. In short, three domains of reality are, on this perspective, distinguished—namely, the *empirical* (experience and impression), the *actual* (events and states of affairs, that is, the actual objects of direct experience), and the *nonactual* or, metaphorically, the "*deep*" (structures, mechanisms, powers, and tendencies).

Now, not only is it the case that these domains are ontologically distinct, according to transcendental realism, but, and crucially, they are unsynchronized, or out of phase as it were with one another. Thus, while experiences are out of phase with events, allowing the possibility of contrasting, as well as revisions to, experiences of a given event, so events are typically unsynchronized with the mechanisms that govern them. On the latter structure/event noncorrespondence, for example, autumn leaves are not in phase with the action of gravity for the reason that they are also subject to aerodynamic, thermal, and other tendencies. In consequence, transcendental realism supports an alternative conception of science. This is the identification of the structures and mechanisms that govern the events of experience. And because the underlying structures are not straightforwardly manifest in events (or "appearances"), this goal of science can be recognized as necessary, possible, and nontrivial.

To recap, according to transcendental realism, the world is composed, in part, of objects that are structured and (to use Bhaskar's term) intransitive—*structured* in the sense of being irreducible to the events of experience,[16] *intransitive* in the sense of existing and acting independently of their identification. According to empirical realism, in contrast, the world consists only of experience and the events of (and which, in effect, are constituted by) experience. From these alternative theories of ontology flow different conceptions of science. Specifically, from the perspective of empirical realism science is necessarily restricted to seeking out constant conjunctions of events (including probabilistically formulated ones), whereas from the perspective of transcendental realism, the primary concern is not with events (or their hoped-for constant conjunctions) at all but with identifying the structures and mechanisms that underlie and govern them.

If transcendental realism provides a contrasting perspective on both reality and science to that of positivism, what is the theory of knowledge that is involved? Clearly, if a knowledge of structures cannot be obtained merely through sense experience, it is hardly intelligible that they can be created out of nothing, as it were. What is at issue here, then, is a transformational conception of knowledge. From the transcendental realist perspective, knowledge progresses as existing theories, hunches, hypotheses, anomalies, and the like, come to be transformed in, and through, the laborious social practice of science. In science, in other words, human beings intervene in and manipulate reality; they confront it on the basis of theory, through practice, through experiment, and in doing so come to transform their (always historically transient) account of it.

From the transcendental perspective now being elaborated, then, knowledge is obtained or revised through transformative social activity, and reality is viewed as structured and intransitive. In addition to this conception of knowledge and theory of ontology, a social theory is supported whereby human beings and institutions are of the sort that knowledge of social structures and the like is possible. Human beings are thus recognized as possessing transformative capacities, as being able, knowledgeably and capably, to intervene in and to manipulate reality so that, amongst other things, it is more assessable, more easily revealed.

The transcendental realist perspective, of course, also entails a theory of philosophical method, of how its results are obtained. Given that science is revealed as a laborious social practice concerned with revealing structures governing phenomena of interest, and given the open nature of the world, it follows that methodological reasoning must be constructively involved at every stage of research. Something more specific can be said, however, about its central mode of reasoning or method involved. Empirical realism, with its focus upon generalizations about conjunctions of events can, at best, support debates about whether these are better revealed by methods of induction or by those of deduction. As is often noted, of course, such discussion never seems to lead anywhere. It is vital to recognize, then, that the essential mode of inference warranted by the transcendental realist perspective is neither induction nor deduction but one that can be styled *retroduction* or *abduction* or "as if" reasoning. It consists in the movement (on the basis of analogy and metaphor, amongst other things) from a conception of some phenomenon of interest to a conception of some totally different type of thing, mechanism, structure, or condition that is responsible for the given phenomenon. If *deduction* is, for example, to move from the *general* claim that all grass is green to the particular inference that the next lawn to be seen will be green, and *induction* is to move from the particular observations on green grass to the general claim that all grass is green, then *retroduction* or *abduction* is to move from the particular observations on green grass to a theory of a mechanism intrinsic to grass that disposes it to being green. It is the movement, paradigmatically, from "surface" phenomena to some "deeper" causal thing(s).

In sum, two perspectives, best characterized as empirical realism and transcendental realism, have been elaborated and contrasted, and attention has been drawn to the differing associated conceptions of knowledge, science, people, and methodology. As yet I have not provided any argument for accepting transcendental realism as the more satisfactory theory, nor have I given reason to suppose that even if transcendental realism were accepted, constant conjunctions of events would not be a pervasive eventuality. These two issues can now be dealt with together.

Positivism and Transcendental Realism Contrasted

With the transcendental realist alternative to positivism in mind, including its causal as well as perceptual criterion for ascribing something as real, it becomes meaningful to question the conditions under which experience is in fact found to be significant for science. Specifically, it becomes meaningful, and, given the contrast between empirical realism and transcendental realism, appropriate, to question or elucidate the conditions, if any, under which the sought-after constant event conjunctions of Humean science are actually found to occur.

Consider first the situation in the natural sciences. The relevant factors here have been noted and previously addressed by Bhaskar (1979). The first observation is that, outside astronomy at least, most of the constant conjunctions of events held to be significant in natural science in fact only occur in situations of experimental control—that is, they are not typically spontaneously occurring. The second observation is that the results or "laws" supported in controlled experimental activity are nevertheless frequently applied with success outside of the experimental situation.

These observations raise certain problems for Humean accounts which tie laws to constant conjunctions of events. For, if scientific laws, or significant results, only occur in such restricted conditions as experimental setups, then this bears the inhibiting implication that science and its results, far from being universal, are effectively fenced off from most of the goings-on in the world. In other words, most of the accepted results of science are not of the form "whenever event X then event Y always follows" after all, but are of the form "whenever event X then event Y always follows, as long as conditions E hold," where conditions E typically amount to a specification of the experimental situation. This also bears the rather counterintuitive implication that any actual regularity of events that a law of *nature* supposedly denotes does not, in fact, generally occur independently of human intervention. But, in addition to such problems, and at least as serious, the constant conjunction view of laws leaves the question of what governs events outside of experimental situations not only unanswered but completely unaddressed. In doing so it also leaves the observation that experimentally obtained results *are* successfully applied outside experimental situations without any valid explanation.

In order to render Bhaskar's observations intelligible it is necessary to abandon the view that the generalizations of nature consist of event regularities, and to accept instead the transcendental realist account of the objects of the world, including of science, as intransitive and structured. That is, experimental activity and results, and the applications of experimentally determined knowledge outside of experimental situations, can be accommodated only through invoking the transcendental realist ontology of generative structures, powers, mechanisms, and necessary relations, and so on, that lie behind and govern the flux of events in an essentially open world. The fall of an autumn leaf, for example, and as already noted, does not typically conform to an empirical regularity, precisely because it is governed, in complex ways, by the actions of different juxtaposed and counteracting mechanisms. The path of the leaf is governed not only by gravitational pull, but also by aerodynamic, thermal, inertial, and other tendencies. On this transcendental realist view, then, experimental activity can be explained as an attempt to intervene in order to *close* the system, in order, in other words, to isolate a particular mechanism of interest by holding off all other potentially counteracting mechanisms. The aim is to engineer a closed system in which a one-to-one correspondence can obtain between the way a mechanism acts and the events that eventually ensue. In other words, on this view, experimental activity can be rendered intelligible *not* as creating the rare situation in which an empirical law is put into effect but as intervening in order to bring about those special circumstance under which a nonempirical law, a power, a tendency, or way of acting of some mechanism can be empirically identified. The law itself, of course, is always operative—if the triggering conditions hold, the mechanism is activated, whatever else is going on. On this transcendental realist view, for example, a leaf is subject to the gravitational tendency even as I hold it in the palm of my hand. Through this sort of reasoning, then, transcendental realism can render intelligible the application of scientific knowledge outside of experimental situations. The context or *milieu* under which any mechanism will be operative is irrelevant to the law's specification. Once activated, the mechanism is operative whatever event pattern ensues.

In short, although the traditional conception of science is the seeking of constant conjunctions of events, in practice such event regularities that have been elaborated have been restricted in the main to situations of experimental control. Transcendental realism, unlike empirical realism, can render this situation intelligible. And it follows from the transcendental realist perspective that the traditional Humean conception rests upon an inadequate analysis, and illegitimate generalization, of what emerges as a special case—wherein a single and stable aspect or mechanism, or set thereof, is physically isolated and thereby empirically identified.

It will not have gone unnoticed that most of the discussion on this point has referred to the situation in the "natural" sciences. However, it is not difficult to reason that the transcendental realist perspective must carry over to the social realm. To see this, it is necessary only to consider two often noted problems of contemporary economics. The first is that significant event regularities of the sought-after kind have yet to be turned up in the social realm. The second is that many economists appear to share the intuition that human agents possess the capacity of real choice even if these same economists are unable to reconcile this insight with their understanding of scientific explanation. Now, if choice is real, any agent could always have done otherwise, each agent could always have acted differently than he or she in fact did. A necessary condition for this, clearly, is that the world, social as well as natural, is open in the sense that events really could have been different. Put differently, if under conditions X an agent chose in fact to do Y, it is the case that this same agent could really instead have done not Y. Choice, to repeat, presupposes that the world is open and actual events need not have been.

But the possibility of choice not only presupposes that events could have been different; it also entails that agents have some conception of what they are doing and wanting to achieve in their activity. That is, if choice is real, then human actions must be intentional under some description. Now all agency (whether human and intentional or otherwise) is inherently transformational. Its exercise thus necessitates that there are real material cases that proceed it. Just as acid cannot corrode without materials to break down, nor a spider set its trap without objects to hang its web on, so human activity cannot take place without means, media, and resources of some kind—conditions which, through human agency, come to be transformed. The intentionality aspect of human agency is, in turn, bound up with knowledgeability. For agents must have some knowledge at least of the conditions that render their intended acts, when they are, as feasible. In turn again, of course, knowledge presupposes sufficient endurability in the objects of knowledge to facilitate their coming to be known. Now, if event regularities, or at least significant ones, do not, as widely reported, generally occur in the social realm, then the enduring objects of knowledge must lie at a different level—at that of structures that govern, but that are irreducible to, events, including human activities, of experience.

But are there any real material causes or facilitating structures that can be said to be clearly social? If we accept as criterial for the social the property of depending upon human agency, then it is easy to see that the answer is yes. Items such as (societal) rules, relations, and positions clearly both depend on human agency and condition our everyday (physical) activities. The human (intentional) activities of speaking, writing, driving on public roads, cashing checks, playing games, giving lectures, and the like would be impossible without such social material conditions as rules of grammar, highway codes, banking systems, and so on. Now, if it is the dependency of such structures upon human agency that marks them as being social, it is their ability, in turn, to make a difference (to enable as well as to constrain) physical states, or actions, that (as with nonperceivable objects of the natural realm such as gravitational and magnetic fields) establishes that they are real.

At a very general level, then, the transcendental realist ontology carries over to the social realm. Now it was observed that, in the natural realm, constant event conjunctions appear to be spontaneously occurring (at least outside astronomy) only in conditions of experimental control. Of course, the feasibility of experimental control in the social realm is rather limited. Are there, then, *any* grounds for expecting significant constant event conjunctions to be a feature of the social realm? If natural and social realms are similar in that both are characterized by structures underlying the events of experience, they are dissimilar in that social, unlike natural, structures depend for their existence on human agency—including human conceptions and action. If the human race were to disappear tomorrow, so too would social structure. Human agency and social structure then presuppose each other. Neither can be reduced to, identified with, or explained completely in terms of, for each requires, the other. The point of relevance here, of course, is that because social structure is dependent on the human agent, it is only ever manifest in human activity. Thus, given the open nature of human action, the situation that any agent could always have acted otherwise, it follows that social structure can *only* ever be present in an open system. Thus, any economic laws must usually be manifest merely as tendencies and only rarely—usually in cases where they are consciously brought about (e.g., the occurrence of annual holidays)—as event regularities, so that the Humean project in its economic guise must, as a general approach, be recognized as misguided.

From Transcendental to Critical Realism

Before returning to the question of how all this ties in with Post Keynesianism, indeed as a preliminary to that discussion, let me briefly elaborate key features of the perspective opened up by these consider-ations with specific regard to the objects of *social* science. While the general perspective on reality as structured and intransitive has been stylized as transcendental realism, the specific version of it that has been developed for, or, more accurately, extended to include the specificities of, the social realm can, following Bhaskar once more, be gathered under the heading of *critical realism*. If a key feature of critical realism is the hermeneutic insight of the concept-dependent nature of social material, an equally fundamental aspect is the recognition that social structure is also dependent upon human activity or praxis. It is through human activity that social structures come about and endure (when they do), whether or not individuals have a discursive awareness that, or how, this is so. Thus, irrespective of whether or not people of a particular culture are, for example, discursively aware of the rules of grammar of their language, the existence and any endurability of such rules are undoubtedly dependent upon the speech acts in which agents engage.

At issue here, clearly, is a specific assessment of the nature of the relationship between social structure and human agency. Because social structure depends upon human agency, it cannot be treated as fixed. At the same time, neither can it be treated as the creation of individuals, for individual intentional action presupposes its prior existence. Structure then can be neither *reified* nor interpreted as a *creation* of individuals. Rather, the relevant conception here must be of *reproduction* or *transformation*—individuals reproduce or transform social structure which, at the moment of any individual act only, can be treated as given. More specifically, individual agents draw upon existing social structure as a, typically unacknowledged, condition for acting, and through the action of all individuals taken in total social structure is, typically unintentionally, reproduced or transformed. Of course, if the transformation of social structure is rarely the reason that agents have for acting in the way they do, they will always have some conception of what they are doing in their activity. Human acts are always intentional under some description. The point, though, is that whatever the motivations and intentions of each and any individual, human action in total is always reproductive/transformational. In short, social structure is neither created by nor independent of human agency, but rather is the typically unmotivated condition of all our motivated productions, the noncreated but drawn upon and reproduced/transformed condition of our daily economic/social activities. Structure and human agency, in sum, each presuppose, although neither can be reduced to, identified with, or explained completely in terms of, the other.

With this transformational conception of social activity in place, various consequences of, and for, the critical realist perspective easily follow. The first to note is that, because of the ever present transformative potential of the human agency on which social structures depend, the latter will at most be only relatively enduring, being inescapably space-time bounded or geohistorically grounded. Social science, then, is necessarily historical and geographical in nature.

A second consequence or implication of all this, clearly, is that the phenomena to be explained, the event-analogs of the social world, the phenomena that social structures govern, are, of course, social activities. On this critical realist conception, then, the goal of economics is primarily to identify the structures governing, the conditions surrounding, facilitating as well as being transformed through, some human activities of interest. Social explanation entails providing an understanding of certain practices and activities of interest, that is, identifying and understanding the unacknowledged conditions of these practices, their unconscious motivations, the tacit skills drawn upon, as well as unintended consequences. While society and economy are the skilled accomplishments of active agents, they remain to a degree opaque to the individuals upon whose activities they depend. The task of science is to describe all that must be going on (whether or not adequately comprehended by the agents involved) for some manifest social phenomenon, for some set of practices or activities, to be possible.

A third consequence, or better requirement, of the critical realist perspective is that, with social activities acknowledged as both drawing upon and also reproducing social structure, some explicit elaboration is required of the point of contact between human agency and social structure. If, as is clearly the case, human agency and social structure are different kinds of things, it is necessary, in other words, to develop some conception of their coming together; one that allows the possibility of the individual acting for his or her own reasons while, in so doing, simultaneously contributing to the reproduction of social structure.

In order to elaborate this point of contact between human agency and structure, it is essential to consider the nature of social relations. In fact, two types of relations are distinguishable—*external* and *internal* relations. Now, two objects or aspects are said to be externally related if neither is constituted by the relationship in which they stand to the other. Bread and butter, coffee and milk, or two passing strangers provide examples. In contrast, two objects are said to be internally related if they are what they are by virtue of the relationship in which they stand to the other. Landlord and tenant, employer and employee, hunter and prey, magnet and its field are examples that spring easily to mind. In each case you cannot have the one without the other, each, in part, is what it is, and does what it does, by virtue of the relation in which it stands to the other.

Of particular relevance here are the internal relations that hold between social *positions*. If it is the case, say, that presidents exercise different rights, obligations, tasks, duties, powers, and so on, to the rest of us, or that, say, teachers exercise different rights and obligations to students, it is equally the case that the relevant rights, tasks, powers, and so on exist independently of the particular individuals fulfilling these roles. At issue then is a system of relational defined position-practices, a system of positions, with associated practices, obligations, and powers defined in relation to other such positions, and into which agents essentially slot. With reflection it should be clear that all social structures and systems—the economy, the state, international organizations, trade unions, and households, and the like—depend upon or presuppose social relations of this form.

It is the position-practice system, then, and specifically the concept of a position into which individuals slot, that provides the concept of the contact point between agency and social structure. Notice, of course, that at any one time a particular individual will occupy any of a number of positions—parent, worker/boss, immigrant/native, male/female, old/ young, member of religious or political or community organization, and so on. If, then, we understand a group or *collectivity* as consisting in, or depending upon, or as a set of people distinguishable by their current occupancy of, a specific social position, then we have a conception that (i) renders intelligible the often noted, but reputedly difficult to sustain, sense of a group or collective interest and thus the basis for a theory of collective action, and one that (ii) allows the possibility of a conflict of interest at the level of the individual. Put differently, on this relational conception any specific collectivity must be understood both in terms of its relations to other groups—especially those against which it defines itself and/or is opposed—as well as with regards to the complex of internal relationships within the collectivity itself. Notice, too, that such a conception allows, in stark contrast to contemporary orthodox economics, a focus upon a range of distributional questions and issues—such as resources to groups as well as people to positions. In short, the need to provide an account of the point of contact between human agency and social structure gives rise to the concept of the position-practice system, a conception that in turn gives impetus to a range of insights and per- spectives with which contemporary orthodox economics cannot contend.

There are clearly numerous other consequences of this critical realist perspective that cannot be explored here, but one last point should be emphasized. On the Humean or positivist conception, policy formulation or intentional change is necessarily limited to the amelioration of events or states of affairs while the emphasis is upon control. This follows because of the focus on relationships of the form "whenever event X then event Y." The most that can be achieved or hoped for under such a scenario is to fix "event X" with the expectation that "event Y" must follow—that is, with the expectation that fixture events are thereby determined. From the *critical* realist perspective, in contrast, the goal of human emancipation can now be seen to be a real possibility. Specifically, policies, plans, and strategies can be formulated not with the objective merely to fix events and states of affairs in order to control the fixture, but with the aim, instead, of replacing structures that are, for example, unwanted and restrictive by those that are needed and empowering, to facilitate, in short, a greater or more desirable or equitably distributed range of human opportunities. Moreover, there opens up the possibility, unique to social (as opposed to natural) science, of facilitating social emancipation through explanatory critique. This follows from a recognition that social structures, unlike natural ones, are concept- and practice-dependent. This bears the consequence that, because it lies within the competence of social science to change such conceptions, so it can facilitate a transformation in social practices and thereby in social structure. Specifically, it lies within the potential of social science both to identify discrepancies between social objects and general beliefs about those objects, and also to provide an explanation of such discrepancies—that is, to identify the social causes responsible. When this is achieved, the basis is clearly laid for the possibility (although it will never be sufficient for the realization) of rational, intentional, social transformation.

It warrants emphasis here that the real possibility for emancipatory change revealed by the foregoing analysis, however it is pursued (i.e., whether or not it hinges fundamentally upon explanatory critique as interpreted here) is not a potential that is merely consistent with, but one that is facilitated by the explanatory function of science—at this point, of course, more adequately, nonpositivistically, conceptualized.

Let us take stock. I have argued that there are empirical and theoretical (ontological) grounds both for questioning the Humean or positivist perspective on knowledge, science, people, and their inter-connections that urderpins contemporary economic orthodoxy, as well as for accepting the transcendental realist alternative in its place. The elaboration of the latter in the context of the social realm, a perspective gathered under the heading of critical realism in this social context, supports, amongst other things, a transformational conception of social activity, a view of social material as highly relational, a focus upon questions of distribution amongst others, and a conception of policy and, generally, intentional change as structure-transformative and potentially emancipatory. With this perspective achieved, the question that can at last be explicitly addressed is how this critical realist perspective relates to Post Keynesian contributions and their links to those of other nonorthodox traditions. It is this issue, then, that I consider next.

Rendering the Nominal Features of Post Keynesianism Intelligible

It should already be clear how I am suggesting that the more generalized or abstract of the features of Post Keynesianism noted at the outset can be rendered intelligible, that is, how they can be seen to fall in place as part of a coherent whole or project. Such features can all be interpreted as criticisms of some (or every) manifestation of the results of positivism elaborated above and/or some aspects of attempts to elaborate an alternative perspective along something very much like critical realist lines.

Consider first the noted results of positivism—specifically, its ontology of constant conjunctions of events and consequent account of science, its conception of human agents as passive sensors of atomistic facts, and its view of methodology as an inconsequential distraction. It is clearly an explicit opposition to the first of these, to the positivist ontology of atomistic events and their constant conjunctions, that underpins the Post Keynesian rejection (see especially Davidson, 1981, 1989) of the usual econometric assumption of an ergodic and/or stationary economy. This opposition is also, of course, implicit in the Post Keynesian criticisms of the universal orthodox reliance upon axiomatic-deductive reasoning. In similar fashion, a rejection of the second positivist result, of the account of human agents as passive receivers of atomistic facts, is equally manifest in numerous different forms in Post Keynesian contributions. By far the most prominent and emphasized of these, of course, is the pervasive emphasis upon the real-world prevalence of fundamental economic uncertainty, and how this enters into economic decision making. The fact that the nature and extent of uncertainty is a factor so often highlighted in Post Keynesian writing and yet constitutes an insight that is so little developed (see Lawson, 1985) is presumably accounted for by a Post Keynesian perception that this indisputable fact is so destructive of contemporary economic orthodoxy. Finally, and as noted at the outset, an opposition to the orthodox dismissal of methodology is manifest in the transparently, and usually explicitly acknowledged, methodological nature of Post Keynesian contributions.

Now if an effective (albeit typically unacknowledged) opposition to the results of positivism can explain the high frequency of Post Keynesian discussions of ergodicity, uncertainty, and methodology, and the like, other prominent features of Post Keynesianism are straightforwardly explicable as (again typically unacknowledged) expressions of the critical realist alternative. Most obviously, the significant Post Keynesian emphases upon viewing events as shaped by economic and political institutions, upon viewing economies as dynamic historical processes, upon raising questions of distribution as well as exchange, and upon accepting the goal of human emancipation, can all be viewed in this way.

The first of these issues, of course, rests straightforwardly upon the transcendental realist conception of society as structured and intransitive. Behind the events of experience, behind the activities of human agents, are the structures or conditions that govern and produce, but are irreducible to, them. Economic and political institutions are obviously highly significant examples.

The second issue, the stipulation that economies must be viewed as dynamic historical processes, is in turn given substance, grounding, and bite by the critical realist transformational conception of social activity.

On this conception, as we have seen, social structures are inescapably geohistorically grounded, being drawn upon and reproduced/transformed through inherently transformative human social activity. Finally, of course, the interdependent but distinct natures of agency and social structure allow the possibility of human emancipation through rational, intentional, structural transformation. In particular, the grounding provided by the position-practice system for dealing with questions of distribution, and by the concept- and practice-dependent nature of social structure for facilitating questions of human emancipation via explanatory critique, have already been explicitly noted.

Explaining Diversity and Conflict at the Level of More Concrete Substantive Theory

From the perspective of the foregoing realist analysis, then, the more general or abstract of the commonly identified characterizations of Posts Keynesianism appear to fall easily into place—as reactions to the results of positivism and/or manifestations of insights of the critical realist alternative. But what about the more concrete substantive claims of Post Keynesians, claims that appear often to be totally unrelated to each other or even in conflict? Surely, it is impossible to render these, or rather the noted diversity and the like, coherent?

So far, I have argued that Post Keynesianism, both in its reaction to economic orthodoxy and in the more generalized of its positive contributions, can be rendered intelligible and coherent by viewing it as, or as a tradition noted in, or adhering to, an essentially philosophical perspective. It is important here, then, to acknowledge that there are always limits to what philosophical (or methodological) reasoning can achieve. In essence, I think, the task of methodology or philosophy of science is, in the manner of Locke, to act as a ground-clearing device. Certainly it can be utilized to assess critically the self -interpretations and claims to scientificity made by economists of whatever tradition or outlook; but it cannot license any particular substantive theory. At its most constructive, it serves, as with critical realism specifically, to provide a set of perspectives on the nature of economy, society, people, and their interrelations, and on how to understand them. But it cannot do the work of science for it. Thus, although critical realism emphasizes, for example, the aim for science of uncovering the structures and conditions responsible for manifest phenomena, it cannot *do* the job of uncovering. It is a perspective, in other words, that is ontologically bold, but substantively cautious or open.

The upshot, then, is that at the level of highly concrete substantive theory, it is clearly possible for competing theories to be maintained by different economists, each of whom, nevertheless, may broadly adopt the critical realist perspective. For, to repeat, critical realism *per se* does not license any particular substantive claim.[17] Of course, where critical realism is accepted, the aim will be to discriminate between competing accounts on the basis of explanatory power and the like (see Lawson, 1989a). However, the extent to which this is possible will be severely dependent upon, amongst other things, the context of analysis. But, more generally, all theory is fallible; it is historically specific and potentially transformable. It is, then, not surprising, and indeed it is perfectly desirable, that competing accounts are sought—even if the aim must be continually to seek to determine, and then provisionally at least to maintain, those accounts that provide the more adequate (explanatorily powerful) expressions of the relevant aspect(s) of reality.

If, then, Post-Keynesianism is to be rendered intelligible as an acceptance or manifestation of something like the critical realist perspective, it is not surprising *per se* to find that the specific claims or viewpoints of individual Post-Keynesians diverge when considering matters of a highly concrete substantive sort. In other words, from the realist perspective elaborated, the diversity of substantive Post-Keynesian thought *can* be accommodated. Moreover, it can be accommodated along with the contrasting high degree of homogeneity to be found at the level of more abstract perspective. Indeed, I can imagine no other way in which these nominally contrasting features can be reconciled. If coherency is desirable, then, if Post-Keynesians do believe there is a consistent basis to their contributions, it would seem to follow that something very much like the explanation here being provided has to be accepted.

Links with Other Traditions—The Claimed Roots of Post Keynesianism

Finally, all of this also facilitates an explanation, or interpretation, of the remaining Post Keynesian perception noted at the outset, that it is a tradition rooted in the (often conflicting) contributions of classical economists, as well as Marx and Keynes. Keynes is an obvious example that fits the bill here—at least this is true of the Keynes of the later 1930s. While his invective against the then contemporary orthodoxy centers on the neglect of fundamental uncertainty, his ridicule of Tinbergen's efforts to introduce econometrics into economics turns precisely upon ontological considerations—that is, on the inappropriateness of applying, at least in the social realm, methods that in effect presuppose atomism and closure (although this is not always Keynes's language, of course) to a world or environment that is essentially organic/holistic and open:

There is first of all the central question of methodology,—the logic of applying the method of multiple correlation to unanalysed economic material, which we know to be non-homogeneous through time. If we were dealing with the action of numerically measurable, independent forces, adequately analysed so that we were dealing with independent atomic factors and between them completely comprehensive, acting with fluctuating relative strength on material constant and homogeneous through time, we might be able to use the method of multiple correlation with some confidence for disentangling the laws of their action. . . .

In fact we know that every one of these conditions is far from being satisfied by the economic material under investigation. . . .

To proceed to some more detailed comments. The coefficients arrived at are apparently assumed to be constant for 10 years or for a larger period. Yet, surely we know that they are not constant. There is no reason at all why they should not be different every year. [Keynes, 1973d, p. 285][18]

Marx too, of course, or at least the later Marx of the *Grundrisse* and of *Capital*, is easily seen to accept a commitment to the sort of realist perspective here at issue. Most obvious, or indicative, perhaps, of numerous relevant, well-known, and explicitly philosophical/methodological comments, passages, or tracts is his well-known assessment that "all science would be superfluous if the outward appearance and essence of thing directly coincided" (*Capital*, III, ch. 48). This view indeed underpins his criticism of the then contemporary orthodox political economy—leading Marx to note "That in their appearances things often represent themselves in an inverted form is pretty well-known in every science except Political Economy" (*Capital*, I, ch. 19).

What about the "classical economists," those writing throughout the classical period—from the time of Adam Smith until about 1870? Rather than attempt to isolate explicit philosophical comments and passages for all such claimed progenitors of Post-Keynesianism, the hypothesis at issue here can, I think, be substantiated in a more general way. The point I am getting at is that, whilst the economists in question tended, more or less without exception, to interpret society as driven by divergent interests and conflict, positivism, in its structure, encourages a quite different image of society that resonates with those who view, or present, society as a harmonious, nonconflictual affair, and specifically as the unproblematic result of individuals optimizing their own welfare, and so on. In other words, the emphasis in positivism upon atomistic events and their connections serves to conceal, to detract attention from, the underlying structures which are irreducible to events. In particular, it detracts from the social structures, including class relationships and structures of power, that are irreducible to, though manifest in, human activities, as well as societies that are irreducible to people. In short, society and economy become unstructured, uniform, and unchanging. The social world contains no unsolved mysteries, no hidden structures of power, no oppressive relations, only the passing flux of experience as described in common sense. Hence, amongst other things, those who argue for significant change (especially upon emancipatory or related criteria—but indeed on any basis) can be safely dismissed (along with "methodologists") as deluded or misguided.

It is clear, of course, and this is the point, that most of the economists writing up until the late nineteenth century adopted something approaching the antithesis of this position. In Marx's case this is hardly contentious. Ricardo, too, is usually recognized as having elaborated a conflictual account of capitalism, an outline of a system governed by, amongst other things, the perpetual warring of different factions—and especially that between landowners and the owners of capital but also that between laborers and employers.[19] And this sort of vision seems to be shared generally by writers of this period. Perhaps Adam Smith, given the manner in which he has recently been portrayed, will be regarded as constituting an exception here, but I think he is not. However, given the predominant interpretation of Smith, at least amongst orthodox economists, and given in addition the penchant of some Post Keynesians for tracing their lineage to Smith in particular, some explicit, albeit necessarily brief, consideration of his arguments as contained in the *Wealth of Nations* seems warranted here.

Recent conventional wisdom has it, of course, that Smith is an unflinching exponent of laissez-faire views whereby a spontaneous, natural, harmonious order establishes itself under the guidance of some "invisible hand," provided only that governments do not interfere in economic matters. There are passages in the *Wealth of Nations* that do lend themselves to such a reading. But the overall picture to be found there is rather less simple or straightforward than this. Indeed, Smith's vision of the economy might just as easily be characterized as one of perpetual conflict between opposing interests giving rise to inevitable disorder in need of remedial action. Unfortunately, it is possible here to provide only the briefest substantiation of this.

The main divisions of society, according to Smith, are between landlords, wage earners, and those who receive profits. And it appears neglectful not to acknowledge that, in Smith's view, these groups are perpetually in conflict—with significant consequences for the economy. Most obviously, people of a shared or similar position in the economy collude to raise their power over resources. Notably, in the workplace, not only do workers combine in an attempt to raise wages, or to resist wage cuts—action resulting sometimes "in the most shocking violence and outrage"—but equally "masters" combine to reduce wages:

We rarely hear, it has been said, of the combinations of masters; though frequently of those of workmen. But whoever imagines, upon this account, that masters rarely combine, is as ignorant of the world as of the subject. Masters are always and every where in a sort of tacit, but constant and uniform combination, not to raise the wages of labour above their actual rate. To violate this combination is every where a most unpopular action, and a sort of reproach to a master among his neighbours and equals. We seldom, indeed, hear of this combination, because it is the usual, and one may say, the natural state of things which nobody ever hears of. Masters, too, sometimes enter into particular combinations to sink the wages of labour even below this rate. These are always conducted with the utmost silence and secrecy, till the moment of execution, and when the workmen yield, as they sometimes do, without resistance, though severely felt by them, they are never heard of by other people. Such combinations, however, are frequently resisted by a contrary defensive combination of the workmen; who sometimes too, without any provocation of this kind, combine of their own accord to raise the price of their labour. Their usual pretences are, sometimes the high price of provisions; sometimes the great profit which their masters make by their work. But whether their combinations be offensive or defensive, they are always abundantly heard of. In order to bring the point to a speedy decision, they have always recourse to the loudest clamour, and sometimes to the most shocking violence and outrage. They are desperate, and act with the folly and extravagance of desperate men, who must either starve, or frighten their masters into an immediate compliance with their demands. The masters upon these occasions are just as clamorous upon the other side, and never cease to call aloud for the assistance of the civil magistrate, and the rigorous execution of those laws which have been enacted with so much severity against the combinations of servants, labourers, and journeymen. The workmen, accordingly, very seldom derive any advantage from the violence of those tumultuous combinations, which, partly from the interposition of the civil magistrate, partly from the superior steadiness of the masters, partly from the necessity which the greater part of the workmen are under of submitting for the sake of present subsistence, generally end in nothing, but the punishment or ruin of the ringleader. [Smith, 1976, pp. 84–85]

Smith also spends much time discussing the conspiracy of monopolists against the public, a conspiracy to collude with others in similar product market positions in order that prices might be made to rise: "People of the same trade seldom meet together, even for merriment and diversion, but the conversation ends in a conspiracy against the publick, or in some contrivance to raise prices" (p. 145). The remarkable point is that, in Smith's account, it is not just that such a tendency is recognized as rife, but it is revealed as a source of perpetual conflict, outrage, and sometimes personal danger. Certainly, any one in authority, including members of parliament, who attempts to resist the activities of monopolists is never going to find things easy. Thus, if any such person opposes the monopolists:

and still more if he has authority enough to be able to thwart them, neither the most acknowledged probity, nor the highest rank, nor the greatest publick services, can protect him from the most infamous abuse and detraction, from personal insults, nor sometimes from real danger, arising from the insolent outrage of famous and disappointed monopolists. [Smith, 1976, p. 47]

Just as notably, because the interests and actions of merchants and manufacturers always run counter to those of the general public, Smith implores the public to be cautious towards any new legislative proposals emanating from this quarter—for the aims of its protagonists will generally be to oppress and also to deceive:

The proposal of any new law or regulation of commerce which comes from this order, ought always to be listened to with great precaution, and ought never to be adopted till after having been long and carefully examined, not only with the most scrupulous, but with the most suspicious attention. It comes from an order of men, whose interest is never exactly the same with that of the public, who have generally an interest to deceive and even to oppress the public, and who accordingly have, upon many occasions, both deceived and oppressed it. [P. 267]

Though brief, these few passages should at least be sufficient to indicate that Adam Smith's portrayal of the economy is hardly reducible simply and unambiguously to a system of spontaneous harmonious order. Furthermore, it is essential to recognize that, for Smith, the basis of conflict does not lie in the caprice of atomistically conceived individuals. Rather, people are recognized as being very much products of their economic/societal positions—with such positions conveying both objective or real needs upon the individuals standing in them as well as governing their objective possibilities for action and development. Indeed, it is easy enough, in places, to read into Smith's account something like the critical realist "position-practice system" elaborated above. Thus, for Smith, people are not born *un*equal in abilities and dispositions. Rather, differences arise almost entirely as a result of unequal access to opportunities, as a consequence of the class structure of society or the specific division of labor that obtains:

> The difference of natural talents in different men is, in reality, much less than we are aware of; and the very different genius which appears to distinguish men of different professions, when grown up to maturity, is not upon many occasions so much the cause, as the effect of the division of labour. The difference between the most dissimilar characters, between a philosopher and a common street porter, for example, seems to arise not so much from nature as from habit, custom, and education. When they came into the world, and for the first six or eight years of their existence, they were, perhaps, very much alike, and neither their parents nor play-fellows could perceive any remarkable difference. About that age, or soon after, they come to be employed in very different occupations. The difference of talents comes then to be taken notice of, and widens by degrees, till at last the vanity of the philosopher is willing to acknowledge scarce any resemblance. But without the disposition to truck, barter, and exchange, every man must have procured to himself every necessary and convenience of life which he wanted. All must have had the same duties to perform, and the same work to do, and there could have been no such difference of employment as could alone give occasion to any great difference of talents. [P. 29]

The image of Smith's perspective as unambiguously harmonious and noninterventionist, then, appears to be called into question by all this—an image still further queried if we observe the quite miserable state into which, in Smith's view, laborers, by virtue of their restricted opportunities, necessarily fall; a state which, apparently, can be remedied only through some kind of government intervention:

> In the progress of the division of labour, the employment of the far greater part of those who live by labour . . . comes to be confined to a few very simple operations; frequently to one or two. But the understandings of the greater part of men are necessarily formed by their ordinary employments. The man whose whole life is spent in performing a few simple operations . . . has no occasion to exert his understanding, or to exercise his invention in finding out expedients for removing difficulties which never occur. He naturally loses, therefor, the habit of such exertion, and generally becomes as stupid and ignorant as it is possible for a human creature to become. The torpor of his mind renders him, not only incapable of relishing or bearing a part in any rational conversation, but of conceiving any generous, noble, or tender sentiment, and consequently of forming any just judgement concerning many even of the ordinary duties of private life. . . . His dexterity at his own particular trade seems, in this manner, to be acquired at the expense of his intellectual, social, and martial virtues. But in every improved and civilized society this is the state into which the labouring poor, that is, the great body of the people, must necessarily fall, unless government takes some pains to prevent it. [Pp. 781–782]

The point, here, is not that Smith's precise claims must be accepted, nor even that these passages contain, necessarily, the central insights of Smith's contribution. But they are indicative of the general vision held. And it is not one of an inevitable, regular flow of some surface harmonious order, but of a reality structured by power relations and opposed interests and moved by, amongst other things, perpetual conflict and tendencies to disorder. In short, it is the sort of vision that only a transcendental realist perspective, or one very much like it, can accommodate.

Links between Post Keynesianism and Other Contemporary Nonorthodox Traditions

An interpretation of Post Keynesianism has been achieved, then, that can render coherent the most prominent nominal features of the project as were noted at the outset—including the claims that its roots lie in the contributions of Keynes, Marx, and the classical economists, amongst others. However, the achieving of this coherency, turning as it does upon what is fundamentally a philosophical perspective, appears to entail consequences that some Post Keynesians may regard as less than desirable. Specifically, with the tradition apparently lacking any significant degree of unity at the level of concrete substantive theory, it seems *a priori* highly likely, and on the face of it *ex posteriori* plausible, that Post Keynesianism is not really very different in structure from other contemporary, and reputedly rival, heterodox traditions—such as, for example, certain strands in the Austrian and Institutionalist schools. Of course, similarities between contemporary nonorthodox traditions such as these have been noted before. O'Driscoll and Rizzo (1985), for example, suggest commonalities between their own Austrian perspective and that of Post Keynesianism:

> In recent years a largely American branch of the Cambridge (UK) school, known as post-Keynesian economics, has arisen to carry forth the subjectivist aspects of Keynes' system . . . , Paul Davidson has conveniently summarized the post-Keynesian perspective in three propositions . . . :
>
> 1. the economy is a process in historical (real) time;
>
> 2. in a world where uncertainty and surprises are unavoidable, expectations have an unavoidable and significant effect on economic outcomes;
>
> 3. economic and political institutions are not negligible, and, in fact, play an extremely important role in determining real world economic outcomes.
>
> The reader will be hard pressed to find any significant differences between then propositions and the arguments of this chapter. What is even more surprising is that Davidson's explication of the meaning of these propositions increases, rather than reduces, the amount of overlap. It is evident that there is much more common ground between post-Keynesian subjectivism and Austrian subjectivism. Cross-fertilization between the two schools is, however, exceedingly rare, although the possibilities for mutually advantageous interchange seem significant. [P. 9]

In parallel fashion, common ground between Austrianism and Institutionalism has also been noted (e.g., Samuels, 1989; Boettke, 1989). There has even been a symposium on the subject.[20] Moreover, it is clear that the commonalities regularly highlighted here consist in the sort of features noted at the outset as characteristic of Post Keynesianism. Thus, for example, Samuels (1989) finds of Austrianism and Institutionalism that, amongst other things, "each tends to define itself, in part, in terms of its contrast with neoclassical economics"(p. 60); "each is internally heterogeneous" (p. 60); "both schools comprise more a paradigm than a fully detailed body of particular theories" (p. 61); "both schools are preoccupied (relative to neoclassicism) with methodological, philosophical (including epistemological), and political economy issues and foundations" (p. 61); and so on.[21]

Perhaps, then, it is time for some fuller reconciliation between the different traditions grounded in a shared philosophical perspective. If this suggestion is resisted, any response must at least address the fact that the substantive basis for separate traditions remains to be laid. Specifically, if Post Keynesians prefer to go down their own separate path in a coherent way, it would appear that they still have to produce a reasonably concrete substantive economic program that can both (a) be clearly seen to be differentiated from that of other traditions, *and* (b) unite Post Keynesian economists. Whether such is possible remains to be seen. At this point in time anyway there is little evidence (that this browser at least is aware of) that such a program is seriously in the offing. But what the full implications of all this, if it is correct, will be for Post Keynesianism (and indeed for supposedly competing nonorthodox traditions), and in particular what the more desirable or likely responses or paths of development may be, are questions, of course, that I can only leave as open.

Final Comments and Conclusion

The arguments of this article can be summarized as follows. The usual or most prominent nominal features of Post Keynesianism *can* be rendered intelligible as aspects of a coherent position. In particular, it is possible to render intelligible how it is that specific broader features of perspective (an emphasis upon uncertainty, historical processes, etc.) both arise and attain general agreement, while at the same time more concrete substantive claims are marked by diversity and often opposition. However, the achieving of this coherence appears to necessitate, in effect, nothing more (so far at least) and nothing less than adopting (at least the results of) what is essentially a philosophical perspective—one stylized here as critical realism. Whether or not this conclusion is a welcome one, I am not aware of any other equally explanatory powerful interpretation than can render the manifest phenomena, results, or claims of this tradition intelligible. There are, of course, advantages of the interpretation here being sustained. In particular, it casts favorable light upon the Post Keynesian claim for a lineage that stretches through Keynes and Marx to the classicals. It also, however, leaves open the possibility that Post Keynesianism is not, and perhaps is not able to be, significantly different from alternative contemporary nonorthodox schools—schools that numerous Post Keynesians appear to regard as oppositional. Maybe this is an important realization to face up to. However, for those who prefer to reject such an inference, one particular response appears to be unavoidable. This, of course, is that it is beholden upon them to develop a program that can both differentiate *and* unite Post Keynesians (or whomever) not merely in terms of broad perspective but also, and specifically, at the level of relatively concrete substantive economic theory.

Notes

For helpful comments on an earlier draft the author is grateful to Paul Dalziel, Sheila Dow, Geoff Harcourt, Prue Kerr, Steve Pratten, and Leslie Turano.

1. On this point the following remarks are typical:

Post-Keynesian economics can be seen as covering a considerable assortment of approaches. It has sometimes been said that the unifying feature of post-Keynesians is the dislike of neoclassical economics. [Sawyer, 1988, p. 1]

[P]ost-Keynesian economics is often portrayed as being distinguished more by its dislike of neoclassical theory, than by any coherence of agreement on fundamentals by its contributors. [Hodgson, 1989, p. 96]

It is less controversial to say what post-Keynesian theory is not than to say what it is. Post-Keynesian theory is not neoclassical theory. [Eichner, 1985, p. 51]

[P]ost-Keynesians tend to define their program in a negative way as a reaction to neo-classical economics. [Arestis, 1990, p. 222]

Some have argued that what unites post-Keynesians is a negative factor: the rejection of neoclassical economics. [Dow, 1992, p. 176]

What seems to be striking to outsiders of post-Keynesianism and neo-Ricardianism is that these two schools of thought and their major proponents only seem to have one cementing theme, their rejection of the dominant neoclassical paradigm. [Lavoie, 1992, p. 45]

See also Hamouda and Harcourt (1989, p. 2) and Harcourt (1985, p. 125; 1988, p. 924), amongst many others.

2. This is apparent from a glance at the content of any Post Keynesian contribution. In addition, the following explicit internalist assessments are to be found:

So the methodological content of post-Keynesian writing tends to be high. This contrasts with the minimal attention paid to methodological issues in [neoclassical textbooks] . . . . the post-Keynesian view of methodology as ranging from ideology through to technique requires that it be continually raised as an issue. [Dow, 1992, p. 182]

[T]he post-Keynesian school of thought represents a positive statement of methodology, ideology and content. [Arestis, 1990, p. 223]

[One] approach to specifying post-Keynesian economics is a methodological one. Elsewhere . . . I have attempted to define post-Keynesianism as a shared methodological approach. . . .

. . . Post-Keynesianism can be understood as a subset of political economy which can in turn be understood as a general embracing of a methodology of diverse methods. An attempt will therefore be made to relate post-Keynesianism and political economy in methodological terms. [Dow, 1990, pp. 346–347]

3. A typical example is the following:

The characteristics of the historical and humanistic models employed by Post Keynesians may be summarized in the following three propositions: 1) The economy is a historical process; 2) in a world where uncertainty is unavoidable, expectations have an unavoidable and significant effect on economic outcomes; 3) economic and political institutions play a significant rule in shaping economic events. [Davidson, 1980, p. 158]

Under the third heading above Davidson explicitly notes that the "distribution of income and power is a basic concern of Post Keynesians" (p. 162) and spends some time discussing the Post Keynesian concern for matters of democracy, policy, and distributional issues more generally. In truth, just about all Post Keynesian contributions appear to share this general perspective.

4. This fact is evident from the most cursory glance at Post Keynesian contributions. It is a situation that underpins, for example, the following remarks and assessments:

Notably, over fifty years after the publication of the *General Theory* there is still no consensus amongst [Post Keynesians] as to what are the basic theoretical foundations of their economics. [Hodgson, 1989, p. 96]

[T]here is a sense of confusion, even among some post-Keynesians, as to what post-Keynesianism is. [Dow, 1990, p. 346]

One important feature of existing post-Keynesian literature is its apparent diversity of content. [Dow, 1990, p. 352]

Post-Keynesian economics is thus a portmanteau term which contains the work of a heterogeneous group of economists who nevertheless are united not only by their dislike [of contemporary orthodox economics] but also by their attempts to provide coherent alternative approaches to economic analysis. . . . We say "approaches" because we may identify several strands which differ from each other both with regard to method and with regard to the characteristics of the economy that are included in their models. [Hamouda and Harcourt, 1988, p. 2]

In attempting to tease out some coherence in the Post Keynesian project, Arestis (1990) makes numerous remarks of the following sort: "its boundaries have not been precisely defined" (p. 222); "there is a substantial diversity of theoretical premises" (p. 222); "there is another dimension to this argument in that there are different 'approaches' that comprise post-Keynesian economics which not only differ in terms of method and economic features subsumed in their models but sometimes conflict with each other" (p. 222). And so on.

5. Just about all Post Keynesians who reflect upon their lineage support this claim. For reasons of space I merely report here a recent typical (if highly abbreviated) assessment:

As the name "post-Keynesian" suggests, the work of John Maynard Keynes is a significant influence. But Keynes is not the sole influence on the school, and indeed the earlier writers who influenced Keynes himself are often identified by post-Keynesians as having influenced them directly. . . . Post-Keynesianism has it roots in classical economics. . . .

Adam Smith is regarded as the first key figure. . . .

As far as the content of post-Keynesian economics is concerned, the key classical figures are Mathus, Ricardo and Marx, each influencing different groups within post-Keynesian economics. [Dow, 1992, p. 177)

6. Where other contenders for inclusion, Sraffa for example (along, indeed, with other possible nominal features of Post Keynesianism not focused upon here), seem to be accepted by only a section of Post Keynesians *and* whose inclusion would appear to be especially controversial, my strategy has been to omit them from explicit consideration here. This seems appropriate. If coherence within Post Keynesianism cannot be found amongst those features that appear to be widely agreed upon by Post Keynesians, then the inclusion of controversial features is unlikely to change matters. Alternatively, if coherence can be brought to, or found within, the agreed features, it should then be that much

easier to assess whether, conditional upon coherence being required, those features not considered here do, could, or should not, etc., belong.

7. While many previous commentators appear to reject such a possibility, Hamouda and Harcourt (1989, p. 32) go further in suggesting that "attempts . . . to synthesize the strands [of Post Keynesianism] to see whether a coherent whole emerges . . . [are] a misplaced exercise, and that those who do so search in vain. While most appear to think that any such coherence has not been found because none such exists, a minority view appears to be that the problem reflects, rather, a relative lack of serious attempts so far to establish the nature of the tradition's coherence. Lavoie (1992, p. 46), for example, provides an assessment that appears to place him in the latter camp:

> [Recent surveys] . . . have not really attempted to pull together the common elements of various stands and authors. For instance while Arena's survey is quite analytical, he insists more upon the differences than the similitudes (Arena, 1987). Hamouda and Harcourt (1989) present an exhaustive survey but they are more descriptive than analytical, centring their attention on the identity and personality of the economists concerned rather than their ideas. They unexpectedly conclude that the search for a coherent vision is a futile endeavour. Coherence within each strand . . . is sufficient in their view. Their conception . . . is thus similar to that of Dow (1985:73) who claimed that post-Keynesians had a Babylonian methodological approach, i.e., one that was eclectic, without being able to identify the essentials. . . . But this only leads critics . . . to conclude that post-Keynesians and their allies have not yet provided a suitable alternative to neoclassical theory (Backhouse, 1988).

8. It must be noted that although previous contributors do not appear to have claimed as much for philosophical perspectives, some forms of realism have been discussed elsewhere in the context of assessing Post Keynesianism—see especially Arestis (1990) and Dow (1990, 1992).

9. Note that this formulation is intended to be quite general. The measurable event-types X and Y can, where appropriate, be scalars, vectors, or matrices, and the relationship can be simple or complex, deterministic or probabilistic, and so on.

10. In the light of this unhesitant belief that deductivism is universal and unchallengeable the following remark by Whitehead (1925) seems particularly pertinent:

> When you are criticizing the philosophy of an epoch, do not chiefly direct your attention to those intellectual positions which its exponents feel it necessary explicitly to defend. There will be some fundamental assumption which adherents of all the variant systems within the epoch unconsciously presuppose. Such assumptions appear so obvious that people do not how what they are assuming because no other way of putting things

has ever occurred to them. With these assumptions a certain limited number of types of philosophical systems are possible and this group of systems constitutes the philosophy of the epoch.

11. Thus, for example, the desire to elaborate constant conjunctions of events necessarily orientates the research process to examining premises that ensure that under any given set of events or states of affairs X then the same thing Y always follows. The obvious (if noncompulsory) premise that serves this purpose is the assumption of economic rationality—that with respect to his or her situation (including preference ordering, etc.), each individual always optimizes. In addition, with a "system" of supposed event regularities of the sought-after form, some system solution concept ensuring equation consistency is obviously desirable. This, of course, is achieved, amongst other ways, through concepts of equilibrium—the requirement that all actions are mutually compatible; and so on (see Lawson, 1994d).

12. For conceptions of positivism similar to, or which include, the interpretation sustained here, see, for example, entries on the term in Outhwaite and Bottomore, 1993; Bullock, Stallybrass, and Trombley, 1988; or Gould and Kotb, 1964.

13. This interpretation of Hume is, if not uncontested, the most prevalent and, I think, most convincing one.

14. I say "fruitfully" because although the noted result is derivable from positivism as interpreted here—indeed the Humean theory of knowledge was probably motivated by the aim of showing how it was that supposedly justified scientific knowledge arose (so rendering methodological discussion irrelevant)—positivism is hardly internally consistent, while those who draw upon it usually do so only selectively. Thus, there *are* some orthodox economists who engage in explicit methodological thinking even if, given their perspective, and as Hahn (1985) notes, it has achieved very little.

15. For further discussion of transcendental realism, see Bhaskar, (1978, 1979, 1986, 1989) and Lawson (1989a, 1989b, 1992, 1994a, 1994b, 1994d).

16. Notice that this usage of the term structure is to be distinguished from that of econometricians as denoting a putative relationship between measurable events.

17. The same is true, of course, of positivistic claims. This is why criticisms of mainstream or neoclassical economics that focus upon the unrealistic, nonexplanatorily adequate nature of mainstream substantive assumptions are usually met with the retort that the assumptions in question are not essential anyway, or some such. Deductivism, though, *is* essential to that project (Lawson, 1994d), just as something very much like critical realism seems necessary to any sustainable alternative.

18. The above-noted comment is made in response to a request for a book review on Tinbergen's work. A fuller elaboration is found in the review eventually published in the *Economic Journal*. Of course, it is not just in his reactions to econometrics that Keynes's attachment to an essentially transcendental realist, antipositivist, conception of the social realm is to be found. As early as 1926 Keynes argues that the atomic hypothesis in particular is inappropriate for social material:

> The atomic hypothesis which has worked so splendidly in physics breaks down in psychics. We are faced at every turn with the problems of organic unity, of discreteness, of discontinuity—the whole is not equal to the sum of the parts, comparisons of quantity fail us, small changes produce large effects, the assumptions of a uniform and homogeneous continuum are not satisfied. [Keynes, 1973d, p. 262]

In his later economic writings, of course, he writes explicitly about tendencies that persist giving rise to events ("mean positions") that are in no sense inevitable or "natural":

> But we must not conclude that the mean position thus determined by "natural" tendencies, namely, by those tendencies which are likely to persist, failing measures expressly designed to correct them, is, therefore, established by laws of necessity. The unimpeded rule of the above conditions is a fact of observation concerning the world as it is or has been, and not a principle which cannot be changed. [Keynes, 1973a, p. 254]

See Rotheim (1993) on this last point, and for an assessment of chapter 12 of the General Theory from a critical realist perspective, see Lawson (1990, 1994c).

19. Indeed, Ricardo is acknowledged amongst some as having provided, or attempted, the "'theoretical foundations for the bourgeoisie in its clash of interest with the land-owning class" (Rubin, 1979, p. 365).

20. In the *Journal of Research in the History of Economic Thought and Methodology*, vol. 6, 1989.

21. It is equally necessary to acknowledge here, of course, that, just as suggested commonalities between traditions are occasionally observed by some, such suggestions are usually immediately and summarily rejected as illusory by others. Thus Davidson (1989), for example, is quite dismissive of the specific claims of commonality between Post Keynesians and Austrians noted by O'Driscoll and Rizzo, just as Miller (1989) rejects the specific claims of commonality between Austrians and Institutionalist as made by Samuels (1989) and Boettke (1989). However, it is not clear that these "rejections" are sustainable. Runde (1993), in examining Davidson's "rejection" in particular, argues explicitly as much. Runde's insight is that Davidson and perhaps O'Driscoll and Rizzo also write on two different levels—corresponding, in effect, to the transcendental realist and the empirical realist perspectives,

respectively. In both cases, the transcendental realist perspective, if implicit, is the more dominant. Runde's argument, in essence, is that while it is the shared implicit perspective of transcendental realism (or certain of its results) that O'Driscoll and Rizzo emphasize in arguing for commonalities, it is the empirical realist stream in Austrian thought compared with the transcendental realist aspects of Post Keynesianism that Davidson draws attention to in arguing for opposition.

References

Allais, M. "The Economic Science of Today and Global Disequilibrium." In M. Baldassarri, et al. (eds.), *Global Disequilibrium in the World Economy.* Basingstoke, UK: Macmillan, 1992.

Arena, R. "L'école Internationale d'été de Trieste (1981–85): Vers une Synthèse Classico-Keynésienne?" *Economies et Sociétés,* 1987, *21,* 205–238.

Arestis, P. "Post-Keynesianism: A New Approach to Economics." *Review of Social Economy,* Fall 1990, *48* (3), 222–246.

Backhouse, R. "The Value of Post Keynesian Economics: A Neoclassical Response to Harcourt and Hamouda." *Bulletin of Economic Research,* 1988, *40,* 35–41.

Bhaskar, R. *A Realist Theory of Science,* 2nd ed. Leeds: Harvester Press, 1978 (1st ed., 1975).

———. *The Possibility of Naturalism.* Leeds: Harvester Press, 1979.

———. *Scientific Realism and Human Emancipation.* London: Verso, 1986.

———. *Reclaiming Reality.* London: Verso, 1989.

Boettke, P. J. "Evolution and Economics: Austrians as Institutionalists." *Research in the History of Economic Thought and Methodology,* vol. 6, pp. 73–91. 1989.

Bullock, A.; Stallybrass, O.; and Trombley, S., eds. *The Fontana Dictionary of Modern Thought.* London: Fontana Press, 1988.

Davidson, P. "Post Keynesian Economics." *The Public Interest,* 1980, special ed., pp. 151–173 (reprinted in D. Bell and I. Kristol [eds.], *The Crisis in Economic Theory.* New York: Basic Books, 1981).

———. "The Economics of Ignorance or the Ignorance of Economics?" *Critical Review,* 1989, *3,* 467–487.

Dow, S. C. *Macroeconomic Thought: A Methodological Approach.* Oxford: Basil Blackwell, 1985.

———. "Post-Keynesianism as Political Economy: A Methodological Discussion." *Review of Political Economy*, 1990, 2–3, 345–358.

———. "Post Keynesian School." In D. Mair and A. Miller (eds.), *Comparative Schools of Economic Thought*. Aldershot, UK: Edward Elgar, 1992.

Eichner, A. S. *Towards a New Economics: Essays in Post-Keynesian and Institutionalist Theory*. London: Macmillan, 1985.

Gould, J., and Kolb, W. L. *A Dictionary of the Social Sciences*. London: Tavistock, 1964.

Hahn, F. "In Praise of Economic Theory." The 1984 Jevons Memorial Fund Lecture, University College, London, 1985.

Hamouda, O. F., and Harcourt, G. C. "Post-Keynesianism: From Criticism to Coherence?" In J. Pheby (ed.), *New Directions in Post-Keynesian Economics*. Aldershot, UK: Edward Elgar, 1989). Reprinted from *Bulletin of Economic Research*, January 1988, 40, 1–34. [Page references to the former.]

Harcourt, G. C. "Post-Keynesianism: Quite Wrong and/or Nothing New." In P. Arestis and T. Skouras (eds.), *Post Keynesian Economic Theory: A Challenge to Neo-Classical Economics*. Sussex: Wheatsheaf Books, 1985.

———. "Post-Keynesian Economics." In J. Eatwell, M. Milgate, and P. Newman (eds.), *The New Palgrave: A Dictionary of Economics*. London: Macmillan, 1988, pp. 924–928.

Hodgson, G. "Post-Keynesian and Institutionalism: The Missing Link." In J. Pheby (ed.), *New Directions in Post-Keynesian Economics*. Aldershot UK: Edward Elgar, 1989, pp. 94–123.

Hodgson, G.; Tool, M.; and Samuels, W., eds. *Edward Elgar Companion to Evolutionary and Institutionalist Economics*. Aldershot, UK: Edward Elgar, 1994.

Keynes, J. M. *The Collected Writings of John Maynard Keynes*, vol. 7, *The General Theory*. London: Royal Economic Society, 1973a.

———. *The Collected Writings of John Maynard Keynes*, vol. 8, *A Treatise on Probability*. London: Royal Economic Society, 1973b.

———. *The Collected Writings of John Maynard Keynes*, vol. 10, *The General Theory and After: Part II Defence and Development*. London: Royal Economic Society, 1973c.

———. *The Collected Writings of John Maynard Keynes*, vol. 14, *The General Theory and After: Part II Defence and Development*. London: Royal Economic Society, 1973d.

————. *The Collected Writings of John Maynard Keynes*, vol. 29, *The General Theory and After, A Supplement*. London: Royal Economic Society, 1979.

Lavoie, M. "Towards a New Research Programme for Post-Keynesianism and New-Ricardianism." *Review of Political Economy*, 1992, *4* (1), 37–78.

Lawson, T. "Uncertainty and Economic Analysis." *Economic Journal*, December 1985, *95*, 909–927.

————. "Abstraction, Tendencies and Stylised Facts: A Realist Approach to Economic Analysis." *Cambridge Journal of Economics*, March 1989a, *13* (1), 59–78 (reprinted in T. Lawson, G. Palma, and J. Sender [eds.], *Kaldor's Political Economy*. London: Academic Press, 1989; also in P. Ekins and M. Max-Neef [eds.], *Real-Life Economics: Understanding Wealth Creation*. London: Routledge, 1992).

————. "Realism and Instrumentalism in the Development of Econometrics." *Oxford Economic Papers*, 1989b, *41* (1), 236–258 (reprinted in N. De Marchi and C. Gilbert [eds.], *The History and Methodology of Econometrics*. Oxford: Oxford University Press, 1990).

————. "Keynes and the Analysis of Rational Behaviour." In R. M. O'Donnell (ed.), *Keynes as Philosopher-Economist*. London: Macmillan Academic and Profession Ltd., 1990.

————. "Realism, Closed Systems and Friedman." *Research in the History of Economic Thought and Methodology*, 1992, *10*, 149–169.

————. "Realism, Philosophical." In G. Hodgson, M. Tool, and W. Samuels (eds.), *Edward Elgar Companion to Evolutionary and Institutionalist Economics*. Aldershot, UK: Edward Elgar, 1994a.

————. "Methodology." In G. Hodgson, M. Tool, and W. Samuels (eds.), *Edward Elgar Companion to Evolutionary and Institutionalist Economics*. Aldershot, UK: Edward Elgar, 1994b.

————. "Economics and Expectations." In S. Dow and J. Hillard (eds.), *Keynes, Knowledge and Uncertainty*. Aldershot, UK: Edward Elgr, 1994c.

————. "A Realist Perspective on Contemporary 'Economic Theory'." *Journal of Economic Issues*, 1994d.

Marx, K. *Capital, vol. I. A Critical Analysis of Capitalist Production*. London: Lawrence and Wishart, 1974a.

————. *Capital, vol. III. A Critique of Political Economy: The Process of Capitalist Production as a Whole*. London: Lawrence and Wishart, 1974b.

————. *Grundrisse: Foundation of the Critique of Political Economy* (rough draft). Middlesex: Penguin Books (in association with New Left Review), 1981.

Miller, E. S. "Comment of Boettke and Samuels: Austrian and Institutionalist Economics." *Research in the History of Economic Thought and Methodology,* vol. 6, 1989, pp. 151–158.

O'Driscoll, G. P., and Rizzo, M. J. *The Economics of Time and Ignorance.* Oxford: Basil Blackwell, 1985.

Outhwaite, W., and Bottomore, T., eds. *The Blackwell Dictionary of Twentieth-Century Social Thought.* Oxford: Blackwell, 1993.

Rotheim, R. "On the Indeterminacy of Keynes's Monetary Theory of Value." *Review of Political Economy,* 1993, 5 (2), 197–216.

Rubin, I. I. *A History of Economic Thought,* trans. and ed. by D. Filzer. London: Pluto Press, 1979 (first published as *Istoniya Chonomicheskoi mysli,* 1929).

Runde, J. "Paul Davidson and Austrians." *Critical Review,* 1993, 7, 381–397.

Samuels, W. J. "Austrian and Institutional Economics: Some Common Elements." *Research in the History of Economic Thought and Methodology,* vol. 6. 1989, pp. 53–72.

Sawyer, M. *Post-Keynesian Economics.* Aldershot, UK: Edward Elgar, 1988.

Smith, A. *An Inquiry into the Nature and Causes of the Wealth of Nations,* ed. by R. H. Campbell and A. S. Skinner. Oxford: Clarendon Press, 1976.

Whitehead, A. N. *Science and the Modern World.* Cambridge: Cambridge University Press, 1925.

PART III

BEYOND THE MARKET:
SOCIAL AND INSTITUTIONAL ECONOMICS

[T]he object of dissent is the conception of the market as the guiding mechanism of the economy or, more broadly, the conception of the economy as organized and guided by the market. It simply is not true that scarce resources are allocated among alternative uses by the market. The real determinant of whatever allocation occurs in any society is the organizational structure of that society—in short, its institutions. At most, the market only gives effect to prevailing institutions. By focusing attention on the market mechanism, economists have ignored the real allocational mechanism. Hence the hiatus between economics and the other social studies, all of which are concerned with various aspects of the institutional structure of society. Economics is more advanced than those others—in the wrong direction.

—Clarence E. Ayres, "A New Look at Institutionalism: Discussion,"
American Economic Review Supplement

7

INSTITUTIONAL ECONOMIC THEORY: THE OLD VERSUS THE NEW

GEOFFREY M. HODGSON[1]

When the history of institutional economics is updated to take account of recent developments, further interest will be added to an already engrossing tale. Remarkably, the institutionalist school of Thorstein Veblen, John Commons, Wesley Mitchell and others was a very prominent paradigm amongst U.S. economists in the 1920s and 1930s. This was followed by, depending on your point of view, one of the several postwar 'counterrevolutions' in economic theory, or an important moment in the unfolding neoclassical and formalistic renaissance. Yet, since the mid-1970s, there has been an equally remarkable growth in what has been dubbed the 'new institutional economics', not via a re-emergence of traditional institutionalism, but mainly through developments in the heart of modern orthodox theory itself. The irony, of course, is that the original institutionalism of Veblen and others emerged largely out of a critique of orthodox assumptions.

After clarifying some of these orthodox fundamentals, a primary task of this paper is to demonstrate the extent to which the new institutional economics relies upon them. Aspects of the old institutionalist critique will be highlighted, with a view to demonstrating the difficulty in sustaining institutionalist theory upon such orthodox propositions, and the need to surpass them, partly along the lines suggested by Veblen and others long ago. The paper concludes with some remarks on the fate of the old institutionalism and its present potential.

This is not a comprehensive 'point-scoring' exercise between the two institutionalisms. The object is not to suggest that the old institutionalism is in all respects satisfactory, nor to conclude that the new variety has nothing to offer, but merely to indicate that the old institutionalists had good grounds for their critique of orthodoxy in regard to assumptions about human agency, even if Veblen and his followers did not provide an adequate alternative. Consequently, whatever its merits, the 'new' institutionalism is to be criticised for proceeding largely on pre-Veblenian assumptions.

New Institutionalism, the Abstract Individual and 'Economic Man'

Despite the claim of its title, the new institutionalism rests upon some long-established assumptions concerning the human agent. These derive from the long tradition of classic liberalism spanning the work of John Locke and John Stuart Mill. Other notable members of this formidable association are Jeremy Bentham, David Hume and Adam Smith. From the outset, classic liberalism has overshadowed economics: it is much easier to identify the few dissenters to this domination—such as Karl Marx and Thorstein Veblen—than the many conformists. It has remained dominant in our discipline, despite its partial eclipse in other intellectual circles in the first two-thirds of the twentieth century. With the rise of the new right in the 1970s and 1980s, classic liberalism has re-emerged on a wide front.

What unites the mentors of classic liberalism listed above, despite their wide-ranging and sometimes conflicting opinions, is the view that, in a sense, the individual can be 'taken for granted'. To put it another way, the individual, along with his or her assumed behavioral characteristics, is taken as the elemental building block in the theory of the social or economic system. It is this idea of the 'abstract individual' that is fundamental to classic liberalism as a whole. According to this conception, as Steven Lukes (1973: 73) puts it, 'individuals are pictured abstractly as given, with given interests, wants, purposes, needs, etc.' In general, the heyday of this idea in western thought dates from the seventeenth to the nineteenth centuries.

Of course, to raise this question is to tread on a philosophical minefield, and it is beyond the scope of this present work to attempt to chart a route across. The notion of the abstract individual can be seen to relate to the doctrine of 'methodological individualism' and be likewise opposed to their joint enemy: holism. However, these terms are rarely well-defined, and many ambiguities and controversies exist.[2] Consequently, these terms are not adopted here.

We may, however, fire off a few Very-lights to illuminate this dangerous terrain. Basing analysis on the abstract individual involves a form of reductionism. Wholes are seen to be explained in terms of this elemental unit. But the individual, as Arthur Koestler (1967: 86) puts it, is itself not an 'indivisible, self-contained unit'. Thus there is no primacy in explaining institutions in terms of individuals, as there is no primacy in explaining the behavior of individuals in terms of institutions. For example, in rejecting the application of the abstract individual to the theory of the firm, Neil Kay (1979: 211) remarks: 'The individual is a holistic concept no less and no more than the concept of the corporation'. The individual, as a fundamental unit, 'cannot be taken as obvious' (Giddens, 1984: 220). As Solomon Asch (1952: 257) wrote several decades ago:

> the unit is not an individual but a social individual, one who has a place in the social order . . . To understand the individual we must study him in his group setting; to understand the group we must study the individuals whose interrelated actions constitute it.

What has to be made clear, however, is that an economist is not necessarily absolved from criticism if he or she is found to admit that individuals, or their wants and preferences, are changed by circumstances. Indeed, all intelligent economists, from Smith to Hayek inclusive, admit that individuals might so be changed. What is crucial is that the classic liberal economist may make such an admission but then go on to assume, for the purposes of economic enquiry that individuals and their preferences must be taken as given. Thus the demarcating criterion is not the matter of individual malleability *per se*, but the willingness, or otherwise, to consider this possibility as an important or legitimate matter for economic enquiry. The oft-repeated statement by orthodox economists that tastes and preferences are not the *explanda* of economics thus derives directly from the classic liberal tradition, and is an object of criticism for this paper. It involves, as quoted above, taking the individual 'for granted'.

Whilst the idea of the abstract individual is fundamental to the standard versions of 'economic man' in the textbooks, the textbook, neoclassical version involves additional assumptions. These concern the nature and exogeneity of individual preferences, a pre-twentieth-century disregard for serious real-world problems of information and knowledge, and the adoption of rather mechanical, equilibriating models of economic phenomena which are redolent of classical mechanics (which, of course, prevailed at a similar time to classical liberalism itself). The Austrian offshoot of the classic liberal tradition does not share these assumptions, but it retains the idea of an abstract and purposeful individual. In all cases the processes governing the determination of individual purposes, tastes and preferences are disregarded.

The important point to be established here is that the assumption of the abstract individual which is fundamental to classic liberalism is fundamental to the 'new institutional economics' as well. Furthermore, standard conceptions of rational 'economic man' are commonplace. These propositions will be supported by examining some key contributors to the new institutionalism. One of the latter is Oliver Williamson (1975; 1985), who was one of the first to popularize the term. Other contributions include Andrew Schotter's (1981) developments in the realm of game theory. In addition we shall examine some recent work by Friedrich Hayek (1982). These three authors can be taken as representative of some key developments in new institutionalist theory.[3]

Notably, these three authors have not been selected because of any closeness to neoclassical orthodoxy. Indeed, their views differ from orthodoxy in several respects, most dramatically in the case of Hayek. It would thus stretch the term too far to define Hayek as a neoclassical economist. The three are selected because they are prominent but, to different degrees, atypical. It is relatively easy to demonstrate the links between neoclassical orthodoxy and classical liberalism. What is important is to find those themes that link up with the important outliers as well.

A wider survey would include other new institutionalist writers such as Douglass North and Robert Thomas (1973), Mancur Olson (1965; 1982) and Richard Posner (1973) and their contributions spanning such diverse issues as economic history, economic growth and the economics of law. All these writings share a prominent new institutionalist theme: to explain the existence of political, legal, or more generally social, institutions by reference to a model of individual behavior, tracing out its consequences in terms of human interactions. However, in terms of theoretical fundamentals, Williamson, Schotter and Hayek have been more innovative. In contrast, North, Olson, Posner and Thomas are the closest to orthodox neoclassical theory, particularly in the adoption of standard, mechanical versions of maximizing rationality, without regard to serious problems of information.

Thus it should not be overlooked that the new institutionalism has this prominent neoclassical wing, reflecting the enduring hegemony of Walrasian and Marshallian ideas in economic theory.[4] At the other extreme are Austrian theorists such as Hayek who depart from the prevailing neoclassical approach, by recognizing the gravity of information problems in real-world decision making, and by eschewing equilibriating models of the economic process. However, both Austrian and neoclassical institutionalists share an attachment to the fundamental assumptions of neoclassical liberalism as outlined above.

Williamson and Orthodox Theory

Williamson's work largely derives, of course, from the seminal paper of Ronald Coase (1937). Superficially Williamson's work seems to be a departure from much of orthodoxy. First, he claims to be influenced, in addition, by Herbert Simon and the behavioralist school, and if this influence were substantial it would suggest a break from the neoclassical axiom of maximizing behavior, even if the work of Simon offers only a partial retreat from classic liberalism itself. Secondly, the central aim of Williamson's theory, to explain the nature and existence of key economic institutions such as the firm, is an innovation of radical importance and contrasts with the earlier tendency of orthodox theory to regard institutions simply as given rigidities or constraints.

However, on closer inspection it is evident that Williamson's break from neoclassical theory is partial and incomplete, and much of the core neoclassical apparatus is retained. In fact, Williamson's claimed departure from orthodoxy sits uneasily alongside his repeated invocation that agents are marked by 'opportunism' (i.e., 'self-interest seeking with guile'). Self-interested behavior, of course, is a typical feature of economic man.

Williamson argues that the existence of firms and their internal supersession of the market mechanism is due to the significant transaction costs involved in market trading. In Williamson's (e.g., 1985: 32) hands this Coasian idea is repeatedly linked with that of Simon: 'Economizing on transaction costs essentially reduces to economizing on bounded rationality'. This awkward formulation is characteristic of its author's prose, and, like much jargon-ridden language, obscures as much as it explains. Essentially, a problem is that Williamson has taken only part of Simon's (1957) argument on board and he is influenced too much by common but inaccurate interpretations of behavioralism.

Simon's argument, of course, is that a complete or global rational calculation is ruled out, thus rationality is 'bounded'; agents do not maximize but attempt to attain acceptable minima instead. But it is important to note that this 'satisficing' behavior does not simply arise because of inadequate information, but also because it would be too difficult to perform the calculations even if the relevant information was available.[5]

Given this point a prevailing orthodox interpretation of Simon's work can be faulted: the recognition of bounded rationality refers primarily to the matter of computational capacity and not to additional 'costs'. Furthermore, 'satisficing' does not amount to cost-minimizing behavior. Clearly, the latter is just the dual of the standard assumption of maximization; if 'satisficing' was essentially a matter of minimizing costs then it would amount to maximizing behavior of the orthodox type.

Basically, Williamson adopts the orthodox, cost-minimizing interpretation of Simon and not the one which clearly prevails in Simon's own work. In Williamson's work 'economizing on transaction costs' is part of global, cost-minimizing behavior, and this is inconsistent with Simon's idea of bounded rationality. Whilst Williamson recognizes some of the informational problems, the fact that the cost calculus remains supreme in his theory means that he has not broken entirely from the orthodox assumption of maximization.

Consistent with the retention of the basic orthodox model of optimizing behavior, Williamson assumes that individual preferences are unchanged by the economic environment and the institutions in which individuals are located. Elsewhere (Hodgson, 1988: Chapter 9) I argue that an important difference between the market and the firm is that actors tend to behave in a different manner with differing goals. To some degree the firm sets up a 'trust dynamic', as Alan Fox (1974) puts it. The whole point about trust is that it is undermined by the cost calculus. As Kenneth Arrow (1974: 23) remarks: 'If you have to buy it, you already have some doubts about what you've bought'. Trust is thus not best explained as a phenomenon resulting simply from the rational calculation of costs and benefits by given individuals. In any social order based on a degree of trust, the regime affects the preferences, goals and behavior of the individuals concerned. Trust is thus both a cause and a consequence of individual plans and purposes. The existence of such an order cannot be explained satisfactorily by arguing in one direction only, by starting from the abstract individual.

To conclude, therefore, Williamson's work retains orthodox assumptions of maximizing behavior with given preferences and reflects some of the still-prevailing presumptions of classic liberalism. Despite its apparent novelty, Williamson's work lies close to the neoclassical pole of the new institutionalist spectrum.

Schotter and the Critique of Free Markets

The style and approach of Schotter's (1981) work is very different from that of Williamson. First, Schotter attains high standards of rigor, clarity and elegance, using the mathematical tools of game theory. Secondly, unlike the conservative and apologetic flavor of much new institutionalism, Schotter develops a forceful critique of 'free-market' economics. He thus breaks with classic liberal policy conclusions. However, as in all game-theoretic models, the abstract individual is retained.

In Schotter's models, agents have the choice of different strategies to obtain the maximum payoff. The conception of the agent is still that of maximizing economic man: the only slight difference is that there is not necessarily a single, determined outcome. Agents maximize, but they may, for example, mix strategies randomly in certain proportions as they seek to optimize.

Schotter's argument is based on games that are played over and over again. It is argued that as the games '. . . are repeatedly played, the players develop certain societally agreed to rules of thumb, norms, conventions and institutions which are passed on to succeeding generations of players' (p. 12). Within this framework, Schotter shows that institutions and routines are, far from being market 'imperfections', actually necessary to supply vital information, particularly about the future strategems of other agents. Whether through evolution or conscious design, institutions provide rich information upon which agents can develop expectations regarding the future behavior of other actors.

In contrast, if action was unstructured and completely fluid it would be much more difficult, by observing behavior that was subject to continuous change, to form such expectations. The orthodox model of price adjustment under perfect competition is a case in point. In this ideal case, information is signalled principally through the price system. In contrast, if there are market restrictions and imperfections, much more information is transmitted, and other than through price. The web of institutions within and around the market place serve as 'mechanisms that supply information about the potential actions of other economic agents' (p. 157).

Consequently, the rigidities in a market system should not be treated as a restrictive assumption to be imposed upon a 'more general' model. Rigidities are not a 'special case'. These so-called 'imperfections' help to impose coherence and order on the market system. Markets function coherently *because of* these imperfections, and not *despite* them as mainstream theorists presume.[6]

In a later work, Schotter (1985) highlights the important policy conclusions of his theory, in terms of a critique of the free-market economics of the new right. Clearly, his argument that institutions and rigid conventions are actually functional to the decision-making process, both inside and outside the market, is a counter to the new right view that, as far as possible, all such rigidities and conventions should be dissolved.

In this later (1985) work his analysis is described as an 'immanent critique' of orthodox theory, because it shares some of its basic assumptions but draws untypical conclusions. It is as an internal critique that

Schotter's work is best appraised. Arguably, game theory cannot serve as a wider foundation for an economic theory of social institutions, partly because of its continuing adoption of the assumptions of maximizing economic man. Thus there is a tension in Schotter's work between his adoption of orthodox assumptions and his attempt to describe some of the informational functions of institutions.

For instance, despite a brief reference to bounded rationality (1981: 148–49), Schotter underlines a standard assumption of game theory that agents make use of '*all* relevant information', and nothing is ignored in the determination of their optimal strategy (p. 160). However, as Herbert Simon argues, such global calculations are impossible because of the limited computational capacity of any computer or human brain. A function of institutions that is not encompassed by Schotter's model is that they facilitate actions when such global calculations are impossible.[7]

It is typical of game theory to take the individual, and his or her purposes and interests, as exogenous or given. The factors influencing the formation of the individuals purposes and goals are not taken into account. Of course, no example from life can show conclusively that individual preferences and purposes are molded by culture and institutions. It is simply suggested that the orthodox view is handicapped by its refusal to investigate these possible influences and processes and may ignore some important features of the phenomena at hand.

Consider the example of the situation facing the soldier in battle. Should he go into attack with his comrades and risk death, or desert and risk capture and punishment? It is quite possible, following Edna Ullman-Margalit (1977) and others, to present the options in game-theoretic terms and consider the payoffs of the various eventualities. What this payoff matrix analysis seems to leave out is factors such as training and leadership in the formation of the soldier's own perceptions and preferences, and the blind routinization of many actions before and during battle. As the film *Full Metal Jacket* depicts with dramatic effect, the training process is designed to subliminate many actions and responses in a battle situation: to condition soldiers so that they become reflexes or habits. Furthermore, it is difficult to encompass the function of charismatic leadership in war without accepting that it may actually mold and develop individual motivation (Keegan, 1976). The experience of army discipline and war itself actually changes the person, making him capable of intentions and acts that he would not have entertained before.

Another prominent example in the discussion of the emergence of behavioral norms is why (nearly all) people drive on the left in the U.K. and on the right in most other countries (e.g., Sugden, 1986). Clearly the emergence and reproduction of this norm can be explained in terms of the obvious dangers and disadvantages in driving on the 'wrong' side of the road. Likewise, there are similar reasons for the acceptance of priority conventions for traffic at crossroads (Schotter, 1981). Whilst the game-theoretic explanation of these phenomena has a superficial attractiveness, other closely related examples cannot be explained so easily and they result in a challenge to utilitarian or game-theoretic explanations.

Take, for instance, the introduction of the law making the wearing of seat belts compulsory in the U.K. in 1983. Contemporary surveys show that a large number of drivers did not wear seat belts before the law was enacted, but afterwards this number was reduced to a tiny minority. Of course this switch of behavior can be explained by reference to the penalties of breaking the law, the disutility of being singled out for the disapproval of others, and so on. There is also the matter of the prominent information campaign on the safety benefits of the seat belt which may have drawn the drivers' attention to the benefits of wearing the seat belts and the 'costs' of doing otherwise.

But are these explanations entirely convincing? After all, the chances of being detected not wearing a seat belt by the police are relatively small. In addition the information campaign was well under way before 1983, but its independent effects do not seem to have been so great as the enactment of the law.

A more convincing explanation is that the law itself had a powerful legitimizing influence on the drivers. Consequently their goals and preferences actually changed in favor of a safer course of action. The authority of the law had the effect not simply of changing behavior by the introduction of penalties or the perception of costs and benefits. In addition it changed those individuals themselves and their goals. The practice of wearing seat belts became embodied in habit and widely rationalized by a widespread belief in their contribution to reducing injury and death.

In addition, Schotter's theory highlights some of the important functions of institutions and conventions, but throws insufficient light on the processes through which an institution grows and dies. It is simply assumed that an institution will arise because it is efficacious in the context of rational behavior by agents. By excluding such matters as uncertainty and tactical surprise,[8] new institutional models such as Schotter's do not involve the possibility of institutional breakdown through the disruption of conventions and routines. This matter will be raised further in the discussion of the old institutionalism below.

Hayek and Spontaneous Order

The economists of the Austrian school contrast with the majority, neoclassical view in several very important respects, particularly in the rejection of equilibrium theorizing and in the greater emphasis given to problems of information and the role of knowledge in the economic process. However, in other respects the neoclassicals and Austrians share common ground. This is particularly the case in regard to their inheritance of classic liberal ideology. Whilst the Austrians do not endorse the rigid preference functions of neoclassical theory, economic agents are still regarded as rational maximizers, in a sense. Indeed, for the Austrians, action is purposeful and by definition rational (Mises, 1949). They are 'maximizers' in the obvious sense that they are pursuing their own purposes to the greatest possible extent.

Furthermore, in making the formation of expectation and decision exogenous, Hayek again conforms to the individualistic tradition in economic theory. Just as neoclassical theorists put the formation and molding of individual tastes and preferences beyond the scope of their analysis, for Hayek (1948: 67) the task of explaining the springs of conscious action is a matter for 'psychology but not for economics . . . or any other social science'.

In general, Austrian theorists seem to argue either that individuals bear no significant influence on the environment, or that it is beyond the scope of economic theory to inquire any further as to how purposes and actions may be determined. Whilst the analyses may be different they have a common effect: to exclude such matters entirely from the domain of economic inquiry. Despite his theoretical radicalism, Hayek takes the orthodox view that choice is the 'first cause', without asking what are the preconditions of and influences on choice itself. *De gustibus non est disputandum* is a slogan behind which both neoclassicals and Austrians can unite.

A consequence of this insular attitude is to disregard the impact of advances in psychology and other social sciences in the understanding of the processes and structures governing human action. Particularly, the link between the cognitive processes and the formation of goals and expectations, on the one hand, and the social and cultural environment, on the other, is downplayed or ignored.

A view advanced here is that there are external influences molding the purposes and actions of individuals, but that action is not entirely determined by them. The environment is influential but it does not completely determine either what the individual aims to do or what he or she may achieve. There are actions which may be uncaused, but at the same time there are patterns of behavior that may relate to the cultural or institutional environment within which the person acts. Action, in short, is partially determined, and partially indeterminate: partly predictable but partly unforseeable.

This line of discussion is relevant to Hayek's (1982) concept of 'spontaneous order'. Much of his argument that norms and conventions can arise, as it were, spontaneously, through the interaction of individuals is interesting and instructive. Note, however, that it is still based on the idea of the abstract individual. An order is defined essentially as a state of affairs in which people can *'form correct expectations'* because of the existence of some pattern or regularity in social life. (Hayek, 1982: Volume 1, 36). Thus when Hayek writes that 'a spontaneous order results from the individual elements adapting themselves to circumstances' (p. 41) he means that behavior may adapt given the information and constraints that are presented. The adaptation in behavior results primarily from a change in information or perception, not from a change in the fundamental nature of the given individual or of his or her preferences.[9]

Hayek's recent work is an advance on much orthodox thinking, in that norms and conventions do not appear mysteriously from outside, and he attempts to explain them in a sophisticated way as the unintended consequences of inter-related individual acts.[10] But, characteristically, he still regards individual purposes and preferences as being exogenous to the system. But order does not simply affect perspectives and expectations, it affects individuals themselves.

Similarly, Robert Sugden (1986: vii) argues that 'if individuals pursue their own interests in a state of anarchy, order . . . can arise spontaneously'. However, it is not considered that the individual's 'own' interests may themselves be molded and structured in a social process. As Anthony Giddens (1982: 8) puts it, both human subjects and social institutions are *'constituted in and through recurrent practices'*. Thus, despite their laudable appeals to an evolutionary conception of the emergence of social institutions, Hayek, Sugden and others do not consider the evolution of purposes and preferences themselves.

For the purposes of their theoretical enquiry, individuals are regarded as if they are born with a fixed personality; they are not constituted through social processes. The analysis has then to proceed from these given individuals to examine the spontaneous order that may emerge; it does not consider the kind of individual that may emerge from a social order of a given type, and contribute further to the evolution of the social order in the future.

Once the preferences and purposes of the individual are taken as endogenous, then the idea of the 'spontaneous order' can take different forms. A process of cumulative, or circular, causation is possible. There can be a 'virtuous' circle where civilized behavior is both built up by, and contributes to, cohesive social norms. But also the circle can be 'vicious', in that a shortage of solidarity and trust may accelerate a propensity for individuals to further diminish their tolerance or altruism, thus advancing the process of social decay.

The fact that an order may appear to be spontaneous, and resulting from individuals pursuing their ends, itself gives it no sanctity or moral priority over any other order that may arise. The fact that a given order has emerged and reproduced itself through time indicates that it is molding and forming individual goals and intentions as much as it is a reflection of them. More than in the limited sense of forming expectations, the order helps to form the individual, just as the acts of the individual help to form the order.

A fully evolutionary view would take into consideration both the emergence, and effect of, the cultural and institutional framework on the purposes and actions of the individual. In this richer sense we are able to appreciate the significance of the past in structuring the present, as well as the intended or unintended consequences of present acts in forming the institutions of the future.

Old Institutionalism versus the Older Orthodox Assumptions

It is beyond the scope of this work to give a full critique of the orthodox assumptions outlined above. For instance, given some well-known defences of the maximization hypothesis (Friedman, 1953; Boland, 1981) it is not sufficient to retort that it is unrealistic, even despite profound misgivings by neoclassical theorists themselves (e.g., Arrow, 1982) when faced by the difficulties of reconciling the hypothesis with data on choices in situations of uncertainty or risk.

As many defenders of orthodox theory have pointed out, no scientific theory can ever be fully realistic. Some simplifying assumptions must be made. It should be added, furthermore, that facts do not speak for themselves, and are always infused with the concepts and theories of the observer. This does not, of course, mean that the orthodox assumptions are valid. The argument here is that orthodox theory cannot be refuted or dislodged simply by pointing at 'facts' or the 'real world', despite an acceptance that facts have a role in theoretical discourse and evaluation.

Veblen's Critique of Economic Man

Veblen's famous (1919) critique of economic man as 'a lightning calculator of pleasures and pains' is sometimes dismissed as a caricature.

However, as well as its rhetorical force, Veblen does foreshadow some of the later and more elaborate theoretical critiques. The ironic 'lightning calculator' phrase suggests that the problems of global calculation of maximization opportunities are ignored by the neoclassical theorists. This reminds the modern reader of Simon's (1957) idea of limited computational capacity and 'bounded rationality'.

In describing economic man as having 'neither antecedent nor consequent', Veblen identifies the inert and mechanistic picture of the agent in neoclassical theory. Of course, he was off the mark to associate this picture with Austrian theorists such as Carl Menger, but regarding neoclassical theorists and the utilitarian calculus of pleasure and pain his strictures are accurate. What Veblen failed to create was an adequate alternative picture, reinstating choice through a recognition of uncertainty and indeterminacy. In places Veblen's argument veers back toward determinism, in others there is scope for the individual as a 'prime mover'.

What is not widely recognized is that Veblen gave further grounds for rejecting orthodox assumptions, other than on the basis of their unrealism. As Thomas Sowell (1967) points out, Veblen (1919: 221) accepted that to be 'serviceable' a hypothesis need 'not be true to life'. He understood that economic man and similar conceptions were 'not intended as a competent expression of fact' but represented an 'expedient of abstract reasoning' (p. 142).

Veblen's crucial argument against orthodox theory was that it was inadequate for the theoretical purpose at hand. His intention was to analyse the processes of change and transformation in the modern economy. Neoclassical theory was defective in this respect because it indicated 'the conditions of survival to which any innovation is subject, supposing the innovation to have taken place, not the conditions of variational growth' (Veblen, 1919: 176–77). But what Veblen was seeking was precisely a theory as to why such innovations take place, not a theory which muses over equilibrium conditions after technological possibilities are established. 'The question', he wrote, 'is not how things stabilize themselves in a "static state", but how they endlessly grow and change.' (Veblen, 1954: 8).

Thus in his criticisms of orthodox theory Veblen put great stress both on the processes of economic evolution and technological transformation, and the manner in which action is molded by circumstances. He saw the individual's conduct as being influenced by relations of an institutional nature: 'Not only is the individual's conduct hedged about and directed by his habitual relations to his fellows in the group, but these relations, being of an institutional character, vary as the institutional scene varies' (Veblen, 1909: 245). He rejects the continuously calculating, marginally adjusting agent of neoclassical theory to place stress on inertia and habit instead: 'The situation of today shapes the institutions of tomorrow through a selective, coercive process, by acting upon men's habitual view of things, and so altering or fortifying a point of view or a mental attitude handed down from the past' (Veblen, 1899: 190).

It is particularly in regard to the medium- and long-period that tastes and preferences, as well as technology, must be seen to change. Bearing the influence of the institutionalists, this argument was put eloquently by Frank Knight:

> Wants are usually treated as *the* fundamental data, the ultimate driving force in economic activity, and in a short-run view of problems this is scientifically legitimate. But in the long-run it is just as clear that wants are dependent variables, that they are largely caused and formed by economic activity. The case is somewhat like that of a river and its channel; for the time being the channel locates the river, but in the long run it is the other way (1924: 262–63).

Habits, Genes and Evolution

Habits play a crucial role in Veblen's theory that is worthy of examination here. Economic institutions are seen as complexes of habits, roles and conventional behavior. Habits are essentially nondeliberative, and even unconscious, contrasting with the Austrian view that all action is purposeful, and with the neoclassical idea that all action is determined by single-valued preference functions. To some extent the idea of habits conflicts with the presuppositions of classic liberalism, in the sense that it undermines notions such as 'the individual is the best judge of his welfare', and of 'consumer sovereignty' and of the general inviolability of individual judgment.[11]

Notably, both Veblen, modern neoclassical theorists and new institutionalists such as Williamson appeal to a Darwinian evolutionary analogy. In particular, since Armen Alchian's classic (1950) article the basis for the supposition that firms are maximizing profits has often been the suggestion that such firms are 'fittest', more likely to survive, and more likely to become typical as less able firms drop out.

However, as Sidney Winter (1964) argues, the neoclassical appeal to Darwinian notions of evolution is unsuccessful because the mechanisms involved in the sustenance and procreation of such maximizing behavior are not specified. As yet, no neoclassical theorist has explained satisfactorily how a firm, once it happens to maximize, will continue to do so. Generally, neoclassical theory has failed to explain how the characteristics of a 'fit' firm are passed on to other, succeeding, new firms. Consequently the neoclassical invocation of Darwin fails.

According to modern biology, in the natural world the mechanism through which characteristics are passed from one generation to the next is the gene. The neo-Darwinian argument is that particular genes contribute to characteristics and behavior which are conducive to survival. Through 'natural selection' genes aiding survival will tend to become more prominent in succeeding generations. In contrast, in neoclassical theory there is no explicit and equivalent mechanism to pass on analogous characteristics from one firm to the next.

However, once we move outside the confines of orthodox economics, and incorporate some of the features of the above discussion of social institutions, we can find mechanisms which play a similar evolutionary role to that of the gene in the natural world. Such mechanisms are organizational structures, habits and routines. Whilst these are more malleable and do not mutate in the same way as their analogue in biology, structures and routines have a stable and inert quality and tend to sustain and thus 'pass on' their important characteristics through time.

Furthermore, habits and routines can enable the survival and transmission of behavioral patterns from one institution to another. As an important type of example, the skills learned by a worker in a given firm become partially embedded in his or her habits, and these will survive if the person changes employer, or if they are 'taught', explicitly or by imitation, to a colleague. Thus the habits of employees, both within the particular firm and the social culture, act as carriers of information, 'unteachable knowledge' (Penrose, 1959), and skills.

Veblen's ideas on this topic became part of his critique of orthodox capital theory. Not only did he criticise the orthodox failure to distinguish between capital-as-goods and capital-as-money, but also he made some relatively undeveloped remarks concerning the nature of production. For him, production was not a matter of 'inputs' into some mechanical function, but an institutional ensemble of habits and routines: 'the accumulated, habitual knowledge of the ways and means involved . . . the outcome of long experience and experimentation' (Veblen, 1919: 150).

The idea that routines within the firm act as 'genes' to pass on skills and information is adopted by Nelson and Winter (1982: 134–36) and forms a crucial part of their theoretical model of the modern corporation. Despite making no reference to the earlier work of Veblen, their work is much closer to the old institutionalism than the new.

As Nelson and Winter suggest, routines do not act as genes in the strict biological sense. In contrast to Darwinian biology, the inheritance of *acquired* characteristics is possible. Thus the true analogue to social and economic evolution in the science of biology is not the work of Charles Darwin—as Veblen believed—but the earlier notion of Jean Baptiste Lamarck. He argued that mutations occur because an organism passes on newly acquired adaptations of behavior to its offspring through heredity. Lamarckian theory has fallen out of favor in biology because of its failure to explain or find evidence for a mechanism through which acquired characteristics could be passed on to offspring. However, in contrast, in the social world acquired characteristics, that is, the changed features of habits and routines, can be inherited. Thus in some senses Lamarckian theory applies to social and economic evolution. Ironically, only by abandoning orthodox presuppositions can a tenable evolutionary analogy find in economics a proper place.

The Fate of Institutional Economics

Several limitations of the old institutionalism have been briefly mentioned already. It has been noted for instance that for Veblen and his contemporaries, problems of knowledge and uncertainty are not given the central place as in the later writings of Keynes, Hayek or Shackle. In addition, Veblen's duality between institutions on the one hand and technology on the other contains many problems and dangers. For instance, institutions can be regarded merely as constraints on some pre-eminent and unqualified technological progress, giving science and technology an objective and hallowed quality and an unproblematic source of social evaluation concerning worth and welfare.

Such pitfalls are evident in Veblen's work, and perhaps even more so in some of the later institutionalists. But perhaps the greatest deficiency in Veblen's work was his failure to develop sufficiently the fundamentals of an alternative economic theory. This is particularly important in regard to the absence of an alternative conception of human agency to replace the neoclassical one he was so keen to reject. In facing the fundamental problem of all social theory—the relations and articulations between action and structure—Veblen's rather nineteenth-century view of science got him into some contradictions and tangles which David Seckler (1975) has enumerated. This, however, is not too surprising. Most of Veblen's work was completed before Albert Einstein, Werner Heisenberg and other theoretical physicists shook modern science to its foundations.

In evaluating Veblen as an economic theorist it should be noted that his works are not as innovative or pathbreaking as those of the founding fathers, such as Adam Smith; they do not contain a highly complex and comprehensive, interconnected structure of concepts and arguments, as in the economic writings of Marx; nor the intense flashes of insight and understanding which change, irreversibly, one's perception of the world once they are understood, as in the *General Theory* of Keynes; nor the extended, diligent effort to reconcile formal arguments and assumptions with the perceived facts of the world, as in Marshall's *Principles*; nor the sustained development of a single, crucial theme, as in the work of Simon. Indeed, Veblen had an explicit hostility to intellectual 'symmetry and system-building' (1919: 68). In sum, as Sowell (1967: 198) concludes, 'Veblen can neither be dismissed nor classed among the immortals'.

Veblen's hostility to theoretical system-building opened the door for an even more impressionistic approach to economics amongst his followers. Thus it is not difficult to see how institutionalism eventually became bogged down after Veblen's pioneering work. After establishing the importance of institutions, routines, and habits, it underlined the value of largely descriptive work on the nature and function of politico-economic institutions. Whilst this was of value it became the predominant practice for institutionalist writers. They became data gatherers *par excellence*. Gunnar Myrdal (1958: 254), an institutionalist himself, has gone so far as to state that traditional American institutional economics was marked by a flagrant 'naive empiricism' and did not give due precedence to matters of theory.

The error here was largely methodological and epistemological, and committed by many institutionalists with the exception of Veblen himself and a few others. It was a crucial mistake simply to clamor for descriptive 'realism', by gathering more and more data, or by painting a more and more detailed picture of particular economic institutions. Contrary to the empiricist view of many institutionalists, the facts do not speak for themselves. There are no perceived facts without pre-existing concepts or theories.

Whilst empiricism remained the dominant implicit and explicit philosophy for Anglo-American theory, the theoretical development of institutionalism became frozen. It reached a plateau in the U.S.A. and in the U.K. it never became established. In some quarters institutionalism became synonomous with a naive descriptive approach, by both practitioner and critic alike. When formalistic and mathematical developments in economics accelerated rapidly after the second world war, the old institutionalism was left behind. It had no alternative, comprehensive theoretical system to challenge the neoclassical renaissance.

However, with economics today in a degree of disarray, there is an opportunity for renewed theoretical development. This is particularly in regard to modern developments in social theory which overcome the pitfalls of either abstract individualism or crude holism.[12] These have been pictured by Tony Lawson (1987: 969), who rightly remarks that 'individual agency and social structures and context are equally relevant for analysis—each presupposes each other. Thus any reductionist account stressing analytical primacy for either individual agents or for social "wholes" must be inadequate'.

Both the new and the old institutionalism have something to offer but, above all, the old warnings about proceeding on classic liberal assumptions should not be ignored. In this respect the old institutionalism retains some advantages over the new.

Notes

1. In part, this paper originally derives from talks given at Birmingham Polytechnic, Copenhagen Business School and Roskilde University from December 1987 to March 1988. A paper along these lines was presented at the History of Economics Society, June 1988 annual meeting at the University of Toronto; the Economic and Social Research Council, European-North American Workshop on Institutional Economics, June 1988, London; and the first *Review of Political Economy* Conference in Malvern, August 1988. The author is grateful to participants at all these sessions, to Bob Coats, Tony Lawson and Ian Steedman, and especially to Richard Langlois as discussant at Toronto, for probing questions and critical remarks, and for the comments of anonymous referees. The author has been molded in the process.

2. For discussions and critiques of methodological individualism see Hodgson (1988: Chapter 3) and Lukes (1973: Chapter 17).

3. Langlois' (1986) important collection of essays in the new institutional economics includes works by Schotter and Williamson, whilst for Langlois himself the work of Hayek in particular is formative. However, the collection also contains essays by Heiner and Nelson. Heiner's is highly innovative and does not easily fit into either the new or the old institutionalist category, and Nelson and Winter's (1982) evolutionary theory of routines as genes is very close to the old institutionalism, particularly of Veblen.

4. The neoclassical institutionalism of North, Olson et al. has been critically discussed by Field (1979; 1981; 1984) and Mjoset (1985).

5. Hence Simon's fascination with the analysis of the game of chess. In principle, the players have all the information with which to calculate an

optimal strategy, leading to a win or at least a draw. However, the game-theoretic analysis is so complex that it cannot be completed even with a mammoth computer, and the devised computer algorithms to play chess do not attempt to derive the optimal solution but to obtain one which is 'good enough' (see, for example, Simon, 1976).

6. Unfortunately, Schotter does not refer to other theorists that have reached this conclusion. See, in particular, the work of Richardson (1959; 1960). For other references see Hodgson (1988).

7. Cognitive theory deals with cases where, due to both computational limitations and radical uncertainty, individuals are forced to use pre-existing conceptual schema to be selective and reject much of the given information. Cognitive anthropologists argue that these schema are molded by culture and social institutions. For related discussions on imperfectly used information see Heiner (1983), on the role of culture see Hargreaves Heap (1986–87) and for references to cognitive theory see Hodgson (1988). Despite the neglect of such information problems by Veblen and others, they are regarded as crucial by many modern contributors to the old institutionalist *Journal of Economic Issues* (Melody, 1987).

8. Uncertainty (in the sense of Knight and Keynes, i.e. involving no calculable probability) does not play a central role in game theory because the actors are aware of both the menu of strategic options and the payoffs in each case. As George Shackle (1972: Chapter 36) points out in his critique, game theory excludes the phenomenon of tactical surprise: 'Surprise is the exploitation of the opponent's lack of knowledge, or of his reliance on what he wrongly believes to be knowledge' (p. 423). In reality, Shackle argues, the '. . . most powerful resource available to a real-life contestant may be to exploit the ignorance of . . . contestants concerning the ultimate conditions of the contest' (p. 426). For this reason the structure of competition and markets is not adequately represented by the game-theoretic tableau.

9. Of course, the (slightly) hidden agenda behind the theory of 'spontaneous order' is to provide further liberal arguments for the minimal state. Whilst in some important cases, such as the emergence of language, the theoretical argument carries considerable force, in others, such as the evolution of money, the legitimizing and statutory functions of the state are downplayed. A similar neglect of the state is found in Williamson (1985).

10. The characterization of Hayek's recent work does, however, contain some problems. In the 1970s and 1980s Hayek has put increasing emphasis on the evolutionary aspect of his theory, the stressing the role of 'cultural selection' on the basis not of individuals but groups (Hayek, 1982; 1988). Whilst this to some extent undermines Hayek's earlier commitment to the 'abstract individual' (see Gray, 1984), it creates problems for, and internal contradictions in his thought. In particular, to embrace any genuine notion of socioeconomic

evolution must be to undermine Hayek's (1948) earlier view that changing tastes and preferences are not to be explained. For further inconsistencies created by Hayek's increasing attachment to evolutionary explanations see Viktor Vanberg (1986).

11. Note, however, that Michael Polanyi (1957; 1967) manages to retain a good dose of classic liberal individualism whilst putting great stress on the function of habits and tacit knowledge. Hayek in particular has been influenced by Polanyi's work. Whilst the stress on habits and tacit knowledge is positive, its function in Polanyi's and Hayek's work is to rule out any attempt to assemble such uncodifiable information for the purposes of a central plan. They go too far, however, in ruling out the possibility and desirability of *some* cautious central planning and state intervention, to establish guidelines and conventions for the economy as a whole, as in the case of industrial policy, indicative planning, and Keynesian demand management, for example.

12. See in particular Giddens (1984).

References

Alchian, A. A. 1950: Uncertainty, Evolution and Economic Theory. *Journal of Political Economy* 58, 211–22.

Arrow, K. J. 1974: *The Limits of Organization*. New York: Norton.

———. 1982: Risk Perception in Psychology and Economics. *Economic Inquiry* 20, 1–9.

Asch, S. E. 1952: *Social Psychology*. New York: Prentice-Hall.

Boland, L. A. 1981: On the Futility of Criticizing the Neoclassical Maximization Hypothesis. *American Economic Review* 71, 1031–36.

Coase, R. H. 1937: The Nature of the Firm. *Economica* 4, 386–405.

Field, A. J. 1979: On the Explanation of Rules Using Rational Choice Models. *Journal of Economic Issues* 13, 49–72.

———. 1981: The Problem with Neoclassical Institutional Economics: A Critique with Special Reference to the North/Thomas Model of Pre-1500 Europe. *Explorations in Economic History* 18, 174–98.

———. 1984: Microeconomics, Norms and Rationality. *Economic Development and Cultural Change* 32, 683–711.

Fox. A. 1974: *Beyond Contract: Work, Power and Trust Relations*. London: Faber and Faber.

Friedman, M. 1953: The Methodology of Positive Economics. In Friedman, M., *Essays in Positive Economics*, Chicago: University of Chicago Press, 3–43.

Giddens, A. 1982: *Profiles and Critiques in Social Theory*. London: Macmillan.

———. 1984: *The Constitution of Society: Outline of the Theory of Structuration*. Cambridge: Polity Press.

Gray, J. 1984: *Hayek on Liberty*. Oxford: Basil Blackwell.

Hargreaves Heap, S. P. 1986–87: Risk and Culture: A Missing Link in the Post Keynesian Tradition. *Journal of Post Keynesian Economics* 9, 267–78.

Hayek, F. A. 1948: *Individualism and Economic Order*. Chicago: University of Chicago Press.

———. 1982: *Law, Legislation and Liberty*, 3-vol. combined ed. London: Routledge and Kegan Paul.

———. 1988: *The Fatal Conceit: The Errors of Socialism*. In Bartley, W. W., editor, *Collected works of Friedrich August Hayek*, vol. I, London: Routledge.

Heiner, R. A. 1983: The Origin of Predictable Behavior. *American Economic Review* 73, 560–95.

Hodgson, G. M. 1988: *Economics and Institutions: A Manifesto for a Modern Institutional Economics*. Cambridge: Polity Press and Philadelphia: University of Pennsylvania Press.

Kay, N. M. 1979: *The Innovating Firm: A Behavioral Theory of Corporate R and D*. London: Macmillan.

Keegan, J. 1976: *The Face of Battle: A Study of Agincourt, Waterloo and the Somme*. London: Jonathan Cape.

Knight, F. H. 1924: The Limitations of Scientific Method in Economics. In Tugwell, R. G., editor, *The Trend of Economics*, New York: Alfred Knopf.

Koestler, A. 1967: *The Ghost in the Machine*. London: Hutchinson.

Langlois, R. N., ed., 1986: *Economics as a Process: Essays in the New Institutional Economics*. Cambridge: Cambridge University Press.

Lawson, A. 1987. The Relative/Absolute Nature of Knowledge and Economic Analysis. *Economic Journal* 97, 951–70.

Lukes, S. 1973: *Individualism*. Oxford: Basil Blackwell.

Melody, W. H. 1987: Information: An Emerging Dimension of Institutional Analysis. *Journal of Economic Issues* 21, 1313–39.

Mises, L., von, 1949: *Human Action: A Treatise on Economics*. London: William Hodge.

Mjoset, L. 1985: The Limits of Neoclassical Institutionalism. *Journal of Peace Research* 22, 79–86.

Myrdal, G. 1958: *Value in Social Theory*. New York: Harper.

Nelson, R. R. and Winter, S. G. 1982: *An Evolutionary Theory of Economic Change*. Cambridge, MA: Harvard University Press.

North, D. C. and Thomas, R. P. 1973: *The Rise of the Western World*. London: Cambridge University Press.

Olson, M., Junior, 1965: *The Logic of Collective Action*. Cambridge, MA: Harvard University Press.

———. 1982: *The Rise and Decline of Nations*. New Haven: Yale University Press.

Penrose, E. T. 1959: *The Theory of the Growth of the Firm*. Oxford: Basil Blackwell.

Polanyi, M. 1957: *Personal Knowledge: Towards a Post-Critical Philosophy*. London: Routledge and Kegan Paul.

———. 1967: *The Tacit Dimension*. London: Routledge and Kegan Paul.

Posner, R. 1973: *Economic Analysis of Law*. Boston: Little, Brown.

Richardson, G. B. 1959: Equilibrium, Expectations and Information. *The Economic Journal*. 69, 223–37.

———. 1960: *Information and Investment*. Oxford: Oxford University Press.

Schotter, A. 1981: *The Economic Theory of Social Institutions*. Cambridge: Cambridge University Press.

———. 1985: *Free Market Economics: A Critical Appraisal*. New York: St. Martin's Press.

Seckler, D. 1975: *Thorstein Veblen and the Institutionalists*. London: Macmillan.

Shackle, G. L. S. 1972: *Epistemics and Economics*. Cambridge: Cambridge University Press.

Simon, H. A. 1957: *Models of Man: Social and Rational*. New York: Wiley.

———. 1976: From Substantive to Procedural Rationality. In Latsis, S., editor, *Method and Appraisal in Economics*, Cambridge: Cambridge University Press.

Sowell, T. 1967: The 'Evolutionary' Economics of Thorstein Veblen. *Oxford Economic Papers* 19, 177–98.

Sugden, R. 1986: *The Economics of Rights, Co-operation and Welfare*. Oxford: Blackwell.

Ullman-Margalit, E. 1977: *The Emergence of Norms*. Oxford: Oxford University Press.

Vanberg, V. 1986: Spontaneous Market Order and Social Rules: A Critical Examination of F. A. Hayek's Theory of Cultural Evolution. *Economics and Philosophy* 2, 75–100.

Veblen, T. B. 1899: *The Theory of the Leisure Class: An Economic Study of Institutions*. New York: Macmillan.

———. 1909: The Limitations of Marginal Utility. *Journal of Political Economy* 17, 235–45 (reprinted in Veblen, 1936).

———. 1919: *The Place of Science in Modern Civilization and Other Essays*. New York: Hübsch.

———. 1936: *What Veblen Taught*. New York: Augustus Kelly.

———. 1954: *Essays in Our Changing Order*. New York: The Viking Press.

Williamson, O. E. 1975: *Markets and Hierarchies: Analysis and Anti-trust Implications: A Study in the Economics of Internal Organization*. New York: Free Press.

———. 1985: *The Economic Institutions of Capitalism: Firms, Markets, Relational Contracting*. London: Macmillan.

Winter, S. G., Junior, 1964: Economic 'Natural Selection' and the Theory of the Firm. *Yale Economic Essays* 4, 225–72.

8

SOCIAL ECONOMICS: A SOLIDARIST PERSPECTIVE

WILLIAM R. WATERS

The major concern of social economics is explaining the economy in its broadest aspects; that is, showing how man deals with the ordinary business of using human and physical resources to achieve a level of material comfort. Explanation includes cultural, political, and ethical details as they are needed for a full understanding. As in any economics, there are three parts to social economics. First is the philosophical base of the social economist, which may or may not be a reflection of the philosophical base or ethos of the society he is studying. Social economics (or any economics) builds upon it. It is the "hard core" in the recent popular literature of the philosophy of science. The second part of the discipline is a description of the significant characteristics of the economy. The economist must observe the multiplicity of economic reality and abstract those characteristics that are substantive. The two together, the philosophical premises and the empirical observations, will determine the third part of the discipline, social economic policy. Policy formulation is thus a mix of the first two.

This paper is one social economist's sketch of the three components of social economics. It starts with an introduction to the philosophical base, then continues with an outline of the significant core of the economic system, contending that it differs from the empirical base routinely offered by economists in principles courses and otherwise. Finally, it refers to social economic policy, the social architectonic dimension needed for human social economic development.

The Hard Core

Contemporary literature in the philosophy of science, especially the work of T. J. Kuhn and Irme Lakatos, has made scientists more aware of preconceptions. The deepest premises of the scholar lie quietly concealed. They are neither defined rigorously nor defended against refutation. Scientists are usually not concerned with them. They are sustaining parameters; they change only as a scientific revolution occurs. Then, new sets of "research programs" are launched. This acceptance of premises occurs among scientists operating with the normal paradigm. There is always a minority of scientists/ economists who do not wish to discuss the hard core because they are very critical of it. These critical economists believe it is defective and that, as a consequence, unfortunate social economic policy is promoted. One of the most popular of Keynes' insights rings true.

. . . The ideas of economists and political philosophers, both when they are right and when they are wrong are more powerful than is commonly understood. Indeed the world is ruled by little else. Practical men, who believe themselves to be quite exempt from any intellectual influence, are usually the slaves of some defunct economist. Madmen in authority, who hear voices in the air, are distilling their frenzy from some academic scribbler of a few years back. I am sure that the power of vested interests is vastly exaggerated compared with the gradual encroachment of ideas . . . soon or late, it is ideas, not vested interests which are dangerous for good or evil. [Keynes, pp. 383–84]

Keynes' successful leadership of a scientific revolution was in response to what he perceived to be a defective social philosophical base laid by academics and to its consequent harmful policy implications.

Spiro Latsis made the hard core of a conventional economics broadly known. Elba Brown-Collier used Latsis' formulation to contrast the premises of neoclassical macroeconomics with that of Post-Keynesian economics. Her treatment suggests another contrast: the classical hard core with solidarism. Conventional "classical" hard core combines a set of four premises about the economy:[1]

a. The *law of nature* prevails. As such, the economy is self regulating. While there are exceptions to the self-regulating process, for example, those described by Smith in *The Wealth of Nations* which include government control of law and order, military defense and public projects unable to make it on their own, such intervention is an imperfect state of affairs.
b. The *individual*, the basic unit of the economy, is governed by the laws of nature. He (she) is a part of the "natural lawfulness" and as such acts according to a pattern of self love; that is, behaves in a

calculated, self-interested manner. The individual maximizes utility. Such selfish conduct is not disruptive of social harmony however. Rather, nature provides a restraining force to protect harmony, namely, the effectively operating competitive market. The impersonal forces of the market are the source of the significant decisions made in the economic sector of society.

c. *Certainty.* By the great power of reason, economic scientists are able to understand the workings of the economy. They have correct knowledge of its relevant features. Uncertainty is ruled out, allowing economic theorists to develop determinate models and for the discipline to be acclaimed a science. Keynes' exogenous variable, investment, depending as it does on non-predictable "animal spirits," is ruled out of macro models by conventional or "Neo-Keynesian" economists because it precludes determinateness. One can't build a scientific, heuristic system with a key variable that is erratic.

d. *Contracts.* Classical (conventional economic) research programs assume people behave most significantly by negotiation. Economic and political behavior is characterized by contractual behavior; for example, typical labor arrangements in industrialized economies are handled via wage contracts between employers and employees.

We need not elaborate further on this hard core of contemporary economic science except to note its once revolutionary nature. A child of the 17–18th century Enlightenment, it offers a substitute for medieval thinking. Each of four premises replaces one prominent in Medieval Christian social thought but the first is especially radically different; that is, the premise that society operates according to a set of natural laws, so that decision-making by authorities is reduced to a minimum. As argued below, solidarism is a social philosophy diametrically opposed to the conventional hard core.

Before suggesting a contrasting solidarist philosophy, it may be helpful to first discuss the Enlightenment hard core as described by the solidarist, Goetz Briefs, and the origin of the concept of utility, a key note of the conventional paradigm.

While the philosophy of science controversy, involving Popper, Kuhn, Lakatos, et al., may have been responsible for bringing the underlying premises of conventional economics to the attention of mainstream economists, recognition of these premises was in the literature all the while for those who would seek out the works of Pesch, Briefs, Mueller and other solidarists. Goetz Briefs especially felt it necessary to frequently identify for his readers the philosophical premises of "market liberalism" that developed out of the social philosophy of the Enlightenment. These premises, as he explained them, approximated the hard core of conventional economics described above. Writing in 1944, he argued that one must be aware of them to understand the historical evolution of the West, ". . . of [the development of] the dominant liberal societies in the Western world from self-interested individualism to a society of competing vested-interested groups to one dominated and ruled by the strongest of the groups"; that is to say, to Briefs, there is a logical and natural social progression from individualism to vested-interest pluralism to totalism, given its philosophical foundations. We of the West have arrived at the second stage, vested-interest group pluralism; historical logic propels us toward what Briefs termed totalism because a society of competing self-interest groups is unstable. The strongest of the group is likely to take over. No one can predict what will happen. Briefs was not a determinist: man has both the capability and wisdom to build something better in response to changing social conditions. But historical logic propels history in this direction. The original liberal society was a combination of liberalism and individualism, where liberalism is a philosophy of negation, "of emancipation from a previous state of society;" individualism springs from the negation. The individual (rather than the institutions of society) determines the whole range of economic affairs regarding "work, investment, disinvestment, savings, buying, selling, technology, in addition to strict rights of private property and freedom of contract"; the individual is self liable, success and failure are his; the consequence is the supreme rule of self interest, "the motor that drives economic life"; and "competition is the mechanism which holds the market forces in check and directs the factors of production toward their optimum allocation." [Briefs, p. 239]

Also important to market liberalism and the hard core of its economies is the origin of the concept of utility as a keynote of conventional economics. With the exception of some eighteenth century Italian economists, the concept of the individual optimizing utility is a Franco-British phenomenon. The French, however, appear to have had a more direct and clear-cut role in its development than the British. British scholarship was distracting. A contemporary group of neo-Liberals in France demonstrate the full descent of classical economics with utility as its central component as stemming from a synthesis, effected by the Abbé de Condillac, of Cartesian rationalism ("without the innate ideas") and Lockean sensationalism. Condillac delineated value as utility, and with it as the center piece, the "science" was handed down from Condillac to Turgot, to Say, to Walras, developing along the way.

These French scholars say that the rationally-calculating individual existed early and consistently in the French economics literature. There would have been no need for the British to "discover" utility in the marginal revolution of the 1870s had not their writers, Adam Smith, Ricardo, and others, chosen to travel on a wasteful detour trying to show labor as the source of value. Michael Lutfalla points out that, with his synthesis, Condillac could not help but derive value [in economics] from utility and did so in his tract, *Le Commerce et le Gouvernement consideres l'un relativement a l'autre*, of 1776, a year of great prominence in the publishing of tracts on liberty. To Condillac, "exchange [is] derived from a comparison of individual utilities." [Lutfalla, pp. 2–3] The point is that conventional economics, as a natural science, developed in a more consistent and orthodox way in France than in Britain. Thinking of conventional economics as achieving allocative and technical efficiency and maximizing welfare in a state of Paretian optimality, one does not need the British contributions.

The hard core of solidarism is an alternative to the classics. It is, in fact, older than classicism. To repeat Briefs' phrase, it is the ethos "of the previous state of society from which liberals emancipated themselves." [Briefs, p. 239] The contrast of classicism and solidarism is striking. There are also four components of the hard core of solidarism:

a. Societal decision-making stems from *institutions* endowed with the values of the culture in which they are formed, this in contrast to the premises of natural lawfulness and self-regulation of conventional economics. Philosophical anthropology, as Franz Mueller calls it, is therefore most significant, both in how societies are formed and in how we study them. The law of nature of conventional economics is replaced with value-laden institutions and social groups. Government is one of the important institutions. Government's role is a positive but limited one, constrained by the principle of subsidiarity.

b. The basic economic unit is the *person* whose decisions are at times rational in the calculating mold of conventional economics but are apparently more often non-rational (a preferable term to irrational which is commonly in use among conventional economists). It is hard to get convincing evidence that men and women make decisions as described in conventional theory; they appear to act much more erratically than that and are driven by a variety of habits and biases. But the significant difference between the individual of conventional economics and the person of solidarism is that the latter is sacred, and as such each person must respect the sacred status of every other person and in turn may expect respect. The person may not always act for the common benefit, but that is what is expected of him (her), especially in group decision-making. It is assumed that an effective and equitable economy cannot be built on calculated self interest; significant decisions must be made for the common good. A corollary is *cooperation* as a basic organizing principle of social behavior. This contrasts with the concept of competition as the organizing principle of social control in conventional economics. To organize a society on a principle of cooperation is possible since competition is not needed to counter self-love and human greed, the role expected of competition in conventional economics. One may note the recent literature on cooperation. For example, Robert Axelrod shows that cooperation can thrive even in a world made up mainly of egoists. Even more might be done, says Bryce Jones, where enlightened self-interest is "seasoned with the integrating attitudes of justice, duty, loyalty and trust—community." [Compare his review of Axelrod, p. 261] This does not deprive competition of a place in the economy. Rather, it is a rejection of the notion that competition (or the competitive market) is the organizing tool whereby the significant economic questions are answered. It recognizes that people (authorities) make the more crucial decisions and should do so collegially or cooperatively.

c. *Uncertainty.* The premise of certain knowledge, along with the law of nature in the conventional paradigm, is what make economics a "science." There is no place in Walras' general equilibrium system, in the neo-Keynesians' macro model or in Friedman's monetarism for a significant exogenous variable of uncertain value. Science requires determinateness. Solidarism does not accept this principle of certainty, so to the solidarists economics is not a natural science. Economics does not attain "scientific status" because free decision-making is not compatible with the rationalistic assumption of certainty. Economics is a softer discipline—a moral science.

d. *Status.* The sacred person has a status in society that assures him of certain rights that are more basic than contracts. For example, one may not contract away freedom. It has been questioned whether a person may even be permitted to trade labor services. As persons, men and women have inalienable rights. This view conflicts in part with the classical principle of behavior by contract leading to the end of Paretian optimality. Ellerman pushes the dilemma of freedom and the right to trade away freedom to its logical conclusion. If men and women have the freedom and right to contract out their labor, for how long may they do this? A lifetime? Half a lifetime? It is only the law of the land that prevents voluntary slavery, not the philosophical premises of conventional economics. To Ellerman the status of the person must be protected and decision-making in

economic and political settings is that of person to person, as distinguished from person using someone as a non-person or as a thing.
[Compare Ellerman, 1984 and 1986] The philosophical premise of
person as opposed to the Enlightenment-bred concept of the individual is both a Christian concept, and is so used by many solidarists,
[see Goetz Briefs' "Person and Ethos: Person and Individual in
European Thought," reprinted in the *Review of Social Economy*,
December, 1983] and a Kantian one. [For the latter compare
Ellerman, 1986, and Etzioni.]

Illustrations of the continuing spread of the influence of the
classical hard core and the evolution toward utility maximizing and to
contracting, away from community and status are the popularization of
cost-benefit and public choice analyses. Another illustration is the
theorizing of Judge Bork, both in industrial organization economics and
constitutional law. In his theory of constitutional law the only right
(status) protected by the Constitution and its Amendments are those
"gratifications" specified by the Founders and Amenders. Beyond
protecting these, Justices have no legitimate authority; ". . . the point is
that the cases cannot be reconciled on any bases other than the Justices'
personal beliefs about what interests or gratifications ought to be
protected" [Bork, p. 12] Moreover, the specified rights are simply
gratifications that the nation decided to protect constitutionally.

A right is a form of property, and our thinking about the category
of constitutional property might usefully follow the progress of
thought about economic property. We now regard it as thoroughly
old hat, passe and in fact downright tiresome to hear rhetoric about
an inherent right to economic freedom or to economic property.
We no longer believe that economic rights inhere in the individual
because he is an individual. The modern intellectual argues the
proper location and definition of property rights according to
judgments of utility—the capacity of such rights to forward some
other value. [Bork, p. 18]

Franz Mueller refers to the movement from status to contract as the
root problem of contemporary society: ". . . Whether it be called
bourgeois, civil, secular, contractual or rational-legal society, it is this
pragmatic co-existence, this more or less deliberate social construction in
which individual interests are contractually conjoined for more advantageous results, which may be regarded as the root-cause of the social
question of our age." [Mueller, p. 28]

The Empirical Dynamic

An economics comprises three divisions: the philosophical premises mentioned above; the subject matter of the discipline which consists of observing and selecting facts to explain the nature of the economy; and proposals for betterment that result from a commingling of the first two. In short, any economics comprises a hard core, a description of the reality and economic policy.

This section pertains to the second of the divisions, the empirical reality—the task of describing the nature of the economy. Textbooks and the rest of the economics literature are available to teach the elements, but that version is presented by writers schooled in what some social economists consider an alien hard core. Popular observations of the structure and behavior of economic life have been colored by Enlightenment philosophical assumptions: the law of nature, the self-regulatory character of the system and the omnipresence of contractual negotiations. The describers of our economy focus upon utility-calculating individuals and social control by competitive markets. This is a distortion to one whose focus is on the person, his (her) sacred status, the natural propensity to behave cooperatively, and commonplace decision-making by authorities.

The combination of classical philosophical premises and observations of the reality gives us the following: man acts to maximize utility in consumption and production. Such behavior establishes the impersonal forces of supply and demand that determine prices and quantities. Price is the governing parameter to which entrepreneurs respond, being guided by the rational behavioral principles (a) marginal cost equals marginal revenue and (b) the price of labor (and each other factor) equals the value of its marginal product. If markets should operate in a reasonably effective manner, the greatest allocative and technical efficiency will result, leading to Paretian optimality and maximum economic welfare. Where there are serious imperfections, government is directed to intervene. The role of government is very limited, however, because it is believed that government generally makes matters worse. It is usually better to leave things alone. On the macro side, stability is inherent in the system given a proper supply of money, although occasional adjustments of aggregate demand may be called for from time to time. The normal operation of the macro economy with the appropriate adjustments maximizes real income in the short run, and for the future growth of income per capita will proceed depending on the size of saving.

This conception of the nature of the modern economy reflects the description found in the elementary principles texts, as well as in advanced theory courses. It is clearly compatible with the philosophical premises laid down by French and British social philosophers of the Enlightenment period of the eighteenth century, further developed by nineteenth century utilitarian economists and twentieth century positivists.

Is this an objective rendition of the nature of modern society? Not to those who have either inherited or chosen a different hard core. A solidarist, say, observes the economic reality differently and selects other details of the economy as fundamental. A serious problem of objectivity surfaces. The very content of economics, its empirical reality, depends on the hard core that premeates society.

In describing the economic reality, two issues confront us: First, how do we deal with the serious question of objectivity mentioned above? Secondly, what is the realistic alternative to the conventional empirical reality described above?

Schumpeter chose the first issue as the topic of his 1949 presidential address to The American Economic Association, namely, the interference of ideology with the most conscientious attempt at objectivity. His answer to the question of how can you avoid it was that you can't. Ideology will always interfere with objectivity. But, he continued optimistically, it is no misfortune because without ideology we might not proceed at all. It is through ideology that we operate scientifically.

> That prescientific cognitive act which is the source of our ideologies is also the prerequisite of our scientific work. No new departure in any science is possible without it. Through it we acquire new material for our scientific endeavors and something to formulate, to defend, to attack. Our stock of facts and tools grows and rejuvenates itself in the process. And so—though we proceed slowly because of our ideologies we might not procede at all without them. [Schumpeter, 1949, p. 359]

In short, while it is difficult (impossible?) to avoid the hazards of nonobjectivity in the explanation of the economy, it is still necessary to proceed. We must seek an empirical reality.

In dealing with the second issue, one wonders how realistic it is to limit observations to static allocation of physical and human resources on the micro side and to growth of national income on the macro. It is clear, however, why mainstream economists do it. It permits the formulation of determinate models, a prerequisite for a natural science and compatible with that part of the classical hard core that assumes certainty of knowledge. But in doing this, theorists are excluding the heart of the economic process, namely, developmental activity and its effect, dynamic efficiency. The consequence is that the source of economic change is either left out of conventional descriptions and analyses or pushed into the background as peripheral.

An alternative to the empirical reality is to recognize that wherever Western culture dominates, the crucial part of the economic process is creative response to economic change. In the words of a popular commentator on Western culture, the sources of modern technology "are entirely directed towards the production of the means of constant change." [Burke, p. 17] A realistic explication of the nature of the economy focuses upon this mechanism of change. The empirical reality is dynamic. Starting with this emphasis, the central role is given to the creative person as an alternative to the utility-calculating individual and is thus more compatible with a solidarist philosophical position than with the dominating classical one.

The economic process is summarized in the appendix. It is essentially Schumpeterian centering upon a creative vision, supported by funding that gives the economic creator access to society's resources and brings forth an innovation. Characteristics of the innovational process, including some Schumpeterian favorites such as dynamic competition, resistance, creative destruction and the universality of cyclical behavior in a private enterprise society are listed. On the lower left are some other essential ingredients of the economic process that are not purely Schumpeterian but appear to be significant components of the economic reality, namely, the apparently natural working together of firms, industries, and governments, the key contributing role of government and the cooperation and solidarity of workers, managers, and owners as partners in the work place. This framework requires some explanation.

At the heart of economic reality is the change of old production functions and the creating of new ones. Initiating economic improvement is the triad of vision, innovation, and fund creation. Innovation or the launching of the vision in the economy is the most vital. While the ideas and inventions (visions) are necessary, as is the third, financial support to permit access to scarce resources (capital), the most difficult work is in the promoting, organizing, and launching of technological and non-technological changes. It is the innovation that constitutes the creative economic activity and brings forth substantial differences in society. So what is termed here the empirical dynamic is essentially Schumpeter's theory of economic development, but the work of others since Schumpeter enrich it, especially Braudel, Gras, McNeill, Myrdal, Olson, Scherer, Solterer, and Weiner.

An elemental concern is the question of priority of saving or investment which separates most social from conventional economists on the macro level. Two rebels from the conventional paradigm are the "true" Keynes and his pupil, Joan Robinson. Both rejected the orthodox view given in the 1776 "inquiry into the nature and causes of the wealth of nations" that priority in the process of improving the performance of an economy be given to saving. Smith's explanation is a direct deduction from the Enlightenment hard core wherein, given the laws of natural liberty, domestic order, tranquility, and protection from enemies, producers will save in order to invest. Given saving, the process of change, according to the orthodox view, proceeds by small businessmen and their workers taking opportunities to improve the productive mechanism by using labor in a more specialized way. Technological improvements resulting from division of labor occur automatically. In short, in a paper setting of law and order, saving arises to promote an end, the improvement in the wealth of nations that the businessmen had no intention of bringing about. [Smith, Book I, chapters 1, 2, and 3, pp. 420–26, 650–51] This view that saving performs the initiating role in development dominates economics in an unconscious but decisive way.

Keynes' refutation of this position is noteworthy. Saving is not the key component in the economic drama; investment is. This erratically exogenous variable is hardly automatic or subordinated to a natural lawfulness. It is not measurable within the macro system: estimates of the profitability of the new capital are made by businessmen who are often inflicted with "animal spirits." Saving isn't the spark to bring economic expansion; in fact, in the short run it has the opposite effect.

Joan Robinson in her important *Accumulation of Capital* argues that innovation brings profit, not the other way around. Economic growth and process are not primarily a matter of allocating profits (saving) among the economic variables of capital and labor but of making decisions about new productive processes. Since initiation is on the investment and not the saving side, investment is not likely to be stimulated by lowering taxes and cutting wage rates.

Schumpeter's position on the priority of investment over savings is patently clear, although unlike Keynes and Robinson he neither wished to be a rebel nor to reject the classical tradition of self-regulation. Nevertheless, to him the funds (savings, financial capital) are not prior; rather, the process of change originates on the investment side with the innovating entrepreneur. The economic system accommodates the entrepreneur by creating the funds. History illustrates lack of development when change is started on the funding side. Iberia's development in the 16th and 17th centuries, for example, was retarded rather than quickened by the expansion of new circulating media flowing in from Mexico and Peru. Inflationary influence from new precious metal is almost wholly destructive. [Schumpeter, 1939, I, chapter vi] Producers and investors, not savers or consumers, are the key to development. They initiate the process and typically work out the funding. This is often a difficult task, but bankers cooperate by forcing saving. Producers proceed when they get funds to force new products upon the consumers, who typically resist them.

Among the significant characteristics of the empirical dynamic are that the entrepreneur, as coordinator of the agents of production, is the creative actor in the economy. The truest entrepreneur is an upstart whose ideas are generally ridiculed in the beginning. Being unwelcome helps to explain the bad statistical record of important innovations. Typically illustrative was the launching of a remarkable steamboat by John Fitch to ply the Delaware River between Trenton and Philadelphia in 1786, twenty years before the state of the technical arts made it feasible. Creative economic activity may or may not be technological. Regarding technical activities, Boretsky says, "there has been a remarkable consistency between the relative growth in U.S. productivity and the relative intensity of overall technological progress in the economy over time." [Boretsky, p. 9] From his tabulation, "American genius created new inventions, and hence, the origins of new industries, every five years or so." [Boretsky, pp. 9 and 14] Yet the greater proportion of entrepreneurial work may not be technological. Williamson, for example, submits "that the modern corporation is mainly to be understood as the product of a series of organizational innovations that have had the purpose and effect of economizing on transaction costs." [Williamson, p. 1537] The innovational function and the function of vision have their sources both within and outside of large corporations. We may expect new ideas to arise chiefly from mavericks on the outside. Even so, as long as the large corporation continues to contribute a major part of the gross national product, it will share significantly in the developmental process. Internal or corporate entrepreneurship has been referred to as intrepreneurship. The journalist Barnhart describes its origin in Signode Industries, a high technology plastics company in the Chicago area, as occurring when "venture teams" are formed with the goal of creating new kinds of business for the corporation. New capital is devoted

> to products generated by Signode's venture teams, interdisci-
> plinary groups of managers plucked from their jobs to create the
> future. [Barnhart, p. 1]

Innovators are not benign. Creative economic activity destroys established techniques and damages the economic interests of those attached to them. Schumpeter borrowed a concept from the French to describe the process. According to the Marxist geographer David Harvey in two books on urbanization in a capitalist culture,

> The long swathes of "creative destruction.. (a phrase coined . . . in Second Empire Paris) trailing across the physical and social landscape are hard to ignore. [Harvey, 1985a, xi]

> Machinery, buildings, and even whole urban infrastructures and life-styles are made prematurely obsolescent; "creative destruction" becomes necessary to the survival of the system. [Harvey, 1985a, p. 27]

> The geographical and technological landscape of capitalism is torn between a stable but stagnant calm incompatible with accumulation and disruptive processes of devaluation and "creative destruction." [Harvey, 1985b, p. 138]

Innovators require financial capital or funds to acquire resources. Whether in a private or socialist society, expansionary economic activity has usually been financed by forced savings. In private enterprise economies, support for new things has been typically made available with demand deposit creation. Corporate savings or retained profits have augmented the supply in our century. There are problems of social justice involved in a private enterprise economy because the people making the decisions about the use of the resources are not those who have legal claim to them. On the other hand, the high rate of failure of innovations means that in a private enterprise economy failure is borne significantly by private capitalists and entrepreneurs rather than by ordinary citizens. Private capital subsidizes the many unsuccessful efforts of the innovators.

The private enterprise system rests upon the interaction of the entrepreneur demanding and the banking system supplying capital. Not only must innovational activity recur continuously for economic improvement to continue, but there must be the necessary funding created to complement it. Theoretically, the amount of credit created for funding innovations could be matched by an equal amount of credit destroyed as the projects become successfully completed. But Solterer observed that this doesn't happen. "Credit in general is never completely self-liquidating. Some money power will always remain and expand." His "law of increasing system expenditure" proposes that in a society where there are revitalizing effects of innovation and reorganization ". . . the sum of all expenditures in terms of the same monetary unit always increases and the purchasing power of that unit declines irregularly until it is replaced by another one." [Solterer, pp. 19 and 20] It follows that in all societies reorganizing to improve the material welfare of their people, money is endogenous; the financial sector responds positively to the developmental needs of the society.

Natural to the developing process is resistance to the new things. On the frontispiece of Marshall's *Principles* is the inscription, *natura non facet saltum.* It supports the view of conventional economics that progress is gradual and harmonious. An alternative view is that it is anything but. Innovations destroy established techniques and products. Understandably, conflict results. The more effective or dynamic the innovation, the stronger the resistance or opposition. The many kinds of resistance to creative economic activity include impediments arising from legal and political institutions, the pseudo-theological spirit that says God didn't mean for us to have the new thing, the counter-offensive of those groups who are threatened by the innovation, the arduous task that confronts the innovator of having his plan financed, and the difficulty of creating the demand. [Schumpeter, 1934, p. 86] The resistance is understandable. It is a legitimate conservative force in society. Innovations, according to Rosenbloom, serve to

raise havoc with individual and organizational identities. The system responds hemeostatically by seeking to maintain itself. . . . This resistance is not a negative force directed against technology but a type of conservative dynamism by which corporations . . . and other social systems . . . attempt to maintain a stable state in the face of forces which by their nature tend to destroy it. [Rosenbloom, p. 27]

Resistance to new things rests within the potential innovator himself. If he is to be successful, he must first convince himself that the great difficulties involved are worth the personal effort. It is always easier to remain in some established pursuit. In innovating, the entrepreneur is acting freely in the highest sense of the word—he must rise above the set patterns and established methods of the environment. It is much easier to follow them. Schumpeter says that "this mental freedom presupposes a great surplus force over the everyday demand and is something peculiar and by nature rare." [Schumpeter, 1934. p. 86]

In proceeding to construct a realistic conception of the nature of a developed economy, a helpful observation is that economies are organized into regions dominated by large urban centers. This constitutes another significant characteristic of the empirical reality. The core areas of the very large urban centers (Gras called them metropolises) supply economic leadership in commerce, industry, education and, especially, finance over their entire region. They are economic capitals, "the focus of local trade and centers through which normal economic relations with the outside are established and maintained." [Gras, p. 186] The economic history of the Western world, if not the whole world, even during ancient times, is competition among the centers: Florence and Venice, New York and Philadelphia, Chicago and St. Louis, New York and Tokyo. The city and metropolitan competition is an important piece of the empirical economic dynamic. Braudel and Labasse continue the work of Gras.

What the concept of the economic capital does for development theory and history is to bring order to innovational activity. Labasse shows this in his work on financial space. He says that the core of economic activity of a region is its financial center that uses links of communication and transportation to connect it. One can see an economy, he says, by examining the center of its financial life because financial activity is closely related to economic activity in general. [Labasse, pp. 5–11]

The empirical dynamic, with its focus on economic capitals, is a piece of a broader historical dynamic. Notice the kinship to McNeill's *World History*. In the structure of a developing economy offered in this paper, economic innovations are clustered in regions dominated by progressive urban centers, and the process stops in one and starts up in some other center. McNeill explains things similarly, but his focus is on cultures rather than economics:

. . . in any given age the world balance among cultures was liable to disturbance emanating from one or more centers where men succeeded in creating an unusually attractive or powerful civilization.

In successive ages the major foci of such disturbance to the world altered. It therefore becomes possible to survey the epochs of world history by studying first the center or centers of primary disturbance, and then considering how the other peoples reacted to or against what they knew or experienced (often at second or third hand) of the innovations that had occurred in the prime centers of cultural creativity. [McNeill, p. vi]

Another key element of the empirical reality is cyclical phenomena. "Cycles are not like tonsils, separable things that might be treated by themselves, but are, like the beat of the heart, of the essence of the organism that displays them." [Schumpeter, 1939, p. v] Being aware of this prepares us for certain long term social policy implications. The temporary obsolescence of major industries (such as steel and automobile in the 1970s and 1980s) becomes more understandable as possibly occurring in the "resting" period of a long run Kondratieff. Not that a scholar should affirm any logical necessity or wish to forecast long-run prosperities or depressions, only that he should be aware of recurring pulsations of economic activity. Scherer points to a sustained down-swing in our own time. In the 1930s and 1960s real output per hour of work in the private nonfarm economy rose about 2.6 percent per year; in 1968 it fell to 1.4 percent and continued downward during the 70s. A reasonable explanation is the decline in the rate of technological innovation, he says, although that is difficult for economists to measure.

> Whether or not cyclical movements of the Kondratieff-Schumpeter sort actually occurred is much debated by economists. That need not detain us; my argument does not require the assumption that history repeats itself in regular cycle. What I propose is merely this: that from the 1940s into the late 1960s there was a distinct surge of economic activity very much like a Kondratieff-Schumpeter upswing. . . . Thereafter, although the evidence is far from complete, the United States entered a period that has all the earmarks of a Kondratieff-Schumpeter downswing. [Scherer, pp. 263-64]

Cyclical behavior, including the long wave, merits a place in a list of basic components of the empirical reality. Compare Stolper's argument on its feasibility.

Also significant to the dynamic empirical is the role of government in the economy. Conventional economics, with its background in Enlightenment philosophy, raises prejudices against government. History, however, appears to show that no economy has ever developed independently of government, even in the remarkable century of *laissez faire* (1780–1880). It probably never will. Most times government is a partner in the economic process; sometimes silent about its participation, however. Often innovators use government; at other times, government restrains development with unfavorable legislation, judicial opinions, or by creating a stormy climate for business. Conventional economics, because of the philosophical premises that underlay it, greatly restricts governmental intervention in the economy.

To social economists, there is still another important relation of government to the economy. Political integration is crucial to the development process. Weiner's article on political integration in less developed countries can be just as useful in evaluating the need for integration in developed countries. Since Western economies are always in a state of potential development, his remarks about responsibilities of public education, national solidarity, and integration of social groups with one another are relevant.

> ... there are many different kinds of integration problems ... there are innumerable ways in which societies and political systems can fall apart. A high rate of social and economic change creates new demands and new tasks for government which are often malintegrative. Since modern states as well as modernizing states are often taking on new functions, it would be quite inappropriate to view integration at some terminal state. ... Once the state takes on the responsibilities of public education and invokes sentiments of "national" solidarity, then the integration of social groups to one another becomes an issue. ... The challenges of integration thus arise out of the new tasks which men create for themselves." [Weiner, pp. 74–75]

There are also unfavorable aspects of the economic process that must be recognized as a part of the empirical reality. By creatively responding to changing conditions, private and public entrepreneurs innovate to improve productivity and introduce new forms of organization. But there are times when and areas where they diminish welfare. Myrdal has explained the frequent detrimental effects of development in one part of a region upon the whole region, or in one region or another. [Myrdal, pp. 23–38] At all times the process involves creative destruction, so there is social damage to some people.

The development process does not continue indefinitely. It stops in one place and starts up somewhere else. Why it declines has not been an important question to scholars, but it should be. In 1982, however, Olson addressed it directly in his *Rise and Decline of Nations: Economic Growth, Stagnation, and Social Rigidities*. Factors of deceleration, according to Olson, are lack of flexibility (rigidities) and the resistance power of special interest groups. This topic of comparative regional decline deserves much more attention than scholars have given it thus far.

Economic Policy

Theories of economic policy stem from a commingling of the divisions of economics treated in parts one and two; that is, they arise out of one's conception of economic reality on the one hand, and out of philosophical premises on the other. The specific policy that develops out of solidarism is much broader than that of conventional economics; it reflects a focus upon the person in his (her) fourfold capacity as (a) member of a household (the focus of conventional economics), (b) as inhabitant of a rich but fragile earth, (c) as worker, and (d) as innovator. This broader structure of economic policy may be explained analogously by reference to the economists' tool, the production function. Conventional economics restricts itself to the efficiency and equity of the dependent variable, output/income. Its formal object of policy is limited to efficiency of production and equity of income distribution. Social economics, on the other hand, insists that in addition there be analytical consideration of what conventional economic insists are "independent" variables, namely, the factors of production, land and labor. In other words, unlike conventional economics, social economics opts for full analytic treatment of physical and human resources. The broad range of economic policy is viewed within the fundamental framework of the production function. [shown below]

output or income (conventional or welfare-state economics)	stems from	land (resources economics) and labor ("community" economics comprising collegial participation in production and creative or innovational economic activity)

Each of these subdivisions of social economics (welfare, resources, and community) is identified below, but because this paper has a solidarist perspective special attention is given to labor, to the person as worker and innovator. We begin this identification of kinds of economic policy by reference to policy in *conventional* economics. There are two ideological positions within conventional economics differentiated by the degree to which there is faith in the automaticity of the economic system and in the market's handling of efficiency and equity. They are laissez faire and welfare-state economics. The former is less sophisticated analytically because to "market liberals" the law of nature minimizes the need for interventionist policy. Its most impressive form of conventional policy analysis is the social economics of von Wieser, kept alive in the current literature by Ekelund. The key point of Wieserian policy is the destruction of privilege as a means of social improvement, rather than government intervention to compensate for the imperfections of the market. Social institutions need to be reformed but not much, because the reformation itself is quite automatic:

> ... self-interested, utility maximizing behavior [creates and alters] institutions along semi-predictable lines. These institutions, in turn, constrain future economic actors until forward-looking and creative entrepreneurs break out of the mold to alter institutions once more. [Ekelund and Thornton, p. 9]

The other theory of policy within the conventional discipline is welfare-state economics. In France, it is referred to as Walrasian for it stems from the scientific analysis developed out of Leon Walras' pure theory. Walras' role as the intellectual grand-pere of conventional interventionist policy is not recognized in the English-speaking world, but his influence, indirectly through Hicks, Samuelson, and others, is quite obvious. Walras' own views on intervention, although little known here, are clear. His other books (in addition to the one on the elements of pure theory) as well as his advocacy of full nationalization of the land, are a major inspiration for income redistribution and government unemployment policies. With the publication in 1987 of Walras' many, formerly unpublished articles, known as *Mélanges*, by the Auguste and Leon Walras Center in Lyon, the influence will be even stronger. [Hébert and Potier]

Conventional economic policy is important, but in the eyes of a social economist is limited since it deals only with the dependent variable of the macro economic production function, output/income. It defines as exogenous matters relating to the person as conservator of natural resources and as collegial participant in the workplace. These matters are endogenous in social economics.

Resources economics, or what an important pioneer, Nicholas Georgescu-Roegen, calls bioeconomics, was developed not just to supplement but to replace conventional policy views. "The term bioeconomics is intended to make us bear in mind continuously the biological origin of the economic process and thus spotlight the problem of mankind's existence with a limited store of *accessible* resources unevenly located and unequally appropriated." [Georgescu-Roegen, p. 361] At the end of the same article he states,

. . . two pillars of standard economics must . . .. be abandoned and replaced with entirely different—nay opposite—principles. First of all, we must discard the principle of discounting the future which has served as the basis for Harold Hotelling's famous study of the economics of irreplaceable resources . . . and continues to do so. . . . Second, instead of the traditional principle of rational behavior that of maximizing "utility" (whatever that may mean)—our policy toward natural resources in relation to future generations must seek to *minimize regrets*. From what it seems, it is precisely because we have always maximized utility that we are going soon to greatly regret our past policy. [Georgescu-Roegen, p. 375]

Some work is progressing in this sub-discipline but its popularity is very limited due to the powerful influence of conventional economics. One excellent example is Herman Daly's ingenious revision of the basic macroeconomic flow model. He added a physical flow of matter-energy that is linear rather than circular, "beginning with the depletion of low-entropy resources from the environment and ending with the pollution of the environment with high-entropy wastes." [Daly, p. 279]

Some of the most important work in this mode was done by E. F. Schumacher, one of two men selected by Keynes to wear his mantle. [Hession, p. 1][2] The two-fold message of this great social economist is that (a) production should be made compatible with the conservation of resources, and (b) methods and equipment used in the production should leave ample room for human creativity.

The greatest danger invariably arises from the ruthless application, on a vast scale, of partial knowledge, such as we are currently witnessing in the application of nuclear energy, of the new chemistry in agriculture, of transportation technology, and countless other things. [Schumacher, p. 36]

This final section on economic policy deals with the person in his (her) capacity as worker. It is the study and social-architectural design of conditions for (a) collegial participation in the workplace, and (b) creative economic activity. Participatory employment is dealt with first and innovational activity next; sometimes, however, it is difficult to keep the two apart.

The eminent labor economist, Ray Marshall, sketched the history of the worker in modern societies as a four-stage historical evolution, starting with industrial democracy, moving next to social democracy and leading to workplace participation and finally economic democracy. [Marshall, Ray, chapter V] The oldest stage, industrial democracy, is collective bargaining that, according to Marshall, increased the efficiency and equity of the economy by removing labor groups from a competitive position and by forcing managers to adopt a more productive way of producing than being competitive at the expense of the worker. The second stage, social democracy, is the welfare state, "a companion process whereby the government took labor out of competition by regulation." [Marshall, Ray, p. 113] Conventional economics deals adequately with these two stages of the development but not with the others.

Today, democratic principles are being extended beyond these stages to workplace participation and economic democracy. Economic democracy is worker ownership, a position pushed mainly by European theorists. [Marshall, Ray, p. 113] This requires considerable restructuring of the economy—a task improbable but not impossible as evidenced by the exciting social reconstruction in the Basque country of Spain, best described by Ellerman, 1984.

Five principles of policy may be drawn from this Mondragon experiment: (a) Firms are structured for net job creation and local economic development, not for individual or company gain. (b) Labor has priority over capital. Each firm is labor- not capital-based. The ranking of the four main ingredients of a business firm in a capitalist society, capital, management, product, and workers is reversed. [Mollner, p. 260] (c) Worker participation in production is collegial. Each worker is a member of a cooperative team. It is more difficult (but not impossible) to apply this principle to privately-owned firms than to cooperative ones such as those in Mondragon. Collegial practice may be based on a union or church affiliation, or simply on the commonality of the vision of a democratic workplace. [Ellerman, 1985, p. 261] The key idea in the firm, as in the economy generally, is cooperation, not competition. (d) The firm enjoys an autonomy with regard to public powers. Both government and private corporations pursue aims in honest collaboration with each other. Finally, (e) the firms' aims are subordinate to the demands of the common good. These principles have their roots in Heinrich Pesch's 4,000-page work written in German between 1904 and 1923 and not yet translated into English; in later Catholic Social Doctrine; in the teaching of Father Jose Maria Arizmendi; in the application of the teaching of his students in Mondragon; and in an updating of it by Pope John Paul in *Laborem Exercens* in 1981.

Illustrations of collegial participation and economic democracy range from a typical large Japanese firm to the highly developed team-control concept used in the production of Saab automobiles in Sweden. Two American examples, the Olga Company, Inc., Van Nuys, California, and the Rexworks, Inc., Milwaukee, are cited here.

The CEO of Olga, Jan Erteszek, says that employee participation in his firm makes it a new corporate form, "common venture enterprise," with four principles. First, the purpose of business is not gain exclusively although it exists in a profit-making environment, but to produce a useful product or service in a climate of integrity. Second, the business is a community—

> . . . in fact, it is the central community of our times. More people spend more of their waking hours in a business institution than in any other environment. Thus, business must address itself to the whole person, both to one's physical and spiritual needs. [Erteszek, p. 326]

Third, in the common venture enterprise,

> it is seen that some men invest capital while other invest talent, administrative skills, know-how (and some even invest total lives in their place of work). To the extent that all of these people are investors, they must all participate in the fortunes of the company. [Erteszek, p. 326]

Fourth, the steady employee is fully employed—"he is a full citizen of the business institution in which he works. Unemployment is not only an economic but a moral issue." [Erteszek, p. 326]

The second, the Rexworks case, is one of a genre of firms or divisions of firms that are struggling, threatened with closure, and, in desperation, introduce a collegial and worker-ownership program that so increases efficiency that the unit survives as a profit-making enterprise. That is to say, the more humanistic worker program is introduced for the wrong reason, for efficiency, rather than because it better conforms to the dignity of the person. Whatever the reason, society is improved. Rexworks of Milwaukee was the Construction Machinery Division of Rexnard. The parent company threatened to close it with the loss of jobs. It survived when nine managers purchased it with the help of a $20 million line of credit from First Bank Milwaukee. The new owners treated the 480 workers in a spirit of community, an open management style, and a very dynamic quality circle program. Also, they initiated a very fair profit sharing/stock program dispersing 25% of the company stock that only Rexworks employees can own. The company buys it back when the owner/worker retires. With the innovations and others (quarterly employee meeting and rotation among different jobs, for example), the old division and new firm is doing quite well, even in the face of German and Japanese competition. [Stollenwerk, pp. 253–56]

Community-developed programs that reflect man's dignity are being introduced all over the industrialized world so there is reason to be optimistic. But collegial participation and worker ownership are only a part of the solidaristic requirement. The institutionalization of opportunities for creative economic activity is hardly begun. Some explanation is required.

In Schumpeter's model of intact capitalism, the banking system, even though it creates credit, a very crucial function in the developmental process, plays a *conservative* role in the economy. It evaluates the investment proposals of entrepreneurs and allocates scarce funds to the chosen ones. The entrepreneur performs the *progressive* function of demander of these limited funds. His (her) ideas when introduced successfully change the economy. As recognized above, the interaction of the entrepreneurial vision and capital financial support is necessary for development in any economy. There is a natural tension between the conservative banking and the progressive innovational forces. A sound social economy requires an institutional arrangement to democratize the banking function (a process of evaluation of these creative ideas), and to extend the opportunity to innovate to people throughout the society. A model to demonstrate that it can exist is found in Mondragon. Again Ellerman explains it best.

This crucial institution in the Mondragon complex of cooperatives is the empresarial (entrepreneurial) division of the bank, the Caja Laboral Popular. The caja is a super-structural or second tier credit cooperative with a membership of cooperatives, a cooperatives' cooperative, It has technical, managerial, and financial resources comparable to those of a major corporation. But very significantly, the resources are applied to the social goals of community and regional development with locally based small and medium sized businesses. [Ellerman, 1984, pp. 273–74]

The Empresarial Division is a "factory factory." Together with the Caja Laboral Popular as a whole it is the prototype of a new kind of economic development organization which institutionalizes the function of the small business entrepreneur. . . . [Ellerman, 1984, p. 274]

Entrepreneurship, according to Ellerman, has been successfully institutionalized and socialized in Mondragon. Its record of starting more than a hundred firms, including some of the largest manufacturers in Spain, with only three failures (as of Ellerman's report in 1984) is remarkable when contrasted with the high business failure rate in America. It does more than design and launch new enterprises. It guides and gives counsel to firms entering new markets, launching new products, making major expansions, changing equipment and technology, or reorganizing a business's structure [Ellerman, 1984, pp. 275, 280–81]

In short, the Caja Laboral Popular rationalizes what was targeted in the mid-section of this paper as the core of the empirical reality, the interaction of vision and finance capital, and does so in a solidaristic way that institutionalizes the personal equity of creative economic activity. This, together with collegial participation, is the core of economic policy of a social economics with a solidarist perspective.

Conclusion

An assumption of this paper is that there are three components to any economic science: philosophical premises, the empirical reality, and economic policy. This implies, of course, that there is not a single, but a number of economics. Two were contrasted here: the orthodox, classical, neoclassical, conventional kind that remains very dominant in the face of periodic and convincing criticism, and a solidarist variant of social economics. Space limitations preclude a lengthy summation of the components and their combination to form the totality, but several insights are offered in conclusion.

First, regarding the most basic component, philosophical premises: a *methodenstreit* continues between advocates of a broad, soft, moral science and those favoring a narrow, scientific discipline, based upon a deterministic mathematical system. And for good reason—the issue of which economics is valid is very important. The dispute is about method, and is between those who accept an Aristotelian outlook on the nature of economic studies and those who have adopted the "modern" Enlightenment approach. The Aristotelian view, as so convincingly explained in Ron Stanfield's book on Polanyi, identifies the study of economic life as focused on satisfying the material needs of the community to permit it to survive and reproduce itself. This view dominated Europe during the Middle Ages but fell out of favor almost completely with the rise of the social philosophy of the Enlightenment and its legitimate offspring, classical economics.[3] The latter focuses upon the decision-making behavior of the individual and the maximization of individual and collective welfare. In simplest terms, it is a conflict of broad against narrow economics, of social against mainstream.

Robbins' famous essay is a defense of the latter but, as a matter of fact, it needs no defense. Since it is based on the paradigm that dominates, its hard core is below the surface of its practitioners' consciousness and taken for granted. Its philosophical premises are encrusted in Western industrialized societies as an ethos. Robbins' definition of the discipline as the study of rational behavior, involving maximizing utility in the relationship between ends and scarce means which have alternative uses [Robbins, p. 16] keeps winning out over what Robbins posits as the older tradition of Marshall-Cannon, represented in Marshall's view of the science as the study of mankind in the ordinary business of life and human behavior connected with the attainment and use of the material requisites of well-being. [Marshall, Alfred, p. 1] The philosophical premises identified with solidarist social economics, namely, the sacred person as economic unit, cooperation as a significant guiding force of economic behavior, and status rather than contractual arrangements as the essence of human rights in society, go beyond the Marshall-Cannon perspective of the nature of economics.

Regarding the topic of the second part of this paper, the economists' collection of observations of what is significant about the economy, priority goes to the entrepreneur, the creative coordinator of the factors of production in an ever-changing society. His (her) creative responses to changing conditions contribute continuously to historical development. But supporting and surrounding this key variable in the empirical reality are the institutions that finance his (her) proposals, that provide public leadership (the role of government) and, as such, are always involved negatively or positively in the developmental process, and that supply business leadership from the money centers of the regions. All of this is in contrast to the lesser but still important activities of supply and demand and marginal analysis. The dynamic variable, it is suggested, must be put in the forefront over the more static realities of utility, general equilibrium, and circular flow. Such an intellectual attitude stresses the remarkable changes taking place. Just as electrical, automotive, chemical, and petroleum production was an infinitesimal part of the GNP at the turn of the century, so biotechnical, superconductive and related products are an insignificant part of the GNP today but are predicted to constitute the majority proportion of the GNP within but a few decades. [Compare Rifkin]

The third component of the paper and of any economics is policy, the commingling of premise and the empirical. In a social economics with a solidarist perspective there is a need to go beyond conventional welfare economics of either the Wieserian or Walrasian kinds, however important they may be. Collegial and cooperative participation in production and creative economic activity are at the heart of economic policy.

Great strides are being made all over the industrialized world to introduce participative involvement in production, notwithstanding powerful resistance. The motive for teamwork is often the wrong one, however; efficiency is the motive rather than that it suits the nature of the person. Some illustrations of collegial participation are most persuasive, for example, the work teams in the Volvo plant. The opposition and skepticism throughout the automotive industry in Sweden was strong but with the sour attitudes of the workers the way they were in the 1960s absenteeism rose, quality declined, and companies had trouble recruiting people in the welfare state. Something had to be offered besides pay, such as a different working environment, more varied jobs, greater employee responsibility for quality, and an active role in decision-making. It has worked well. [Lohr]

Another striking illustration of the efficiency of the solidarist way is a report that an industry that had been dominated by America for fifty years until the 1980s was captured by a high-wage nation, West Germany. In the textile machinery industry, the "explanation for our [U.S.] manufacturers' failure is also the secret of their [WG] success." The firms in Germany came to view their industry as a trade association of specialists. Each company was guaranteed protection against competition from other association members during downturns. The association procedures pooled advertising expenses, established foreign marketing agencies and did many other things to foster cooperation. [Sabel and Herrigel]

> The trade association and cooperative banks that help institutionalize flexibility in West Germany strike us as collusive. The close relations between skilled workers and managers would discomfort many bosses and trade unionists here. Many Americans believe that the only way to encourage innovation is to remove obstacles to competition, including anything that smacks of cooperation.
>
> Recently, however, economists, public officials and managers have begun to concede that competition can be a barrier to innovation. [Sabel and Herrigel]

The genuine reason for collegiality is that it conforms to the nature of the worker as a person, but it also appears to promote efficiency.

Finally, there is the aim to institutionalize creative entrepreneurship as the key to a humanistic policy and an effective developing economy with sound social goals. Some guidelines were mentioned in the description by the Mondragon experiment above. Here I am restricted to two statements by Josef Solterer, one of the first and most persuasive scholars to see the connection of man's dignity and creative economic development.

... to deprive men of the opportunity to act responsibly is resented by them perhaps more than to deprive them of the fruit of their labor. Largely because of historical reasons, our society is organized in such a way that many are excluded from acting entrepreneurially in economic affairs. [Solterer, 1950, p. 19]

The entrepreneurs or business leaders are the makers of a new order; their acts of innovation have a vastly greater significance than do simple acts of exchange: entrepreneurial activity is order-forming. Business leaders are essentially organizers, in whose acts we can see more clearly certain meanings of social justice. [Solterer, 1951, p. 16]

Appendix: The Empirical Reality

The Economic Process:

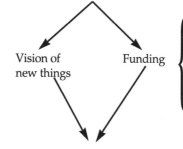

Kinds of Vision:
  technological
    changes
  new sources
    of supply
  demand creation
  new forms of
    organization

Vision of
new things

Funding

Kinds of Funding:
  self financing
  normal saving
  forced saving
  (credit creation
    in money
    centers)

Combination
of vision and funding
is innovation by the business
entrepreneur or public innovator who
creatively coordinates:

land
labor
capital
technology

Economic development, for
  example, Chicago 1793 is
  so different from Chicago
  1893 and Chicago 1993
Decline of nations and
  economies

Other ingredients of the
  process:
    government
    consensus
    cooperation in the
      work place

Some characteristics of
  the process:
    resistance (development blocks)
    creative destruction
    cyclical behavior
      alternating loci of development

Notes

This paper was presented as the Presidential Address, the Association for Social Economics, December 29, 1987, Chicago IL. The author wishes to express his gratitude to Brother Leo V. Ryan, C. S. V., and Professor Bala Batavia, Chair, Economic Department, DePaul University for released time that made it possible.

1. Conventional, classical, and neo-classical economics are interchangeable here. Said Keynes, "The classical economists was a name invented by Marx to cover Ricardo and James Mill and their *predecessors*, that is to say for the founders of the theory which culminated in the Ricardian economics. I have been accustomed, perhaps perpetrating a solecism, to include in the classical 'school' the *followers* of Ricardo, those that is to say, who adopted and perfected the theory of the Ricardian economics, including (e.g.—J. S. Mill, Marshall, Edgworth and Professor Pigou." [*Keynes*, p. 3] I mean for it to cover even more: classical, neoclassical, Austrian, monetarist, Neo-Keynesian (that is Keynesianism after the Hicksian synthesis), supply-side and rational expectations economics. What makes it conventional, orthodox, and/or classical is the set of philosophical premises, called the hard core below, but especially the self-regulatory character of the economy.

2. Schumacher's daughter reported, as relayed by Hession, ". . . that Keynes had singled out Schumacher as one worthy enough to be his successor. Sir William Early of the British Treasury had been visiting with Keynes prior to 1946 and at one point in the conversation Keynes said: 'If my mantle is to fall on anyone, it could only be Otto Clarke or Fritz Schumacher. Otto Clarke can do anything with figures, but Schumacher can make them sing.'" [Hession, p. 1]

3. Campbell shows he understands this when he writes in his excellent article on Constitutional economics, ". . . there are at least two different kinds of 'economics' which the founding fathers wished to maintain: first, the classical liberal visions coming from Adam Smith with an emphasis on the market and economic freedom; second, the tradition of household management [from Aristotle] which provides virtue. The first is preserved in due process; the second in the doctrine of police powers." [Campbell, p. 15]

Resources

Axelrod, Robert. *The Evolution of Cooperation*, New York. 1984.

Barnhart, Bill. "One Firm's Capital Idea: Intrepreneurship Spurs Growth." *Chicago Tribune*, Business Section, May 26, 1985.

Boretsky, Michael. "The Role of Innovation," *Challenge*, November-December, 1980.

Bork, Robert H. "Neutral Principles and Some First Amendment Problems," *Indiana Law Journal*, Fall, 1971.

Burke, James. *The Day the Universe Changed*, Boston, 1985.

Braudel, Fernand. *The Perspective of the World*, New York, 1984.

Briefs, Goetz. "The Solidarist Economics of Goetz Briefs," *Review of Social Economy*, December, 1983.

Brown-Collier, Elba K. "The Neoclassical and Post-Keynesian Research Programs: The Methodological Issue," *Review of Social Economy*, September, 1970.

Campbell, William F. "Two Traditions of Constitutional Economics," *The Intercollegiate Review*, Spring, 1987.

Ekelund, Jr., Robert B. "Power and Utility: The Normative Economics of Friedrich von Wieser," *Review of Social Economy*, September, 1970.

Ekelund, Jr., Robert B. and Mark Thornton. "Wieser and the Austrian Connection to Social Economics," *Forum for Social Economics*, Spring, 1987.

Ellerman, David P. "Entrepreneurship in the Mondragon Cooperative," *Review of Social Economy*, December, 1984.

———. "A Kantian Approach to Normative Economics" presented at the History of Economic Society Meeting, New York, June 2–4, 1986.

Erteszek, Jon J. "Corporate Enterprise and Christian Ethics," *Review of Social Economy*, December, 1982.

Etzioni, Amatai. "Toward a Kantian Socio-Economics: Relevant Kantian Positions," *Review of Social Economy*, April, 1987.

Georgescu-Roegen, Nicholas. "A Bioeconomic Viewpoint," *Review of Social Economy*, December, 1977.

Gras, N. S. B. *An Introduction to Economic History*, New York, 1922.

Harvey, David. *Consciousness and the Urban Experience*, Baltimore. 1985a.

———. *The Urbanization of Capital*, Baltimore, 1985b.

Hébert, Claude and Jean-Pierre Potier. "The Surprising History of the *Mélanges d'economic politique et sociale*," *History of Economics Society Bulletin*, Fall, 1987.

Hession, Charles H. "E. F. Schumacher as Heir to Keynes' Mantle," *Review of Social Economy*, April, 1986.

Jones, Bryce J. Review of Robert Axelrod's *The Evolution of Cooperation*, *Review of Social Economy*, October, 1985.

Keynes, John M. *The General Theory of Employment, Interest and Money*, New York, 1936.

Labasse, Jean. *L'espace financier*, Paris, 1974.

Lakatos, Irme. "Falsification and the Methodology of Scientific Research Programs," from Lakatos and Alan Musgrove, *Criticism and the Growth of Knowledge*, Cambridge, England, 1979.

Latsis, Spiro J. "A Research Programme in Economics," in *Method and Appraisal in Economics*, edited by Spiro Latsis, Cambridge, 1976.

Lohr, Steve. "Making Cars the Volvo Way," *New York Times*, Tuesday, June 23, 1987.

Lutfalla, Michael. "Nineteenth Century Enlightenment: French Economic Liberals, 1789–1815," presented at the History of Economics Society Meeting, Pittsburgh, 1984.

McNeill, William. *World History*, New York, 1967.

Marshall, Alfred. *Principles of Economics*, New York, 1948.

Marshall, Ray. *Unheard Voices: Labor and Economic Policy in a Competitive World*, New York, 1987.

Mollner, Terry. "Mondragon, a Third Way," *Review of Social Economy*, December, 1984.

Mueller, Franz. *The Church and the Social Questions*, Washington, 1984.

Myrdal, Gunnar. *Economic Theory and Underdeveloped Regions*, New York, 1957.

Olson, Mancur. *The Rise and Decline of Nations: Economic Growth, Stagnation, and Social Rigidities*, New Haven, 1982.

Rifkin, Jeremy. *Algeny: A New Word, A New World*, New York, 1983.

Robbins, Lionel. *An Essay on the Nature and Significance of Economic Science*, London, 1948.

Rosenbloom, Richard. Review of Donald Schon's *Technology and Change, Bulletin of the Atomic Scientists*, September, 1968.

Robinson, Joan. *The Accumulation of Capital*, London, 1959.

Sabel, Charles F. and Gary B. Herrigel. "Losing a Market to a High-Wage Nation," *New York Times*, Sunday, June 14, 1987.

Scherer, F. M. *Innovation and Growth, Schumpeterian Perspectives*, Cambridge, MA, 1984, Chap. 14.

210   *William R. Waters*

Schumacher, E. F. *Small is Beautiful*, New York, 1975.

Schumpeter, Joseph A. *Business Cycles: A Theoretical, Historical and Statistical Analysis of the Capitalist System*, two volumes, New York, 1936.

———. *Theory of Economic Development*, Cambridge, MA, 1934.

———. "Science and Ideology," *American Economic Review*, March, 1949.

Smith, Adam. *An Inquiry into the Nature and Causes of the Wealth of Nations*, New York, 1937.

Solterer, Josef. "The Entrepreneur in Economic Theory," *Review of Social Economy*, March, 1950.

———. "Schumpeter and Quadragesimo Anno," *Review of Social Economy*, March, 1951.

———. "Structure of a Pluralistic Economy," *Review of Social Economy*, March, 1958.

Stanfield. J. Ron. *The Economic Thought of Karl Polanyi: Lives and Livelihood*, New York, 1986.

Stollenwerk, James. "Rexworks: A Case Study of Applied Social Economic Justice," *Review of Social Economy*, December, 1984.

Stolper, Wolfgang F. Review of Kondratieff's *Long Wave Cycle*, *Journal of Economic Literature*, December, 1984.

Weiner, Myron. "Political Integration and Political Development," *Developing Nations*, edited by Frank Tachau, New York, 1972.

Williamson, Oliver. "The Modern Corporation: Origins, Evolution Attributes," *Journal of Economic Literature*, December, 1981.

9

COMPARISON OF MARXISM AND INSTITUTIONALISM

WILLIAM M. DUGGER AND HOWARD J. SHERMAN

It is our view that Marxism and institutionalism have much in common—and that it is useful in the United States to stress the common ground among all critical economists. We also recognize that there are different viewpoints within each of these paradigms. There are liberal and radical institutionalists, but there are also official and independent, critical Marxists. By official Marxism, we mean that version of Marx that was held by the Soviet Union and all of the Communist parties during the Stalin era (1928–1953). We recognize that liberal institutionalists and official Marxists have little or nothing in common, but we believe that modern, radical institutionalists and modern, critical (nonofficial) Marxists have much in common. It should be stressed that the dichotomy mentioned within each school is a drastic oversimplification. In reality, there is a wide spectrum of views within each school. We use a dichotomy only to highlight certain differences within each school.

The Questions

Of the two coauthors, the radical institutionalist will give the institutionalist answers to a set of questions, while the Marxist will give the critical Marxist answers to the same set of questions. We will then jointly compare the answers. The questions include:

I. Fundamental Relationships

a. What are the most important relationships in society?
b. How are technology and ideas related?
c. Is there class conflict?
d. How is class related to technology and ideas?
e. Can all social explanations be reduced to technology? To ideas? To class?
f. What is the role of the individual?

II. Dynamics

a. Can the social sciences be ahistorical?
b. Is there social evolution?
c. Is evolution teleological and predetermined?
d. What causes historical evolution?
e. Is evolution a simple, linear process?

The mere fact that questions like these can be formulated is important. Since these questions are meaningful and significant for both Marxism and institutionalism, the two clearly share certain common understandings of society. Otherwise, meaningful and significant questions like these could not be asked of the two. The two schools would simply talk past each other. Of course, much of that does occur, but a case can be made that this is a consequence of a lack of fundamental understanding of their own school of thought by those who do the talking past. It is that set of common understandings that allow us to ask questions of each other that needs to be explored. Of course, differences exist as well and should not be ignored, but enough internecine squabbling has taken place.

On the Marxist side, as noted above, the answers given are those of modern, critical, independent Marxists. These answers are quite different than those that would have been given by official Marxists in the time of Stalin or even Brezhnev.

On the institutionalist side, the answers formulated come from the radical institutionalist tradition, which traces itself back to Thorstein Veblen [see Dugger 1989, 1992]. The answers are not necessarily those that would be given by a liberal institutionalist in the Veblen-Ayres or the Commons traditions, and they most certainly are not those that would be given by a new institutionalist in the Oliver Williamson or Douglas North tradition. Radical institutionalists have been derisively referred to as "middle-class radicals." The label, while intended to be derogatory, is quite descriptive [for further discussion, see Dugger and Waller 1992].

The Institutionalist Paradigm

What are the most important relationships in society? Power relationships are the most important relationships in society. Power means the ability to get others to do what you want them to do. Because of myths and misconceptions, weaker groups and individuals often do not understand their own interests, and they end up serving the interests of others. Myths and misconceptions are not harmless. They enable one group to dominate another and to exercise power over them. Enabling myths are those that enable one group or individual to get others to do what is wanted of them, even when it is not in the interest of the dominated group or individual. Power relationships based on enabling myths were the principal focus of Thorstein Veblen, the founder of institutional economics. Power relationships are relationships of domination that allow one person or group to implement new technologies and to reap the benefits of doing so at the cost of whomever. Power relationships make it possible to defend existing rights (including, but not restricted to, property rights) and to create and acquire new rights. Power relationships determine whose rights count and whose voice is heard. They also determine whose rights do not count and whose voice is not heard. Power relationships come before property and before income because power relationships determine both. Power is prior. It is foundational.

Power relationships are interwoven with the Veblenian dichotomy—the distinction first made by Veblen between socially useful activity and selfish aggrandizement [see Veblen 1919, 279–323]. Selfish activity, especially that of the powerful, is overlaid with ceremonial justification, while useful activity is simply a matter of fact. Hence, ceremonialism versus instrumentalism is a theme that runs through much of institutionalism. Radical institutionalists emphasize the need to take collective action against ceremonialism, while liberal institutionalists see ceremonialism being weakened "naturally" by the spread of education, enlightenment, and new technology.

How are technology and ideas related? Technology, the way we do things, and ideas, the way we think about what we do, are mutually related. They interact in two senses. Ideas are distillations of and rationalizations for the way we do things. In this first sense, ideas are determined by technology. New technology created the industrial revolution, with the rise of the factory system. The new technology changed our ideas about the world around us and about ourselves. It also transformed dying feudalism into dynamic capitalism. So, technology, rather than ideas, was the driving force in the latest historical transformation of our world. But ideas are also essential in devising new ways to do things and new things to do. So, in a second sense, technology is determined by ideas. Technology and ideas interact to determine each other. Nonetheless, there is a senior partner in the interaction between technology and ideas. In the conventional view, necessity is the mother of invention. We need more things and we need new things, so we think up ways to produce them. Doing so helps us all enjoy the good life, produced by the genius of a few great inventors and by the accumulated capital of a few great entrepreneurs. Again, in the conventional view, ideas are the senior partner. But in the institutionalist view, invention is the mother of necessity. Technology is the senior partner. In our current age, corporate researchers think up new things and new ways to produce them, then set about selling them to individual consumers and justifying the extravagance of some consumers in the face of real want for many others. This is the revised sequence: producers sell consumers what producers want to produce. The revised sequence is a direct contradiction of consumer sovereignty and makes the conventional wisdom regarding the good life a cruel joke.

Ideas, condensed into the conventional wisdom, are justifications and rationalizations of the status quo. Ideas, formulated by scientific advance and spreading enlightenment, are also powerful debunkers of the conventional wisdom.

Is there class conflict? Institutionalists do not deny class conflict, but consider it too abstract for theory building and too diffused and misconceived for supporting political reform programs. In institutional analysis, cultural lag is generally substituted for class conflict. A cultural lag exists when racist, sexist, and classist myths, shrouded in the verities of tradition, are used to justify and rationalize the exploitation of the weak and of the outsider by the strong and by the insider. Institutionalist Gunnar Myrdal explained that racism, for example, involves a vicious circle. Racist myths are used to justify discrimination against minorities of a different color. This pushes their educational attainment down and handicaps their attainment of good health, nutrition, and family life. Their low levels of living, caused by the discrimination, are then used as evidence of their alleged inferiority, and such "evidence" is used to justify even further discrimination. The same kind of vicious circle exists with respect to sexism and classism.

Here is where institutionalists emphasize the positive rule of advancing science and spreading enlightenment. The most important thing that anthropological studies can do is debunk the racist and sexist myths that hold down women and minorities of a different color. Social Darwinism and male chauvinism are myths and systematic distortions of human knowledge that must be dispelled by responsible social scientists. The most important thing that heterodox (institutionalist, Marxist, Post Keynesian) economic studies can do is debunk classist myths that hold down the poor. Classist myths have coalesced into neoclassical economics. Responsible economists must band together to expose neoclassical economics. Neoclassicism is not just irrelevant because it is based on unrealistic assumptions and tenuously long threads of deductive reasoning. Rather than just being irrelevant, it is pernicious. Would that it were only irrelevant then it would be ignored. But, in a very real sense, it is perfectly relevant—as a justification and rationalization of continued inequality, that is.

How is class related to technology and ideas? This is a most perplexing question to institutionalists, as they do not emphasize class in their analysis. The more narrowly defined "economic interest group" or vested interest is used instead. Furthermore, the cultural concept of cultural lag is used in place of the economic concept of class interest to explain social conflict. Struggles over the implementation of new technologies and over the acquisition of new rights or the loss of old ones are seen either as a clash between new ways of doing things against established traditions and myths or as a clash between a narrow interest group against an established community.

The strength of institutionalism is its willingness to consider factors other than class. For example, the struggle over nuclear power plants is not seen as the working class versus the capitalist class, but as an established community defending itself against a reckless industry. Considerable insight is gained by applying the institutionalist formulation rather than the class formulation to the nuclear power issue. A weakness of institutionalism is that sometimes institutionalists ignore class altogether. For example, the struggle over the eight-hour-day is seen as a succession of unions versus a succession of captains of industry struggling over the working rules of their particular industries. Considerable insight is lost by applying the institutionalist formulation to the eight-hour-day issue and ignoring the class formulation.

In class analysis, members of a class should acquire a class consciousness and when they do not, they are said (by official Marxism) to suffer from false consciousness. But what people believe and why they have come to do so is often given short shrift. In institutional analysis, people in conflict over particular issues and problems are understood to base their thoughts and actions on the best meanings and beliefs available to them. Although those meanings and beliefs are frequently distorted by enabling myths, the myths are not given short shrift. They are taken as the basis of the problem. How people came to believe them is an important element of theory building and problem solving.

Can all social explanations be reduced to technology? To ideas? To class? Institutionalism is holistic, not reductionist. Its explanations are not reduced to one particular set of factors, so technology, ideas, and class are all important. Institutionalism is the broad study of the social provisioning process in its cultural context. As such, it does not assume that technology or ideology or class structure is constant. Instead, institutional explanations attempt to weave together the interplay between all relevant factors, whatever they may be. Furthermore, with nothing assumed constant, change pervades all institutional explanations. The importance of change to institutional explanations makes technology a central explanatory factor, for technology often changes dramatically. Institutionalists believe that the march of science and new technology has the capacity to fundamentally alter social relations and to improve the quality of human life. But institutionalists are not simple technological determinists. Although technology clearly plays a leading role in social change, social change cannot be explained simply in terms of new technology. Ideas play an important role in social explanations, particularly the enabling myths of inegalitarian societies and the debunking of those myths by the advance of science and the spread of enlightenment. Class also plays a role in social explanations, but it does so in a very narrow and specific sense: how existing rights (property rights and other rights) affect social relations is a crucial explanatory element in any social theory. The attempts to expand existing rights and to create new rights play important roles in social explanation. The struggles over rights involves the state, so the state also plays an important explanatory role.

What is the role of the individual? To oversimplify, institutionalism relies on methodological collectivism rather than on methodological individualism. Since institutionalism is a cultural science, the individual is seen as a product of culture. The individual is not a cultural marionette, because individuals can and do transform their culture through collective action and even through individual action. In fact, culture itself is continually changing through the myriad of actions, inactions, and choices of individuals separately and collectively. Nonetheless, individuals do not act or choose in a vacuum. They act and choose within a particular cultural context.

To explain the individual, institutionalism must begin with the context in which individuals find themselves. This is essential, for it means that economics is not merely the study of how individuals allocate scarce resources to meet alternative uses. Institutional economics asks how specific resources come into use—how science and technology affect the availability of resources. Furthermore, it asks how property rights affect the use of resources. Also of major import is how individuals come to "want" specific things. This is the essence of the revised sequence.

To defend the individual against oppression, institutionalists must not assume that the resources available to individuals are fixed by nature nor that their preferences are spontaneously generated from within themselves. Instead, the myriad of property rights, civil rights, beliefs and myths, scientific knowledge and technology, and distribution of income and wealth all affect the resources available to them, the preferences they have, and the choice sets they face.

Can the social sciences be ahistorical? With the German Historical economists, the institutionalists share an appreciation for the importance of time and place. One obvious example of the need for historical specificity is the analysis of the free trade doctrine. As the German scholars realized full well, free trade was great for the British in 1870 since British industries were firmly established by then and since British interests were protected by the British navy. But free trade was disadvantageous for the Germans in 1870 since their infant industries faced imports from mature British producers at home and faced British interests backed up by the British navy abroad. Economic relations and policies must be continually reevaluated in the light of changing circumstances. Economic doctrine and theory must evolve along with changing circumstances.

Societies and their problems continue to change. What resolved a particular problem in one time and place may not resolve it in another. What was considered a problem in one time and place may not be considered a problem in another. So economic policy must also change as social problems change. History being the record of change, historical understanding is essential to adequate policy. If we do not know history, not only are we doomed to repeat its mistakes, but we are also doomed to ignorance about the types of problems that are continually emerging.

Furthermore, economic laws—to the extent that they can be made anything more than common sense observations—must be considered in terms of the specifics of different times and different places. Economic law itself is specific to time and place. The very categories that economic law deals with are products of historical change. Capital, labor, and land—the factors of production—did not even exist a few hundred years ago in anything resembling their current forms.

Is there social evolution? The fact of social change is the only constant in institutional economics. Human societies have undergone the most profound kinds of change and continue to do so. Social relations continually evolve. Hunting and gathering societies have evolved into herding and farming societies. The handicraft system changed into the putting-out system, and the putting-out system changed into the factory system. The industrial revolution changed almost everything. And even now, the leading industrial country of the world (the United States) is de-industrializing. Stateless and classless societies have evolved into societies stratified into classes and ruled by nation-states. Societies in which the people provisioned themselves with no thought of property rights have changed into societies in which many of the people think of little else. Only a few hundred years ago, many infants did not survive into adulthood. Now, many adults fear that they will live too long—so long that they use up their savings and fall into destitution. Only a few hundred years ago, when men went to war they had to hack off each others arms and legs with sharpened lengths of steel. Killing was hard and dirty work. Now, they can incinerate themselves by the millions with just the push of a button. Killing is now easy and clean. So, of course, we do much more of it.

Yes, there is social evolution, because change never stops. But is social change really what is meant by social evolution? Change means doing and thinking differently. Progress means doing and thinking better. Until recently, most institutionalists believed that societies progress—they get better. But in recent years, this faith has begun to falter. We still believe that societies change, but we are not sure that societies will make progress through that change.

Is evolution teleological and predetermined? Radical institutionalists would answer with a resounding NO. In the face of experience over the last half century, their belief in progress has been shaken to its roots. And social "progress" generally means not just change, but movement from a lower to a higher form. Biological evolution means only adaptation to the environment. The fittest (not necessarily the "best"—whatever that may mean) survive. But some institutionalists used to think that social evolution generally means progress. Belief in progress—that society has improved and will continue to improve—may give us the strength to get up every morning, but it also moves us quite close to a teleological conceptualization of evolution.

A teleological conceptualization of evolution imputes a direction to change and insists that change moves society along some scale of values. A strand of institutionalist thought puts considerable emphasis on the idea that societies have progressed and will continue to progress because of the dynamic and beneficial effects of new technology and in spite of the static and detrimental effects of entrenched institutions. That belief in progress is as close to teleological as one can get without being a member of the choir. And yet, it is from that very strand in institutionalism that the loudest objections to Marxism are heard—objections to Marxism because of its teleology.

There is enough teleology lurking about institutionalism to make us formulate our thoughts far more carefully than we have done in the past. Institutionalism done well is not teleological. It does not conceptualize society as moving toward some predetermined end. Marxism done well is not teleological either. To build for the future, we should focus on the best in the two research traditions.

What causes historical evolution? Societies evolve (change) because of two basic forces: (1) cumulative causation (an idea usually attributed to Gunnar Myrdal but discussed in Veblen [1919, 68–80] and (2) blind drift [Veblen 1964, 25]. Societies are not moving toward equilibrium, but they are continually changing. Once a particular change has begun, it initiates or induces further changes that reinforce the original movement. Social change is driven by forces that are not offsetting (equilibrium), but by forces that are reinforcing (cumulative causation). For example, regression toward racism and inequality began in the United States some 20 years ago, and it has gathered momentum in a vicious circle. Only a massive push in the other direction will reverse the decline. But this does not mean that societies just move back and forth like a pendulum, with no permanent change taking place.

Racial inequality may be a bad example, but on many fronts, dramatic and permanent change has taken place. And, it has taken place in a cumulative fashion. The powerful use their power to become more so. The weak, disadvantaged by their weakness, get weaker. This is cumulative causation: From those who have not, it shall be taken. To those who have, it shall be given. However, massive, concerted collective action can reverse a vicious circle and turn it into a virtuous circle. This too is cumulative: if the underdogs can join together in mutual defense against the top dogs, they can gain self-confidence and power. Their first taste of power can give them more self-confidence, which leads to more power, and so on in a cumulative circle.

Societies are continually changing in a cumulative fashion, but they do not necessarily move in a particular, desired direction. They do not necessarily move from a lower to a higher level—and, in fact, the words "higher" and "lower" are often misleading with respect to social evolution. Societies are simply changing, moving in the direction of least resistance or in the direction of most power. This is blind drift. Social change is not necessarily progress—continued movement in one direction. Social change is drift, random movement, but not offsetting movement. At least it has been in the past. It need not continue to be drift in the future. Societies can control—to a degree—their own futures. Up till now, they generally have not done so.

Is evolution a simple, linear process? Evolution is never simple, never linear. It is often complex, moving in many directions at once, under the impact of many different forces. Vast increases in agricultural production have taken place, but the distribution system has broken down. Farmers cannot sell their output at prices sufficient to keep them on the farm, and millions of people at home and abroad go hungry while grain speculators grow rich in the great trading pits of the world. The Soviet planning system developed ways of accumulating vast quantities of capital but applied it inefficiently. Advances in medical science, nutrition, and public sanitation have doubled the life span, but old people worry that they will live too long and run out of income. There is nothing linear about social change.

Furthermore, social change often leads to a dead end. The globe is littered with the ruins of dead civilizations—dead ends of evolution, societies destroyed by their own avarice, superstition, or stupidity; societies destroyed by disease and change in climate; societies destroyed by other societies. To paraphrase and update Veblen, society seldom falls back on its common sense to find ways out of precarious institutional situations such as that which we now face at the end of the twentieth century [Veblen 1964, 25]. But we never stop trying, either.

The Marxist Paradigm

What are the most important relationships in society? For Marxists, all of society may be divided into the "social structure" (also called the social superstructure) and the "economic structure" (also called the economic base). The social structure consists of all ideas and all noneconomic institutions such as the family, government, political parties, education, and religion. The economic structure consists of the relations and the forces of production. The forces of production consist of land, labor, capital, and technology. The relations of production are the relations of classes of people within the economic process such as slave and slave-owner.

All Marxists agree that the economic structure affects the social structure. Critical Marxists, however, also emphasize that the social structure affects the economic structure. Thus, the crucial relationships are between social ideas, noneconomic institutions, economic (class) relations, and the forces of production.

For critical Marxists, power is important in society, but it is a derivative of class relations. (For a full discussion of class and power, see Sherman [1987, chap. 8].) Because the capitalist controls capital, the capitalist is able to hire and fire workers as well as to exploit workers; that is the face of economic power. Because the capitalist class has economic power, it also has political power. A crude example was the ability of Ross Perot to spend $60 million on an election campaign. But Marxists have also written reams of literature on the subtle aspects of power, from the para-meters of a privately owned media to the legitimation of the status quo by foundation-funded academics to the implicit threats of capital to leave a region if the environmental controls are too stiff. (This literature is discussed in detail in Sherman [1987, chap. 9].)

How are technology and ideas related? In the official Marxian view, the economic base determines the social superstructure. Furthermore, within the economic base, the forces of production determine the relations of production. Since technology is the most dynamic part of the forces of production, it follows that ideas are ultimately determined by technology.

Critical Marxists agree that the economic structure affects the social structure, but they emphasize that the social structure also affects the economic structure. Furthermore, critical Marxists agree that the forces of production affect the relations of production, but they also insist that the relations of production affect the forces of production. It follows that ideas and technology interact (see detailed discussion in Sherman [1979]).

What are the key interactions? Suppose there is a rigid class structure such as feudalism in medieval Europe. Suppose that technology begins to change. Suppose there are improvements in agriculture, leading to a large increase in the agricultural surplus. A big surplus encourages trade, leading to cities, in which people specialize in certain crafts. Merchants arise who buy and sell the agricultural goods as well as the craft products. But all of this new technology is out of place in feudalism; a feudal noble does not want to become a merchant, nor does he wish to allow his serfs to escape and become craftspeople or merchants. The feudal lords put restrictions on craft technology, prohibit lending for interest, and charge heavy tolls on merchants, thus holding back economic progress.

Is there class conflict? In the late medieval period, the frictions between a rigid class system and growing technological possibilities led to friction between the interests of various classes. The city folk in crafts and trade wanted an end to all feudal regulations and restrictions. The serfs were attracted by the freedom in the cities and wanted to escape the feudal manors. The feudal nobility fought to maintain the status quo. (See discussion of the origins of capitalism in Sherman [1987, chap. 3].) These class frictions were reflected in political fights and upheavals and eventually in the English revolution of 1648 and the French revolution of 1789. Moreover, such class conflicts are surely the background for the famous democratic protest writings of the period by people such as Voltaire, Jean Jaques Rousseau, and Thomas Paine. Such writing did not merely reflect society, but played an active role in changing it.

In the United States today, the fight over taxation of capital gains certainly reflects class interests and leads to class conflict. Presidential actions and congressional debates give vent to those interests. Ideological warfare ensues over whether taxes on capital gains are good or bad. Typically, throughout history each class presents its ideological standard as the good of the whole nation. Thus, President Bush did not argue for lower capital gains taxes on the grounds that they would benefit his wealthy friends; rather, he claimed the lower taxes would lead to more investment, which would lead to more employment for all Americans. Whatever the rhetoric, this is class conflict.

How is class related to technology and ideas? In the view of critical Marxism, a given level of technology will support only a given range of class relations. Thus, if technology is so primitive that a worker cannot produce any surplus in one day beyond his or her own subsistence, then exploitation is impossible. Slavery was not profitable in most primitive hunting and gathering civilizations of the old Stone Age because a slave could only produce enough to keep the slave alive.

At the same time, a given level of class relations can only make use of a certain range of technology. A slave society, for example, can only make use of simple implements and simple forms of organization. If a slave is given a complex mechanism, the only rational response is to destroy it so one can rest or to transform it into a weapon in order to escape slavery. (See discussion of the literature on slavery in Sherman [1987, chap. 3].)

A ruling class must have ideas that are congenial to its rule. If most people in the United States believed strongly in socialism, then capitalism would be overthrown. A ruling class will usually attempt to make its own ideas the dominant ideas of its society—and usually it will succeed. If it does not succeed, a revolution is imminent. In the United States, the ideas of capitalism are dominant because of many things including the media, the education system, organized religion, the necessity of keeping a job, and the fact that capitalism is the only reality.

In summary, technology affects class, but class also affects technology. Class relations affect ideas, but ideas also affect class relations. *Can all social explanations be reduced to technology? To ideas? To class?* Some Marxist writers have tried to reduce all social explanations to technological change. But critical Marxists deny that understanding of society can be reduced to technology. Modern critical Marxists emphasize that the "mode of production" includes both technology and class relations. The previous section showed how technology does, indeed, affect class relations. Yet it also showed how class relations affect technology, so technology cannot be seen as a prime mover with nothing moving it. One must always be able to explain technological change by its relation to the rest of society. Why is there interest in a particular problem at a given time? Who does the research? How is the research funded?

There is a tendency in neoclassical economics to reduce all explanations to psychological factors. Given the preferences of individuals, a pattern of demand will emerge, so certain things will be produced. This explanation suffers the same kind of fatal flaw as does the official Marxist view of economic reductionism—namely, the fact that official Marxism cannot explain technology itself while neoclassical economics cannot explain ideas themselves. Somehow, one must explain the evolution of ideas. In his Presidential Address to the American Economic Association, John Kenneth Galbraith [1973] made the simple point that consumers are not born with preferences for television sets. One must explain the emergence of these preferences from the rest of social relations. So ideas are not a final prime mover. The last section showed not only that ideas affect class relations, but that class also affects ideas.

Since both ideas and technology affect class, all explanations cannot be reduced to class. In fact, society is an integrated organism, so only its relationships can explain it. It is wrong to try to isolate one particular factor as the only active factor.

What is the role of the individual? It has been shown above that individual ideas affect society, while society also affects individual ideas. The individual is part of society, so it is wrong to ever visualize an individual outside of society. To ask if the individual affects society is like asking if the legs of a person affect that person—both are silly questions. Every individual affects society, so "great" individuals certainly do affect society. But what an individual can accomplish certainly depends on what situation that individual has inherited. If Albert Einstein had been born into a primitive society, he could not have invented the theory of relativity. That theory was possible only when others had done a lot of previous theoretical work, when technology had reached a high enough level to make the concepts relevant, and when class relations were such as to encourage such research. Having said all that, the personality of Albert Einstein certainly affected his research and his research certainly affected society.

On the methodological level, critical Marxists do not agree with the individualist methodology of neoclassical economics. Neither do they agree with the extreme collectivist methodology, used by Hegel to discuss the state as if it were alive or by official Marxists to discuss a class as if it had a will beyond its members. Critical Marxists use a moderate relational or holistic view in which class relations are quite real but must be supported by observations—not assumptions—about the individuals in those classes.

Can the social sciences be ahistorical? Social science certainly can be ahistorical since neoclassical economics is ahistorical. It claims that its laws are valid for all societies. But ahistorical social science distorts social understanding, so social science should always be historical.

To be historical means acknowledging that each type of society has its own laws. Laws—or social regularities—are specific to particular societies. Different societies perform differently. Thus, the Soviet Union, under central planning from 1928 to 1988, suffered no unemployment because central planning necessarily prevented it. Cyclical unemployment is, as Wesley Mitchell showed in many books [see, e.g., Mitchell 1913], a typical characteristic of capitalist societies; it did not exist under feudalism—nor did it exist in the Soviet system [Mitchell is discussed extensively from a Marxist view in Sherman 1991]. The characteristic evils and problems of feudalism or of the Soviet system were very different from those of capitalism and from each other. Of course, any two societies may have some particular thing in common. For example, both the U.S. and Soviet systems made use of money and paid workers a money wage. In addition to historical specificity, to be historical in approach also means to explain historical evolution. That is discussed in the next section.

Is there social evolution? If one means by evolution a progression from lower to higher or from worse to better forms of society, then no such progression is necessary or guaranteed. As in Darwin's theory of biological evolution, the most one can say is that an organism or a society adapts itself to its environment. That organism or society that adapts itself to its environment will survive.

In the case of society, evolution operates by and through the operation of human intelligence, though the decisions are not always rational and are subject to various biases. If a human being sees that one society is doing a superior job of providing a better life to its citizens than another society, then a human being will normally choose the social system that looks better. Thus, a primitive tribe that is conquered by the British Empire might begin to adopt and emulate the customs of the British even if they were not forced to do so. The coercion to become an integral part of the British Empire or the Roman Empire was both economic and military.

But adaptation is only in small part a process of conscious adaptation. The least fit societies will die out both by external competition and by internal revolution, caused by the clash between rigid class systems and changing technology. Both nature and technology constitute the environment to which a society must adapt or else not survive. Marx spoke of the conflict between the frozen class relations (defended to the last gasp by the ruling class that benefits from them) and the changing forces of production (including better technology, more capital, and more education).

Is evolution teleological and predetermined? It was shown above that all we can predict is survival of the fittest society—but that is defined as adaptation to the environment, not necessarily as a "better" society as human beings would define it—so there is no teleological goal that society must follow.

When Marx speaks of social evolution as the result of the conflict between class relations and the forces of production, does that mean that history is predetermined by forces external to human beings and that human beings have no free will? No, critical Marxists believe that human beings make their own history, though under given conditions. "Class relations" are human relationships, not a mere abstraction. When there is a clash between a rigid class society and the possibilities of material progress for adaptation to the environment), class relations will change if, and only if, human beings become aware of the situation and are motivated to do something about it. When the U.S. South was a slave society, industrial improvement was retarded by slave relations. The slaves were not interested in greater productivity, while the slaveowners desired it only within such limits as would retain their power over the slaves. The elite of every Third World country desires economic development but holds it back when the necessary specific measures would undermine its own power—for example, they resist paying taxes necessary for governments to build roads, schools, and so forth.

The fact that the ruling class is holding back development may or may not lead to a revolutionary change. It will lead to that change only if a sufficient number of people become aware of the issues and are motivated to change it. So it is people who make changes—within given circumstances.

What causes historical evolution? In broad terms, this question has already been answered. Societies, like animal populations, change because the process weeds out the unfit and leads to survival of the fit. Specifically, as also shown above, the process is never ending, but we may begin the story with the possibility of improving forces of production held back by the unyielding class relations. Suppose, for example, that the Great Depression had lasted another 20 years in the United States and Europe. Can anyone not agree that there would have been very drastic changes in those societies?

As an actual example, consider the former Soviet Union. Its system of class relations led to rapid progress up through the 1950s and had wide support. But the class relations (including central control and planning as well as political dictatorship by a small elite) eventually led to slower and slower growth, with decline in the late 1980s. That decline caused the ruling class to first try to reform the system. Then a coalition of some parts of the old ruling class with other rising groups destroyed the old system and set about building a new one. This example shows how certain conditions of conflict and tension in the society lead to the change of human ideas, and those changed ideas lead to a change in the class relations.

Is evolution a simple, linear process? The popular propaganda of official Marxism pointed toward a simple progression from slavery to feudalism to capitalism to socialism to communism in all societies. This view was never defended by serious Marxist scholars. Society does evolve, as shown above, but the process is complex, resembling the very complex tree of biological evolution with its many branches. Societies may regress in some cases (either by external invasion or internal causes such as environmental destruction). Societies may jump over any given step that others have gone through. Societies may change at very different rates.

All of this shows anything but a linear path of evolution. If one needed more evidence, the fact that the Soviet Union is regressing to capitalism from some kind of non-capitalist system should convince anyone that evolution is nonlinear. Soviet society was deep in trouble and had to change. But it could have changed in various directions. In fact, its people (including a large part of the ruling class) thought that they could get the best parts of European and U.S. capitalism while retaining the beneficial aspects of their old system (such as full employment). By hindsight, one can understand how this mistaken view became so widespread in a desperate situation. At any rate, the Soviet collapse is an example of historical evolution but certainly not a simple linear path.

Comparison of the Two Paradigms

A Framework for Comparison

Before comparing the answers to basic questions, a framework for comparison is needed. Systems of thought can be related in five ways, in order of increasing convergence: (1) they can be unrelated to each other, (2) contradict each other, (3) compete with each other, (4) complement each other, or (5) coincide with each other.

1. When systems of thought are unrelated, they clatter past each other like noisy trains blowing wind, but they have no real effect on each other. They are on different tracks—the basic terms used and relations emphasized are different and cannot be translated one to the other without destroying the original meaning. The systems of thought are also going in different directions—explaining different things and dealing with different problems. Being unrelated, they simply go past each other. The truth or untruth of one is meaningless in terms of the truth or untruth of the other. In the terminology of Thomas Kuhn [1962], the two paradigms are not comparable.

2. Systems of thought can contradict each other. They are like trains on the same track—the terms used and relations emphasized can be translated into each other. But they are headed straight toward each other and will crash. One can be true only at the expense of the untruth of the other. The usual case is a combination of cases (1) and (2), that is, the paradigms appear to contradict each other, but it is difficult or impossible to translate from one to the other.

3. Systems of thought can compete with each other. In this case, they are like trains racing each other to the same destination but on different tracks. The terms they use and the relations they emphasize mean different things, but the things they try to explain and the problems they try to resolve are the same. The truth or untruth of one is operationally significant to the other, but their competition does not necessarily mean that the truth of one is at the expense of the untruth of the other because the meanings of their basic terms and relations are different. In this case, the two paradigms have

much in common, but in so far as one can translate from one to the other, differences remain.

4. When systems of thought are complements, they move together as in a convoy. They are on close and parallel tracks because the basic terms used by each, and relations emphasized by each, either have the same meanings or can be translated one into the other without doing serious damage to the original meanings of the terms and relations. The problems dealt with and the explanations attempted are not the same, even though the terms and relations used can be translated to mean the same thing or at least to be meaningful in both systems. The truth or untruth of each paradigm is meaningful to the other. Each paradigm can be true with respect to different problems or different explanations.

5. Systems of thought can coincide. Their terms and relations, though named differently, mean the same things and the problems dealt with and explanations offered, though named differently, also mean the same. In such case, they are actually one paradigm, expressed differently.

What are the most important relationships in society? Power is the most important relationship in institutionalism, while class is the most important relationship in Marxism. The two schools of thought do not crash into each other (contradict each other) nor do they clatter past each other (fail to relate). Instead, they compete in some respects but clearly complement in other respects. They are important and meaningful, one to the other.

To see how the two systems complement each other, note that the institutionalist relationship "power" can be translated into the Marxist relationship "class" or "relation of production." Power means the ability to get others to do what you want. This can be translated into the ability of capitalists to get workers to work an amount of time for an amount of money, the product of that labor being owned by the capitalist. Furthermore, note that the Marxist term "superstructure" can be translated into the institutionalist term "enabling myth." The superstructure refers to ideas, like neoclassical economics, that affect the economic structure by justifying it as efficient.

At least some of the basic terms of the two can be translated into each other, but those terms are often used to explain different things or to resolve different problems. Power is used by institutionalists to explain the acquisition of rights and the imposition of burdens in the evolution of working rules in a going concern. The concepts of class or relations of production are used by Marxists, however, to explain the conflict of classes in the economy. The two views complement each other. Using both systems of thought enlarges the scope of problems and relations that can be explained.

But using both systems of thought also shows areas where the two compete. Both institutionalism and Marxism try to explain change, but their explanations compete. Marxism explains change in terms of class conflict, and radical institutionalism does so in terms of cultural lag. One involves a struggle against class interest, while the other involves a struggle against outmoded ideas. Even a correct translation still leaves some issues in dispute. Institutionalists and Marxists understand each others' terms, but the terms compete. Both explanations may be true, depending on the nature of the case in question.

How are technology and ideas related? Here the two schools coincide on a broad front and compete in a narrow range. They coincide to the extent that the meanings of the different terms used by each can be readily translated into each other. If the Marxist economic base (particularly the forces of production) is translated as the institutionalist concept of technology, and if the institutionalist concept of enabling myth is translated as the Marxist concept of social superstructure, then both schools can be said to explain how technology, or forces of production, determine ideas or social superstructure. Of course, neither system of thought is simple. Each emphasizes the enormous complexity and mutual interaction between technology and ideas or between the forces of production and social superstructure. Nevertheless, they coincide on a broad front, particularly in the emphasis each puts on the importance of the industrial revolution. The two schools of thought also compete in their treatment of technology and ideas because radical institutionalists use the concept of cultural lag, and Marxists use the concept of class interest to explain the friction-creating part of the complex and mutual relationship between technology and ideas. The institutionalist cultural lag emphasizes enabling myth (the neoclassical myth of consumer sovereignty is one) as a factor that distorts how people come to understand their own economic interests. However, class interests are perceived by Marxists as one of the factors affecting culture (with other factors being ideologies such as racism, sexism, and neoclassical economics). They compete in the sense of having different emphases, but the concepts are also complementary.

Is there class conflict? Here the schools compete to some degree. They use different terms and emphasize different relationships to explain the same kinds of thing—social conflict and change. In Marxism, class interests are one important cause of behavior, though personal experiences of race, gender, and ethnicity as well as ideological blinders, also play key roles. Class interests conflict, and the conflict of interests gives rise to considerable ideological warfare—and in times of crisis may result in political upheaval. Certainly, in the Marxist view, class interests may be modified by other group interests or by the weight of the prevailing ideology (remember Herbert Marcuse's *One Dimensional Man*). The conflict between class interests, though, will sometimes lead to confrontation and crisis. Yet the form of crisis may be racial (as in the U.S. Civil War), national (as in the collapse of the Soviet Union), or even religious struggle (as in the English civil war of 1648). Systemic changes occur during times of crisis.

According to radical institutionalists, people generally believe in enabling myths that distort their understanding of their own economic interests (particularly the poor and the outsider) and make it difficult for them to act collectively. The conflict between economic interests then is indirect and cultural. Changes occur through the spread of enlightenment and as the advance of science debunks the myths of racism, sexism, and classism.

But here the schools appear to contradict each other. To the extent that institutionalism insists that conflict takes the form of cultural lag and that change takes place incrementally through institutional adjustment due to spreading enlightenment, and to the extent that Marxism insists that drastic change sometimes takes place relatively suddenly through class conflict culminating in crisis, the two schools of thought contradict each other. The two views of change are complementary with respect to incremental reforms (differing only in emphasis) but are competing or even contradictory with respect to revolutionary change.

Reconciliation is possible on the institutionalist side if to cultural lag and gradual change through institutional adjustment, the Marxism of class conflict and sudden change due to crisis is added. Reconciliation is possible on the Marxist side if to class conflict and change through crisis, the institutionalism of cultural lag and change through institutional adjustment are added. (Note that there is a huge Marxist literature, beginning with the Frankfurt school and Jurgen Habermas, that concentrates solely on issues of ideology, consciousness, and cultural lag and on the role they play in reform and revolution.) Of course, both schools acknowledge the interaction of ideology, class interest, and institutional structures. The issue is one of exact causes and degree of discontinuity in social evolution.

How is class related to technology and ideas? In answering this question, the two schools have usually clattered past each other, with no benefit to either. This is because the two schools are unrelated unless class interest from Marxism and power relation from institutionalism are carefully translated one into the other. But with successful translation of concepts used by both, considerable enrichment is possible. For example, the concept of ceremonial encapsulation may be translated by radical institutionalists in order to enrich the thought of critical Marxists. The benefits of a new technology are captured by a vested interest, and the burdens of the new technology are passed on to the local community when the technology is ceremonially encapsulated. Ceremonial encapsulation allows for significant insight into how powerful corporations (capitalist class) can implement new technologies and reap substantial profits while imposing substantial costs on impacted communities. Nuclear power plants in populated areas and center-pivot irrigation systems on the Great Plains are examples of ceremonial encapsulation. Similarly, the insights of Marxists into interest conflict and revolutionary processes might be translated to the benefit of radical institutionalists. The scenario of forces versus relations can be translated in order to sound remarkably similar to the tensions of technology versus institutions (including the Veblenian concept of resistance, and even sabotage, by vested interests).

Can all social relations be reduced to technology? To ideas? To class? On this question, the two schools of thought coincide. Neither believes that all social relations can be reduced to technology or to ideas or to class. Both schools of thought are strongly opposed to such reductionism and view society as a complex set of relationships that is forever changing. Nonetheless, both schools of thought view technology as a vital part of the dynamics of change. Technology is not necessarily progressive. Both schools of thought accept the Galbraithian revised sequence, for example [Galbraith 1967, 211–218].

Some competition also exists. Important differences come into play when the two schools of thought explain how technology affects the rest of the social system. Radical institutionalism emphasizes cultural lag: the forward thrust of new technology meeting the past-bound resistance of institutionalized thought patterns. Marxism emphasizes class conflict: the struggle for the income, status, and power generated by new forces of production, a struggle taking place in the workplace and also in all of society. Note, however, that critical Marxists do not deny, but rather emphasize the power of past-bound thought; however, radical institutionalists do not deny, but emphasize the power of vested interests.

What is the role of the individual? On this question, the two schools of thought coincide. Neither takes individual preferences or beliefs as given. Both schools of thought treat preferences and beliefs as variables to be explained rather than assumed. Both schools of thought construct theories of the individual. That is, both schools of thought try to explain how the context in which individuals find themselves affects the individuals and how the individuals in that context affect the context itself.

Can the social sciences be ahistorical? The answers to this question by institutionalists and Marxists coincide. Any ahistorical social science, such as neoclassical economics, is inadequate. Any adequate social science must be historical, with specific laws applying to each social-economic system.

Is there social evolution? Both institutionalists and Marxists believe that evolution exists in the sense that both incremental and drastic changes do occur, so they coincide to that degree. Both have had extensive controversies among themselves regarding whether social evolution means progress to better societies. In the nineteenth and early twentieth centuries, both did believe in "progress" to "better" societies. After lengthy discussion, changes in the social milieu, and new social experiences, however, most scholars in both schools have slowly changed their views. Most members of both groups have concluded that there is evolutionary change, but not necessarily "progress."

Is evolution teleological and predetermined? At one time, both schools tended to think that evolution was predetermined by historical forces to progress to better societies. Official Marxism said it was inevitable that society would pass from feudalism to capitalism to socialism. But few, if any, contemporary critical Marxists agree; they believe that evolution changes in complex ways, with no direction from God or Marx or "history." Similarly, at one time many institutionalists believed that progress was somehow ordained in spite of entrenched interests and enabling myths. Now, most institutionalists have given up that crutch, as have most Marxists. Their views thus coincide in a nonteleological and nonpredetermined evolution.

What causes historical evolution? Critical Marxists, using a reconstructed version of the old Marxian approach, conclude that there are situations in which class relationships hold back the improvement of the forces of production (including technology). Such a situation leads to tensions and conflicts within society; these human conflicts will then lead to change and to the evolution of a new society.

Institutionalists point to the process of cumulative causation, in which one change leads to another so that society gathers momentum in one direction, eventually leading to change of existing institutions and relationships. Such cumulative changes may benefit either the ruling elite or the underdogs. The direction of change is simply a blind drift so long as there is not conscious control by all of society. If there is conscious control, society can choose its direction within the existing parameters. (This institutionalist view sounds somewhat like Engels's notion that society would someday pass from the realm of necessity to that of freedom [Engels 1888].)

Is evolution a simple, linear process? Contemporary Marxists reject the old, official Marxist view that society must evolve along a simple, linear path through predetermined stages. They see evolution as a very complex process that includes diffusion, regression, jumps, and other adaptations. Institutionalists have never doubted that society evolves in exceedingly complex and contradictory ways—and modern institutionalists are clear that societies may not "progress," but may dead end and disintegrate. Thus, at an earlier period, considerable differences existed between Marxists and institutionalists in this area, even though both believed in progress. Now their views coincide on this issue, both having reached a more limited, but more viable, understanding.

Conclusion

At one time, it was true that Marxists and institutionalists had conflicting views in a number of the areas we have explored. Now, however, they coincide in some basic issues, but for the most part they have differing, though complementary, approaches. One can learn much by studying both with an open mind.

The clearest convergence between modern Marxists and modern institutionalists is on two basic points: (1) a nonreductionist relational or holistic view of ideas, structures, and the individual; and (2) a nonstatic historical or evolutionary view of society as process. The clearest differences in emphasis and rhetoric—and perhaps in substance—are in the areas of the conceptualization of class versus power and in the notions of what kind of conflicts lead to revolutionary changes.

In the limited space of this article, issues were discussed with extreme brevity. No attempt was made to discuss the extensive literature in each area or to provide extensive citations. We did not attempt final answers to our questions. Moreover, we did not discuss detailed economic issues, such as the concept of markets, or issues of high-level methodology, such as the role of ethical values in analysis—these issues must be left to later articles. Our modest aim was to start a dialogue between Marxists and institutionalists, with a road map of some of the important questions to be explored and with the purpose of enlightenment for both.

Note

The authors are grateful to David Fairris for his criticisms on an earlier draft.

References

Dugger, William M. *Radical Institutionalism.* New York: Greenwood Press, 1989.

————. *Underground Economics.* Armonk, N.Y.: M. E. Sharpe, 1992.

Dugger, William M., and William T. Waller, Jr., eds. *The Stratified State.* Armonk, N.Y.: M. E. Sharpe, 1992.

Engels, Frederick. *Ludwig Feuerbach.* New York: International Publishers, n.d. (Original published in 1888).

Galbraith, John Kenneth. *The New Industrial State.* Boston: Houghton Mifflin, 1987.

————. "Power and the Useful Economist." *American Economic Review* 63, no. 1 (March 1973): 469–78.

Kuhn, Thomas. *The Structure of Scientific Revolutions.* Chicago: University of Chicago Press, 1968.

Marcuse, Herbert. *One Dimensional Man.* Boston: Beacon Press, 1964.

Sherman, Howard J. "Technology vis-a-vis Institutions: A Marxist Commentary." *Journal of Economic Issues* 13, no. 1 (March 1979): 175–193.

————. *Foundations of Radical Political Economy.* Armonk, N.Y.: M. E. Sharpe, 1987.

————. *The Business Cycle: Growth and Crisis Under Capitalism.* Princeton, N.J.: Princeton University Press, 1991.

Veblen, Thorstein. *The Place of Science in Modern Civilization and Other Essays.* New York: B. W. Huebsch, 1919.

————. *The Instinct of Workmanship.* New York: Augustus M. Kelley, 1964.

PART IV

THE CHANGING FACE OF RADICAL POLITICAL ECONOMY

There is a long agenda awaiting socialist economists. They cannot even begin to face the real problems unless they openly reject the utopian elements of the Marxist tradition. Marx would surely have revised his own ideas if he had lived a hundred years longer—he would have been a "revisionist." There were many things he could not possibly foresee: nuclear weapons, for instance. Great man though he was, he could also just occasionally be wrong.

. . . Western mainstream economists escape reality by retreating into mathematical abstractions and an artificial world of formulae. Those who claim to believe in "praxis" should not take refuge in some "socialist" equivalent of general equilibrium never-never land. "Marxist scholars have interpreted his doctrines in this way and that. The point however is to change them."

—Alec Nove, *The Economics of Feasible Socialism*

10

POSTMODERNISM, MARXISM, AND THE CRITIQUE OF MODERN ECONOMIC THOUGHT

JACK AMARIGLIO AND DAVID F. RUCCIO

If postmodernism as critique has exhausted itself in cultural and literary circles, this result stands in sharp contrast to the situation within contemporary economics. The destabilizing effects of postmodernism are only beginning to be noticed in the area of economics, and the resistance of philosophers and historians of economic thought to the critical currents of postmodern theory is precisely because they have understood (correctly, we think) the mostly nihilistic implications of adopting epistemologically "relativist" and antiscientistic stances. Add to this the fact that most economists remain firmly committed to the modernist premises of their enterprise—to the unified rationality of the intentional economic subject/agent, to determinism in causal explanations, to a notion of economic knowledge (for both subjects and economic scientists) that treats cognition as a "mirror of nature"—and what emerges is a picture of a discipline in which the transition from high modernism (if it has even reached that stage) to postmodernism has largely been arrested.[1]

This characterization is not only true of mainstream economic theories (especially neoclassical and Keynesian); to different degrees it holds as well for most Marxian approaches, from orthodox and classical versions to the more recent analytical Marxism and others. So, while it is now increasingly fashionable to declare postmodern thought to have been merely a passing fad (from what tried-but-true point of view, one wonders?), it remains the case that the challenges unleashed by post-modernism to the unified, rational subject, to all forms of determinism, and to traditional epistemology have hardly been met, let alone negated, in the field of economics.

This situation may now be changing.[2] A "new" philosophy of eco-nomics—one that is not wedded to repetitious and stale renegotiations of logical positivism and/or the legacy of Karl Popper but, instead, is pursuing the alternative paths created by postmodern approaches to science and language—has developed in recent years with great vigor and scope.[3] This new philosophy is evident in projects that range from Stephen Resnick and Richard Wolff's (1987a) antideterministic reconfiguration of Marxian epistemology and methodology, Donald McCloskey's (1985) focus on economic "rhetoric," and Arjo Klamer's (1990) antimodernist anthropological investigations of economic "conversations" to Philip Mirowski's (1991) revelation of contemporary neoclassical economic theory's ill-fated reliance on the metaphors and methods of nineteenth-century physical science, Diana Strassmann's (1993a) and Julie Nelson's (1992) depictions of the gendered writing strategies of most economic theory, and finally to our own attempts (Amariglio 1990; Ruccio 1991) to unearth the "postmodern moments" of twentieth-century economic thought. While it cannot be said that these departures from traditional economic philosophy all acknowledge the progenitors of postmodern theory (and here we include the works of Nietzsche, Foucault, Derrida, and Lyotard, among others)—indeed, some of them explicitly refuse the connection to postmodernism, and to poststructuralism and deconstruction—it is our view that the discursive forms and timing of their critiques have been made possible mostly as a result of the spread of postmodern theory and culture in the West during the past twenty-five years. Each of these projects exemplifies a shift away from debates about the "growth of scientific knowledge" and the meaning of "falsifiability" and toward an investigation of the discursive elements of the production of economic theories and the social conditions implied in "reading" economic writings; and certainly such a shift has been stimulated by postmodern concerns with textuality and power as well as a fundamental disbelief in the self-professed disinterestedness of positive economic analysis.

In writing about the development of these postmodern projects, we wish to make clear our strong difference with those (most often noneconomists) who, perhaps unwittingly, collapse the issue of the nature of contemporary economic processes and the issue of the quality and character of current economic theory.[4] In this paper, we do not treat postmodernism as a surrogate for discussing something called "late capitalism." Aside from our skepticism about such a term, we do not regard the changes that are now occurring in cultural and social theory as a corollary to or a reflection of the emergence of "consumerism" or whatever other fetishized sign under which all postmodern theory is supposed to exist. We do not deny the effectivity of economic processes on postmodern discursivity (or the reverse). What we do reject is the simplistic— and, we believe, mistaken—way in which the theory of late capitalism (or, what is often taken to be the same, postindustrial or consumer society) has been read and the even more facile way in which it has been used to support the view that there is a more-or-less simple transposition of the economic processes that are said to underlie this phase of capitalist development to the theoretical and cultural level. Deducing a ubiquitous culture of "consumerism" (and then postmodernism) from the idea that the realization of surplus-value is decidedly problematic in the present world (but when has it been otherwise in the history of capitalism?) simply will not do.[5]

In any event, no effort is made here to characterize the "modes of production" that can be said to exist at present. And, certainly, no implication about economic processes should be derived from our discussion of the postmodern moments of contemporary economics. Here, we concentrate our efforts on economic thought, on depicting and evaluating the postmodern moments of, first, mainstream and then, Marxian modes of theorizing about the economy.

In doing so, we note immediately that there is good reason to see much of contemporary economic thought as exemplifying what has been called economic modernism. Although neoclassical, Keynesian, and Marxian economic theories (to name just three) differ from one another, in some places considerably, we also think that there are some conceptual contrasts that serve as the foundational axes around which each of these discourses is composed. Together, these contrasts or distinctions comprise the common modernity of these otherwise different theoretical frameworks. We will concentrate on only three of them here: (a) order and disorder (i.e., the related questions of ontological structural patterns and causal determinism), (b) centering and decentering (here, we limit our attention to the composition and nature of the economic subject), and (c) certainty and uncertainty (both as epistemological discursive norms and as descriptions of an ontological reality).

Our view is that economic modernism both constitutes these contrasts as fundamental to any discourse viewed as economic theory and emphasizes one side of the contrast in preference to the other. In general, the modernist preference is for order, centering, and certainty. The reasons for this are not hard to fathom. Many economists, both mainstream and radical, regard as impossible, "nihilistic," and ultimately inappropriate as theory or science most attempts to complicate economic thinking along the lines of disorder, decentering, and uncertainty.[6] That is, even when these latter elements are allowed in as objects of analysis (but not, of course, as epistemological norms), they are always mastered or brought under control by ordering of disorder (discovering the pattern underlying seemingly anarchic economic events); by the centering of decentering (showing that the chaos of desire and the individuation of society do find their limit in some original and intentional subjectivity); and by making certain, or at least probable, uncertainty (demonstrating both that there are reasonable, if not absolute, grounds for knowledge and the action based on it and that most degrees of uncertainty can be calculated by agents and economists alike). Thus, while modern economic thought may not entirely discard— and may even relish the challenge of theorizing—disorder, decentering, and uncertainty, it does so in the conceit that these elements are, in the end, superseded by the discursive ordering and analysis that are presumed to make up modern scientific activity.

Mainstream Economics and Its Critics

Neoclassical economic thought, while constituted by the tension implicit in these dualities, does put forward at least one compelling story that shows nicely the robust connections among the preferences for order, centering, and certainty in economic modernism. Often told by employing the trope of irony (perhaps modernism's characteristic literary strategy), the story of the "invisible hand" emerges as the result of the initial positing of disorder, decentering, and uncertainty and then deriving a set of consequences that seems to be remote—an unlikely possibility—in the stipulation of the initial conditions.[7]

Drawing upon Adam Smith as the original source, neoclassical economists begin with the premise that civil society, rather than being governed by an overarching religious authority or state, is fractured into a plethora of individuated and competing human atoms who take actions on their own behalf without knowing in advance either the actions of others or, for that matter, the potential consequences of their own actions.[8] Of course, the apparent chaos that is suggested by the interaction of the teeming mass of uncertain individual actors is shown to converge toward a well-ordered, "general equilibrium" solution—in which all individuals maximize their utility and economy-wide opti-mality is achieved—by virtue of decentralized markets. Thus, the modernist paradox is solved by showing that (a) economic coordination can be achieved (market transactions are mostly orderly processes) as the outcome of (b) the unintended (or not necessarily intended) actions of self-interested, rational agents (the centered, cognitive subject is the first and only source of all decisions and actions), the consequence of which is (c) that uncertainty is eliminated (as each agent's expectations tend to correspond with the actual results achieved, at least to the extent that each individual's plans for self-satisfaction are realized through market transactions). Indeed, in this last matter, agents come to see markets as the primary means to make their expectations correspond to actual outcomes, and vice versa. In this way, and barring market imperfections and noneconomic obstacles, the initial uncertainty is eliminated through a process of learning: agents come to "know" the consequences of their market behavior through understanding the processes in and through which their individual desires are realized in the myriad transactions that obtain between themselves and others.[9]

In this neoclassical story, then, the initial premise of apparent anarchy is overcome by the order, centering, and certainty that are taken to be both essential attributes and effects of market processes. The unfolding of this story gives rise to the characteristic optimism and progressivism—the utopian vision—of modernism since it confirms post-Enlightenment beliefs in the efficacy and social beneficence of rationally directed, free, and individual choice.

Even within the confines of mainstream economic theories, however, the dualities that in our view are representative of such modernist stories are, in fact, unstable and often begin to unravel and/or to deconstruct themselves. Thus, in the ceaseless pursuit to update the kind of market story we have just presented, economists in this century have frequently embraced indeterminism, disequilibria, and chaos, "partly" rational or even rule-driven subjects, and radical uncertainty which they perceive as part and parcel of modern market processes.[10] But these elements—these discursive methods and conceptual concerns also comprise the postmodern moments whose nihilistic potential, if and when pursued, calls into question the coherence and consistency of such narratives.

These postmodern moments also serve as an organizing point for a critique of neoclassical and Keynesian theories insofar as they allow critics to discern the "weak links" in the totalizing stories of these theories and they beckon toward different theoretical, oppositional stances. While, to date, these postmodern moments have been mostly domesticated and contained by the modernizing aspects of economic theory—for example, uncertainty is shown to be about degrees of either objective or subjective rational belief, thus keeping alive empiricist notions of objective reality beyond the subject or the inherent wholeness and intentionality of the subject—they are often picked up and pushed toward their deconstructive limits by opponents and critics of the mainstream. For example, within Post Keynesian and feminist economics (to name just two), concepts of disorder, decentering, or uncertainty often play a key role in criticisms of neoclassical and mainstream Keynesian theories. For Post Keynesians influenced by the work of G. L. S. Shackle, "true uncertainty," seen as diametrically opposed to certain or even probable knowledge, is touted as the basis for a thoroughgoing reconsideration of economic theory (in some places, as in his 1966 book, Shackle states categorically that "uncertainty is ignorance" [119]).[11] While Shackle's work is embedded in a form of subjectivism and, therefore, preserves the humanist centering characteristic of economic modernism, the radicality of his view of the impossibility of economic knowledge under economic uncertainty and, therefore, of knowledge-based choice is sufficient to summon up the charge of nihilism.[12] Shacklean Post Keynesians regard their work otherwise, that is, as establishing a different economic theory in which the relativism of true choice on the part of economic agents, at least in regard to knowledge, (implied in, among other things, the ideas of "degrees of potential surprise" and "possibility" in choosing courses of economic action in contrast to the probability of their occurrence which, if known in advance, means that no meaningful decision is required) leads to alternative conceptions of the macroeconomy more consistent with radical readings of Keynes than with the mainstream Keynesian view that has been prevalent in the discipline.[13]

Other Post Keynesians court similar charges of nihilism in pursuing the disorganization of a monetary system and the ever-present disequilibria that arise in market situations. The entire apparatus of general equilibrium, often considered to be the hallmark of modern economic theorizing, is called into question by the claim that transactions made "outside equilibrium" are not only common but constitute the norm. In this view, the mostly disorderly nature of decentralized markets is stressed, although it is true that explanations are often given in which some order is indeed uncovered to explain the ever-present tendencies outside and away from equilibrium. Often this approach leads to the demand that institutional analysis be included in a theory of markets so as to reveal the underlying structural constraints or determinants that account for the existence of such permanent disequilibria. By giving credence to institutional analysis these Post Keynesians bring the wrath of other economists down on themselves by appearing to appeal to "ad hoc" explanations, that is, explanations that have no universal theoretical application or validity because they focus on the conjunctural and, therefore, transitory nature of institutions and their effects. Also, these Post Keynesian views are often dismissed as atheoretical because they lack the appropriate "microfoundations"—the idea that all economic behavior should be explained at the level of individual, rational actions—which are presumed to be a necessary condition for economic theory proper.[14] Although even Post Keynesians resort to concepts of the centered subject (especially in their approaches to investment decisions), the mainstream reactions against their work on the issue of microfoundations indicate the degree to which they can be read as having displaced "economic man" as the founding element of economic theory and, thus, as having "decentered," if not their views of the essential nature of the subject, at least their explanations of economic order and causality.

Feminist economics, though still in its initial stages, also draws out some of the more postmodern aspects of contemporary economic theory and adds to them a concern with gendering. In fact, the very pluralizing of economic subjectivity which is implicit in some recent feminist work and the displacing of the autonomous subject by structural forces that are said to "socially construct" all economic subjects uses gender as a means to fracture the totalizing (and male) edifice of traditional neo-classical and Keynesian theories.[15] Though some feminists are very hesitant to embrace postmodern theory, others have utilized post-modern critiques of science and epistemology to deconstruct the con-ceptions of truth, rationality, and action that are tightly conjoined in modern economic theory.[16] The problematic underpinnings of main-stream economic thought are highlighted by the additional insight that the reigning modernist notions of knowledge and subjects are deeply gendered and, therefore, exclude through their assumptions of univer-sality and uniformity socially constructed differences (in the forms of cognition, goals, and actions) between differentially gendered subjects. By bringing to the fore gendered knowledges and subjectivities, feminist economists have begun to construct new theoretical perspectives tending more toward decentered (and therefore more disorderly) economic totalities and a sort of "uncertainty" regarding the nature and effects of rationality and knowledge on economic processes.[17] It is no accident, then, that defenders of the traditional neoclassical and Key-nesian faith, even those sympathetic to some types of feminism, have had the most difficulty in accepting the fragmenting of economic theory that the introduction of such gendered notions of subjectivity and knowledge represents.[18]

Marxian Economics

While we are indebted to the elucidation and deployment of the postmodern moments of mainstream theory by some Post Keynesians and feminists, we have found that the pull of modernism on those theoretical frameworks has been strong enough to blunt their critical edge. We have also found that the modernist cast of much Marxian theory has had a similar effect, restraining Marxian criticisms of the mainstream economics tradition and of the economic system it so often celebrates. In the remainder of this paper, therefore, we turn our attention to identifying and criticizing modernism within Marxism and to posing a postmodern Marxian alternative. In so doing, we point out how the three contrasts we specified in the case of mainstream economics also help to constitute much of Marxian economic and social thought and how, "in the last instance," the emphasis of modernist Marxism is on forms of order, centering, and certainty.[19] Likewise, however, we argue that the postmodern moments of Marxian economics— particularly the emphasis on disorder, decentering, and uncertainty— can be exploited and developed in order to undo those contrasts and, thus, to accomplish a "rupture" with key elements of modernist Marxian discourse.[20]

The dialectical tensions in the order/disorder, centering/decentering, and certainty/uncertainty contrasts get played out in a variety of ways in the Marxian tradition. To name just a few here, these tensions constitute the differentiations and oppositions between the realms of production and circulation, between markets and planning, and, ultimately, between capitalism and socialism. Indeed, there is a sense in which modernist Marxism's critique of capitalist social formations comes down to the contrast between one socioeconomic system (capitalism) in which anarchy, fragmentation, alienation, and uncertainty are the rule and a different one (socialism) in which social order and unification, rational planning, unalienated and self-conscious subjects, fulfilled expectations, and true knowledge are key constituents. That is, modernist Marxian economic and social theory makes clear that, at least at the level of "objective" and historically determined reality, the choice between capitalism and socialism is equivalent to the preference that one may have for living *either* in a society in which, depending on one's viewpoint, the remnants of "premodernism" hold sway ("barbarism," ethnic, national, and racial hostilities, underdevelopment, and the like) or the "underside" of modernism (for some, postmodernism, in which social fragmentation is created but never resolved) is dominant or in a society in which modernity—here identified with a rationally and communally planned "progressive" socioeconomic order—has truly succeeded (by coming to complete fruition).[21]

We return below to a more extended discussion of the role that the three contrasts mentioned above play in the endgame distinction between capitalism and socialism. However, to clarify what is at stake in adhering to such dichotomies, we now turn our attention to the specific contrasts drawn in modernist Marxism between production and circulation and between market and plan.

Production and Circulation

The distinction between the spheres of production and circulation is often conceptualized in modernist Marxism as the difference between the production of value, on the one hand, and the realization of that value, on the other. In many versions, production is seen as structured and stable, at least to the extent that the production of value (including surplus-value) is organized and controlled—ordered in a despotic fashion—by capitalists.[22] Yet, although surplus-value may be produced within the confines of capitalist enterprises, the realization of that surplus value (and therefore of money profits) depends upon the existence of demand for the commodities adequate to allow them to be sold at their values. Numerous Marxist economists have found in Marx's discussions of the realization problem in volume 1 of *Capital* (1977) the general form of crisis within capitalism. That is, because of the absence of foreknowledge of demand, and because demand is decentralized and is attendant upon millions of individual households and other firms, the problem for capitalists in realizing the surplus-value created in their enterprises and under their control is that the realm of circulation is quixotic at best and anarchic at worst. For example, some capitalists may face a problem of "underconsumption" if the sum total of wages paid to workers is insufficient to meet their initial output decisions. Similarly, capitalists may be victims of the absence of appropriate "proportionalities" among "departments" of production, such as the possible disproportionality that can occur between the wage-goods and capital-goods sectors, which results from the lack of conscious coordination between these sectors. Here each firm makes calculations about its needed rates of input and consequent rates of output on the basis of its own estimates, but it lacks the foreknowledge of other firms' plans. One consequence, then, is that individual firms and even whole sectors can "miscalculate" the needs of other firms and households, resulting in the observed disproportionality.

Since uncertainty reigns in the sphere of circulation, individual capitalists suffer from the unplanned character of markets, and some are unable to appropriate (in the form of money) the surplus-value that, in their view, they have worked hard to bring forth. Capitalists who are unable to sell their commodities at their value, or even to sell them at all, thus find themselves in the predicament of not being able to achieve the expected rate of profit. They respond, in turn, by making decisions to cut back on production and, if realization problems persist, to forestall new purchases (of labor power, machinery, and/or raw materials). The crisis of accumulation that the problem of realization sets off, then, is one that stems from the original distinction between production and circulation under capitalism insofar as the disorder of the market is blamed for eventually disrupting production and throwing the entire economic system into a temporary if not prolonged crisis.

We should note, however, that there is a different but related story often told in modernist Marxian economic thought which focuses alternatively on the "anarchy of production." Although capitalists may exhibit class solidarity and coordination—for example, in their participation in the state or in relation to demands from contending classes (such as workers, bankers, or landowners)—no such coordination exists in the realm of production. The very fragmentation of capitalist firms, the competition among them, and the necessity to make individual production decisions that are guaranteed by the possession of private property rights over means of production create a situation in which each capitalist is forced to make decisions that, for the capitalist class as a whole, lead to a lower rate of profit. Such a situation may obtain if, in order to expand production, capitalists' demand for laborers exceeds the available supply, thus depleting the "industrial reserve army." When workers' bargaining power is strengthened, wages will be bid up and the rate of profit will decline. The rate of profit may also exhibit a "tendency" to fall if, in order to stem the distribution of some of their surplus-value to other, more productive firms in their sector, capitalists are forced to increase the "organic composition of capital" (the ratio of dead to living labor), thereby decreasing the source of surplus-value. Once again, the diagnosis is that the problem stems essentially from disorder in the capitalist market system, even though here the problem begins in the sphere of production and is the result of the "anarchy" that reigns because of the very existence of private capitalist firms.

Both cases are governed, as in the story of the invisible hand told in modernist neoclassical economics, by the master trope of irony. In this instance, however, rational capitalists who appear to be in control are forced, by virtue of their position in a disorderly, uncertain, and anarchic system of unplanned markets and individual competition, to make decisions that, rather than creating a general equilibrium, more or less inevitably lead to economic instability and crises.[23]

Market and Plan

In this analysis the diagnosis suggests the cure: planned production and coordination among firms. This cure, so the story goes, can be practiced only within the bounds of socialism since the elimination of competitive market forces and private productive property serves as the necessary condition of existence for the emergence of coordination and planning. A more orderly form of economic organization is possible in socialism as long as a central planning board is able to calculate accurately the needed balance between inputs and outputs within and among different industries and branches of production. The fact that enterprises would no longer be motivated to engage in individual attempts at increasing, or at least maintaining, maximum rates of profit through strategies of increasing the rate of exploitation of workers means that these same enterprises can rationally plan—with social goals in mind, and with the foreknowledge of the plans of other firms—not only their output levels but also even the amount of "surplus" that they will be able to retain in order to expand production through additional capital formation.

Hence, the superiority of socialist production lies precisely in the elimination of the disorder and uncertainty that are said to characterize capitalist production and circulation The order that is made possible by planning is presumed to be preferable to the anarchy of capitalist production since the former eliminates the tendency for crises (most importantly, by eradicating the crucial conditions for the existence of exploitation and, therefore, the necessity for producers to sell their commodities at their values) while the latter always tends toward system-wide crises. Capitalist production, circulation, and distribution are thus seen to be fundamentally predicated on the absence of social and economic stability while socialist production, circulation, and distribution are seen to be governed by the real possibility of such stability.

Subjectivity

As we have seen, the modernist Marxian conception of the differences between production and circulation, market and plan are made to serve the ultimate distinction between capitalism and socialism. But this last distinction rests as well on other key modernist premises, such as the centrality of subjectivity in constructing an ethics of system choice. At first sight, this privileging of subjectivity would seem to be one of Marxism's objects of scorn. After all, one of Marxism's strong points has always been the critique of bourgeois individualism. Marxists have in the past argued not only that any form of subjectivity—including individuality—is a product of historical circumstances, and is therefore contingent and conjunctural (and not universal or eternal), but also that the appropriate agent of history is never the abstractly conceived individual but, instead, classes. In this sense, the Marxian tradition, even when thoroughly modernist, has been able to resist the Cartesian idea of the centered subject and its use in the hands of Adam Smith and others as the starting point for economic and social analysis. Yet, we think it would be a mistake to conclude that this resistance has meant the complete displacement or elimination of the centered individual subject from Marxian theory.[24]

In place of the Cartesian concept of the individual subject, many western Marxists seized upon Marx's early writings in opposition to mechanistic and Stalinist Marxism to "reintroduce" a subject whose essential nature is indeed alienated in the historical process. Such Marxists resurrected Marx's idea that class societies come to produce a rupture between the individual's species-nature and the conditions for its realization. Thus, the history of class societies is, at least in part, the history of the emergence of stunted, one-sided, and increasingly disaffected forms of subjectivity. While in pursuit of this idea Lukács and the Critical Theorists alike were careful not to reinstitute the Feuerbachian notion of an abstractly conceived "man," they read Marx as postulating an essential species-being that, in the process of its becoming, that is, its coming to self-consciousness, was capable of eventually realizing itself. Thus, the basic potential wholeness of the human subject was asserted, though now as the end to some teleological process of historical development rather than as an ever-present essence.[25]

In this way, although western Marxists challenged the idea of the eternal, self-motivated individual whose every action reaffirms its essence, their reading of the "early Marx" and the consequent interpretation of commodity fetishism and reification has served to reinscribe the notion of the centered subject perhaps as the historical origin (as in the state of primitive communism, with its putatively "organic" individuals) and certainly as the attainable goal of the "end of history." Thus, modernist Marxism's break with its non-Marxist siblings is more over the question of the possibility of the realization of the centered subject in socialist rather than capitalist social formations than a preference for the decentered subject of postmodernism.[26] In fact, as is now well established, the modernist Marxist criticism of postmodernism is precisely on the point that postmodernists deny the historical possibility of the centered subject (whether now, in the past, or at some distant point in the future) and, therefore, see decentered subjectivity everywhere and at all times. In contrast, modernist Marxists see the decentered subject as the unfortunate historical product of capitalism and, thus, not to be treated as a universal, abstract, and historically transcendent form of subjectivity. For contemporary modernist Marxists, the decentered subject is a deformation of capitalism whose eradication under socialism, where "wholeness" and true self-consciousness are at least historically feasible, is to be desired. The reification of the decentered subject by post-modern thinkers, according to such modernist critics, speaks volumes about the irreducibly reactionary political project of postmodernism.

As we have suggested, in Marxian economic theory this question of the form of subjectivity is best rendered in the debates over the meaning of Marx's discussion of commodity fetishism. The typical reading is that general commodity relations distort the subjects and their consciousnesses to the degree that they come to attribute the qualitative relations among themselves to the commodities that they possess and exchange. This "false consciousness" is a misperception, but it is also the "true" expression of the onesidedness and alienation that is the lot of subjects in a totally commodified social formation. The consequences for the economy of this fetishism of commodities—this perversion of economic subjectivity—are several: capital is treated as a "thing" and not a social relation, money is understood to be the source of self-expanding value, surplus is viewed as arising in exchange, technology is seen as constituting the forms of the labor process, profit is attributed to some quality of the means of production and/or productive activities of capitalists instead of exploitation, and much else.

The overthrow of capitalism, once again, promises a solution to all of this. In socialism, commodity fetishism is banished as production no longer is for exchange but for use, thus eliminating the crucial condition for fetishism to arise. In the modernist Marxist tradition, then, socialism is additionally preferred to capitalism in that the crippling and distorting forms of subjectivity that reflect general market relations under capitalism are replaced by those forms of subjectivity in which agents are now able to "see" clearly (since these relations are now transparent) the social relations behind their interdependent economic links. As a result, as Marxism purports to show, socialism creates the conditions for true knowledge of economic processes and disallows the "errors" about capital, money, profit, and the like that were caused primarily by reification. There is no discrepancy now among the socioeconomic totality, knowledge, and subjectivity, and this finally leads to the true centering of the now "total" subject.

We have argued that, as in mainstream economics, the dichotomies of order/disorder, centering/decentering, and certainty/uncertainty show up in crucial places in modernist Marxian economic thought. The conventional distinctions between production and circulation, market and plan, and capitalism and socialism are in fact built upon these contrasts. In addition, modernism in Marxian economic theory has given preference (although not exclusively) to order and so forth. In the final section, using a few examples, we present our objections to this modernism and begin to sketch the postmodern Marxism that, in our view, is itself suggested by the postmodern moments in Marx's texts and subsequent Marxisms.

Postmodern Marxism

To be clear, we have no interest in diminishing the significant achievements associated with the utopian imagery created by the oppositions characteristic of modernist Marxism. If nothing else, preserving the idea that alternatives both to mainstream economic theory and to the economic and social systems it so often ends up celebrating is vitally important. Indeed, we are strong advocates of socialism and may even, under many circumstances, prefer planning to markets. However, we do not think that modernism has done Marxism proud since, to our mind, it has built up a theoretical edifice with political consequences that are questionable. For example, we think that the modernist tendency has overemphasized both the existence of disorder in capitalism and the negative consequences of the types of disorder that arise there. Likewise, it has exaggerated the orderly nature of socialism, and especially of planning, and has viewed as unduly positive the consequences of such order

To take just the last point, for example, we see no evidence that planning means stability and order, nor do we think it implies a "better" method to get at the "true" needs of individuals and/or enterprises. Planning, both in theory and as it has been practiced historically, is a process in which contention, conflict, and difference enter at every stage. Like all other "overdetermined" processes, not only is it the result of many determinations but its effects are always multiple and are played out in a variety of often contradictory ways. Planning differs from markets in the degree to which some people's desires and plans are calculated and realized more heavily than others, but it does not diverge from markets either in the ability to forecast accurately the effects of the decisions taken or in the controversies and potential "inequalities" that may result. As Ruccio (1986a, 1986b) has shown, planning, like markets, is always the site of class conflict insofar as planners must make decisions on how to allocate the surpluses that are produced among many different classes. Indeed, it is precisely because planning under socialism often presumes the end of class conflict and announces itself as the establishment of socially rational order that class discourse is neglected. This neglect shows up in the inability of planners to account for the conflicts and difficulties that arise in the course of planning other than as "mistakes" in calculation and technical inefficiencies. The determinants and outcomes of plans are thus often as unpredictable as market solutions are said to be.

But this last comment should not be taken to be one of criticism. In our view, if socialist planning announced itself as nothing more than an activity in which the desires of exploited classes were given priority, this would suffice to give it credence. However, this has not generally been the case. Instead, the defense of planning has been its promise to mediate different demands and to make rational choices from the standpoint of society as a whole, thus eliminating the social uncertainty that previously stemmed from market conditions. Where mistakes arise, then, the promise to correct them always follows since the possibility of getting it right—of ordering the process accurately and of acquiring and employing correct information about needs and so on—is implicit in the very (modernist) idea of the plan. Since planning is advertised as preferable to markets precisely because of this possibility, it is no accident that the political consequences of its presumed historic "failures" have led not only to the abandonment of socialism but to a rejection of planning *tout court*.[27]

Markets, of course, do not do much better. Yet, in our view, markets are stereotyped by modernist Marxism in that they are seen as disorderly and thereby incapable of meeting social needs. Modernist Marxists have tended to exaggerate the negative consequences of market disorder, to see only one side of the disharmonies that are characteristic of markets.[28] In our view, the reactions to "disequilibria" on the part of market participants can be, and often are, the impetus for the production of new goods and services (and, of course, for not producing other goods and services) and for changes in the way existing goods and services are produced. It is in this sense that the disorderliness of markets can (at certain times, in particular circumstances) lead to the satisfaction of social needs.

But just as crucially, the degree of disorder has, we think, been overstated by modernist Marxists. In their rush to criticize and to distance themselves from economic discourses, such as neoclassical economics, that celebrate the existence of markets and generally express a preference for markets to all other forms of social exchange and distribution of produced goods, modernist Marxists (ironically, like their neoclassical counterparts) have tended to neglect the implications of an insight long provided by the Marxian tradition; that economic institutions and identities are socially and historically constituted in a capitalist social formation. One possible implication of this social constitution of institutions and identities is that the activity of capitalist market exchange mostly takes place on a regular and orderly basis. Consider, for example, the "normal" activity of consumers. They often shop in the same locations, purchasing many of the same goods, even when prices vary (sometimes considerably) from one marketplace to another and new products are placed on the shelves. In this sense, the participation of individual consumers in markets is a much more stylized and ritualistic activity than is usually presumed. Similarly, firms often negotiate long-term contracts with other firms (both suppliers of inputs and distributors of outputs) precisely in order to "stabilize" deliveries and to avoid the "disorder" attendant upon the continual recontracting and renegotiating that would be necessary every time the price or quality of a commodity changes. In neither case—and these may be the norm rather than the exception—do markets exhibit the disorder frequently emphasized by modernist Marxists or, for that matter, implicit in those neoclassical stories that portray the instantaneous reactions of consumers and producers through the metaphors of supply and demand, "fish auctions," and *tâtonnement*. Instead, markets can be seen as sites (symbolically/culturally constituted) in which consumers and firms are usually guided by tradition and habit, set prices, make contractual commitments, and otherwise "arrange" their transactions to contain or eliminate disorder.

This "anthropological" approach to markets is consistent with those views found in other economic discourses that focus on conditions of stability in capitalist exchange.[29] In most modernist versions of economic analysis, these conditions are themselves essentialized so as to find the "origin" or essence of market stability in some unique subjective attribute or institutional arrangement. For example, while neoclassicals may have no particular recourse to "institutions" as ultimate explanatory variables, they do have the possibility of explaining the recourse to consumer and producer habit and ritual through such concepts as "risk averse" behavior, concern for "present" as opposed to "future consumption," and "lack of foresight." In these cases, habit and ritual are reduced to and are said to originate in an individual's preference for acting habitually. Yet, in our view rationality itself can be seen as habitual and routine. That is, so-called rational behavior must be learned (and, thereby, turned into a "habit" of mind and action), can be considered to require repetition (at least if consistency is to be achieved), and, of course, is itself a matter of culture and discourse (that is, it only arises within certain cultures and discourses and varies accordingly). The ritualistic nature of rationality is usually ignored by most neoclassicals who wish to use the notion of rationality as a term opposite to habit and convention and to essentialize it, in fact, as an alternative origin for economic and social behavior. Many

Marxists, institutionalists, and Post Keynesians, on the other hand, see social convention and habit in market behavior as stemming essentially from sociocultural norms (usually conceived as "outside" of markets and "historically determined") and/or a rational economic strategy in the face of fundamental uncertainty.[30] In either of these last cases, once again, habit and ritual have an essential time and place of origin, do not arise for the most part in the process of exchange itself, and are not "overdetermined" in their constitution.

We stress this last point since it bears as well on the concepts of habit and ritual we wish to endorse here. We see no reason to view habit and ritual as necessarily "orderly" because we see no reason to view the constitution of habitual or ritualistic behavior as other than always contingent and overdetermined. In this regard, we note that there are, of course, many forms of habitual economic behavior that are normally viewed as disorderly. The activities and behavior of commodity traders and their markets—indeed, most forward markets and forms of speculation, which proceed according to well-defined rules—provide one such example. While the habit and ritual of market transactions may permit the discursive introduction of more order than that which is found in the atomistic view of instantaneous markets comprising both the self-consciousness of neoclassical theory and the critique of the same by modernist Marxists, we think that the conjunctural and overdetermined nature of habit and ritual (they must always be reconstituted in each moment) makes it impossible to treat these as mere synonyms for socioeconomic order.

Even with the introduction of habit and ritual, then, capitalist markets cannot be seen as uniformly orderly processes. In addition to the provisos we note above, there is no guarantee that a particular market will come into existence when it is called for (i.e., when either side of a potential transaction or some outside observer finds it "necessary") or that a market, once it exists, will continue to exist over time (e.g., that an object, once produced, will successfully complete the process of circulation). Markets, in this sense, are not self-organizing or self-regulating activities; they are always being broken up and need to be created anew. And this formation and re-formation of the activity of market exchange is predicated on the existence of processes and institutions throughout the social formation in and through which the means and identities of such transactions are continually being created and destroyed. When markets are understood in this manner, they are seen to be "socially embedded" (indeed, socially constructed) institutions that are disorderly precisely because they are not the expression of any underlying essence whether a given economic rationality (as presumed by classical and, later, by neoclassical economists) or a universal law of value (as often put forward by modernist Marxists). As with habit and ritual (or symbol and sign), markets are disorderly at least to the extent that their continued existence must be reproduced in each moment, and this reproduction requires its determination by myriad institutions and subjects, themselves requiring such reproduction. Change and dislocation, therefore, are the rules rather than the exceptions.

But it is this same disorderliness that characterizes what we understand to be the activity of planning; any act of planning requires, and differs according to the particular constitution of, a whole host of economic and social conditions: from forms of calculation to social identities (of the planners and the recipients of plans), legal entitlements, and so on. And, as with markets, the conditions that "overdetermine" the activity of planning cannot but produce particular kinds of disorder—both in the activity itself and in its effects. Nor can disorder be considered uniquely unfortunate in its effects. The new possibilities and struggles that both give rise to and are consequences of an economic plan may be viewed by important segments of the populace and even the planners themselves to be preferable to planned and/or expected outcomes. Indeed, the disorder brought about by struggles over the distribution of the economic surplus, for example, may give rise to future plans in which the concerns of new or previously marginalized groups and classes are now therefore included. Therefore, it is a mistake, at least from our perspective, to focus primarily, as modernist Marxism has done, on the negative consequences of disorder, whether of markets or of planning.

The postmodern Marxian conception of the relationship of social needs to markets and planning also runs counter to the usual modernist Marxist story that sees planning as promising to satisfy the range of social needs which markets are incapable of meeting.[31] Frequently this story is supplemented by the argument (often said to be drawn from the manuscripts of the "young Marx") that there are two sets of needs, one "true," the other "artificial." So-called true needs are considered to be universal and "authentic"; they are seen as "basic" to humanity and therefore would continue to exist under socialism. Socialist planners are seen as possessing the unique ability to accurately calculate and arrange production to satisfy these authentic needs. On the other hand, there are "false" needs or desires, the "distorted" products of markets, "created" (by advertising, the media, and so on) merely for the purpose of satisfying the capitalists' drive to produce and realize surplus-value—needs that would, therefore, be reduced or eliminated under socialism.

From this perspective, what socialism represents is the transcendence of use-value over exchange-value inasmuch as the latter is seen to represent, among other things, the transitory and mostly artificial needs created purely by the market.

The problem is that, while modernist Marxists have distanced themse!ves (correctly, in our view) from the neoclassical presumption that consumer "preferences" are "exogenous," and, therefore, from the idea that human needs exist prior to and independent of the economic and social situation in which they are "expressed," they continue to hold onto a distinction between two sets of needs: one that is "constructed" (by markets) and another that is "intrinsic" and therefore "true." Like Veblen, who distinguished between the conspicuous consumption of the elite and the "normal" consumption of seemingly everyone else (and who failed to understand, as both Mary Douglas [Douglas and Isherwood 1979] and Pierre Bourdieu [1984] have argued, that all patterns of consumption, from working-class to capitalist, involve some form of "differentiation" within and across social groups), modernist Marxists have exaggerated both the extent to which markets create needs and the extent to which planning merely responds to and thereby satisfies needs. From a postmodern perspective, there is no origin or singular place where needs are created and of which they are an expression. Certainly, markets and particular market participants participate in creating needs, but so does the activity of planning, for example, who the planners decide that some goods will be available in larger or small quantities, thereby creating the distinction between goods that are for "basic consumption" and other goods that are forms of "luxury consumption."

In this sense, the determination of use-value cannot be considered independent of either exchange-value or "plan-value." At the same time, the needs that are "satisfied" (or not) by either markets or planning are only partly determined by those activities; they are also constituted by the diversity of identities and subjectivities— racial, gender, ethnic, class, and so on—that are produced in the two (capitalist and socialist) social formations. Thus, postmodern Marxism refuses the distinction between markets and planning in terms of one (planning) being able to satisfy social needs that the other (markets) cannot and, instead, focuses on the different ways in which each—together with many other social activities—participates in determining and satisfying needs and desires in particular economic and social settings.

None of this is to deny what Marxists (but also many others) have long pointed out: that markets can be and often are disorderly, that such disorders can have negative consequences (since the lives of individuals are often forcibly disrupted, not to mention those of firms, sectors, regions, or entire nations), and that the needs of many individuals and groups are often not met in particular market circumstances (hunger, starvation, and famine are not only possible but recurrent for significant sections of the population in many market economies, including the most developed). However, there is nothing either in the actual history or in the concept of socialist planning that avoids these "criticisms." There may, of course, be many situations when some form of planning is preferred to markets; what we object to is the idea that planning is in general any more orderly than markets, that order is always preferable to disorder, and that either activity is capable (or not) of satisfying and of participating (or not) in the determination of social needs. What we oppose, then, is the terms in and through which modernist Marxists have distinguished between markets and planning and, on the basis of such distinctions, expressed a preference for socialism over capitalism.

Our view is that, in contrast to modernist Marxism, the post-modern moments of Marxian theory—those elements of the Marxian tradition that emphasize disorder, decentering, and uncertainty—can constitute key aspects of a new Marxian economic discourse. The distinctiveness of this discourse can be viewed by rethinking such oppositions as that between capitalism and socialism with this emphasis in mind. For example, Marx's analysis of a capitalist economy can be read more in terms of the idea of historical conjuncture and contingency than of "laws of motion" and necessity. It is just this reading that Louis Althusser and his school have contributed to the Marxian tradition with the concept of overdetermination. For example, in the work of Resnick and Wolff, Antonio Callari (1986; Wolff, Roberts, and Callari 1982), Bruce Roberts (1987, 1988), Bruce Norton (1986, 1988, 1992), and John Roche (1988), among others, the processes of the creation and realization of economic value are seen to depend at every moment on the concatenation of forces—economic as well as noneconomic—that combine to produce a unique effect, whether that be the money form of value, capital, surplus-value, and so forth. For postmodern Marxism, there are no laws of motion of capitalism, no essences to be discovered in economic processes, no essential determinants of any economic effects, and no inexorable or preordained trajectory for the capitalist economy (and, therefore, no necessary sequence of stages or phases of capitalism). For postmodern Marxism, likewise, there is no subject of history, no teleological historical process, and therefore no necessary end to any process of change and/or transition. If taken seriously, the notions of over-determination and process without a subject—two of Althusser's main contributions—imply a radical contingency and uncertainty about social and economic processes. In this sense, postmodern Marxism gives priority to disorder insofar as it becomes impossible to discern in advance, or even ex post, the necessary pattern of determinants or effects for any event and/or for historical change. One implication for the contrast between capitalism and socialism is that postmodern Marxism sees all outcomes in either social formation as always contingent. Thus, it cannot be taken for granted nor understood as the necessary effects of the concept that, for example, socialist planning will mean more or less certainty, more or less order in comparison to capitalist markets. Likewise, capitalist markets imply nothing in particular about the necessity for economic crises, the meeting of individual needs, and so forth. The effects of markets and planning depend crucially on the concrete conditions of existence of each and are not given in advance in the form of their respective concepts. In this sense, postmodernism unmoors Marxism from the modernist tendency to find abstract order in concrete disorderly events by emphasizing that the conjunctural analysis of overdetermined social sites is the Marxist method pure and simple. While many Marxists and other modernists find, of course, this "everythingism" to be nihilistic, we reject this interpretation insofar as, far from denying or preventing theoretical scientific analysis, postmodern Marxism indicates its ever-present significance and possibility.[32] Indeed, we are willing to borrow from Marx his insight, which he and Engels and certainly others limited to a description of life under capitalism, that overdetermination implies "ever-lasting uncertainty" (Marx and Engels 1978, 476) inasmuch as it implies that "effects" are never strictly deducible from their "cause" (or vice versa). Marxian views of capitalism and socialism, market and plan, and so forth could clearly benefit, in any event, from the deconstruction of all "inevitabilities," "necessary tendencies," and "laws of motion." Whatever light they may have shone on their objects, these concepts have fed into political views and social actions that have been at the heart of some of the key failures of modernist Marxism.

On the question of the decentering of the subject, a different—and postmodern—reading of commodity fetishism is possible. Amariglio and Callari (1993), for example, have argued that, far from setting up a dichotomy between false and true consciousness, Marx's discussion of commodity fetishism produces a new concept of the subject and his/her consciousness. This subject, in this view, is socially constituted both prior to and in the act of exchange, and the consciousness that this subject possesses and enacts serves as a condition for the existence of commodity exchange (as well as a condition for its potential transformation and, even, supersession). The socially constituted subject of commodity exchange therefore "sees" exchange in a certain way (e.g., as the exchange of equal or unequal values) as a function of its overdetermination. But this sight has no privilege as being closer to or further from the "real" conditions that prevail. The ideological and discursive constitution of the subject as an exchanging subject, for example, is only one of many subjectivities enacted by subjects in a capitalist social formation, none of them more "correct" than any of the others in capturing the (partial or otherwise) "truth" of that perceived reality. The form of subjectivity described by Marx in his discussion of commodity fetishism is, in this postmodern view, the "open" subject—a subject that is constantly being constructed anew (and in multiple and contradictory ways) and for which there is no "center" to the resulting construction. Thus, the form of subjectivity that serves to overdetermine the realm of commodity exchange is never finally "sutured" nor is it significantly different in its moment of openness from the forms of subjectivity that would prevail in noncommodity relations.

In this way, we follow Althusser (1971) whose essay on ideology and ideological state apparatuses makes clear the impossibility of an end to ideology. According to Althusser, the process of interpellation that constitutes (concrete) individuals as (concrete) subjects exists in all social formations and is certainly not eliminated under socialism despite the possibility of halting general commodity relations. That is, Althusser's analysis of the process of subjectification implies as well the never-ending recomposition of the individual subject and, therefore, the impossibility of revealing the essence or center of the subject with the supposed end of commodity fetishism. While Althusser's understanding of commodity fetishism remains too closely tied to a "last instance" determination by the economy (Althusser and Balibar 1970), his theory of ideology—especially his strong criticisms of the "illusionary" nature of ideology—is based on a notion of the decentered subject. This decentered subject may exhibit many different subjectivities simultaneously (they are interpellated in different ways in different activities), none of which is given privilege as representing the subject's real essence, whether natural or historical. Althusser, too, employs a notion of the "open subject" insofar as he sees the processes of interpellation as incessant and without a goal or end to which they are moving. Indeed, there may never be a point of coalescence or unification of the different forms of subjectivity as a result of their overdetermination; this may explain why some Althusserians embrace the postmodern idea of the fragmented subject.

In any event, the difference between capitalism and socialism that modernist Marxists tend to draw—between the "really" fractured and alienated subject of capitalism and the potentially holistic and unalienated subject of socialism, "socialist man"—can be challenged by drawing out the postmodern moments in Marx's theories of commodity fetishism and ideology.[33] For postmodern Marxism, the difference between the subjects in the two social formations is a matter of the different elements of their overdetermination (e.g., by capitalist class processes in the one, and by communal class processes in the other) and not of the absence or presence of subjective unity and true consciousness in either formation.

Finally, as Althusser, Barry Hindess and Paul Hirst (1975; Hindess 1977), Resnick and Wolff (1987a, 1987b), and others have argued, there is a distinct Marxian notion of knowledge which eschews the premises and logical consequences of classical—empiricist and rationalist—epistemology. We call this notion of knowledge postmodern because, in our view, it tends to demote the idea of certainty and replaces it with forms of cognition that tend toward uncertainty (at least in the sense of indeterminism). The critique of epistemology we refer to is known well enough, at least or readers of *Rethinking* MARXISM, for us not to replicate it here (see also Amariglio 1987). But, we do want to add the idea that this critique not only holds for the practice of economic "scientists" but is meant to describe the modes of production and types of knowledge that are possible for economic agents—the objects of economic analysis—as well. The overdetermination of all events and the basic discursivity of knowledge—knowledge is not a mirror of nature but is constituted in and by discourse—precludes the idea that there is a relation of adequacy of correspondence between one's knowledge and the "real" outside of it. The "relativism" that this concept of knowledge implies is not, to our mind, a statement of the impossibility of knowledge. To the contrary, it indicates the plurality of and (often incommensurable) differences between knowledges and suggests that the means of choosing among them is not a question of finding an interdiscursive form of truth but primarily (although not exclusively) evaluating their perceived theoretical and social effects. The "everlasting uncertainty" of Marx and Engels can therefore be attributed to the irreducible plurality of knowledges and the fact that these knowledges can, at best, produce only contingent and not necessarily transcendental truths.

On this point, then, the distinction between capitalism and socialism as pertaining to the differential possibilities for knowledge (or lack thereof) is modernist in its basic premises. For modernist Marxism, the relativism that marks capitalism is attributed to the fact that it tends to fracture and segregate individuals and groups on the basis of the division of labor and membership in different classes. That is, capitalism produces "one-sided" individuals who lack the ability to perceive the whole and therefore to possess true knowledge. The possibility for seeing the totality, of course, rests historically with the class-conscious proletariat, and Marxism's conceit in this matter is that it claims to provide the working class with the "science" to turn its spontaneous perception of the many-sided (and therefore concrete) totality into a consistent theory of that totality and to eventually transform it. In modernist Marxism, then, socialism marks the moment of the historical transcendence of one-sidedness (abstractness) and allows potentially all of its members to see the whole. Thus, for example, planning can succeed where markets could not in discerning all of the needs underlying the plan and in calculating all of the effects of instituting it. The relativism (one-sidedness) and uncertainty of capitalism is overcome by rational planning whose objective basis the victory of the proletariat, with its full appreciation of the totality—guarantees in advance the superiority of its knowledge and practice.

Postmodern Marxist discourse regards this view as unhelpful and ultimately damaging in distinguishing between capitalism and socialism. For it is clear, to us at least, that socialism has been and will be beset with the multiplicity of knowledges and the radical uncertainty that goes along with the contingency of events and the persistence of ideology. The destruction that has been done, we add, to peoples living under socialist regimes and to the very concept of socialism as a result of the claim by the party or state to have privileged (but not partisan) objective knowledge has been considerable. For us, socialist planning will always be marked by the mediation of different knowledges and subjectivities, and the resulting plan, a contingent act if there ever was one, may need to declare itself as partisan, provisional, and uncertain of its effects if it is to avoid the disasters that have befallen planning mechanisms that have been infused with modernist explanations and ideals, utopian though they may be. The totalizing promise of rational centralized planning is a modernist one. The declared partiality, relativism, and uncertainty of planning is, in contrast, postmodern.

Notes

A shorter version of this paper was presented at the conference "Marxism in the New World Order: Crises and Possibilities" organized by *Rethinking* MARXISM at the University of Massachusetts-Amherst, November 1992; it appears in "Marxism in the Postmodern Age" (Callari, Cullenberg, and Biewener 1994). We wish to thank Joseph Buttigieg, Julie Graham, Sandra

Harding, Arjo Klamer, Ellen Messer-Davidow, Bruce Norton, and the two reviewers, Ric McIntyre and Rob Garnett, for their helpful comments and suggestions.

1. For different discussions of the extent of postmodernism and post-structuralism in economics, see Amariglio (1990), Ruccio (1991), Dow (1991), Samuels (1991), Hargreaves Heap (1993), Rossetti (1990), Milberg (1991), and Williams (1993).

2. Although it would be difficult to discern this shift from recent surveys such as Rosenau (1992) and Rose (1991) where postmodernism in economics is barely mentioned.

3. Of course, as one might expect, these developments have also engendered "the reaction." In the face of the growing multiplicity of positions both in economic theory proper and in the philosophy of economic thought (including methodology), there are some, like Herbert Gintis (1993), who assert the recent forging of a unity in economics and the social sciences. Gintis sees a new form of a unified "scientific" discourse emerging among economists, sociologists, and political scientists (or at least among those very few who count—he uses as support for his view the fact that Nobel prizes have been awarded in economics for "theories of the family, education, and organization," and he indicates that "articles on altruism and political logrolling now appear in the major economics journals" [886]). In supporting this view of an immanent unity, Gintis is clear about his target: postmodernism. In his rush to judgement, Gintis makes the slip of reproducing the very argument that he purports to oppose. To wit, he identifies a significant opposition—postmodernism—to *his* view of social scientific unity (so there *is* considerable disagreement among economists and other social scientists, just as the postmodernists would have it!) but then dismisses it implicitly and with a wave of the hand by defining it out of existence (since "unity" is in fact occurring). It is curious, of course, that his own very recent work and views just happen to comprise the main elements of unity for economics and the social sciences that he ends up describing (adherence to "the theory of games, of transactions costs, of asymmetric information, and of the endogenous enforcement of contracts" [886]). In our view, there is nothing original or particularly insightful in using such exclusionary measures to define the "core" and/or unity of a discipline (see Amariglio, Resnick, and Wolff [1990] for a discussion of these typical measures).

4. We are thinking, in particular, of Jean Baudrillard (1975, 1981), David Harvey (1989), and Fredric Jameson (1991).

5. It is unfortunate that such simplistic renderings have been spawned by Jameson's (1991) more sophisticated use of Ernest Mandel's (1975) classic work on late capitalism. Yet, it is clear to us that Jameson's reading of Mandel is not only selective but tends toward the positions that we criticize here. (An excellent criticism of Jameson's reading of Mandel is contained in Norton

[1994]. For a related and powerful critique of Jameson's relatively uncontradictory conception of both culture and the economy, see Montag [1988].) Jameson has interesting things to say about economic theory in his chapter on markets and the work of Gary Becker but, even here, Jameson is prone to linking any defense of markets to the recent postmodern turn in social and cultural theory. While we can't develop this idea here, we find it bizarre to regard Becker's work on markets as "postmodern." Our discussion below of modernism in economics should clarify why we strongly disagree with Jameson on this point.

6. Both of us have had experiences in presenting our work on postmodernism and economics at academic conferences and at departmental seminars in which both mainstream and radical economists have espoused identical criticisms of postmodernism, however different they conceive the economic theories to which they proclaim their allegiance to be. Similarly, proponents of postmodern approaches to economics, such as these discussed above, can be found within both mainstream and radical economics. What we conclude from this is that the line between modernism and postmodernism cuts through and across—it is layered on but does not displace—the other divisions among and between economic theories.

7. For a discussion of how irony emerged as the prevalent trope of historical writing by the end of the 1800s, see White (1975). In White's view, the "crisis of historicism" that emerged in historical writing toward the end of the nineteenth century was a function of the dominance by then of the "ironic condition of mind." In our view, White correctly links the emergence and dominance of irony with both the development of modernist historiography and the ultramodernist rebellions against it in this century.

8. For a related critical discussion of the Smithian/neoclassical story, see Amariglio, Resnick, and Wolff (1990)

9. That is, agents are conceived to be able to "learn" about all beneficial trading opportunities, to correctly revise their plans in the light of new information, and to "know" that they can indeed realize their plans when a general equilibrium is finally reached.

10. What we have in mind are various economists' attempts to extend the range of earlier general equilibrium models and/or to develop alternatives to such models. The result, in many cases, has been the "discovery" of situations in which the existence, uniqueness, and stability of general equilibrium solutions for a wide variety of economic models cannot be guaranteed. This has been the case, especially, in the use of game theory in economics—thus leading to a considerable degree of disenchantment among mainstream economists with the ability of game-theoretic methods to "save" the story of the invisible hand. See, for example, the "problems of game theory" discussed by David Kreps (1990).

11. A few of Shackle's numerous works that bear mentioning here are *Epistemics and Economics* (1972), *Decision, Order, and Time in Human Affairs* (1961), *Imagination and the Nature of Choice* (1981), *Uncertainty in Economics* (1955), and *The Nature of Economic Thought: Selected Papers 1955–1964* (1966).

12. Ted Burczak (1994), though, makes the argument that the humanism of both Shackle and Friedrich von Hayek avoids the modernist humanism, at least the brand in which the human subject is seen by the economist as unified, centered, and essentially constituted prior to its participation in markets. In this regard, then, Burczak treats Shackle and Hayek as having a properly postmodern conception of the economic subject. The most frequently cited accusation of nihilism against Shackle and other "fundamentalist Keynesians" appears in Coddington (1983). For an interesting attempt to think seriously about the charge of nihilism brought against Shackle, see Parsons (1993).

13. A forthcoming book edited by Sheila Dow and John Hillard, with papers from a 1993 conference (in which we participated) held at the University of Leeds, is dedicated entirely to the project of discussing and rethinking such radical readings of Keynesian theory and their consequences in the light of Keynes's writings on uncertainty and probability.

14. For a philosophically informed discussion and critique of the charges of ad hoc explanations directed against Keynesian thinkers and the consequent rage for "microfoundations" in recent macroeconomic theory, see DeMartino (1993). DeMartino sees the charges and countercharges that have characterized the debates over microfoundations to have their origin in a mostly unspoken ontological commitment of both critics and defenders to a "necessity/contingency dualism."

15. Some of the recent work in feminist economics in which economic subjects as well as economic discourse are found to be both gendered and socially constructed include Strassmann (1993a, 1993b), Nelson (1992, 1993), and England (1993). Feiner and Roberts (1990) show persuasively how mainstream neoclassical and Keynesian introductory economics textbooks "hide" gender bias by generally employing supposedly universal (but, of course, clearly gender- and race-specific) subjects and their behaviors.

16. We should note that recent feminist economists' criticisms of science and epistemology owe much to other feminists whose relation to postmodernism is mixed and/or ambiguous. This is true not only of the work of Bordo (1987, 1990) and Longino (1990), but also of the "standpoint theorists," such as Harding (1986), Smith (1987), and Hartsock (1984). In looking over the many papers from the 1993 conference on feminist economics held in Amsterdam, we note that Harding, in fact, may be the most important and frequently cited of the sources for feminist economic challenges to mainstream and masculinist epistemology and methodology. For her own balanced take on postmodernism, see Harding (1990).

17. That is why, we should add, quite a few feminist economists have been willing to work largely with Post Keynesian, institutionalist, and Marxian economic concepts since it is in these frameworks that, until now, the challenges to economic modernism have been primarily enunciated, at least in the neoclassical and Keynesian forms.

18. We should also add that other feminist economists, aware of the possible disintegration of the dominant economic frameworks, have reasserted the importance of retaining the centered economic subject as the founding moment of economic theory and have moved to halt the "disorderliness" that more postmodern feminists in economics are seen to have introduced. Such reactions are exemplified by Rebecca Blank (1993) who admits that she has tired of the critical nature of much feminist work in economics, of the absence of "alternative models," and of the more recent attacks (we would argue, inspired by postmodernism in other fields) on the links between post-Enlightenment epistemologies and the maleness of (both natural and social) scientific theory ever since. In this impatience, she is not alone, since in the same volume much of the same irritation with the more philosophical feminist critiques of economics is displayed in Robert Solow's (1993) comments.

19. In the pages that follow, we present a view of modernist Marxism that is an outcome of our own involvement for twenty-five years or more in learning, teaching, and writing about Marxian economic thought. That is, we do not wish to attribute the following characterization of modernist Marxism to any one thinker, although we are utterly convinced in our view that parts—in some cases, large parts—of what we present here can be found in a wide range of texts that have treated for the past century Marxian approaches to economic and social thought. To our way of thinking, most Marxian economic thought during this period of time has been structured by the discursive framework that constitutes for us economic modernism. To put this another way, we believe that a modernist "problematic" has been at work in some of the most important contributions to Marxian economics. In looking over many classic texts for the writing of this paper, we found the modernist discursive contrasts between order and disorder, centering and decentering, and certainty and uncertainty to structure to a large degree the possible views (and even the differences among them) that could be entertained on the nature of and distinctions between capitalist and socialist economies, and much else. We mention here ten texts of relatively recent vintage (primarily since the 1960s), most of them originally in English, that have been frequently used and cited among teachers and students of Marxian economic thought in the United States and perhaps elsewhere. These texts differ radically in their views on quite a lot of the Marxian corpus, so that at first glance it may seem perverse to lump them together. But, as we have already said, while no one of these texts reproduces word for word the modernist Marxism we summarize below, and while some of them put forward criticisms on discrete points that can be likened to our own, we believe that all of these texts are similar in their abiding, prevailing constitution by economic

modernism. We encourage readers to consult the following texts to satisfy themselves, we hope, of our reading: Michel Aglietta, *A Theory of Capitalist Regulation* (1979); Duncan Foley, *Understanding Capital* (1986); John Weeks, *Capital and Exploitation* (1981); David Harvey, *The Limits to Capital* (1984); Jon Elster, *Making Sense of Marx* (1985); John Roemer, *Free to Lose* (1988); M. C. Howard and J. E. King, *The Political Economy of Marx* (1975); Ernest Mandel, *Marxist Economic Theory* (1970); Paul Sweezy, *The Theory of Capitalist Development* (1970); and Paul Baran and Paul Sweezy, *Monopoly Capital* (1968). We want readers to understand that we are greatly indebted in our learning to all of these authors and that we do not intend our discussion below as a dismissal of these works. To the contrary, we hope that we have rendered these texts in a different light, thus adding a new dimension to the discussions and debates that have surrounded these books during the past two or more decades.

20. To be clear, we are not arguing that this rupture can be carried out by merely importing into Marxian economic and social thought the elements of postmodernism as they have been developed outside of Marxism (and, in the minds of some postmodern theorists, in opposition to Marxism). First, because, at least in some quarters, what passes for postmodernism today has become a discursive regularity that has served to dampen what we consider to be the critical potential of postmodernism. Second, because, from our perspective, many Marxists have themselves pioneered key elements of the "disruptive" impulses that we associate with postmodernism. Our aim, therefore, is to locate, build on, and extend what we see as the postmodern moments within the Marxian tradition.

21. Julie Graham and Katherine Gibson (Gibson-Graham 1993) put forward a powerful challenge to the modernist Marxian notions in which capitalism is presented as a "unity" a "singularity," and a "totality." Readers will recognize in these discursive elements the notions of order and centering we are likewise discussing.

22. In their very provocative attempt to overhaul much of Marxian political economy in terms of a probabilistic calculus, Farjoun and Machover (1983) make the argument that, at the level of the economy as a whole, the movements of capital and the consequent differences and fluctuations in profit in response to market conditions can be understood in terms of randomness. However, they conceive of production as a fundamentally orderly sphere because of the control capitalists exercise over the conditions of production. Thus, while we are supportive of their move to indeterminism and probability as a way of raising objections and developing an alternative to traditional forms of determinism in Marxian value theory, we see their argument as reproducing some of the modernist biases we criticize here.

23. Cullenberg (1994) shows that modernist Marxian discourse concerning the tendency of the rate of profit to fall can be generally viewed as having two variants, Cartesian and Hegelian, that rely on treating the capitalist

economy as a totality whose ability to reproduce itself is threatened by a fall in the rate of profit. Cullenberg additionally shows that even contemporary discussions of this "tendency" are structured by the discursive rules of formation that often unwittingly rely on utilizing either notion of totality. That is, Cullenberg sees some of the traditional disagreements among Marxists on the causes and effects or even the possibility of the fall in the rate of profit to be largely about which concept of totality one uses. In our view, both concepts of totality reproduce many of the aspects of ordering, centering, and so forth that we are criticizing here.

24. We are unable here to discuss the important issue of how class itself has often been conceived as a centered—and centering—subject in the Marxian tradition.

25. A recent version of this argument has been put forward by Wilson (1991); see Ruccio (1994) for a critical review.

26. Although, of course, what such subjectivity represents is also different in these traditions.

27. See Ruccio (1992) for a more extensive discussion of the connection between the failure of socialism and the turn away from planning and toward markets.

28. Hindess (1987) discusses and criticizes the "essentialism of the market" (and, from there, of planning) that can be found not only in Marxian thought but also in Hayekian liberalism. His critique is similar to our own. We quote at length:

> To write of essentialism in this context is to say that the market is analysed in terms of an essence or inner principle which produces necessary effects by the mere fact of its presence. In this case certain consequences are thought to follow merely from the fact that goods and services are provided through market exchanges rather than in some other ways. Precisely what those consequences are supposed to be, of course, will vary from one of these positions [Marxism or liberalism] to another: they are anarchic and wasteful, they leave too much power in private hands, they generate indefensible inequalities; they are a realm of freedom and efficiency; they foster a spirit of egoism which undermines the altruism of social policy; under conditions of wage-labour they are the means of capitalist exploitation; and so on. The diversity of markets themselves and of the consequences that are alleged to follow from their existence may be obscured by reference to 'the market'—as if what is at issue is an institutional structure of interactions with roughly similar properties in all significant cases (149–50).

Hindess concludes that such essentialisms "mask extremely complex and hetero-geneous sets of conditions" (150). As a result, "liberalism, Marxism, socialism, and many positions in between, treat market provision and public control as if they represented distinct and incompatible principles of social organization" (151).

29. Here we leave aside the issues raised in the growing anthropological and cultural studies literature, following Baudrillard (1975, 1981) and Marshall Sahlins (1976), regarding the symbolic or significatory order that is enacted and reenacted in exchange and consumption, constituting subjects and social structures (including markets) alike. Baudrillard and Sahlins have contributed especially to a rejection of Marxist "productionism" (the subsumption of consumption to production, or of exchange-value to use-value). In addition to Baudrillard and Sahlins, readers can consult Douglas and Isherwood (1979) and Miller (1992) for a discussion of the "anthropology" of consumption.

30. For a forceful explication of Keynes's notion of convention as the primary determinant of investment behavior under conditions of uncertainty, see Crotty (1993).

31. Richard McIntyre (1992) provides a valuable analysis of what he calls the "conventional Left critique of 'consumer society'" (40) which combines elements of both Marx's and Veblen's views of consumption and human needs under capitalist markets. McIntyre summarizes this critique in the following three points: "1. Individuals' needs are manipulated by corporations. 2. There is a tendency towards 'wasteful' production. 3. Individuals relate to each other mainly through their commodities" (49). As McIntyre points out, the common thread that links Marx's views with Veblen's is that "capitalism distorts humanity's natural development" (51) as represented in manipulation and alienation of authentic human needs. McIntyre opposes this shared institutionalist and Marxist modernist critique with an analysis that owes much to the work of Baudrillard. Among other things, Baudrillard criticizes Marx for removing "use-value from history, making use-value a symbol of transformation beyond capitalism" (53). As McIntyre states, Baudrillard claims that "use-value . . . is just as fetishized as is exchange-value and cannot serve as an objective ground for exchange-value in some ideal world" (53). Thus, "just as the apparent abstract equivalence of commodities is socially constituted, so too is the utility of the object" (53). It follows, therefore, that this social constitution takes place under conditions of markets and planning and that neither situation can be said to correspond to a state of "true" social needs.

32. For the charge of "everythingism" in the work of Resnick and Wolff and their spirited but careful response, see Carling (1990) and Resnick and Wolff (1992).

33. Or, perhaps more accurately, the contributions toward such a theory that Marx developed in his discussions of commodity fetishism and of the ideology of "vulgar economics" is *Capital*—elements on which Althusser and others have been able to build.

References

Aglietta, M. 1979. *A Theory of Capitalist Regulation.* Trans. D. Fernbach. London: New Left Books.

Althusser, L. 1971. *Lenin and Philosophy and Other Essays.* New York: Monthly Review Press.

Althusser, L. and Balibar, E. 1970. *Reading Capital.* London: New Left Books.

Amariglio, J. 1987. "Marxism against Economic Science: Althusser's Legacy." *Research in Political Economy* 10, 159–94. Greenwich, CT: JAI Press.

———. 1990. "Economics as a Postmodern Discourse." In Samuels 1990, 15–46.

Amariglio, J. and Callari, A. 1993. "Marxian Value Theory and the Problem of the Subject: The Role of Commodity Fetishism." In *Fetishism as Cultural Discourse*, ed. E. Apter and W. Pietz, 186–216. Ithaca: Cornell University Press.

Amariglio, J.; Resnick, S.; and Wolff, R. 1990. "Division and Difference in the 'Discipline' of Economics." *Critical Inquiry* 17 (Autumn): 108–37.

Baran, P. A. and Sweezy, P. M. 1968. *Monopoly Capital.* New York: Monthly Review Press.

Baudrillard, J. 1975. *The Mirror of Production.* Trans. M. Poster. St. Louis: Telos Press.

———. 1981. *For a Critique of the Political Economy of the Sign.* Trans. C. Levin. St. Louis: Telos Press.

Blank R. 1993. "What Should Mainstream Economists Learn from Feminist Theory?" In Ferber and Nelson 1993a, 133–43.

Bordo, S. 1987. *The Flight to Objectivity: Essays on Cartesianism and Culture.* Albany: State University of New York Press.

———. 1990. "Feminism, Postmodernism, and Gender-Scepticism. In *Feminism/ Postmodernism*, ed. L. J. Nicholson, 133–56. London: Routledge.

Bourdieu, P. 1984. *Distinction: A Social Critique of the Judgement of Taste.* Cambridge: Harvard University Press.

Burczak, T. A. 1994. "The Postmodern Moments of F. A. Hayek's Economics." *Economics and Philosophy* 10: 31–58.

Callari, A. 1986. "History, Epistemology, and Marx's Theory of Value." *Research in Political Economy* 9, 69–93. Greenwich, CT: JAI Press.

Callari, A.; Cullenberg, S.; and Biewener, C. 1994. *Marxism in the Postmodern Age. Confronting the New World Order.* New York: Guilford Publications.

Carling, A. 1990. "In Defence of Rational Choice: A Reply to Ellen Meiksins Wood." *New Left Review*, no. 184 (November/December): 97–109.

Coddington, A. 1983. *Keynesian Economics: The Search for First Principles*. London: George Allen & Unwin.

Crotty, J. 1993. "Are Keynesian Uncertainty and Macrotheory Compatible? Conventional Decision Making, Institutional Structures, and Conditional Stability in Keynesian Macromodels." In *Macroeconomics on the Minsky Frontier*, ed. R. Pollin and G. Dymski. Ann Arbor: University of Michigan Press.

Cullenberg, S. 1994. *The Falling Rate of Profit. Recasting the Marxian Debate*. London: Pluto.

DeMartino, G. 1993. "Beneath 'First Principles': Controversies Within the New Macroeconomics." *Journal of Economic Issues*.

Douglas, M. and Isherwood, B. 1979. *The World of Goods: Towards an Anthropology of Consumption*. London: Allen Lane.

Dow, S. 1991. "Are There any Signs of Postmodernism with Economics?" *Methodus* 3 (June): 81–85.

Dow, S. and Hillard, J., eds. 1995. *Keynes, Knowledge, and Uncertainty*. Cheltenham: Edward Elgar.

Elster, J. 1985. *Making Sense of Marx*. Cambridge: Cambridge University Press.

England, P. 1993. "The Separative Self: Androcentric Bias in Neoclassical Assumptions." In Ferber and Nelson 1993a, 37–53.

Farjoun, E., and Machover, M. 1983. *Laws of Chaos: A Problematic Approach to Political Economy*. London: Verso.

Feiner, S. F. and Roberts, B. 1990. "Hidden by the Invisible Hand: Neoclassical Economic Theory and the Textbook Treatment of Race and Gender." *Gender and Society* 4 (2): 159–81.

Ferber, M. A. and Nelson, J. A. 1993a. *Beyond Economic Man*. Chicago: University of Chicago Press.

———. 1993b. "Introduction: The Social Construction of Economics and the Social Construction of Gender." In Ferber and Nelson 1993a, 1–22.

Foley, D. K. 1986. *Understanding Capital: Marx's Economic Theory*. Cambridge: Harvard University Press.

Gibson-Graham, J. K. 1993. "Waiting for the Revolution, or How to Smash Capitalism while Working at Home in Your Spare Time." *Rethinking Marxism* 6 (Summer): 10–24.

Gintis, H. 1993. "Review of The *History and Philosophy of Social Science* by Scott Gordon." *Journal of Economic Literature* 31 (June): 886–87.

Harding, S. 1986. *The Science Question in Feminism.* Ithaca: Cornell University Press.

———. 1990. "Feminism, Science, and the Anti-Enlightenment Critiques." In *Feminism/Postmodernism,* ed. L. J. Nicholson, 83–106. London: Routledge.

Hargreaves Heap, S. 1993. "Post-Modernity and New Conceptions of Rationality in Economics." In *The Economics of Rationality,* ed. B. Gerrard, 68–90. London: Routledge.

Hartsock, N. 1984. *Money, Sex, and Power.* New York: Longman.

Harvey, D. 1984. *The Limits to Capital.* Oxford: Basil Blackwell.

———. 1989. *The Condition of Postmodernity.* Oxford: Basil Blackwell.

Hindess, B. 1977. *Philosophy and Methodology in the Social Sciences.* Hassocks, Sussex: The Harvester Press.

———. 1987. *Freedom, Equality, and the Market.* London: Tavistock Publications.

Hindess, B. and Hirst, P. Q. 1975. *Pre-capitalist Modes of Production.* London: Routledge and Kegan Paul.

Howard, M. C. and King, J. E. 1975. *The Political Economy of Marx.* Harlow, Essex: Longman Group.

Jameson, F. 1991. *Postmodernism, or the Cultural Logic of Late Capitalism.* Durham: Duke University Press.

Klamer, A. 1990. "Toward the Native's Point of View: The Difficulty of Changing the Conversation." In *Economics and Hermeneutics,* ed. D. Lavoie, 19–33. London: Routledge.

Kreps, D. 1990. *Game Theory and Economic Modelling.* Oxford: Clarendon Press.

Longino, H. 1990. *Science as Social Knowledge.* Princeton: Princeton University Press.

McCloskey, D. 1985. *The Rhetoric of Economics.* Madison: University of Wisconsin Press.

McIntyre, R. 1992. "Consumption in Contemporary Capitalism: Beyond Marx and Veblen." *Review of Social Economy* 50 (Spring): 40–60.

Mandel, E. 1970. *Marxist Economic Theory.* 2 vols. Trans. B. Pearce. New York: Monthly Review Press.

———. 1975. *Late Capitalism.* London: Verso.

Marx, K. 1977. *Capital*. Vol. 1. Trans. B. Fowkes. New York: Vintage.

Marx, K. and Engels, F. 1978. "Manifesto of the Communist Party." In *The Marx-Engels Reader*, ed. R. Tucker, 469–500. New York: W. W. Norton and Co.

Milberg, W. 1991. "Marxism, Poststructuralism, and the Discourse of Economists." *Rethinking Marxism* 4 (Summer): 93–104.

Miller, D. 1992. *Material Culture and Mass Consumption*. Oxford: Basil Blackwell.

Mirowski, P. 1991. *More Heat than Light*. Cambridge: Cambridge University Press.

Montag, W. 1988. "What Is at Stake in the Debate on Postmodernism?" In *Postmodernism and Its Discontents*, ed. E. A. Kaplan, 88–103. London: Verso.

Nelson, J. A. 1992. "Gender, Metaphor, and the Definition of Economics." *Economics and Philosophy* 8 (1): 103–25.

———. 1993. "The Study of Choice or the Study of Provisioning? Gender and the Definition of Economics." In Ferber and Nelson 1993a, 23–36.

Norton, B. 1986. "Steindl, Levine, and the Inner Logic of Accumulation: A Marxian Critique." *Social Concept* 3 (December): 43–66.

———. 1988. "Epochs and Essences: A Review of Marxist Long-Wave and Stagnation Theories." *Cambridge Journal of Economics* 12: 203–44.

———. 1992. "Radical Theories of Accumulation and Crisis: Developments and Directions." In *Radical Economics*, ed. B. Roberts and S. Feiner, 155–98. Boston: Kluwer Academic Publishers.

———. 1994. "Late Capitalism and Postmodernism: Jameson/Mandel." In A. Callari, S. Cullenberg, and C. Biewener 1994, 59–68.

Parsons, S. D. 1993. "Shackle, Nihilism, and the Subject of Economics." *Review of Political Economy* 5 (1).

Resnick. S. and Wolff, R. 1987a. *Knowledge and Class*. Chicago: University of Chicago Press.

———. 1987b. *Economics: Marxian versus Neoclassical*. Baltimore: Johns Hopkins University Press.

———. 1992. "Everythingism, or Better Still, Overdetermination." *New Left Review*, no. 195 (September/October): 124–26.

Roberts, B. 1987. "Marx after Steedman: Separating Marxism from 'Surplus Theory'." *Capital and Class* 32:84–103.

———. 1988. "What is Profit?" *Rethinking Marxism* 1 (Spring): 136–51.

Roche, J. 1988. "Value, Money, and Credit in the First Part of Capital." *Rethinking Marxism* 1 (Winter): 126–43.

Roemer, J. E. 1988. *Free to Lose: An Introduction to Marxist Economic Philosophy.* Cambridge: Harvard University Press.

Rose, M. A. 1991. *The Post-Modern and the Post-Industrial: A Critical Analysis.* Cambridge: Cambridge University Press.

Rosenau, P. M. 1992. *Post-Modernism and the Social Sciences: Insights, Inroads, and Intrusions.* Princeton: Princeton University Press.

Rossetti, J. 1990. "Deconstructing Robert Lucas." In Samuels 1990, 225–43.

Ruccio, D. F. 1986a. "Planning and Class in Transitional Societies." *Research in Political Economy* 9, 235–52. Greenwich, CT: JAI Press.

——. 1986b. "Essentialism and Socialist Economic Planning: A Methodological Critique of Optimal Planning Theory." *Research in the History of Economic Thought and Methodology* 4, 85–108. Greenwich, CT: JAI Press.

——. 1991. "Postmodernism and Economics." *Journal of Post Keynesian Economics* 13 (Summer): 495–510.

——. 1992. "Failure of Socialism, Future of Socialists?" *Rethinking Marxism* 5 (Summer): 7–22.

——. 1994. "Marx's Critical/Dialectical Procedure: A Review Essay." *Research in the History of Economic Thought and Methodology,* forthcoming. Greenwich, CT: JAI Press.

Sahlins, M. 1976. *Culture and Practical Reason.* Chicago: University of Chicago Press.

Samuels, W. 1990. *Economics as Discourse.* Boston: Kluwer Academic Press.

——. 1991. "'Truth' and 'Discourse' in the Social Construction of Economic Reality." *Journal of Post Keynesian Economics* 13 (Summer): 511–24.

Shackle, G. L. S. 1955. *Uncertainty in Economics.* Cambridge: Cambridge University Press.

——. 1961. *Decision, Order, and Time in Human Affairs.* Cambridge: Cambridge University Press.

——. 1966. *The Nature of Economic Thought: Selected Papers 1955–1964.* Cambridge: Cambridge University Press.

——. 1972. *Epistemics and Economics.* Cambridge: Cambridge University Press.

——. 1981. *Imagination and the Nature of Choice.* Edinburgh: Edinburgh University Press.

Smith, D. E. 1987. *The Everyday World as Problematic: A Feminist Sociology*. Boston: Northeastern University Press.

Solow, R. 1993. "Feminist Theory, Women's Experience, and Economics." In Ferber an Nelson, 1993a, 153–57.

Strassmann, D. 1993a. "Not a Free Market: The Rhetoric of Disciplinary Authority in Economics." In Ferber and Nelson 1993a, 54–68.

———. 1993b. "The Stories of Economics and the Power of the Storyteller," *History of Political Economy* 25 (1): 147–65.

Sweezy, P. M. 1970. *The Theory of Capitalist Development*. New York: Monthly Review Press.

Weeks, J. 1981. *Capital and Exploitation*. London: Edward Arnold.

White, H. 1975. *Metahistory: The Historical Imagination in Nineteenth-Century Europe*. Baltimore: Johns Hopkins University Press.

Williams, R. 1993. "Race, Deconstruction, and the Emergent Agenda of Feminist Economic Theory." In Ferber and Nelson 1993a, 154–53.

Wilson, H. T. 1991. *Marx's Critical/Dialectical Procedure*. New York: Routledge.

Wolff, R.; Roberts, B.; and Callari, A. 1982. "Marx's (not Ricardo's) Transformation Problem: A Radical Reconceptualization." *History of Political Economy* 14 (4): 564–82.

11

TOWARD A SOCIALISM FOR THE FUTURE, IN THE WAKE OF THE DEMISE OF THE SOCIALISM OF THE PAST

THOMAS E. WEISSKOPF

Introduction

What is socialism really all about? The revolutionary events of 1989 in Eastern Europe, and the enormous changes that have taken place in the former Soviet Union since then, have raised this question with renewed acuity.

The idea of socialism developed historically out of opposition to the reality of capitalism. The basic goals of the movement for socialism have thus been formulated in reaction to the perceived ills of capitalism. To condense an enormous literature on the subject of socialist goals, I would suggest that socialism has been committed most fundamentally to the following objectives:

1. *Equity*: as against the capitalist reality of great inequalities of income and wealth, socialism calls for an egalitarian distribution of economic outcomes and opportunities by class, race, gender, region, etc.
2. *Democracy*: as against liberal democracy in the political sphere, which has characterized the most democratic of capitalist societies, socialism calls for economic democracy that enables people to exercise control over their own economic fate.
3. *Solidarity*: as against the celebration of the individual under capitalism, socialism calls for the promotion of solidarity among members of communities extending from the neighborhood to the whole of society—encouraging people to develop the sense and the reality of themselves as social rather than simply individual beings.

In addition to its commitment to these goals that distinguish it from capitalism, socialism has historically been committed to the improvement of people's material standards of living. Indeed, in earlier days many socialists saw the promotion of improving material living standards as the primary basis for socialism's claim to superiority over capitalism, for socialism was to overcome the irrationality and inefficiency seen as endemic to a capitalist system of economic organization. In the present time—at least in the more affluent parts of the world, where capitalism has brought substantial improvements in living standards and where problems of ecological balance loom more important than problems of starvation or malnutrition—this growth objective has receded in importance for socialists. However, the extent to which any resource-using economic or social objective can be achieved—whether it be improving the environment or eliminating hunger—remains dependent on the degree of efficiency with which the system of economic organization operates. I will therefore articulate—as do most socialists, explicitly or implicitly—one additional important socialist objective:

4. *Efficiency*: socialism requires that resources be used wisely and non-wastefully in order that resource-using economic and social goals can be more successfully achieved.

In this paper I seek to explore what kind of socialist system can promise to make good on the socialist commitment to these goals, in light of the manifest failure of the political-economic systems of the U.S.S.R. and Eastern Europe to do so. I will begin in section I by discussing the implications of the events of 1989; this leads me to identify two potentially fruitful models for socialism in the future—market socialism and participatory socialism. Sections II and III explore in turn each of these two forms of socialism; I pose and seek to answer questions with which critics have challenged the advocates of each. I conclude in section IV by articulating the kind of socialism that seems to me to hold the greatest promise of living up to time-honored socialist ideals.

The Implications of 1989

There can be no doubt that 1989 marks a watershed in the history of socialism. Although, as we now know, the disintegration of the political-economic systems of the U.S.S.R. and Eastern Europe had already been underway for at least a decade, 1989 was the year in which the failure of these systems became visible to one and all. As people took to the streets in Eastern Europe, rulers scrambled to dissociate them-selves from the old order. After the failed coup against Mikhail Gorbachev in August 1991, it has become perfectly clear that even in the successor states of the Soviet Union itself there can be no return to the political-economic system of Lenin, Stalin or Brezhnev.

The events of 1989 are clearly the main reason why we (and many others) are now discussing the future of socialism. Of course, the conventional wisdom is that socialism has no future—only a past. As Robert Heilbroner (1989: 4) put it: "Less than 75 years after the contest between capitalism and socialism officially began, it is over: capitalism has won." We on the Western Left reject that conventional wisdom because we argue that where there has been economic failure—in Eastern Europe, in the Soviet Union, if not in all of the Communist Party-directed socialist economies—it has not been a failure of true socialism, but of something very different.

Is there anything, then, for us to learn from 1989? Indeed, I believe there are several important lessons.

First of all, we must recognize that Communist-Party-directed socialism—the type, characteristic of all actually existing socialist systems the world has known[1]—was a worse economic failure than most of us had previously been willing to admit. In the Soviet Union and Eastern Europe, at least, it not only failed to provide much growth and efficiency in its last decade or two, it also failed to achieve real equity, and it was ecologically disastrous.[2] In these respects the accomplishment of CP-directed socialism have been somewhat more impressive in less developed economies such as those of China and Cuba, especially as compared with their own past experience; but even in these more favorable instances, there have been many disappointments. And, of course, all these societies have been extremely undemocratic, and almost always deeply alienating to their workers and citizens.

Second, we cannot simply dismiss this dismal record as having nothing to do with socialism. Of course CP-directed socialism is a far cry from the democratic, egalitarian and solidaristic society that most of us on the Left have advocated. There are even some Western Leftists who have consistently refused to apply the label "socialist" to the societies at issue. Nonetheless, most Western Leftists are to some extent tainted by the record of the CP-directed state socialist countries.

For one thing, these countries have exhibited certain characteristics that have been associated with socialism, not just by CP officials and old-fashioned socialists, but by many contemporary Western Leftists—for example, society-wide control of capital formation, strict limitation of the role of private ownership, strong curbs on the operation of markets, guarantees of employment and basic social services to all citizens. Moreover, many on the Left have compared aspects of the performance of the CP-directed socialist economies—for example, their long-term growth record, their egalitarianism, their social services—favorably with that of capitalist economies. Even when such a favorable comparison is justified by the evidence (e.g., in comparing many of Cuba's social achievements with those of other Latin American countries), to claim that it represents any kind of victory for socialism is to accept that what has been constructed in countries like Cuba is indeed a form of socialism.

Confronted with such concerns, many of us have held out hope that at least some of the CP-directed socialist systems—however distorted and unsatisfactory their current structure—might evolve toward a truer form of socialism.[3] This again lends credence to the notion that the CP-directed socialist systems do have something to do with the socialism that we advocate.

Perhaps, then, 1989 represents the vindication of a small minority of Western Leftists—those who have always sharply criticized the CP-directed socialist systems and who have consistently refused to consider them as having anything whatsoever to do with socialism. There are two main schools of socialist thought on the Western Left that have been "pure" in this respect; I believe that they can usefully be characterized as *liberal-democratic* and *communitarian*, respectively.[4]

Liberal-democratic socialists have stressed the general socialist goal of democracy, arguing in particular that liberal democracy—a political system including constitutionally protected civil rights and liberties, democratic elections, etc.—is an absolute prerequisite for a socialist society worthy of the name. This implies that socialist economic institutions, designed to promote such other socialist goals as equity and solidarity, must be built upon a liberal-democratic political foundation. The construction of socialist society is seen not as the replacement of "bourgeois democratic institutions" by some entirely different and superior form of democracy, but as deepening the democratic nature of these institutions and extending them from the political through the social to the economic arena. From this perspective, the authoritarian character of political rule in all of the CP-directed socialist societies has disqualified them from the very start as exemplars of socialism.[5]

Communitarian socialists are also committed to democracy, but democracy of a less liberal and more participatory kind. In the communitarian vision it is the socialist goal of solidarity which receives the greatest emphasis—people are to develop and sustain solidarity as active participating members of communities ranging from the neighborhood and the workplace to the society as a whole. The political and economic institutions of liberal democratic capitalism are to be discarded; what is envisaged is a revolutionary transformation to an egalitarian participatory society in which people jointly and directly control their own fate. From this perspective, the CP-directed socialist societies are rejected because of their retention of many of the individualistic patterns and hierarchical structures of capitalist societies, as well as for their betrayal of democratic ideals.[6]

Liberal-democratic socialists generally advocate a form of democratic *market socialism*, in which liberal democracy is combined with an economic system characterized by predominantly collective forms of ownership of the means of production and by the use of markets as the predominant means of resource allocation and distribution—subject to some government planning, intervention and regulation. Collective ownership is designed to promote egalitarianism in both economic and political spheres; markets are seen as indispensable both to individual freedom of choice and to efficient resource location; and government regulation is seen as necessary to assure that the general interest prevails over particular interests and to limit the development of substantial inequities.

Communitarian socialists generally advocate a form of democratic *participatory socialism*, in which there is collective social control of the means of production and in which decentralized participatory planning institutions replace the market as a mechanism for resource allocation and distribution. This is a vision of socialism in which, to put it in Marxist terms, both exploitation and alienation are overcome; thus not only private property but also markets must be abolished. Instead of responding as independent self-interested individuals to market signals in the economic arena, people are to develop and sustain themselves as interdependent social beings as they participate together in making consumption and production decisions.

Both the market socialist model envisaged by the liberal-democratic socialists and the participatory socialist model envisaged by the communitarian socialists are sharply differentiated from the CP-directed socialism of the past. In the following two sections of this paper, I will consider market socialism and participatory socialism in more detail.

Market Socialism

The idea of a market-based form of socialism was first given serious attention in the 1920s, when it was promoted by people within the social-democratic wing of Marxism as a desirable alternative to the marketless form of socialism identified with Marx's vision of full communism and embraced by the Bolshevik wing of Marxism. The first systematic theoretical exposition of the functioning of a market socialist economy was undertaken by Oskar Lange in the 1930s, who has ever since been recognized as the pioneer of market socialism.[7] Lange's original model involved both actual markets (in consumer goods and labor), simulated markets (in producer goods) and a limited but critical role for central planning (e.g., in determining the rate of investment and the distribution of income). All enterprises were to be owned by the government, but run according to profit-maximizing rules by independent managers. Since Lange's exposition of his original model of market socialism, a great deal of work has been done by advocates of market socialism—many of them economists from and/or interested in the post–World War II Eastern European countries—seeking to improve upon Lange's model while dealing with various problems raised by critics.[8]

Out of this continuing literature on the conceptualization of market socialism have emerged a variety of different models, but they all share the same central defining purpose. Market socialism seeks to promote socialist goals of equity, democracy and solidarity while largely retaining one major feature of capitalist economies—the market—but largely replacing another major feature of capitalism—private ownership of the means of production. For at least the major sectors and/or the most important enterprises in the economy, market socialists propose some form of social ownership of enterprises.

"Ownership" is a complex concept encompassing a variety of rights, which can potentially be assigned to a variety of different people. For our purposes it will he useful to identify and distinguish two such rights in particular: (l) the right to enterprise control and the right to enterprise income. The right to control confers the prerogatives and responsibilities of management: those who control the enterprise (or their representatives) make the decisions about how the enterprise will be operated, who will work in it and under what conditions, whether or not any aspects of the enterprise are to be expanded, contracted, sold or liquidated, etc. The right to income confers a claim to the surplus generated by the enterprise—that is, the net (or residual) income after fixed obligations have been paid.[9]

The standard capitalist enterprise is owned by private individuals or shareholders who have (ultimate) control over management according to the nature and the amount of their ownership shares; a small number of individuals or shareholders may have predominant control. Under market socialism enterprise control is social rather than private. Control of a market socialist enterprise is held by a community of people, each of whom—in principle—has an equal say in the management of the enterprise; as a practical matter, this (ultimate) control is usually exercised via appointment of managerial staff. There are two principal variants of such social control, depending on the nature of the community in whom control rights are vested:

1. *Public management*: enterprises are run by managers who are appointed by and accountable to an agency of government (at the national, regional or local level), which agency represents a corresponding politically constituted community of citizens.[10]
2. *Worker self-management*: enterprises are run by managers who are appointed by and accountable to those who work in them (or their elected representatives), with control rights resting ultimately with the community of enterprise workers (on a one-person one-vote basis).[11]

In the standard capitalist enterprise, ownership by private individuals or shareholders conveys not only control rights but also income rights—again according to the nature and the amount of their ownership shares. Under market socialism income rights are held socially rather than privately. The surplus of the market socialist enterprise accrues to a community of people in a relatively egalitarian manner. Here again there are two principal variants of such social claims to income, depending on the nature of the community holding the claim:

1. *Public surplus appropriation*: the surplus of the enterprise is distributed to an agency of government (at the national, regional or local level), representing a corresponding community of citizens.[12]
2. *Worker surplus appropriation*: the surplus of the enterprise is distributed to enterprise workers.[13]

These two different ways of assigning control rights and income rights under market socialism can generate a matrix of four different possible market socialist models, since there is no *a priori* reason why each set of rights must be assigned in the same way. As it happens, however, most contemporary advocates of market socialism lean primarily in one direction or the other: there is one school favoring what I will label the "public enterprise model," characterized by public management and public surplus appropriation, and a second school favoring the "worker enterprise model," characterized by worker self-management and worker surplus appropriation.[14]

Although the replacement of private with social control and income rights at the enterprise level is what most clearly distinguishes market socialism from (market) capitalism, advocates of market socialism also generally call for a greater degree of government intervention into markets than is the norm in capitalist economies. Such intervention does not primarily take the form of quantitative controls, of the kind associated with the discredited system of centrally planned socialism. Instead, it involves more extensive government provision of public goods and services, more extensive public capital formation, more extensive government regulation of enterprises and more extensive use of taxes and subsidies to internalize external effects that would otherwise be neglected by individual consumers and producers in the market environment. The objective here is to shape the environment in which the market operates, and to use the market rather than replace it, so that market price and cost valuations will approximate true social benefits and costs.[15] The difference between market socialism and capitalism in this respect is essentially one of degree rather than kind; apart from public control and income rights in enterprises, the economic role of government in a market socialist system differs little from that of government in the more regulated (e.g., social-democratic) capitalist systems.

Market socialism has been challenged both by those who question the ability of markets to function efficiently in the absence of capitalist private property rights, and by those who question the ability of social ownership forms to meet socialist goals in the context of markets. I have discussed elsewhere (Weisskopf 1992) the former line of criticism; here I will focus on the concern that market socialism is not really socialist enough. This latter concern tends to revolve around the following kinds of questions.

1. *Don't market systems systematically undermine efforts to serve general public interests?*
    Markets provide an environment in which people are encouraged to find ways to better themselves at the expense of others—through individual rent-seeking behavior, the formation of self-aggrandizing coalitions, etc. As a result, there would appear to be a systematic tendency for the general social interest to be undermined by the pursuit of particular private interests.
    This line of argument is theoretically plausible; yet it is not decisive. Rent-seeking behavior and self-aggrandizing coalitions of one kind or another can and will occur under any conceivable system of economic organization that permits some people to live better than others. Virtually every system will therefore require

institutions that limit antisocial behavior. The only way in which an economic system of organization per se could eradicate the problem would be if that system, by virtue of its controls on individual patterns of living, precluded any individual from enjoying the gains from self-interested behavior.

Thus a solution to the problem of such behavior could come only at the price of strict limits on privacy and freedom of choice—a price that market socialists are unwilling to pay.

2. *Don't market systems unfairly reward good luck?*

In market capitalist economies people are rewarded for productive contributions due to the property they own (in the form of capital income); such rewards to property ownership not only have very unequal distributional consequences, but they are generally not necessary to assure deployment of the property in production. In market socialist economies people are rewarded primarily for productive contributions due to their own labor.[16] Yet market socialism, like capitalism, maintains rewards to people's natural abilities (in the form of labor income), even though such rewards may not really be necessary to elicit the deployment of those abilities in production. Moreover, worker self-managed forms of market socialism are likely to favor those people who happen to work in prosperous areas or enterprises but do not necessarily work any harder or longer then other people who work in less prosperous areas or enterprises.

A more just system of economic remuneration would arguably link payment solely to differential personal effort and personal sacrifice, not to the luck of the genetic or economic draw. While market socialist systems do not achieve this ideal, they do not depart from it anywhere near as much as do capitalist systems. Moreover, to the extent that unwarranted returns to a person due to their luck in the genetic lottery or in economic circumstances remain, the resulting differentials can be diminished by a progressive system of income taxation.[17]

3. *Won't any kind of market system lead to inequalities that contradict the socialist goals of equity and democracy?*

Critics of the "market" within market socialism suggest that it will generate an elite minority of "coordinators"[18]—for example, public investment bankers, public enterprise directors, self-managed firm managers, even government planners—who end up gaining disproportionate economic and political power, much as do capitalists within a capitalist system.

It is certainly true that under market socialism there must be some people occupying positions of key decision-making responsibility, and in all likelihood such people will have higher incomes as well as greater power than most of the rest of the population. Thus inequalities of income and power would surely develop under market socialism. But they would just as surely be much smaller than under capitalism—because market socialism eliminates most returns to property ownership, which is the predominant source of inequalities under capitalism. While there would still be ample scope for inequalities associated with differential skills, talents and responsibilities, it is hard to see how the equivalent of a propertied capitalist class could emerge from the more privileged strata of a market socialist society.

Although a market system could not assure anything close to full equality of income and power for all participants, neither could any economic system in a complex society. Such societies require sophisticated decision-making institutions of one kind or another; and there are bound to be great differences among people in their ability (or desire) to participate effectively in decision-making processes.

4. *Won't markets undermine solidarity and community?*

Critics of market socialism also argue that markets of any kind tend to breed selfish motives and competitive behavior on the part of producers and consumers, dividing people instead of uniting them, encouraging indifference to rather than empathy for others and discouraging the development of public-spirited community consciousness end solidarity.

To transact effectively in markets, people do have to think mainly in terms of their own individual (or family) welfare, while setting aside consideration for others; markets encourage anonymity, autonomy and mobility rather than community, empathy and solidarity.[19] Market socialism thus admittedly does not provide direct support for a culture of community, empathy and solidarity. Yet it surely does provide a less hostile environment for the development of such characteristics than (market) capitalism because it attenuates, via greater egalitarianism and stronger democracy, the consequences of unfettered markets and unrestricted private property ownership. Although economic institutions are powerful social and cultural forces, they are neither monolithic nor omnipotent; hence community, empathy and solidarity may be fostered in other spheres of life even in a market system.

5. *Will market socialism be any more successful than social-democratic variants of capitalism in achieving socialist goals?*

Advocates of social democracy share the socialist objectives of advocates of market socialism, but they differ as to the best means to achieve them. Where market socialism seeks to promote the public interest, greater equity, democracy and solidarity primarily by transferring capitalist ownership rights to communities of citizens and/or workers, social democracy seeks to do so by government policy measures designed to constrain the behavior of capitalist owners and to empower other market participants. Thus social democrats do not try to do away with either the market or private property ownership; instead, they attempt to create conditions in which the operation of a capitalist market economy will lead to more egalitarian outcomes and encourage more democratic and more solidaristic practices than would a more conventional capitalist system.

Market socialists have traditionally been highly suspicious of social democracy, on the ground that its failure to attack head-on the source of capitalist power—private ownership of the means of production—would ultimately prevent it from attaining socialist objectives. But as models of market socialism have been refined over the years, the distinction between market socialism and social democracy has been somewhat blurred. Partly because of the problematic experience of East European CP-directed socialist economies with limited market-oriented economic reforms, advocates of market socialism have come to support an increasingly wide scope for markets and increasing autonomy for public and/or worker enterprises operating within the market environment.[20] While such proposals do not amount to the restoration of full capitalist private property rights, they do open up opportunities for individuals to receive some forms of capital income.

The elimination of large-scale private property ownership under market socialism certainly leads to a much more equal distribution of income than obtains under conventional capitalism. Both theory and the actual experience of social democracy, however, suggest that government taxation and spending programs can substantially reduce the extent of income and wealth inequalities within a capitalist economy. As far as the pattern of enterprise management is concerned, there is also good reason to question how far market socialism really differs from social democracy. Market socialist enterprise managers, whether accountable to government agencies or to enterprise workers, are expected to operate their enterprises in such a way as to maintain profitability in a market environment; this means that they will typically have only limited leeway to steer the enterprises in a direction much different than would managers accountable to private shareholders.[21] And, indeed, to prevent autonomous public enterprises or worker self-managed firms from acting in their own particular interest, as against the general social interest, it would in all likelihood be necessary for government to regulate them or their markets just as is done by social-democratic governments in a capitalist economy.

At a more fundamental level, market socialism does not dispense with individual gain incentives and the necessarily associated inequalities. Instead, it seeks:

a. to link differences in rewards more closely to corresponding differentials in the actual productive effort contributed by people to the economy; and

b. to reduce the extent of differences in rewards associated with differentials in productive effort, so as to reduce (greatly) the resultant distributional inequity without reducing (much) the incentives they generate.[22]

Again, this is precisely what social democracy tries to do—albeit in a different way than market socialism. Social democracy achieves greater egalitarianism via ex-post government taxes and subsidies, where market socialism does so via ex-ante changes in patterns of enterprise ownership. As for serving the general social interest, market socialists and social democrats agree that, where the unfettered market will not achieve important social goals, the first option is to try to guide the market toward socially optimal behavior (via appropriate taxes, subsidies, etc., to internalize externalities by "planning with the market"); where this is not adequate, the second option is to replace price-and-market mechanisms by quantitative controls and/or direct state operation of enterprises.

On further reflection, one might well ask of market socialists: what compelling reason is there to restrict forms of enterprise ownership to types in which control and income rights accrue to (citizen or worker) communities rather than to private shareholders? Why not simply provide a level market playing field in which all types of enterprises can compete on a truly equal basis? Most contemporary market socialist models in any case allow for individual or small-scale private enterprise. Could not the problems of excessive wealth and power associated with large-scale private enterprise be addressed as easily and successfully via taxation and regulation as via restrictions on private ownership?

To sustain the superiority of the market-socialist over the social-democratic approach to achieving socialist objectives, I would argue as follows. In redefining and reassigning (to workers and/or communities) rights that form the point of departure for markets, market socialism intervenes into the market system before markets operate—while social democracy intervenes (mainly) after markets operate. This makes social democracy much more vulnerable to weakening or disintegration under political challenge, since tax-and-subsidy schemes and government regulation are much easier to reverse than changes in property rights.[23] Moreover, the maintenance of property-owning capitalists under social democracy assures the presence of a disproportionately powerful class with a continuing interest in challenging social democratic government policies. Under market socialism there may well emerge a kind of managerial class with disproportionate power; but its power is likely to be less disproportionate because enterprise control rights and personal wealth will not be so highly concentrated.

Participatory Socialism

Although market socialism has become relatively popular on the Left in recent years, there is a much older socialist tradition that has always rejected the idea of including markets in anything other than a transitional phase following capitalism. Karl Marx wanted to rid the world not only of the inequalities associated with private property, but of the alienation and commodity fetishism associated with the operation of market systems. This was the Marxist tradition embraced by the Russian Bolshevik revolutionaries, and it remained an important part of the ideology—though not the practice—of Soviet socialism for decades after the Revolution of 1917. In point of fact, none of the "actually existing" CP-directed socialist economies of the U.S.S.R., Eastern Europe, China, Cuba, etc., came close to dispensing with markets[24]—even though they limited the operation of markets in many ways.

Contemporary participatory socialists seek to revive this marketless Marxist ideal, but in a manner very different from that of the Bolshevik tradition. First of all, they reject the authoritarian rule associated with the CP-directed socialist economies and insist instead on a democratic political framework. Second, they reject the hierarchical central planning apparatus that has hitherto been utilized as the main alternative to market exchange and insist instead on a process of decentralized planning in which people participate as equals.

Just as in the case of market socialism, ideas and conceptions of a marketless participatory socialism have been developed in various ways by various authors—starting with utopian socialists even before Marx and continuing through anarcho-syndicalists down to present-day advocates of democratic and participatory planning. Most recently, important contributions to the literature on participatory socialism—providing unusual and laudable detail on the actual institutions and functioning of decentralized democratic planning systems—have been published by Pat Devine and by Michael Albert and Robin Hahnel.[25] These and other conceptions of participatory socialism differ in many respects, but they are all based on the replacement of market forces (which allocate resources by generating material incentives for individual economic agents acting in their own best interest)[26] by a system of decentralized and coordinated planning (designed to allocate resources via negotiation among and between appropriately constituted groups of workers, consumers, community residents and citizens in general).

The basic decision-making units of the participatory system are typically workplace workers' councils and neighborhood consumers' councils, in which production and consumption decisions are made collectively by workplace and neighborhood communities, respectively. But these basic decision-making units are embedded in a larger network of related politically constituted bodies, designed to bring to bear relevant considerations and concerns that transcend the scope of individual workplaces and neighborhoods. A critical role in the network of non-market decision-making institutions is played by various planning boards, which are responsible for collecting and dispensing information and for coordinating the decisions of separate councils and entities in such a way that decentralized production and consumption plans emanating from all the workplaces and neighborhoods ultimately converge to a feasible overall pattern of production and consumption. The relevant information to be considered in decision-making includes both quantitative data about production and consumption processes and qualitative evidence about the ramifications of each production and consumption activity.

Advocates of this kind of participatory economic system assert that it can attain far more successfully than market socialism the socialist goals of egalitarianism, democracy and solidarity—because of the absence of markets—while performing at least as efficiently as a market system—in spite of the absence of markets. Advocates of market socialism, on the other hand, find this effort to do without market forces highly quixotic and thoroughly problematical; they question the feasibility of a participatory socialist system, and sometimes also its desirability. Some of the main concerns raised by critics of participatory socialism are reflected in the following questions:

1. *Wouldn't the allocation of resources in a complex economy by means of participatory decision-making institutions place impossible demands on information processing and inordinate demands on people's time?*

Since Adam Smith's original exposition of the mechanism of the "invisible hand," advocates of the market have celebrated its ability to process the enormous amount of information necessary for coordinated economic decision-making in a complex economy and to convey it in a simple way to individual economic actors, so that they have both the information and the incentive to act in an economically efficient manner. Most economists believe that the only other way that resources can be allocated in a complex economy is via a centralized, hierarchical system of administrative commands[27]—the system that he been so deeply discredited by the experience of the CP-directed socialist economies. Participatory socialists take up directly the challenge to develop a third resource allocational mechanism that avoids both the use of markets and the hierarchy of an administrative command system.

To replace the market without using administrative commands, they propose an enormous number and a vast network of decision-making bodies on which individuals will sit, process information, deliberate and arrive at decisions. Precisely because they don't trust the information summarized in and conveyed by market prices, they require these decision-making bodies to consider in detail both the qualitative and the quantitative implications of alternative ways of allocating resources. This places some staggering requirements on the system as a whole:

a. to involve virtually everyone in the society in group decision-making processes;

b. to compile an enormous amount of information about the economy and to make that information available in a timely and accessible way to individuals engaged in economic decision-making at one level or another;

c. to develop a system of accounting—as a supplement if not an alternative to conventional market prices—that enables the social value of different production and consumption activities to be measured and compared, so that individual decision-makers can understand the aggregate social consequences of any given set of decisions;

d. to find a way for the group of people involved in any given decision-making body to arrive in a reasonably harmonious and timely fashion at agreement on decisions: and

e. to develop a system to assure that the myriad plans developed at the ground level of the decision-making network, when aggregated, converge to a consistent pattern of resource allocation for the economy as a whole.

The mere listing of these requirements is enough to generate skepticism about whether and how they can possibly be met. Even if, in principle, institutions and processes can be developed to accomplish the necessary tasks (and Albert & Hahnel and Devine have advanced some ingenious ideas to do so), one is bound to wonder whether the whole system would actually function in practice. Assuming that computer technology could be relied upon to process and disseminate the enormous amount of information needed to make the system work, how would people be persuaded to provide the needed information in an unbiased and disinterested manner? And even if all the needed information could be accurately compiled, wouldn't participatory planning require each individual to dedicate so much time, interest and energy to assessing the information and participating in decision-making meetings that most people would get sick and tired of doing it?

2. *Isn't the process of democratic decision-making sufficiently complex and problematic that it should be applied only to a limited range of critical decision-making areas?*

Advocates of decentralized participatory planning to replace market forces generally place great weight on democracy—both as a desirable goal in itself and as the best means to arrive at decisions that truly reflect people's interests. In so doing, however, they tend to ignore the myriad problems involved in establishing fair and efficient democratic decision-making processes. First of all, choice among alternative voting conventions is complex and critical: when should decisions be made by simple majority, by a supermajority, or by consensus? What will distinguish constitutionally protected rights from those subject to democratic voting? If in principle people's votes on any particular issue should vary according to the extent to which they are affected by a decision, how should the weighing actually be determined in practice?

Explicitly political forms of economic decision-making are favored by advocates of participatory planning over impersonal and individual market processes, on the grounds that people should take explicitly into account the larger social context and the interdependence of their decisions. But won't the politicization of all kinds of decisions lead to excessive conflict, strife and anger and/or to the formation of political blocs and parties which tend to compress the great variety of individual views and preferences into lowest-common-denominator platforms and programs? Direct participatory democracy is generally favored over indirect representative democracy, on the grounds that people should be required to listen to and confront one another as directly as possible in arriving at decisions. But isn't the practice of participatory democracy sufficiently difficult, time-consuming and emotionally draining that it would in practice have to be limited to a relatively small range of decisions?

A system of decentralized and negotiated planning is expected by advocates of participatory socialism to assure egalitarianism in economic decision-making, yet in practice such a system might well enable some people to exercise much greater influence over decisions than others. Disproportionate influence would not arise from disproportionate wealth or income, but from disproportionate interest in and aptitude for the relevant decision-making processes. People are likely to vary greatly in terms of their ability to access and process information, to negotiate with others and to influence group decision-making; so political and economic inequalities can easily emerge in marketless as well as in market societies.

These kinds of concerns about the operation of democratic decision-making processes should not of course be read as a condemnation of democracy, much less as a plea for a purely free-market economic system or an authoritarian political system. Rather, such concerns suggest that democratic political institutions ought to focus on a critical and manageable range of decision-making arenas, rather than be used for all kinds of economic as well as political decisions. Direct voice in economic decision-making through negotiating and/or voting procedures is surely not the only, nor necessarily always the best, way for people to have their interests represented in the societal resource allocation process. People's individual and collective interests can often best be served by a combination of the opportunities for choice and exit provided by markets and the economic policy measures undertaken by democratically elected governments.

3. *Wouldn't it be very wasteful to try to allocate labor without an incentive system that rewards individuals according to the market-determined value of their work contributions?*

Albert & Hahnel (1991a and 1991b) have argued that their participatory planning model actually has an important efficiency (as well as equity) advantage over market systems in its ability to reward people for work according to effort rather than according to result. They propose that the consumption opportunities available to individuals be linked to an individual's input into the production process—in the form of personal effort made or personal sacrifice endured. They criticize the market principle of linking individuals' rewards for work to the market-determined value of their output because the latter depends on variables over which individuals have little or no personal control—for example, natural talent, job location, the vagaries of market demand.

Albert's and Hahnel's proposal would surely lead to greater equity in the reward for labor than the market-based alternative,[28] but their claim of greater efficiency is misguided. They argue that it is most efficient for people to be rewarded according to their personal input because individuals would then be best motivated to supply the one factor which they actually control. Albert and Hahnel suggest that the alternative of a market-determined-output reward system is wasteful and misdirected because it rewards performance due in considerable past to factors beyond the individual's control. But the case for a personal-input reward system is flawed on two counts.

First of all, it is very difficult to observe and measure an individual's sacrifice or work effort and to determine how much of a work result was due to such personal input rather than to other aspects of the work. Measurable indexes of personal input would surely have to be quantitative in nature (e.g., time at work), for how could the quality of a person's effort be adequately measured? Any input-oriented incentive theme would thus tend to encourage the substitution of quantity for quality of effort. Moreover, people would have an interest in understating their natural talents and abilities and in encouraging the perception that good performance had much more to do with their personal input then other factors, while bad performance was mainly the result of bad luck.[29]

Second, even in the absence of any measurement problems, an incentive structure geared to reward individuals according to their personal input would be quite inefficient. Although it would presumably elicit greater work effort and sacrifice on the part of individuals, it would do nothing to assure that such effort and sacrifice were expended in a desirable way. The social good is best served by encouraging activities the results of which are highly valued relative to the cost of undertaking those activities. In order to motivate people to expend their efforts in a desirable way, it is therefore necessary to reward activities according to the value of work output rather than according to the quantity of work input. If market valuations of output do not adequately reflect the general social interest, then it follows that those output valuations ought to be modified accordingly—not that work should be rewarded according to an input measure instead. If one insists on ethical grounds that work be rewarded according to personal input, then one must be prepared to allocate resources by means that do not depend on the motivation of work via individual material reward.

4. *Wouldn't a participatory economic system be viable only if there were a prior transformation of people's basic consciousness from one that is individually oriented to one that is socially oriented?*

Advocates of market socialism assume that people will tend to behave as *homo economicus* and seek to attain the greatest possible individual rewards; they seek to achieve socialist goals by structuring the market environment in which self-interested individuals make their decisions, in such a way that people will choose to undertake economic actions in a socially desirable way. Advocates of participatory socialism are highly critical of such a market-oriented motivational scheme and seek to diminish the role of individual material incentives. But what alternative incentives are available? There are a number of possibilities. On the positive motivational side, people could derive satisfaction (a) from the intrinsic interest of the more enjoyable parts of their work, (b) from the social esteem that might accrue to them for a job well done and/or a social duty performed; (c) from the knowledge that they had met their responsibilities to others in the society, and/or (d) from a vicarious sharing in the enjoyment derived by others from consumption and production activities to which they contributed. On the negative motivational side, people could be discouraged from antisocial behavior by (e) the watchfulness and peer pressure of fellow consumers and workers, and/or (f) the practical inability of getting away with such behavior (whether it is excessively high consumption or excessively low production) in a society committed to egalitarianism.

In order for such mechanisms to add up to a workable system of motivation which could substitute for individual material incentives, there would surely have to be a wholesale conversion of human behavior patterns from homo economicus to what might best be characterized as *homo socialis*—that is, a person whose very consciousness was socially rather than individually oriented. It is a fundamental premise of Marxism that people are strongly influenced by their socioeconomic environment—that people's values and behavior can and will become different as historical and socioeconomic conditions change.   Accepting this premise, one can envisage that in a participatory economic environment people might develop the solidaristic attitudes and cooperative capabilities which would make a participatory socialist system work. What remains to be examined, however, is the process whereby both the needed institutions and the needed values and behavior patterns would emerge. I will return to this question in the final section of the paper.

5. *Wouldn't a participatory economic system tend to be too intrusive in restricting individuality, privacy and freedom of choice?*[30]

Critics of participatory socialism question whether it can adequately protect the legitimate interests of those who hold and wish to act on minority views. True democracy requires not only that people have more or less equal influence over decisions that affect them to the same degree, but that minorities be protected from majority decisions—however equally and fairly they are arrived at—which disadvantage them in important ways. Under participatory socialism there are many important decision-making bodies that are expected to operate by majority vote. Citizens are expected to exercise a great deal of voice in participating in these decision-making bodies. If a decision doesn't go the way of a particular individual or group, however, the opportunities for exit are limited: changing workplaces or neighborhoods in order to enter new decision-making groups remains possible, but one cannot be confident that this would be easy to do in practice.[31]

Although not a goal that is usually voiced explicitly by socialists, freedom of choice—in how to live, what to consume, what kind of work to do, how to express oneself, how to define one's social identity, etc.—is an important value. A participatory system is likely to require people to justify many of their choices along these lines to some kind of collective decision-making body, which in turn is bound to limit the extent to which people can really get their choices accepted—no matter how democratically decision-making bodies are constituted.[32] By enabling individuals to make most choices without reference to what others think about their decisions, a market system provides much greater freedom of this kind. Of course it does so only for people who have the wherewithal to afford alternative choices; thus for a market system to promote meaningful freedom of choice for all, the distribution of income must be reasonably equitable.

In order to avoid the hierarchy of power, income and prestige that tends to develop when people specialize in particular jobs, Albert and Hahnel (1991a and 1991b) have proposed that "balanced job complexes" be established in participatory socialist societies. Under this plan each individual would engage in a variety of work tasks with varying degrees of desirability, combined into a job complex that would be characterized by an average degree of pleasantness comparable to that of every other individuals' job complexes. But many people are likely to prefer doing more specialized work activities than would be permitted under such a balanced-job-complex requirement, which means that enforcement of the requirement might well involve implicit or explicit coercion. Moreover, many people might well prefer to have certain activities carried out by other specialists rather then by participants rotating through from the rest of their balanced job complexes; not just brain surgery and airplane piloting come to mind here, but also such everyday activities as teaching, writing and the performance of music, art and sports. Apart from their inhibition of personal freedom, balanced job complexes designed to avoid specialization seem likely to deprive society of the benefits of activities performed well only by people who have devoted a disproportionate amount of time and effort to them.[33]

These kinds of questions about the desirability of participatory socialism stem from the attribution of fundamental value to a significant degree of individuality, privacy and freedom of choice—in addition to and alongside the more traditional socialist goals of equity, democracy and solidarity. The more weight one places on the former kind of objectives, the more skeptical one will be about the desirability of participatory socialism.

Conclusion

Having raised many of the arguments both for and against the variants of socialism with the strongest claims to a future, I turn now to an attempt to decide on the one that offers the most promise to achieve the basic goals of socialism. The most important choice to be made is between market socialism and participatory socialism. Before turning to that choice, however, it will be useful to consider what kind of market socialism provides the best alternative to participatory socialism.

Public Enterprise versus Worker Enterprise Market Socialism

Market socialism calls for the replacement of private by social control and income rights within a (government-guided) market environment. An important question for advocates of market socialism is whether to base the social rights on communities of *citizens* or *workers*. Should control rights—the rights to manage the enterprise—be vested in governmental agencies (democratically accountable to electorates of citizens) or in workers' councils (democratically accountable to electorates of enterprise workers)? Should income rights—the rights to the surplus generated by the enterprise—accrue to the general public (via government agencies) or to enterprise workers?

Advocates of *public management* stress its advantages vis-à-vis worker self-management with respect to "capital efficiency"—access to capital funds, encouragement of risk-taking, technological progress, etc. Advocates of *public surplus appropriation* stress its advantages with respect to equity at the societal level: channeling the residual income of enterprises into an aggregate "social dividend" recognizes the interdependence of all production activities, protects workers and citizens against the potential risk and inequity of having their capital income tied to the performance of a particular enterprise (which may do well or do badly for reasons of luck rather than merit) and can distribute society's surplus much more equitably than when individual enterprises retain much of their own surplus.

Advocates of *worker self-management* stress its advantages vis-à-vis public management in several different respects: (1) "labor efficiency"— motivation of work effort and quality, disciplining of management, organizational improvement, etc.; (2) democracy: worker self-management at the enterprise level is in and of itself democratic, and may well reinforce democracy at the political level; and (3) solidarity: through greater publication in workplace and enterprise decision-making, workers may gain a stronger sense of solidarity with their fellow workers. Advocates of *worker surplus appropriation* stress its advantages with respect to labor efficiency and solidarity, as workers' incomes are linked collectively to the performance of their enterprises.

Clearly there are significant trade-offs here. Different kinds of social control rights are advantageous with respect to different kinds of efficiency considerations, and different kinds of social income rights are advantageous with respect to different socialist objectives of equity, democracy and solidarity. A reasonable solution to the dilemma of choice—consistent with the overall spirit of compromise inherent in market socialism—would be to encourage a mixture of public and worker control and income rights, emphasizing each in the particular circumstances in which it would do the most good. Such a compromise could take the form of promoting public management in those industries and enterprises characterized by relatively large economies of scale and/or relatively extensive externalities, and promoting worker self-management in industries and enterprises with smaller economies of scale and/or less significant externalities. Since income, unlike control, can easily be shared, it might well be best to promote patterns of enterprise income rights in which there is both a social dividend claim and an enterprise worker claim.

Market Socialism versus Participatory Socialism

To make this choice, socialists must confront two major, separable issues. The first issue is whether and how people could be expected to change from *homo economicus*, as we know him/her in contemporary capitalist societies, to *homo socialis*, as he/she is depicted in the operation of participatory socialist societies. The second issue is how much value we should attach to the opportunity for individuals to exercise such libertarian rights as freedom of choice, privacy and the development of one's own specialized talents and abilities—as compared to the more traditional socialist goals of equity, democracy and solidarity.

In the effort to build a socialist society, market socialists take the terrain of *homo economicus* to be the relevant one—at least for the present and the foreseeable future. If people act essentially as *homo economicus*, it follows that a significant amount of inequality, hierarchy, competition, etc., is a necessary ingredient of an efficient economic system; and this is one important reason for the market socialist acceptance of markets. Participatory socialists, on the other hand, believe that, for the construction of socialism within the foreseeable future, *homo economicus* need not be an unalterable fact. They argue (with Marx) that *homo economicus* is the result of a particular pattern of historical development (and a related pattern of unequal power), which can be changed if people decide do so and act collectively on that desire. The struggle for *homo socialis* can itself help to bring about the desired change in human values and behavior, which would then permit the socialist goals of equity, democracy and solidarity to be achieved with reasonable efficiency under a system dependent on participation and cooperation rather than autonomy and competition.

Many market socialists—for example, Alec Nove (1991; Part 1)—dismiss the idea of *homo socialis* as utopian, and on that basis reject participatory socialism as utterly irrelevant to the fashioning of a "feasible" socialism for the foreseeable future. In the previous section I raised many of the arguments with which skeptics question the feasibility of a participatory economy, and these arguments have made a skeptic of me. I believe, however, that even if we skeptics are wrong about the potential viability of *homo socialis*, there remains a solid reason for turning away from the communitarian vision of socialism.

Consider what it would take to move from here to there. The same Marxist reasoning which suggests that homo socialis is perfectly possible, within an appropriately symbiotic institutional context, suggests that people who have been living in a capitalist institutional environment will be deeply imprinted with the characteristics of *homo economicus*.[34] To transform *homo economicus* into *homo socialis* would thus involve a massive change in people's mind-sets. Such a transformation might conceivably be imposed on a society by an authoritarian elite, but it is virtually impossible to imagine it being generated by a democratic process that respected the current attitudes and preferences of the general public.

This reasoning does not rule out the possibility of any kind of democratic social change from contemporary conditions. It does suggest, however, that such change must be gradual enough so that it is realistic to expect that people—as they are, in their current socioeconomic environment—can be persuaded of the desirability of the change. This seems to me a compelling reason for pursuing socialism in terms of the more modest ambitions of market socialists. Even if one's ultimate hope is to progress to a participatory form of socialist society, a gradual move to some form of market socialism—which would begin to change people's actual socioeconomic environment in a more socialist direction—would appear to be a necessary first step in achieving a democratic transition.

Whether a subsequent transition from market socialism to participatory socialism would in fact be desirable remains an open question. In my discussion of participatory socialism in the previous section, I suggested that certain libertarian objectives associated with personal freedom of choice can best be satisfied only if individuals have the kind of opportunities for choice (and for exit) that a market system alone can provide. While the replacement of markets with a participatory economic system—if feasible—would arguably contribute to a more egalitarian, democratic and solidaristic society, the point is that it would appear to do so at a cost in terms of libertarian objectives.

It is undeniable that such libertarian objectives smack of "bourgeois rights," while the objectives of equality, democracy and solidarity have traditionally been the most strongly associated with socialism. I submit, however, that both kinds of objectives are important ingredients of a good society, and that the task for socialists is to assure the attainment of both in significant measure. I therefore believe that market socialists are right to opt for a significant role for markets, recognizing that this involves a sacrifice of some degree of equality, democracy and solidarity, but expecting that it will deliver more respect for individuality and privacy and more freedom of choice.

Democratic Self-Managed Market Socialism

I have thus concluded with an endorsement of market socialism. To emphasize that democracy should be the essential cornerstone of the socialist project—in the process of transition as well as in the organization of institutions—I include the word "democratic" in my characterization of market socialism. And to emphasize that democracy must be extended from the political to the social to the economic sphere of life, I include also the word "self-managed."

A democratic self -managed market socialism combines

1. *A liberal democratic political framework,* under which government (at all levels) is accountable to citizens via regular democratic elections in a context of civil rights and civil liberties, and participatory democratic mechanisms are promoted at local levels where direct participation is feasible.
2. *Social rights to the control and the income of enterprises* (above a modest size), with these rights to be divided between communities of citizens and communities of workers according to pragmatic criteria.
3. *Markets as the predominant mechanism for resource allocation,* providing informational and incentive benefits as well as freedom of choice, with the opportunities for exit afforded by markets complementing the opportunities for voice afforded by participatory democracy in local politics and enterprise self-management.
4. *A significant economic and social policy role for the state,* whereby the market is rendered the servant rather than the master of society: the national government formulates and implements overall macroeconomic policy, influencing but not controlling the rate and pattern of investment, and also undertakes microeconomic intervention as needed to achieve important goals—not only via taxes and subsidies but also by directly providing certain goods and services (e.g., capital or consumption goods with strong public good characteristics), by assuring general social security (to maintain economic welfare for all), and by pursuing active labor market policies (to keep unemployment down).

However attractive and convincing this vision of socialism may be to its advocates, we must recognize that its general appeal is still very limited. On the Right, it confronts powerful political forces and a powerful ideology favoring capitalism over socialism. On the Left, it faces obstacles even among people upset with the present system, convinced of the need for fundamental change and ready to embrace some form of socialism.

The problem is that the call for market socialism is simply not the kind of clarion call that is emotionally satisfying or politically inspirational; the case for market socialism is all too reasoned, too balanced, too moderate. This is its virtue, but also its Achilles' heel. Who will rally behind its banner? If it is ever to get anywhere, it will need the backing of a strong political movement; and a political movement needs power-ful rallying cries and effective popular mobilization to get off the ground. Democratic self-managed market socialism needs to resonate more fully and more clearly with public hopes and aspirations, or it is likely to remain a socialism for the future but not of the future.

Notes

This paper grew out of my involvement in lively and wide-ranging discussions of Marxism and socialism over the Progressive Economists' Network. I am grateful to countless PEN participants. I would like to mention in particular my indebtedness to Michael Lebowitz for his role in a series of stimulating debates. I would also like to thank Sam Bowles, Michael Goldfield, Fred Moseley, David Kotz, and Victor Lippit.

1. I will consistently use the term "Communist-Party-directed" (or the abbreviated "CP-directed") to describe the kind of socialism that has actually existed in the Soviet Union, Eastern Europe, China, Cuba, Vietnam and North Korea. There are of course many other adjectives that have been used to characterize this type of socialism—"actually existing," "bureaucratic state," "centrally planned," etc.—and some have even called it a form of (state) capitalism. I prefer "CP-directed" because it underlines in a compact way the authoritarian, hierarchical, bureaucratic nature of both the political and the economic system.

2. A complete balance sheet on CP-directed socialism in Eastern Europe and the Soviet Union would have to include also such positive achievement as the public provision of free education and health care (among other social services), the availability of low-cost transportation and housing and greater public access to culture—however modest and restricted some of these benefits may have been. For an insightful attempt to draw such a balance sheet, see Peter Marcuse's (1991) account of his experience in East Germany when the old system was crumbling in 1989–90.

3. This is the implication of a quotation from Serge Mallet that I and my co-authors endorsed in the introductions to all three editions of Edwards, Reich and Weisskopf (1972, 1978, 1986). Mallet (1970: 45) asserts that the societies of the Soviet Union and Eastern Europe are to true socialism "what the monsters of the paleolithic era are to present animal species: clumsy, abortive prototypes."

4. I do not include Trotskyist Marxists among those who have con-sistently rejected CP-directed socialist systems because—although they have been among the most acerbic critics of Stalinism and of the Soviet Union for at least half a century—they do not reject all forms of communist party control over socialism.

5. Liberal-democratic socialists are for the most part not closely associated with Marxism; however, some do consider themselves Marxist and see Communist Parties as having betrayed the principles of Marxism. The most prominent liberal-democratic socialists in the United States are associated with *Dissent* magazine, notably the late Michael Harrington; see, for example, Harrington (1989).

6. Communitarian socialists include Marxists who identify with Marx's long-run vision of a truly communist society as well as "new Leftists" who reject many elements of the Marxist tradition. One of the best known exponents of this school of thought in the United States is Noam Chomsky; for a detailed discussion of what a communitarian socialist society would look like, see Albert and Hahnel (1991).

7. See Lange (1936–37) and Lange and Taylor (1938). Abba Lerner also made seminal contributions to the early literature on market socialism; see Lerner (1934) and (1936).

8. For a brief survey of the history of the idea of market socialism, see Brus (1987); for a recent contribution to the literature on conceptualizing market socialism, see Nove (1991).

9. In this context the enterprise surplus should be defined to include also any capital gains or losses.

10. Examples of recent models of market socialism characterized by public management include those of John Roemer (1991) and Leland Stauber (1977).

11. Examples of recent models of market socialism featuring worker self-management include those of David Schweickart (1980) and David Ellerman (1990)—though in Schweickart's model the national government retains control over net capital formation, and Ellerman does not explicitly use the term "market socialism".

12. For example, in Roemer's model of market socialism, (most of the) enterprise surpluses flow back to the national government to be distributed (in large part) to the general public in an equitable manner as a "social dividend"; in Stauber's model, local government agencies receive enterprise capital income *qua* shareholders and either use it for local public purposes or redistribute it to local citizens.

13. For example, in both Schweickart's and Ellerman's models of worker self-management, the enterprise surplus accrues strictly to its worker—though there are taxes and/or other charges which must first be paid to government.

14. Roemer's and Stauber's models of market socialism represent different kinds of public enterprise models, while Ellerman's is a worker enterprise model; Schweickart's is predominantly a worker enterprise model,

but includes come characteristics of a public enterprise model—for example, government control over net capital formation.

15. Market valuations are expected to reflect "true" social benefits and costs to a much greater extent under market socialism than under capitalism not only because of the greater degree of internalization of externalities, but also because of the more equal distribution of income that results from the socialization of enterprise income rights; thus overall market demand will not disproportionately reflect the demands of a minority of wealthy individuals.

16. The elimination of rewards to property ownership under market socialism is not complete because most market socialist proposals allow for some private ownership of small businesses and for some payment of interest-type returns on individual savings.

17. Progressive taxation is of course also possible in market capitalist systems, but it is surely more likely to be successfully instituted in a market socialist system because of its greater overall economic and hence political equity.

18. This term "coordinator" has been introduced by Albert and Hahnel (1981) to characterize the managers and beneficiaries of the CP-directed socialist economies, but it would seem equally appropriate as a term to characterize any small group of people who are able to parlay critical decision-making roles in a social system into disproportionate political and economic power.

19. See Bowles (1991) for a very suggestive analysis of the impact of markets, as cultural institutions, on the process of human development.

20. This evolution in the thinking of advocates of market socialism toward an increasing role for markets can be seen very clearly in the differences between Brus (1972) and Brus and Laski (1989).

21. Some critics of market socialism have argued that a market socialist system is fundamentally unstable, bound to veer back to a form of capitalism under the pressures on enterprises imposed by competition in a market environment. Certainly market competition restricts the scope of viable options for any kind of producing enterprise; but the argument that it obliterates distinctions among enterprise types is based on a very unrealistic economic model of capitalism—one in which "black-box" firms face no problems of contract enforcement, worker motivation, etc.; only under such restrictive assumptions is there no room at all for discretionary decision-making by firm management and is the market all-determining. For a stimulating debate on these issues, see the exchange between Arnold (1987) and Schweickart (1987).

22. As Miller (1989: 30) has put it: "for markets to operate effectively, individuals and enterprises must receive primary profits, but the proportion of those profits that they need to keep as private income depends on how far they require material (as opposed to moral) incentives."

23. The experience of Sweden since the mid-1970s is often cited to show the vulnerability of social democracy to pressures to move toward a more traditional form of capitalism. For informative analyses of the trials of the Swedish model of social democracy in recent years, see Lundberg (1985) and Pontusson (1987).

24. The period of "War Communism" in the Soviet Union during the civil war years immediately after the Bolshevik Revolution constitutes an exception to this assertion, but of course one associated with exceptional circumstances.

25. See Devine (1988) and Albert and Hahnel (1991a) and (1991b); of the Albert and Hahnel works, the former is a highly accessible popular presentation of their model, while the latter provides a more rigorous and technical presentation of their ideas.

26. Devine (1988) takes pains to distinguish between "market exchange" and "market forces"; the later is distinguished from the former as the process whereby "change [in the economy] occurs . . . as a result of atomized decisions, independently taken, motivated solely by the individual decision-makers' perceptions of their individual self-interest" (p. 23).

27. I refrain deliberately from using the term "central planning" to describe this system, since the literature on such systems demonstrates clearly that their planning mechanisms have been unable to bring about the coordinated fulfillment of any kind of consistent central plan; see, for example, Wilhelm (1985).

28. On the other hand, if equity were really the primary concern, why not reward people according to their need instead of their work input—in other words, why not replace Albert's and Hahnel's version of the socialist distributional principle with Marx's communist principle?

29. It is of course often difficult to measure the result or output of an individual's work, but the difficulties in measuring work output are qualitatively less significant then the difficulties associated with measuring an individual's work input. The former difficulties have mainly to do with distinguishing the contributions of different worker to a joint output, while the latter have to do with disentangling an individual's personal effort from the person's natural abilities.

30. Many of the issues raised here about the desirability of participatory socialism have already been discussed in a persuasive critique of Albert and Hahnel (1991a) by Folbre (1991: 67–70).

31. Of course, changing workplaces or neighborhoods is not that easy to do in practice for many people in market economics either; but the point is that market economies offer individuals or minorities other kinds of opportunities for exit when they make choices that differ from those of the relevant majority.

32. Even the option of switching workplaces and neighborhoods, or forming new ones, does not completely overcome this problem; aside from any difficulties in effecting such switches, there will be societal rules in a participatory economy which every workplace and neighborhood must adhere to, and no doubt many issues of interpretation of those roles which will call for socially determined decisions. Of course, even the most individualistic society must adhere to some rules if it is to survive at all; but the point is that societal rules loom more important in a communitarian society in which people's responsibility to one another is elevated to a guiding principle.

33. As Moore (1980) has argued forcefully in a critique of Marx's vision of full communism, the material basis of cultural complexity is precisely the division of labor.

34. The same surely holds true for people who have been living in a CP-directed socialist institutional environment, where the motivational system remained rooted in individual material incentives.

References

Albert, Michael and Robin Hahnel. 1981. *Socialism Today and Tomorrow*. Boston: South End Press.

———. 1991a. *Looking Forward: Participatory Economics for the Twenty First Century*. Boston: South End Press.

———. 1991b. *The Political Economy of Participatory Economics*. Princeton, NJ: Princeton University Press.

Arnold, N. Scott. Marx and Disequilibrium in Market Socialist Relations of Production. *Economics and Philosophy* 3(1).

Bowles, Samuel. 1991. What Markets Can—and Cannot—Do. *Challenge* (July-August).

Brus, Wlodzimierz. 1971. *The Market in a Socialist Economy*. London: Routledge & Kegan Paul.

———. 1987. Market Socialism. In, *The New Palgrave: A Dictionary of Economics*, John Eatwell, Murray Milgate and Peter Newman (eds.), London: MacMillan.

Brus, Wlodzimierz and Kazimierz Laski. 1989. *From Marx to the Market*. London: Oxford University Press.

Devine, Pat. 1988. *Democracy and Economic Planning*. Boulder, CO: Westview Press.

Edwards, Richard C., Michael Reich and Thomas E. Weisskopf. 1972, 1978, 1986. *The Capitalist System*. Garden City, NJ: Prentice-Hall.

Ellerman, David. 1990. *The Democratic Worker-owned Firm*. Winchester, MA: Unwin Hyman.

Folbre, Nancy. 1991. Contribution to Looking Forward: A Roundtable on Participatory Economics, *Z Magazine* (July-August).

Harrington, Michael. 1989. *Socialism, Past and Future*. Boston: Little Brown.

Heilbroner, Robert. 1989. Interview under the heading No Alternatives to Capitalism. *New Perspectives Quarterly* (fall).

Lange, Oskar. 1936–37. On the Economic Theory of Socialism. Part 1 and 2, *Review of Economic Studies* 4.

Lange, Oskar and Fred Taylor. 1938. *On the Economic Theory of Socialism*. Minneapolis: University of Minnesota Press.

Lerner, Abba. 1934. Economic Theory and Socialist Economy. *Review of Economic Studies* 2.

———. 1936. A Note on Socialist Economics. *Review of Economic Studies* (4).

Lundberg, Erik. 1985. The Rise and Fall of the Swedish Model. *Journal of Economic Literature* 23(1).

Mallet, Serge. 1970. Bureaucracy and Technology in the Socialist Countries. *Socialist Revolution* 1(2).

Marcuse, Peter. 1991. *Missing Marx: A Personal and Political Journal of a Year in East Germany, 1989–90*. New York: Monthly Review Press.

Miller, David. Why Markets? In, *Market Socialism*, Julian Le Grand and Saul Estrin, (eds.). London: Oxford University Press.

Moore, Stanley. 1980. *Marx on the Choice between Socialism and Communism*. Cambridge, MA: Harvard University Press.

Nove, Alec. 1991. *The Economics Of Feasible Socialism Revisited*. London: Harper-Collins Academic.

Pontusson, Jonas. 1987. Radicalization and Retreat in Swedish Democracy. *New Left Review* #165.

Roemer, John. 1991. The Possibility of Market Socialism. Working Paper No. 357, Department of Economics, University of California, Davis.

Schweickart, David. 1980. *Capitalism or Worker Control?* New York: Praeger.

———. Market Socialist Capitalist Roaders. *Economics and Philosophy* 3(3).

Stauber, Leland. 1977. A Proposal for a Democratic Market Economy. *Journal of Comparative Economics* 1(3).

Weisskopf, Thomas E. 1991. The Drive Toward Capitalism in East Central Europe: Is There No Other Way? Working Paper, Department of Economics, University of Michigan.

———. 1992. Challenges to Market Socialism: A Response to Critics. *Dissent* (Spring).

Wilhelm, John. 1985. The Soviet Union has an Administered, not a Planned, Economy. *Soviet Studies* 37.

PART V

WHERE DO WE GO FROM HERE?
NEW PHILOSOPHICAL ISSUES

Two roads diverged in a wood, and I—
I took the one less travelled by, . . .

—Robert Frost, *The Road Not Taken*

12

THE FEMINIST CHALLENGE TO NEOCLASSICAL ECONOMICS

FRANCES R. WOOLLEY

Introduction

There are economists who are feminists. Working within economics, we address feminist concerns, such as gender inequality and androcentric research strategies. This essay is a report on our progress, describing our research agenda, how some of the research priorities have been accommodated within neoclassical economics, and how others fundamentally challenge the neoclassical economic paradigm.

As Michèle Pujol notes (1992, p. 10), feminist economics is not a homogeneous concept. The diverse positions within feminist scholarship as a whole are echoed in feminist economics. A liberal vision of feminist economics can be found in the writings of Barbara Bergmann. She writes: 'what really distinguishes feminist economists is their view that the present assignment of economic duties based on sex is unfair and should be eliminated' (Bergmann, 1983, p. 25). Feminist economists recognise that women are disadvantaged and are committed on equity grounds to improving women's well-being. Brown (1989), like Bergmann, emphasises the fact of women's inferior position: 'Another unifying theme of feminism is the view that in most societies and throughout most of recorded history, women as a group have been in a socially, economically, and politically inferior position to men as a group' (p. 4).

Feminist economists, influenced by critiques of the natural sciences (Harding, 1986), have also begun to question the objectivity of economics. Paula England (1990) asks 'What can economics learn from feminism?' and answers: 'To be more attentive to gender biases in economic work and in the world' (p. 1). More generally, Sandra Harding (1986) has identified two ways in which feminist perspectives expand scientific thought. Feminist empiricism eliminates sexism and androcentrism by applying the tools of scientific investigation in an unbiased way to both women's and men's behavior. Feminist standpoint theory argues that women's experiences, particularly as a disadvantaged group and as a group engaged in caring labour, give women (or feminists) a different and valuable perspective in their scientific investigations. These views form an agenda for feminist neoclassical economics:

i.   to document differences in the well-being of men and women;
ii. to advocate policies which will promote equity; and
iii. to conduct research free from androcentric bias.

The first two items on the agenda correspond to the active, policy-oriented feminism advocated by Bergmann. The third relates to Harding's feminist empiricism and feminist standpoint perspectives. In this essay I make a progress report on the feminist economics agenda, highlight the challenges feminism raises for neoclassical economics, and discuss the relationship between feminist and other challenges to the neoclassical framework. The main point of the paper is to argue that advocating equity-promoting policies and attempting to eliminate bias leads feminist neoclassical economists to challenge their discipline.[1]

Before we consider how feminists challenge neoclassical economics, however, we need to define neoclassical economics. The definition proposed by Robbins—the study of the allocation of scarce resources among different and competing ends—is too broad. Marxist, Austrian, and other varieties of non-neoclassical economics also study the allocation of resources. Alternatively, neoclassical economics can be characterised by the assumptions of methodological individualism, that is, 'individuals are assumed to behave self-interestedly' and 'the analysis is built on the individual' (Nicolaides, 1988, p. 315). While methodological individualism drives much economic research, it does not define the subject, primarily because substantial areas of study lack microfoundations, for example, much of macroeconomics, or theories which aggregate families or firms into individuals or entrepreneurs. Perhaps the most fruitful approach is simply to define neoclassical economics as 'mainstream, orthodox economics' (Blaug, 1980, p. 160) or to 'think of traditional or neoclassical economics as that which is presented in intermediate text books' (Nicolaides, 1988, p. 313). In this essay we shall attempt to take into account both traditional neoclassical views and the new, more institutional, research which is currently entering the economic mainstream.

Documenting the Well-Being of Women

The first item on the feminist agenda is documenting differences in the well-being of men and women. Levels of well-being are determined in part by non-monetary factors, such as health, ties of family and friendship, and disposition. At the same time, money matters. Two major determinants of a woman's well-being are her own income and her share of any family income. A third factor contributing to her well-being is the amount of time she spends working. Let us examine, for earnings, sharing, and time, the absolute position of women, and their position relative to men.

The majority of women in most industrialized countries work. Yet women working full time earn less than two-thirds of men's salaries (Blau and Ferber, 1986, p. 70, U.S. figures). Part of the pay differential is structural. Most women are in poorly paid, predominately female jobs, and many women have less education and training than men. A factor of major importance is that women bear the primary responsibility for child care. Gunderson (1989, p. 51) concludes that: 'Factors originating from outside the labor market (e.g., differences in household responsibilities . . .) are an important source of the overall earnings gap . . .' Finally, women face discrimination: '. . . most studies do find some residual wage gap that they attribute to discrimination' (Gunderson, 1989, p. 51).

Women's own wages are an important determinant of women's well-being, particularly for the large number of women who are unmarried, divorced, single parents or widows. But earnings do not tell the whole story. A woman living with a partner benefits from that partner's income. If we take into account sharing within the family, how does the position of women change? Sen (1984) concludes that there is inequality in the distribution of food within the family. Evidence from rural Bangladesh and West Bengal suggests that women generally receive less calories than men, and, in times of famine, suffer from more malnutrition. More recent studies have confirmed Sen's results. For example, Haddad and Kanbur (1990) conclude on the basis of Philippine data that 'the neglect of intra-household inequality is likely to lead to a considerable understatement of the levels of inequality and poverty' (p. 866). We should not simply project the experience of developing countries onto developed ones, but it is fair to say that we should not assume wage inequalities are canceled out by sharing in the family.

Women earn less than men, and perhaps they have a smaller share of household income. Yet their lower income may be compensated for by greater leisure time. The evidence does not support this hypothesis.

In the United States, men on average spend more time working (including both market and housework) than do women (Juster and Stafford, 1991). However, if one compares men and women with similar labor market commitments, women devote more time to work than do men (Juster and Stafford, 1985, pp. 147–48). Women pay for greater equality in earnings with their leisure time.[2]

If feminist economics fails to take root, it will not be because of a failure to achieve the first item on the agenda, to document differences in the well-being of men and women. There is a large body of evidence to suggest that in terms of income, household sharing, and hours worked, certain women are in a disadvantaged position. The evidence is published in the leading journals of the profession. Where feminist economics encounters less support is in its normative agenda, that is, the commitment to advocate policies which will promote equity.

Policies to Promote Equity

In section 1 we identified inequities in three areas: earned income, share of household income, and leisure time. In this section I shall focus on income inequality, for two reasons. First, government policies, such as affirmative action or equal pay for comparable worth legislation, have aimed at remedying income inequality. Second, other inequalities, particularly inequality in the share of household income, may be alleviated by greater equality in earned income.

How to promote equity depends upon our hypothesis as to what causes inequality between men and women. In this section I shall outline three explanations of the male/female earnings differential, namely taste, statistical, and error discrimination. I consider the implications of each explanation for the choice of government policy, and the challenges each raises for neoclassical economics. These three forms of discrimination are by no means the only models of discrimination. I choose them, first, because they are frequently advanced explanations of discrimination and, second, because they illustrate the point I want to make in this section: *a policy-oriented feminism is not sufficient. It leads to more research or to challenges to neoclassical economics.*

Taste Discrimination

The idea behind taste discrimination is that employers, co-workers or customers have a 'taste' for discrimination, that is, they prefer to hire, work with or be served by, say, men. These preferences translate into lower wages and fewer employment opportunities for women. For example, if employers prefer men to women, they will give male candidates preference when hiring, and offer males higher salaries. Although taste discrimination was originally advanced by Becker (1971) as an explanation for racial discrimination, feminist economists are now using men's preferences to explain occupational segregation (Bergmann, 1986, 1989).

According to the Becker (1971) taste model of discrimination, government policies can increase equity, but at a cost in terms of efficiency. Equal pay combined with affirmative action legislation will improve women's pay and employment opportunities, improving equity. However, it will have two efficiency costs. First, it will make discriminating individuals worse off. The very fact that they discriminate means that they are less well off in a mixed environment than in a gender-segregated one. Second, when employers have a strong preference against hiring women, they may substitute capital for labour instead of hiring a gender-mixed work force, which would cause a departure from the efficient, competitive equilibrium.

However, this efficiency costs story is unsatisfactory, since it suggests that, in a world with taste discrimination, a non-discriminating employer would be able to make substantial profits. S/he could hire women instead of men, pay them slightly less than the going male wage rate, and because s/he had lower costs than other firms, would make profits. With these profits s/he would be able to expand, generating more employment for women, and so on. Just a few non-discriminating employers can, in a competitive market, bid away taste discrimination. The persistence of discrimination over long periods of time is hard to explain in the Becker model.

Bergmann (1989) draws on efficiency wage theory to explain the survival of discriminatory firms in a competitive environment. Efficiency wage theory suggests that increasing wages reduces shirking and turnover, creating efficiency gains which offset the costs of the higher wages groups not discriminated against receive. With this story, discriminating firms will not necessarily be at a substantial disadvantage vis-à-vis non-discriminating firms.

The fundamental issue raised by taste discrimination models is the origin of discriminatory tastes. Feminist and other economists are beginning to answer this question. Paula England and Irene Brown (1990) apply Nancy Chodorow's feminist psychoanalytic theory to labour market segregation. Chodorow argues that because boys are raised by women and have little opportunity to interact with men, they forge their masculine identity out of a rejection of things feminine (England and Brown, 1990, p. 10). Men's identities are threatened if women enter traditionally male occupations as equals. Nancy Folbre (1992) discusses how the process of evolution may have favoured societies in which men and women shared a preference for male control. Geoff Hodgson (1986) stresses the role of institutions in shaping individual's purposes. Variables such as child-rearing practices, cultural evolution or institutions contrast sharply with the variables used to explain tastes in strongly neoclassical models.[3] For example, Stigler and Becker (1977) explain taste changes in terms of prices and incomes. Employers have stable underlying meta-preferences, but will cultivate tastes which are more cheaply satisfied, for example, for immigrant workers. Feminists do not reject price or income explanations of taste changes but add other, less conventional, explanatory variables.

Changing tastes are crucial for feminist economics because many strategies to increase gender equality within and outside the workplace involve changing discriminatory preferences. Yet neoclassical welfare economic policy evaluation almost invariably assumes stable underlying preference orderings.[4] Dropping the assumption of given tastes is problematic. For example, how do we evaluate an affirmative action policy which is expected to increase the acceptance of female employees: in terms of current tastes, in terms of future tastes, or in terms of what tastes would be in a world characterised by gender equality? Or perhaps the notion of welfarism is suspect when tastes are variable? These questions do not have straightforward answers.[5] They raise the first feminist challenge to economics:

Challenge no. 1:   To develop models to explain and evaluate endo-
                    genous preference changes

Statistical Discrimination: A Human Capital Approach

An alternative to the taste discrimination explanation of inequality between men and women is statistical discrimination. There is a body of evidence to suggest that, given two candidates identical in every respect except gender, potential employers, referees and others will rate the performance of the woman as inferior to that of the man. Numerous studies have simulated hiring situations, presenting employers with equivalent male and female candidates, and have found that male candidates are more likely to be hired, or were offered a higher starting salary, in universities, and for managerial, scientific and semiskilled positions (see Nieva and Gutek, 1980, for a survey). To take another example, Ferber and Teiman found that women are more likely to have their articles accepted in journals where the referees do not know the sex of the author (Ferber and Teiman, 1981, pp. 1267).[6] A third example is a study in which groups of students, both male and female, were asked to value two paintings, one attributed to a male and the other to a female. On average the 'male' painting received the higher appraised value (Nieva and Gutek, 1980, p. 268). There is a large body of evidence suggesting that identical work by women is valued less than the same work by men. The question is: why?

One explanation which fits in well with economic theory is that of statistical discrimination. Perhaps women's paintings are, on average, inferior to men's and so worth less in the market. Given two paintings, one will be right more often than not in guessing that the woman's painting has a lower market value. Assigning a lower value to the woman's artwork may be a rational way of reducing the odds of making costly evaluation errors, given the tremendous difficulty of measuring the inherent merit of a work of art. Economists such as Aigner and Cain (1977) have argued that statistical discrimination need not lead to economic discrimination. Although excellent female artists' work may be undervalued, that of unskilled females will be overvalued. On average the evaluation will be correct.

Is there any empirical evidence to support the statistical discrimination hypothesis? As was described in section 1, even after controlling for age, work experience, education, and other variables, most studies find some residual wage differential which they attribute to discrimination. If the statistical discrimination hypothesis is correct, that wage differential represents some unobserved productivity or human capital differential, not proxied by education and so on. What is this variable which employers find so easy to observe and econometricians so elusive? One possibility is women's higher turnover rates. However, as Gronau (1988) has noted, turnover is a 'chicken or egg' problem—are women in relatively low-paid jobs requiring little training because they have high turnover, or do women's higher turnover rates result from their low occupational status? Gronau (1988) deciphers this interrelationship, and finds that 'if women were to reduce their quit rate, increase their labour force experience and tenure, and change their occupational composition, they would obtain only marginally better jobs, and the wage gap would not narrow appreciably'. He concludes: 'Closing the gap therefore requires a structural change'. A range of other factors have been proposed to explain the male-female wage differential, including the greater variability of women (Aigner and Cain, 1977), or that women, exhausted by their household responsibilities, devote less effort to work than men (Becker, 1985), but there is little empirical evidence in support of these factors. Given the number of econometric studies which have found male-female wage differentials not explained by observed productivity or human capital differentials, it seems reasonable to turn to other models of discrimination to explain the wage inequality.

Error Discrimination

A final explanation for the underrating of women's work is error discrimination (England, 1992). People mistakenly over-estimate the difference between an average man and an average woman and, therefore, assign women's work too low a value. Error discrimination can become enshrined in institutional structures, for example, Victorian laws forbidding women from working underground (preventing them, for example, from driving subway trains) remained in force in the U.K. in the 1980s. Moreover, error discrimination creates self-fulfilling prophecies—women are hired for low-grade jobs because they are perceived to be less skilled, they do not learn skills because they are in jobs with no possibility of advancement.

Error discrimination and statistical discrimination have radically different policy implications. If women are disadvantaged because of employers' errors, policies such as affirmative action or pay equity simply correct employers' errors, benefiting women at no cost in terms of economic efficiency. If there is statistical discrimination, requiring employers to change their hiring or pay practices will lower the average quality of the work force (recall—if more men are hired than women it is because men are more productive) decreasing productivity and leading to a fall in economic efficiency. Error discrimination implies that affirmative action and pay equity can be costless, statistical discrimination that they are costly.

The systematic mistakes explanation of discrimination is not one that is universally accepted by feminist economists. First, feminist economists are economists, and are reluctant to dispense with the notion of rationality. Behavior which produces systematic mistakes, that is, outcomes which are wrong on average, or which are not the best choice given current information and the cost of making decisions (i.e., not satisfying), is evidence of irrationality. Second, systematic mistakes suggest that intervening in markets can improve both equity and efficiency. Feminists might consider this an unrealistically rosy view of the consequences of policy intervention. Finally, it seems almost naive to think that those who support discriminatory institutions are honestly mistaken, and are completely uninfluenced by any benefits they might receive from the current *status quo*.

Yet at the same time, when we look at the history of female subordination, it does seem that economists have held mistaken beliefs about the capabilities of women (Pujol, 1992). If the error discrimination hypothesis is true, it fundamentally challenges neoclassical economics, because it suggests that people may not act rationally, and that the outcome of competitive markets may not be optimal.

Challenge no. 2:   To allow that people may make systematic mistakes

The reason for considering policies which promote equity was to show how economists advocating such policies are led away from text-book neoclassical models and toward models where tastes can be endogenized and where judgment errors can persist over time. What, now, for the third item on the feminist agenda? Will moving towards research free from androcentric bias also challenge neoclassical economics?

Toward Research Free from Androcentric Bias

How does bias enter into economic research? The feminist agenda of creating economic research free from androcentric bias is developing in a number of directions. First, feminists aim to do better economics. Economists appeal to 'stylized facts' to motivate their models. Gender bias can cause people to be mistaken about stylized facts. Second, many feminists are concerned that the economic issues affecting women have not been addressed by the profession, or have been marginalized. Economists at times appear unable to 'see' women- or gender-related issues. In this section we shall discuss each of these feminist critiques.

Stylized Facts

Economic models, like maps, are abstract representations which are simpler and more tractable than the real world, yet at the same time do not capture all of the real world's complexity. For a feminist to argue convincingly that her colleagues are using the wrong stylized facts, she cannot simply demonstrate that the assumptions of their models do not correspond to the real world, since no model is ever perfectly realistic. The London Underground map's stylized simplicity is what makes it so easy to use and remember. A feminist also has to show that relaxing a model's assumptions provides predictions which correspond more closely to the real world than those of alternative models.

In this paper I shall take one fairly straightforward but, I think, significant example of a mistaken stylized fact. Economists generally assume, as Gary Becker (1981A) puts it, 'altruism in the family and selfishness in the market place'. Yet it can be argued, that the family-altruism/market place-selfishness dichotomy is in fact incorrect. First, altruism can be found in the market. Paula England (1990, p. 12) argues that male collusion to keep women out of 'their' jobs can be thought of as selective within-sex altruism. Don McCloskey (1989) gives war as an example of a situation where men are public spirited. Second there is little discussion of why conflict is absent from families. One of the few rigorous analyses that conclude there is indeed altruism within the family (Becker, 1974) relies on the assumption that one household member has a large enough share of the household income that all others are supported by him. This is not true for couples where the wife works full- or part-time.[7] Even in 1974 many women worked; today the majority of women work.

Selfishness in the family and altruism in the market place has implications which matter to economists. For example, in the conventional model of the altruistic family, we are unable to explain why it might make a difference to pay family allowance payments to mothers rather than to fathers. The family-altruism/market place-selfishness dichotomy passes the two tests for a mistaken stylized fact. It does not correspond to the real world, and it is unable to explain certain observations, such as the idea that it matters who receives the family allowance check, about the real world. This brings us to our third challenge:

Challenge no. 3:   To correct mistaken stylized facts

In a sense mistakes about stylized facts are the easiest form of gender bias to combat. One simply has to gather the appropriate data and present evidence which shows that a particular view is mistaken. A mistaken view is a public view.

At the same time, correcting mistaken stylized facts is not entirely straightforward. First, women and men have different experiences of the world, and a stylized fact that seems perfectly reasonable to one sex may seem strange or outrageous to the other. Second, as McCloskey (1983) has argued, an overwhelming body of econometric evidence has to be assembled before a model can be considered to be 'disproved'. Take, for example the statistical discrimination model of the previous section. Advocates of the model can always maintain that there are economically relevant differences between men and women, it is just that econometricians have not yet found out what they are. Refutation of a model is highly problematic.

The Invisible Woman

While mistaken stylized facts may be difficult to correct, one can at least argue about an assumption which is in the public domain. The form of gender bias which is hardest to counter is the invisibility of women. Females can disappear from economic analysis in a number of ways. First, results derived on the basis of a male sample are presented as if they applied to all individuals. For example, a recent article on 'The occupational choice of British children' studied only the occupational choice of British boys (Robertson and Symons, 1990). Second, the productive and reproductive activities of women are not recognised as part of economic activity. As Marilyn Waring (1988) points out, the value of household production is not recognised in the national accounts. Third, even when men and women are incorporated into economic models, relationships between men and women rarely are. For example, Robert Barro's celebrated (1974) analysis of the effect of government debt is based on a model of individuals who reproduce themselves asexually. As Bernheim and Bagwell (1988) have shown, if the model is expanded to allow for marriage, it produces absurd results. This brings us to the fourth challenge:

Challenge no. 4:   To incorporate both men and women into economic analysis

There has been progress made in countering the first two aspects of women's invisibility. Women are beginning to appear in economics texts. A survey of the introductory chapters of six intermediate microeconomics textbooks[8] found only one (Gould and Lazear, 1989) which used exclusively male pronouns and characters. The latest planned revisions of the U.N. system of national accounts meets a number of the feminist criticisms raised by Marilyn Waring (Postner, 1992), and there is a growing literature on the value of household production, which is surveyed by Goldschmidt-Clermont (1982, 1987).

However, there is more work to be done. The major problem now is to incorporate women as women, and to describe the constraints and relationships particular to this gender. Women spend much of their time in what feminists refer to as the private sphere, doing housework, caring for children, and so on. Economics tends to regard the private sphere as a black box. This places sources of women's disadvantage, such as long hours spent in housework, unequal sharing of household income, or inability to influence family spending decisions, outside the scope of economic analysis. I shall now consider the economics of the private sphere.

The Private Sphere

Economists usually finesse the private sphere by assuming that the family maximises a single utility function. Family members act as if they all have the same preferences for food, children's clothing, or individual family members enjoying leisure. The family utility function assumption is unsound for feminist and for methodological reasons. A consequence of the family utility function is that conflict within the family cannot be addressed. Marshall's treatment of the family is not unrepresentative:

> . . . the family affections generally are so pure a form of altruism, that their action might have shown little semblance of regularity, had it not been for the uniformity of the family relations themselves. As it is, their action is fairly regular and it has always been fully reckoned with by economists, especially in relation to the distribution of the family income between the various family members, the expenses of preparing children for their future career, and the accumulation of wealth to be enjoyed after the death of him by whom it has been earned (Marshall, 1920, p. 20).

Since families are regulated by a uniform altruism, economics can be assured that family income is distributed equitably between the various family members, and there is no need to inquire into intra-family equity. Conflict disappears. A fundamental question on the feminist research agenda, namely, the position of women in the private sphere, cannot be answered. The family enters a 'black box'.

Treating the family as a single unit is also methodologically unsound. A number of writers have noted the inconsistency between the notion of a single family utility function and neoclassical economics' standard of methodological individualism. Neoclassical (micro-) economics takes as the basic explanatory device the behavior of a rational individual. As Chiappori (1992) puts it 'Modelling a group (even reduced to two participants) as if it were a single individual . . . should be seen as a . . . holistic deviation'. What are the justifications for this deviation?

Early economists such as James Mill justified treating the household as a single individual on the grounds that the interests of women and children were subsumed in the interests of the male household head. Folbre and Hartmann (1988) quote James Mill's *Encyclopedia Britannica* article arguing against the emancipation of women to illustrate this view:

> One thing is pretty clear, that all those individuals whose interests are indisputably included in those of other individuals may be struck off without inconvenience. In this light may be viewed all children, up to a certain age, whose interests are involved in those of their parents. In this light also, women may be regarded, the

interests of almost all of whom is involved either in that of their fathers or in that of their husbands (quoted in Folbre and Hartmann, 1988, p. 188).

The household is treated as a single unit, and the interests of women and children are thereby rendered invisible.

There are few modern defences given for the family utility function assumption. Samuelson (1956) gives the rather weak argument that families reach a 'consensus' because 'blood is thicker than water'. The problem with his argument is that, even if we agree that families are cooperative, there is no reason to believe that the outcome of family cooperation will be a utility function which has all the properties of an individual utility function, that is, that a harmonious family will be as consistent and rational as a single individual. Betts (1991) derives a family utility function using assumptions which guarantee that everyone marries someone with tastes identical to his or her own. Even if we accept this vision of marital harmony, we must admit that it does not include women as distinct individuals, it does not allow any analysis of the private sphere, and is open to the objections advanced to Samuelson's model. Becker's theory of social interactions is the most rigorous justification of the family utility function assumption. Becker showed that, under certain conditions, the household has a single utility function which is identical to that of the head of the household, that is the male income earner (Becker, 1974). Women and children count only to the extent of their husbands' and fathers' caring.

Alternative models of family decision-making which do not arrive at a single family utility function have been developed by Leuthold (1968), Manser and Brown (1980), Apps (1981), Apps and Savage (1989), Ashworth and Ulph (1981), McElroy and Horney (1981), Sen (1985B, 1987), Ulph (1988), Lommerud (1989), Chiappori (1992), Bragstad (1989), Woolley (1990), and Lundberg and Pollak (1992).[9] Feminist critiques have been provided by Janet Seiz (1991), Julie Nelson (1991) and Elaine McCrate (1987). A brief description of the new models of the household gives a guide to their general flavor.

All the models of family decision-making model interaction between two people. One fundamental question that each modeler has to face is: 'How are the asymmetries between men and women captured in this model?' If one is to stay within the neoclassical methodological mainstream, the fundamental explanatory variables must be individuals' tastes, capacities and endowments. So, in Jane Leuthold's (1968) pioneering work, there are asymmetries between men's and women's labor supply, and these arise from differences in their wage rates and in the preferences for leisure versus market work, which may in turn be influenced by the presence of children. In Torunn Bragstad's (1989) model, each member of the household has a 'threshold', which is the maximum amount of untidiness, dirty dishes, and so on he or she can tolerate. Small differences in the thresholds of family members can lead to large differences in the amount of housework performed. McElroy and Horney (1981) argue that a woman will enjoy a greater command over household income the higher her fall-back position, that is, the level of well-being in case of marital breakdown, the greater her partner's concern for her consumption and the lower the price of the goods which she likes to consume.

Does the presence of alternative models of household decision-making provide evidence that it is possible to fight the traditional invisibility of women within the neoclassical economic paradigm? In an obvious sense, it does. The models discussed above are neoclassical models with rational, visible, women. They allow us to answer questions such as: 'Do working women enjoy a greater level of well-being than housewives?'. Apps and Savage (1989) actually estimate the extent of inequality within the household. So, in one sense, the models do provide a non-gendered neoclassical economics.

Yet building models of the family according to the standard economic rules, that is, people maximize their own well-being (which may depend upon the well-being of other people) subject to some set of constraints, fails to yield explanations or predictions about family behavior which are convincing to all economists. Traditional economists and feminists might agree that there is something missing from the models of the family, but would differ in the preferred candidate for the missing element. Ben-Porath (1982) attacks the notion of rationality within the household: maximization of utility "is less compelling in household behavior where those who fail to maximize are not necessarily eliminated' (p. 58). In my own experience, traditional economists often react to models which view the family as two rational utility maximizers by saying something along the lines of 'My marriage isn't like that. We cooperate and make decisions together'. Samuelson's idea that families reach a consensus has broad popular appeal. But there is an infinite variety of possible consensuses—we could agree to go on a cycling holiday or we could agree to visit New York City, but cannot afford to do both. What determines which consensus is reached? The question is rarely asked, so I can only speculate as to likely answers, such as, love, commitment, or perhaps the longevity of family relations which make people sacrifice short-term interest to the long-run good of the family. In a way the real challenge is for traditional economists to articulate clearly the problems with models of family decision-making.

Feminists are fundamentally concerned with how gender is incorporated within economic models of the family. What makes the models apply to a man and a woman living together, instead of to, say, college roommates? One difference between men and women is in the institutional constraints the genders face. Family relations, particularly marriage, are what legal scholars call a 'status', not a freely negotiated contract. The state imposes limits on the terms of, on entry to, and exit from marriage. For example, homosexuals cannot marry. Conventions surround the roles of 'husband', 'wife' and 'mother', and determine socially acceptable behavior. Feminist economists are now beginning the vast enterprise of explaining the emergence of institutions which disadvantage women. For example, Nancy Folbre (1992) discusses how evolution has shaped institutional 'structures of constraint'. This brings us to another challenge.

Challenge no. 5:   To find out what shapes the institutions which privilege or disadvantage women

The literature explaining economic institutions has grown rapidly in the last decade, and has a number of divergent strands. A number of writers connect the search for an individualistic explanation of institutions with political individualism or libertarianism (see, e.g., Rowe, 1989). The transaction cost approach provides insights into the evolution of firms and families (Pollak, 1985). What feminists can add to this literature is a feminist standpoint. Women's experiences of economic institutions are not always the same as men's, and neither are their stylized facts, or reasonable explanations. A feminist economics would draw from non-feminist writers, but would be informed by a feminist perspective.

A second way in which gender enters the new economic models of the family is through tastes. For example, in Bragstad's model, women have a lower threshold for household mess than do men.[10] Recognizing that tastes may be endogenous brings us back to our first challenge: endogenising tastes may be necessary if we are to find satisfactory explanations of women's disadvantage.[11]

A third aspect of gender difference is that women have children. Yet, as Julie Nelson (1991) points out, models of 'families' too often become models of adult individuals in which children play no role. Indeed, my own work (Woolley, 1990) essentially models a 'household' as two childless adults. Nelson (1991) argues that: 'A view of families that focuses only on the prime-age adults makes invisible—unimportant, part of 'nature' not, amenable to study—exactly those activities which have traditionally been of foremost importance to women'.

Does incorporating children into models of the family pose a fundamental challenge to neoclassical economics? Children can be included within models of the family as, say, a public good (Lundberg and Pollak, 1992). Children's welfare or consumption enters as an argument in the parents' utility functions. This approach generates a number of interesting predictions about, for example, the potential effect of differentials in caring on the distribution of household income or the division of household labor. However, as Nelson (1991) has argued, it is open to feminist critiques. First, it treats children as objects not ends in themselves. Second, women's caring for children at times seems a commitment, a responsibility, or even a constraint.

A feminist perspective on children could fundamentally challenge neoclassical economics. First, if, as Nelson suggests, we choose to look after children because of responsibility or commitment, we may want to reconsider our welfare economic evaluation of these choices, perhaps along the lines developed in Sen in his classic essay, 'Rational Fools' (1982). Second, inclusion of children as economic agents and not consumer durables would radically change the new home economics. This brings us to our sixth challenge:

Challenge no. 6:   To develop a better economic model of caring and reproductive activity

Perhaps a feminist might not want to tie herself to one particular view of the family The models developed by Bragstad, McElroy and Horney, and others within the economic paradigm yield insights as to the effect of mess thresholds, divorce laws, and other factors on the well-being of women within the private sphere. At the same time, a richer modelling of institutional structures might allow a better understanding of family relations. Feminists would not deny the traditional economists' view that loving is part of family life—but only one part. People in families can be nurturing and giving, and they can be motivated by their own self-interest. We are best off taking a part from each view of the family, rather than committing ourselves to one.

Conclusions

We are now in a position to appraise each item on the feminist economics agenda.

To document differences in the well-being of men and women. The first agenda item is the one which is the closest to being achieved. There is a substantial literature documenting differentials in women's and men's earnings, leisure time and, most recently, share of household income. The research is published in mainstream economic journals.

To advocate policies which will promote equity. The second agenda item is more problematic. In many neoclassical economic models, policies which promote equity have efficiency costs. Hence a feminist economist has two options. First, to do unbiased research which establishes the relative magnitude of equity gains and efficiency losses. Second, to push back the boundaries of neoclassical economics by endogenising preference structures and institutions. A policy-oriented feminism is not sufficient unto itself.

To conduct research free from androcentric bias. There are two types of gender bias in economics. The first, the use of mistaken stylized facts, is easier to combat than the second, the invisibility of women. Invisibility is more pervasive, more persistent, and harder to fight. I suggested that the most serious example of women's invisibility is the subsuming of women's preferences into the household utility function, but this may reflect my own particular biases as a micro-economist. Certainly, the attempts which have been made to model the household explicitly provoke fundamental questions about neoclassical economics.

Carrying out the feminist economics agenda raises challenges for neoclassical economics. First, inequality between men and women in the labor market and in the household appears to be partially attributable to tastes and institutions. Feminist economists' commitment to greater gender equality brings with it a hope that tastes and institutions can be changed in ways that will promote greater equality between men and women, and a corresponding need for a welfare economic framework within which to evaluate changing preferences and institutions. Second, a feminist economics would make visible traditional areas of female concern, such as household production, child rearing, and caring.

Feminist economists are not alone in examining the origin of tastes, modeling the household, or calling for a more institutional economics. On the one hand, the questions raised by feminists have been addressed by economists trained in the Chicago tradition. Stigler and Becker (1977) endogenise preferences, Becker (1974) models the household, and Landes (1978) and Becker and Murphy (1988) discuss the evolution of marriage and divorce institutions. There are, I think, two reasons why this work is not feminist. First, the stylized facts of these Chicago models seem to many feminists to be wrong. Second, the models encourage an almost complacent acceptance of the status quo. For example, Becker and Murphy (1988, p. 18) conclude 'It is remarkable how many state interventions in the family appear to contribute to the efficiency of family arrangements'. To be a feminist is to believe that it would in some sense be better if the world was characterized by a greater degree of gender equality than is presently the case.

On the other hand, there is an emerging 'neo-neoclassical' economics which is meeting many of the challenges raised by feminist economists. Amartya Sen has suggested that economic man is a rational fool if he does not take time to think about the preference function he is maximizing. Sen's work on meta-preference orderings (1982) and capabilities (1987) provides promising avenues for the development of a welfare economics which incorporates feminist ideas of endogenous preferences (Woolley, 1992). Sheila Dow's (1990) idea of moving 'beyond dualism' is thought-provoking from a feminist perspective. The division between self and other permeates economic thinking. Dow's 'Babylonian thinking' provides a way of breaking down this division, recognizing that at times we think in terms of self-interest, at times in terms of our children's interests, or our family's interests, or social interests. Geoff Hodgson's (1986) insightful critique of methodological individualism, and his call for a synthesis of explanations, involving both individual agency and social structure (p. 219) is very welcome.

Feminist economics can draw from all of these new economic thinkers. What feminism can add to the literature is, first and foremost, a focus on economic justice between men and women, which unifies an otherwise disparate literature, and gives a compelling motivation for continuing to challenge traditional economic thinking. Second, feminists bring new perspectives and experiences which allow them to see, and to seek to explain, economic facts about male-female wage differentials, household production, or family decision-making.

Notes

An earlier version of this paper was presented in Carleton University's Women's Studies seminar. I have benefited from discussions with the participant in that seminar, my colleagues at Carleton, and participants at the University of Manitoba conference on Feminist Criticisms of Economic Theory. Fiona Coulter, T. K. Rymes and a referee provided written comments. David Long provided intellectual support throughout.

1. Other varieties of economics, such as Marxian or post-Keynesian economics, might benefit from feminist scrutiny. I confine my attention to

neoclassical economics. In part this is because the neoclassical paradigm is the one dominant in much of English-speaking economic thought. In part it is because I am trained as a neoclassical economist.

2. When we turn from industrialised to agricultural societies, women's relative access to leisure falls. One study of rural Botswana in 1975 found that women worked on average 12 hours per week more than men; a 1981 study of Nepalese villages found that women worked 23 hours per week more than men (Juster and Stafford, 1991).

3. Nicolaides (1988, pp. 321–22) provides a discussion of this literature.

4. Notable exceptions include Gintis (1974) and Hahnel and Albert (1990).

5. I address these issues in more detail in Woolley (1992).

6. Although Blank (1991) is more cautious in her appraisal of the evidence: 'While the data are consistent with an argument that women fare better under a double-blind reviewing system, the estimated effects are small and show no statistical significance'.

7. To be strictly accurate, Becker's result holds when the wife's earnings are less than the income transfer from husband to wife.

8. Salvatore (1991), Hirschleifer (1988), Frank (1991), Eaton and Eaton (1991), Gould and Lazear (1989), Hyman (1989).

9. There is not sufficient space here to describe the literature in detail; those interested will find a survey in Woolley (1990).

10. It is interesting to note that Becker's (1974) model of the family also incorporates asymmetric tastes. The head (male) is altruistic and the dependent (female) is selfish. The motivation for this assumption is unclear.

11. John Stuart Mill, an early feminist economist, recognised how women's tastes were shaped by their cultural conditioning: 'If women are better than men at anything, it surely is in individual self-sacrifice for those of their own family. But I lay little stress on this, so long as *they are universally taught that they are born and created for self-sacrifice*' (Mill, 1970, p. 172, emphasis added).

References

Aigner, D. J. and Cain, G. C. 1977. Statistical Theories of Discrimination in Labour Markets, *Industrial and Labour Relations Review*, vol. 30.

Apps, P. 1981. *A Theory of Inequality and Taxation*, Cambridge, Cambridge University Press.

Apps, P. and Savage, E. 1989. Labour Supply, Welfare Rankings and the Measurement of Inequality, *Journal of Public Economics*, vol. 39.

Ashworth, J. S. and Ulph, D. 1981. Household models, in Brown, C. V. (ed.), *Taxation and Labour Supply*, London, George Allen and Unwin.

Barro, R. 1974. Are Government Bonds Net Wealth?, *Journal of Political Economy*, vol. 82.

Becker, G. S. 1971. *The Economics of Discrimination*, 2nd ed., Chicago, IL, University of Chicago Press.

Becker, G. S. 1974. A Theory of Social Interactions, *Journal of Political Economy*, vol. 82.

Becker, G. S. 1981A. Altruism in the Family and Selfishness in the Market Place, *Economica*, vol. 48.

Becker, G. S. 1981B. *A Treatise on the Family*, Cambridge, Harvard University Press.

Becker, G. S. 1985. Human Capital, Effort, and the Sexual Division of Labor, *Journal of Labor Economics*, vol. 3.

Becker, G. S. and Murphy, K. 1988. The Family and the State, *Journal of Law and Economics*, vol. 31.

Ben-Porath, Y. 1982. Economics and the Family—Match or Mismatch? A review of Becker's *A Treatise on the Family*, *Journal of Economic Literature*, vol. 22.

Bergmann, B. 1983. Feminism and Economics, *Academe* September/October.

Bergmann, B.1986. *The Economic Emergence of Women*, New York, Basic Books.

Bergmann, B. 1989. Does the Market for Women's Labor Need Fixing, *Journal of Economic Perspectives*, vol. 3.

Bernheim, B. and Bagwell, K. 1988. Is Everything Neutral?, *Journal of Political Economy*, vol. 96.

Betts, J. 1991. Technological Change and the Intra-family Division of Labour, paper presented to the Canadian Economics Association meetings, Kingston, Ontario, June, 1991.

Blank, R. 1991. The Effects of Double-blind Versus Single-blind Reviewing: Experimental Evidence from the American Economic Review, *American Economic Review*, vol. 81.

Blau, F. and Ferber, M. A. 1986. *The Economics of Women, Men and Work* Englewood Cliffs, NJ, Prentice Hall.

Blaug, M. 1980. *The Methodology of Economics or How Economists Explain*, Cambridge, Cambridge University Press.

Bragstad, T. 1989. 'On the Significance of Standards for the Division of Work in the Household' mimeo, University of Oslo.

Brown, L. J. 1989. 'Gender and Economic Analysis: A Feminist Perspective' mimeo, Eastern Washington University.

Chiappori, P. A. 1992. Collective Labour Supply and Welfare, *Journal of Political Economy*.

Dow, S. C. 1990. Beyond Dualism, *Cambridge Journal of Economics*, vol. 14, no. 2.

Eaton, B. C. and Eaton, D. F. 1991. *Microeconomics*, 2nd ed., New York, W. H. Freeman.

England, P. 1990. What Can Economics Learn from Feminism, paper presented at the AEA annual meetings, December, 1990.

England, P. 1992. *Comparable Worth: Theories and Evidence*, New York, Aldine.

England, P. and Brown, I. 1990. Internalization and Constraint in Theories of Women's Oppression, forthcoming in Ben Agger (ed.), *Current Perspectives on Social Theory*.

Ferber, M. and Teiman, M. 1981. The Oldest, the Most Established, and Most Quantitative of the Social Sciences—and the Most Dominated by men: The Impact of Feminism on Economics, in Spender, D. (ed.), *Men's Studies Modified; The Impact of Feminism on the Academic Disciplines*, Oxford, Pergamon Press.

Folbre, N. and Heidi, H. 1988. The Rhetoric of Self-interest: Ideology of Gender in Economic Theory, in Klamer, A., McCloskey, D. N. and Solow, R. M. (ed.), *The Consequences of Economic Rhetoric*, Cambridge, Cambridge University Press.

Folbre, N. 1992. *Who Pays for the Kids? Gender and the Structure of Constraint*, London, Routledge.

Frank, R. H. 1991. *Microeconomics and Behavior*, New York, McGraw Hill.

Fuchs, V. R. 1986. His and Hers: Gender Differences in Work and Income, 1959–1979, *Journal of Labor Economics*, vol. 4.

Gintis, H. 1974. Welfare Criteria with Endogenous Preferences: The Economics of Education, *International Economic Review*, vol. 13.

Goldschmidt-Clermont, L. 1982. *Unpaid Work in the Household: A Review of Economic Evaluation Methods*, Geneva, International Labour Office.

Goldschmidt-Clermont, L. 1987. *Economic Evaluations of Unpaid Household Work: Africa, Asia, Latin America and Ocean*, Geneva, International Labour Office.

Gould, J. P. and Lazear, E. P. 1989. *Microeconomic Theory*, 6th ed. Homewood, IL, Irwin.

Gronau, R. 1988. Sex-related Wage Differentials and Women's Interrupted Labor Careers—The Chicken or the Egg, *Journal of Labor Economics*, vol. 6.

Gunderson, M. 1989. Male-female Wage Differentials and Policy Responses, *Journal of Economic Literature*, vol. 27.

Haddad, L. and Kanbur, R. 1990. How Serious Is the Neglect of Intra-household Inequality, *Economic Journal*, Vol. 100.

Hahnel, R. and Albert, M. 1990. *Quiet Revolution in Welfare Economics*, Princeton, NJ, Princeton University Press.

Harding, S. 1986. *The Science Question in Feminism*, Milton Keynes, Open University Press.

Hirshleifer, J. 1988. *Price Theory and Applications*, 4th ed., Englewood Cliffs, NJ, Prentice Hall.

Hodgson, G. 1986. Behind methodological individualism, *Cambridge Journal of Economics*, vol. 10, no. 2.

Hyman, D. N. 1989. *Modern Microeconomics: Analysis and Applications*, 2nd ed., Homewood, IL, Irwin.

Juster, F. T. and Stafford, F. D. 1985. *Time, Goods and Well-Being*, Ann Arbor, MI, Institute of Social Research, University of Michigan.

Juster, F. T. and Stafford, F. D. 1991. The Allocation of Time: Empirical Findings, Behavioural Models and Problems of Measurement, *Journal of Economic Literature*, Vol. 29.

Lam, D. 1988. Marriage Markets and Assortative Mating with Household Public Goods, *Journal of Human Resources*, Vol. 23.

Landes, E. 1978. The Economics of Alimony, *Journal of Legal Studies*.

Leuthold, J. 1968. An Empirical Study of Formula Income Transfers and the Work Decisions of the Poor, *Journal of Human Resources*, vol. 3.

Lommerud, K. 1989. Marital Division of Labor with Risk of Divorce: The Role of 'Voice' Enforcement, *Journal of Labor Economics*, vol. 7.

Lundberg, S. and Pollak, R. A. 1992. 'Separate Spheres Bargaining and the Marriage Market' mimeo, Department of Economics, University of Washington.

Manser, M. and Brown, M. 1980. Marriage and Household Decision-Making, *International Economic Review*, vol. 21.

Marshall, A. 1920. *Principles of Economics*, 8th ed., London and Basingstoke, MacMillan.

McCloskey, D. 1983. The Rhetoric of Economics, *Journal of Economic Literature*, vol. 23.

McCloskey, D. 1989. Some Consequences of a Feminine Economics, published as Some consequences of a conjective economics, in Ferber, M. A. and Nelson, J. A. (eds), *Beyond Economic Man: Feminist Theory and Economics*, Chicago, IL, University of Chicago Press.

McCrate, E. 1987. Trade, Merger and Employment: Economic Theory on Marriage, *Review of Radical Political Economics*, vol. 19.

McElroy, M. J. and Horney, M. B. 1981. Nash Bargained Household Decision Making, *International Economic Review*, vol. 22.

Mill, J. S. 1970. The Subjection of Women in John Stuart Mill and Harriet Taylor Mill, *Essays on Sex Equality* in Rossi, A. (ed.), Chicago, IL, University of Chicago Press.

Nelson, J. 1991. Towards a Feminist Theory of Family, paper presented at the AEA annual meetings, January 3–5, 1992.

Nicolaides, P. 1988. Limits to the Expansion of Neoclassical Economics, *Cambridge Journal of Economics*, vol. 12, no. 3.

Nieva, V. F. and Gutek, B. A. 1980. Sex Effects of Evaluation, *Academy of Management Review*, vol. 5.

Peters, H. E. 1986. Marriage and Divorce: Informational Constraints and Private Contracting, *American Economic Review*, vol. 76.

Pollak, R. A. 1985. A Transaction Cost Approach to Families and Households, *Journal of Economic Literature*, vol. 23.

Postner, H. 1992. Review of *If Women Counted: A New Feminist Economics*, *Review of Income and Wealth*, vol. 38.

Pujol, M. A. 1992. *Feminism and Anti-Feminism in Early Economic Thought*, Edward Elgar, Aldershot, England.

Robb, R. E. 1978. Earnings Differentials between Males and Females in Ontario, *Canadian Journal of Economics*, vol. 11.

Robertson, D. and Symons, J. 1990. The Occupational Choice of British Children, *Economic Journal*, vol. 100.

Rowe, N. 1989. *Rules and Institutions*, Hemel Hempstead, Herts, Allan.

Salvatore, D. 1991. *Microeconomics*, New York, Harper Collins.

Samuelson, P. 1956. Social Indifference Curves, *Quarterly Journal of Economics*, vol. 52.

Seiz, J. A. 1991. The Bargaining Approach and Feminist Methodology, *Review of Radical Political Economics*, vol. 23.

Seiz, J. A. 1991. Gender and Economic Research, forthcoming in de Marchi, N. (ed.), *The Methodology of Economics*, Boston, MA, Kluwer Nijhoff.

Sen, A. K. 1966. Labour Allocation in a Cooperative Enterprise, *Review of Economic Studies*, vol. 33.

Sen, A. K. 1982. *Choice, Welfare, and Measurement*, Oxford, Basil Blackwell.

Sen, A. K. 1984. Family and Food: Sex Bias in Poverty, *Resources, Values, and Development*. Cambridge, MA, Harvard University Press.

Sen, A. K. 1985A. Well-being, Agency and Freedom: The Dewey Lectures 1984, *The Journal of Philosophy*, vol. 82.

Sen, A. K. 1985B. Women, Technology and Sexual Divisions, *Trade and Development: An UNCTAD Review*, vol. 6.

Sen, A. K. 1987. Gender and Cooperative Conflicts, WIDER Working Paper 18.

Shakespeare, W. 1986. *The Complete Works*, Wells, S. and Taylor, G. (eds), Oxford, Clarendon Press.

Stigler, G. J. and Becker, G. S. 1977. De Gustibus Non Est Disputandum, *American Economic Review*, vol. 67.

Ulph, D. 1988. 'A General Noncooperative Nash Model of Household Behaviour', mimeo, University of Bristol.

Waring, M. 1988. *If Women Counted: A New Feminist Economics*, San Francisco, CA, Harper and Row.

Woolley, F. R. 1990. *Economic Models of Family Decision Making, with Applications to Intergenerational Justice*, unpublished Ph.D. dissertation, London School of Economics.

Woolley, F. R. 1992. 'Welfare Economics and Its Critics: A Feminist Reappraisal', mimeo, Carleton University.

13

AGAINST PARSIMONY:
THREE WAYS OF COMPLICATING SOME
CATEGORIES OF ECONOMIC DISCOURSE

ALBERT O. HIRSCHMAN

In his well-known article on "Rational Fools," Amartya Sen asserted that "traditional [economic] theory has *too little* structure" (1977, p. 335). Like any virtue, so he seemed to say, parsimony in theory construction can be overdone and something is sometimes to be gained by making things *more complicated*. I have increasingly come to feel this way. Some years ago, I suggested that criticism from customers or "voice" should be recognized as a force keeping management of firms and organizations "on their toes," alongside with competition or "exit," and it took a book (1970) to cope with the resulting complications. Here I deal with various other realms of economic inquiry that stand similarly in need of being rendered more complex. In concluding I examine whether the various complications have some element in common—that would simplify and unify matters.

Two Kinds of Preference Changes

A fruitful distinction has been made, by Sen and others, between first- and second-order preferences, or between preferences and meta-preferences, respectively. I shall use the latter terminology here. Economics has traditionally dealt only with (first-order) preferences, that is, those that are *revealed* by agents as they buy goods and services. But the concept of metapreference must be of concern to the economist, to the extent that he claims an interest in understanding processes of economic *change*. Its starting point is a very general observation on *human nature*: men and women have the ability to step back from their "revealed" wants, volitions, and preferences, to ask themselves whether they really want these wants and prefer these preferences, and consequently to form metapreferences that may differ from their preferences. Unsurprisingly, it is a philosopher, Harry Frankfurt (1971), who first put matters this way. He argued that this ability to step back is unique in humans, but is not present in all of them. Those who lack this ability he called "wantons": they are entirely, unreflectively in the grip of their whims and passions.

As I have pointed out before (1982, p. 71), certainty about the existence of metapreferences can only be gained through *changes* in preferences, that is, through changes in actual choice behavior. If preferences and metapreferences always coincide so that the agent is permanently at peace with himself no matter what choices he makes, then the metapreferences hardly lead an independent existence and are mere shadows of the preferences. If, on the other hand, the two kinds of preferences are permanently at odds so that the agent always acts against "his better judgment," then again the metapreference can not only be dismissed as wholly ineffective, but doubts will arise whether it is really there at all.

Changes in choice behavior are therefore essential for validating the concept of metapreferences; conversely, this concept is useful in illuminating the varied nature of preference change, for it is now possible to distinguish between two kinds of *preference changes*. One is the reflective kind, preceded as it is by the formation of a metapreference that is at odds with the observed and hitherto practiced preference. But there are also preference changes that take place without any elaborate antecedent development of metapreferences. Following Frankfurt's terminology, the unreflective changes in preferences might be called "wanton." These are the preference changes economists have primarily focused on: haphazard, publicity-induced, and generally minor (apples vs. pears) *change in tastes*. In contrast, the nonwanton change of preference is not really a change in tastes at all. A taste is almost *defined* as a preference about which you do not argue—de gustibus non est disputandum. A taste about which you argue, with others or *yourself*, ceases ipso facto being a taste—it turns into a *value*. When a change in preferences has been preceded by the formation of a metapreference much argument has obviously gone on within the divided self; it typically represents a *change in values* rather than a change in tastes.

Given the economists' concentration on, and consequent bias for, wanton preference changes, changes of the reflective kind have tended to be downgraded to the wanton kind by assimilating them to changes in *tastes*: thus patterns of discriminatory hiring have been ascribed to a "taste for discrimination" (Gary Becker, 1957) and increases in protectionism have similarly been analyzed as reflecting an enhanced "taste for nationalism" (Harry Johnson, 1965). Such interpretations strike me as objectionable on two counts: first, they impede a serious intellectual effort to understand what are strongly held values and difficult-to-achieve changes in values rather than tastes and changes in tastes; second, the illusion is fostered that "raising the cost" of discrimination (or nationalism) is the simple and sovereign policy instrument for getting people to indulge less in those odd "tastes."

In the light of the distinction between wanton and nonwanton preference changes, or between changes in tastes and changes in values, it also becomes possible to understand—and to criticize—the recent attempt of Becker and George Stigler (1977) to do without the notion of preference changes for the purpose of explaining changes in behavior. Equating preference changes to changes in what they themselves call "inscrutable, often capricious tastes" (p. 76), they find, quite rightly, any changes in those kinds of tastes (our wanton changes) of little analytical interest. But in their subsequent determination to explain all behavior change through price and income differences, they neglect one important source of such change: autonomous, reflective change in values. For example, in their analysis of beneficial and harmful addiction they take the elasticity of the individual's demand curve for music or heroin as given and, it would seem, immutable. May I urge that changes in values do occur from time to time in the lives of individuals, of generations, and from one generation to another, and that those changes and their effects on behavior are worth exploring—that, in brief, de valoribus *est* disputandum?

Two Kinds of Activities

From consumption I now turn to production and to human activities such as work and effort involved in achieving production goals. Much of economic activity is directed to the production of (private) goods and services that are then sold in the market. From the point of view of the firm, the activity carries with it a neat distinction between process and outcome, inputs and outputs, or costs and revenue. From the point of view of the individual participant in the process, a seemingly similar distinction can be drawn between work and pay or between effort and reward. Yet there is a well-known difference between the firm and the individual: for the firm any outlay is unambiguously to be entered on the negative side of the accounts whereas work can be more or less irksome or pleasant—even the same work can be felt as more pleasant by the same person from one day to the next. This problem, in particular its positive and normative consequences for income differentials, has attracted the attention of a long line of economists starting with Adam Smith. Most recently Gordon Winston has distinguished between "process utility" and "goal utility" (1982, pp. 193–97). While such a distinction makes it clear that the means to the end of productive effort need not be entered on the negative side in a calculus on satisfaction, it keeps intact the basic instrumental conception of work, the means-end dichotomy on which our understanding of the work and production process has been essentially—and, up to a point, so usefully-based.

But there is need to go further if the complexity and full range of human activities, productive and otherwise, are to be appreciated. Once again, more structure would be helpful. The possible existence of wholly *noninstrumental* activities is suggested by everyday language: it speaks of activities that are undertaken "for their own sake" and that "carry their own reward." These are somewhat trite, unconvincing phrases: after all, any sustained activity, with the possible exception of pure play, is undertaken with some idea about an intended outcome. A person who claims to be working exclusively for the sake of the rewards yielded by the exertion itself is usually suspect of hypocrisy: one feels he is "really" after the money, the advancement or—at least—the glory, and thus is an instrumentalist after all.

Some progress can be made with the matter by looking at the varying predictability of the intended outcome of different productive activities. Certain activities, typically of a routine character, have perfectly predictable outcomes. With regard to such tasks, there is no doubt in the individual's mind that effort will yield the anticipated outcome—an hour of labor will yield the well-known, fully visualized result as well as entitle the worker, if he has been contracted for the job, to a wage that can be used for the purchase of desired (and usually also well-known) goods. Under these conditions, the separation of the process into means and ends, or into costs and benefits, occurs almost spontaneously and work assumes its normal instrumental character.

But there are many kinds of activities, from that of a research and development scientist to that of a composer or an advocate of some public policy, whose intended outcome cannot be relied upon to materialize with certainty. Among these activities there are some—applied laboratory research may be an example—whose outcome cannot be for any single day or month; nevertheless, success in achieving the intended result steadily gains in likelihood as the period during which work is carried on gets longer. In this case, the uncertainty is of a probabilistic nature and one can speak of a certainty equivalent with regard to the output of the activity in any given period so that, once again, the separation of the process into means and ends is being experienced and work of this sort largely retains its instrumental cast. I now come to a more puzzling kind of nonroutine activities. From their earliest origins, men and women appear to have allocated a considerable portion of their time to undertakings whose success is simply unpredictable. These are activities such as the pursuit of truth, beauty, justice, liberty, community, friendship, love, salvation, and so on. As a rule, these pursuits are of course carried on through a variety of exertions for apparently limited and specific objectives (writing a book, participating in a political campaign, etc.). Nevertheless, an important component of the activities thus undertaken is best described not as labor or work, but as *striving*—a term that precisely intimates the lack of a reliable relation between effort and result. A means-end or cost-benefit calculus is impossible under the circumstances.

The question now arises why such activities should be taken up at all, as long as their successful outcome is so wholly uncertain. Moreover, they certainly are not always pleasant in themselves—in fact some of them can be quite strenuous or highly dangerous. Do we have here then another paradox or puzzle, one that relates not just to voting (why do "rational" people bother to vote?), but to a much wider and most vital group of human activities? I suppose we do—from the point of view of instrumental reason, noninstrumental action is bound to be something of a mystery. But I have proposed an at least half-rational explanation: these noninstrumental activities whose outcome is so uncertain are strangely characterized by a certain fusion of (and confusion between) striving and attaining (see my 1982 book, pp. 84–91). He who strives after truth (or beauty) frequently experiences the conviction, fleeting though it may be, that he has found (or achieved) it. He who participates in a movement for liberty or justice frequently has the experience of already bringing these ideals within reach. In Pascal's formulation: "The hope Christians have to possess an infinite good is mixed with actual enjoyment . . . for they are not like people who would hope for a kingdom of which they, as subjects, have nothing; rather, they hope for holiness, and for freedom from injustice, and they partake of both" (*Pensées*, 540, Brunschvicg edition, my translation).

This fusion of striving and attaining is a fact of experience that goes far in accounting for the existence and importance of noninstrumental activities. As though in compensation for the uncertainty about the outcome, the striving effort is colored by the goal and in this fashion makes for an experience that is very different from merely agreeable, pleasurable or even "stimulating": in spite of its frequently painful character it has a well-known "intoxicating" quality.

The foregoing interpretation of noninstrumental action is complemented by an alternative view which has been proposed by the sociologist Alessandro Pizzorno (1983). For him, participation in politics is often engaged in because it enhances one's feeling of belonging to a group. I would add that noninstrumental action in general makes you feel more like a "real person." Such action can then be considered, in economic terms, as an *investment in individual and group identity.* The feeling of having achieved belongingness and personhood may of course be just as evanescent as the fusion of striving and attaining to which I referred earlier. The two views are related attempts at achieving an uncommonly difficult insight: to think instrumentally about the noninstrumental.

But why should economics be concerned with all this? Is it not enough for this discipline to attempt an adequate account of man's instrumental activities—a vast area indeed—while leaving the other, somewhat murky regions alone? Up to a point such a limitation made sense. But as economics has grown more ambitious, it becomes of increasing importance to appreciate that the means–end, cost-benefit model is far from covering all aspects of human activity and experience. Take the analysis of political action, an area in which economists have become interested as a natural extension of their work on public goods. Here the neglect of the noninstrumental mode of action was responsible for the inability of the "economic approach" to understand why people bother to vote and why they engage from time to time in collective action.

Once the noninstrumental mode is being paid some attention it becomes possible to account for these otherwise puzzling phenomena. It is the fusion of striving and attaining, characteristic of noninstrumental action, that led me to a conclusion exactly opposite to the "free ride" argument with respect to collective action:

> since the output and objective of collective action are . . . a public good available to all, the only way an individual can raise the benefit accruing to him from the collective action is by stepping up his own input, his effort on behalf of the public policy he espouses. Far from shirking and attempting to get a free ride, a truly maximizing individual will attempt to be as activist as he can manage, ... [1982, p. 86]

The preceding argument does not imply, of course, that citizens will never adopt the instrumental mode of action with respect to action in the public interest. On the contrary, quite a few of them may well move from one mode to the other, and such oscillations could help explain the observed instability both of individual commitment and of many social movements in general.

A better understanding of collective action is by no means the only benefit that stands to flow from a more open attitude toward the possibility of noninstrumental action. As has been argued earlier, a strong affinity exists between instrumental and routine activities, on the one hand, and between noninstrumental and nonroutine activities, on the other. But just as I noted the existence of nonroutine activities that are predominantly instrumental (in the case of an applied research laboratory), so can routine work have more or less of a noninstrumental component, as Veblen stressed in *The Instinct of Workmanship*. Lately the conviction has gained ground that fluctuations in this component must be drawn upon to account for variations in labor productivity and for shifts in industrial leadership. It does make a great deal of difference, so it seems, whether people look at their work as "just a job" or also as part of some collective celebration.

"Love": Neither Scarce Resource Nor Augmentable Skill

My next plea for complicating economic discourse also deals with the production side, but more specifically with the role of one important prerequisite or ingredient known variously as morality, civic spirit, trust, observance of elementary ethical norms, and so on. The need of any functioning economic system for this "input" is widely recognized. But disagreement exists over what happens to this input as it is being used.

There are essentially two opposite models of factor use. The traditional one is constructed on the basis of given, depletable resources that get incorporated into the product. The scarcer the resource the higher its price and the less of it will be used by the economizing firm in combination with other inputs. A more recent model recognizes the possibility of "learning by doing" (Kenneth Arrow, 1962). Use of a resource such as a skill has the immediate effect of improving the skill, of enlarging (rather than depleting) its availability. The recognition of this sort of process was a considerable, strangely belated insight.

Because the "scarce resource" model has long been dominant, it has been extended to domains where its validity is highly dubious. Some thirty years ago, Dennis Robertson wrote a characteristically witty paper entitled "What Does the Economist Economize?" (1956). His often cited answer was: love, which he called "that scarce resource" (p. 154). Robertson explained, through a number of well-chosen illustrations from the contemporary economic scene, that it was the economist's job to create an institutional environment and pattern of motivation where as small a burden as possible would be placed, for the purposes of society's functioning, on this thing "love," a term he used as a shortcut for morality and civic spirit. In so arguing, he was of course at one with Adam Smith who celebrated society's ability to do without "benevolence" (of the butcher, brewer, and baker) as long as individual "interest" was given full scope. Robertson does not invoke Smith, quoting instead a telling phrase by Marshall: "Progress chiefly depends on the extent to which the *strongest* and not merely the *highest* forces of human nature can be utilized for the increase of social good" (p. 148). This is yet another way of asserting that the social order is more secure when it is built on interest rather than on love or benevolence. But the sharpness of Robertson's own formulation makes it possible to identify the flaw in this recurrent mode of reasoning.

Once love and particularly public morality is equated to a scarce resource, the need to economize it seems self-evident. Yet a moment's reflection is enough to realize that the analogy is not only questionable, but a bit absurd—and therefore funny. Take, for example, the well-known case of the person who drives in the morning rush hour and quips, upon yielding to another motorist: "I have done my good deed for the day; for the remainder, I can now act like a bastard." What strikes one as funny and absurd here is precisely the assumption, on the part of our driver, that he comes equipped with a strictly limited supply of good deeds; that, in other words, love should be treated as a scarce resource—just as Robertson claimed. We know instinctively that the supply of such resources as love or public spirit is not fixed or limited as may be the case for other factors of production. The analogy is faulty for two reasons: first of all, these are resources whose supply may well increase rather than decrease through use: second, these resources do not remain intact if they stay unused; like the ability to speak a foreign language or to play the piano, these moral resources are likely to become depleted and to atrophy if *not* used.

In a first approximation, then, Robertson's prescription appears to be founded on a confusion between the *use of a resource* and *the practice of an ability*. While human abilities and skills are valuable economic resources, most of them respond positively to practice, in a learning-by-doing manner, and negatively to nonpractice. It was on the basis of this atrophy dynamic that the U.S. system for obtaining an adequate supply of human blood for medical purposes, with its only partial reliance on voluntary giving, has been criticized by Richard Titmuss, the British sociologist. And a British political economist, Fred Hirsch (1976), has generalized the point: once a social system, such as capitalism, convinces everyone that it can dispense with morality and public spirit, the universal pursuit of self-interest being all that is needed for satisfactory performance, the system will undermine its own viability which is in fact premised on civic behavior and on the respect of certain moral norms to a far greater extent than capitalism's official ideology avows.

How is it possible to reconcile the concerns of Titmuss-Hirsch with those seemingly opposite, yet surely not without some foundation, of Robertson, Adam Smith, and Alfred Marshall? The truth is that, in his fondness for paradox, Robertson did his position a disservice: he opened his flank to easy attack when he equated love to some factor of production in strictly limited supply that needs to be economized. But what about the alternative analogy that equates love, benevolence, and public spirit to a skill that is improved through practice and atrophies without it? This one, too, has its weak points. Whereas public spirit will atrophy if too few demands are made upon it, it is not at all certain that the practice of benevolence will indefinitely have a positive feedback effect on the supply of this "skill." The practice of benevolence yields satisfaction (makes you feel good), to be sure, and therefore feeds upon itself up to a point, but this process is very different from practicing a manual (or intellectual) skill: here the practice leads to greater *dexterity* which is usually a net addition to one's abilities, that is, it is not acquired at the expense of some other skill or ability. In the case of benevolence, on the other hand, the point is soon reached where increased practice does conflict with self-interest and even self-preservation: our quipping motorist, to go back to him, has not exhausted his daily supply of benevolence by yielding once, but there surely will be *some* limit to his benevolent driving behavior, in deference to his own vital—perhaps ethically compelling—displacement needs.

Robertson had a point, therefore, when he maintained that there could be institutional arrangements which make *excessive* demands on civic behavior just as Titmuss and Hirsch were right in pointing to the opposite danger: the possibility, that is, that society makes *insufficient* demands on civic spirit. In both cases, there is a shortfall in public spirit, but in the cases pointed to by Robertson, the remedy consists in institutional arrangements placing less reliance on civic spirit and more on self-interest whereas in the situations that have caught the attention of Titmuss and Hirsch there is need for *increased* emphasis on, and practice of, community values and benevolence. These two parties argue along exactly opposite lines, but both have a point. Love, benevolence, and civic spirit are neither scarce factors in fixed supply, nor do they act like skills and abilities that improve and expand more or less indefinitely with practice. Rather, they exhibit a complex, composite behavior: they atrophy when not adequately practiced and appealed to by the ruling socioeconomic regime, yet will once again make themselves scarce when preached and relied on to excess.

To make matters worse, the precise location of these two danger zones—which, incidentally, correspond roughly to the complementary ills of today's capitalist and centrally planned societies—is by no means known, nor are these zones ever stable. An ideological-institutional regime that in wartime or during some other time of stress and public fervor is ideally suited to call forth the energies and efforts of the citizenry is well advised to give way to another that appeals more to private interest and less to civic spirit in a subsequent, less exalted period. Inversely, a regime of the later sort may, because of the ensuing "atrophy of public meanings" (Charles Taylor, 1970, p. 123), give rise to anomie and unwillingness ever to sacrifice private or group interest to the public weal so that a move back to a more community-oriented regime would be called for.

Conclusion

I promised, earlier on, to inquire whether the various complications of traditional concepts that have been proposed have any common structure. The answer should be obvious: all these complications flow from a single source—the incredible complexity of human nature which was disregarded by traditional theory for very good reasons, but which must be spoon-fed back into the traditional findings for the sake of greater realism.

A plea to recognize this complexity was implicit in my earlier insistence that "voice" be granted a role in certain economic processes alongside "exit," or competition. The efficient economic agent of traditional theory is essentially a silent scanner and "superior statistician" (Arrow, 1978) whereas I argued that she also has considerable gifts of verbal and nonverbal communication and persuasion that will enable her to affect economic processes.

Another fundamental characteristic of humans is that they are *self-evaluating* beings, perhaps the only ones among living organisms. This simple fact forced the intrusion of metapreferences into the theory of consumer choice and made it possible to draw a distinction between two fundamentally different kinds of preference changes. The self-evaluating function could be considered a variant of the communication or voice function: it also consists in a person addressing, criticizing, or persuading someone, but this someone is now the *self* rather than a supplier or an organization to which one belongs. But let us beware of excessive parsimony!

In addition to being endowed with such capabilities as communication, persuasion and self-evaluation, man is beset by a number of fundamental, unresolved, and perhaps unresolvable tensions. A tension of this kind is that between instrumental and noninstrumental modes of behavior and action. Economics has, for very good reasons, concentrated wholly on the instrumental mode. I plead here for a concern with the opposite mode, on the grounds 1) that it is not wholly impervious to economic reasoning; and 2) that it helps us understand matters that have been found puzzling, such as collective action and shifts in labor productivity.

Finally I have turned to another basic tension man must live with, this one resulting from the fact that he lives in society. It is the tension between self and others, between self-interest, on the one hand, and public morality, service to community, or even self-sacrifice, on the other, or between "interest" and "benevolence" as Adam Smith put it. Here again economics has concentrated overwhelmingly on one term of the dichotomy, while putting forward simplistic and contradictory propositions on how to deal with the other. The contradiction can be resolved by closer attention to the special nature of public morality as an "input."

In sum, I have complicated economic discourse by attempting to incorporate into it two basic human endowments and two basic tensions that are part of the human condition. To my mind, this is just a beginning.

References

Arrow, Kenneth, J., "The Economic Implications of Learning by Doing," *Review of Economic Studies*, June 1962, *29*, 155–73.

———, "The Future and the Present in Economic Life," *Economic Inquiry*, April 1978, *16*, 160.

Becker, Gary S., *The Economics of Discrimination*, Chicago: Chicago University Press, 1957.

——— and Stigler, George, "De Gustibus Non Est Disputandum," *American Economic Review*, March 1977, *67*, 76–90.

Frankfurt, Harry G., "Freedom of the Will and the Concept of a Person," *Journal of Philosophy*, January 1971, *68*, 5–20.

Hirsch, Fred, *Social Limits to Growth*, Cambridge: Harvard University Press, 1976.

Hirschman, Albert O., *Exit, Voice, and Loyalty*, Cambridge: Harvard University Press, 1970.

——, *Shifting Involvements: Private Interest and Public Action*, Princeton: Princeton University Press, 1982.

Johnson, Harry G., "A Theoretical Model of Economic Nationalism in New and Developing States," *Political Science Quarterly*, June 1965, *80*, 169–85.

Pizzorno, Alessandro, "Sulla razionalità della scelta democratica," *Stato e Mercato*, April 1983, No. 7, 3–46.

Robertson, Dennis H., "What Does the Economist Economize?," in *Economic Commentaries*, London: Staples Press, 1956, 147–55.

Sen, Amartya K., "Rational Fools: A Critique of the Behavioral Foundations of Economic Theory," *Philosophy and Public Affairs*, Summer 1977, *6*, 317–44.

Taylor, Charles, *The Pattern of Politics*, Toronto: McClelland and Stewart, 1970.

Winston, Gordon C., *The Timing of Economic Activities*, Cambridge: Cambridge University Press, 1982.

14

THE METHODOLOGY OF ECONOMICS AND THE CASE FOR POLICY DIFFIDENCE AND RESTRAINT

WARREN J. SAMUELS

The "testing of hypotheses" is frequently merely a euphemism for obtaining plausible numbers to provide ceremonial adequacy for a theory chosen and defended on *a priori* grounds.

—Harry G. Johnson

. . . our choice is between forming these notions carelessly and forming them carefully. The harder the task, the greater the need for steady patient inquiry.

—Alfred Marshall

Introduction: The Argument

I propose in this address to make a case for the position that economists, and also noneconomists, must be diffident and restrained in making policy recommendations. The case rests upon a view of the nature and especially the limits of economic knowledge. The case involves certain fundamental considerations which are widely ignored or forgotten and, in any case, typically left unapplied.

The perspective taken is predicated upon certain understandings concerning (1) the social construction of the economy, (2) the transcendental importance of scarcity, (3) the importance of values in the social construction of the economy, and (4) the importance of power in determining and choosing between values.

The operative premise is that the economy is not given to man but is largely constructed through human action both individual and collective. That is why economic policy is important, for the determination and administration of policy is one means through which the economy is created and re-created.

Scarcity is the existential condition of the economy. Economics not only studies scarcity and how people individually and aggregatively cope with scarcity but is itself immersed in scarcity: The latter is because of the circumstance that noneconomists desire policy recommendations from economists, *and* economists are quite willing if not eager to provide them. Common, therefore, to both the economy and economics is the ineluctable necessity of choice: Choice consequent to scarcity of resources having alternative uses and choice consequent to the typical mutual exclusivity of and thus conflict between policy alternatives.

Values are important in either or both of two respects: First, values are the effective basis on which choices are made.[1] Second, values are the product of both choices *per se* and the operation of the economy. Values are important in perceptions of "reality" and thereby the development of economic theories based on them. While the very notion of "values" is honorific, it must be understood that values conflict. In a sense, choices ultimately are between conflicting values.

Power can be defined and modelled in various ways, but most fundamentally power governs whose interests, whose values, count. Moreover, power, or power structure, is not something given, but it, too, is a social construction, something open to reconstruction.

In all these respects economics is important, so much so that it behooves us to be attentive to the limits of our work and, therefore, to the reasons we must be diffident and restrained in making policy recommendations. In affirming this position, I am most assuredly *not* arguing that economists should be silent in matters of policy. I *am* arguing that economists must dutifully and constantly pay attention and give explicit effect to the limitations of their tools, models, theories, paradigms, lines of reasoning, and so on. Economists should set an example for noneconomists by being thoughtful, diffident and restrained in jumping to policy conclusions. Every bit as dangerous as the "empirical leap" from limited inductive studies to universal generalizations is the "policy leap" from narrow and presumptive analyses to drawing policy implications and making policy recommendations. This policy leap is dangerous precisely because policy is important: Policy is a means through which the economy is socially created and re-created, and that is not something to be undertaken either lightly, thoughtlessly or blindly. Indeed, the ultimate danger of *laissez faire* or noninterventionist thinking is that it obfuscates both the inevitability and the importance of economic policy.[2]

Having now stated the argument, I shall next present the supporting case and then defend the case against the major objections that can be made against it.

The Supporting Case

Economics is largely comprised of a set of *models*.[3] Each model deals with a particular problem and comprises a set of variables structured in a particular way. Certain variables are excluded, and those included are postulated to have certain relationships. The relationships generally are functional rather than causal; the value of one variable varies with the value of another, rather than necessarily in a relation of causal dependence.

Models are, therefore, constrained by (1) the choice of problem to which the model is addressed; (2) the variables included within the model (as well as by their further particular specification for econometric and other purposes, in contrast with their general specification); and (3) the relationships posited to exist between the included (endogenous) variables. Whatever conclusions for analysis and implications for policy may be derived from the model depend upon and in a fundamental sense are tautological (circular) with the assumptions on which the model rests. In other words, the conclusions and implications are not independent but are derived from the assumptions; the assumptions give rise to the conclusions and implications; choice of assumptions constitutes choice of conclusions and implications.

Models may not readily give effect to an important characteristic of economic life, namely, that particular variables can be both cause and consequence in a process of cumulative causation.

It also will be noted that models can be (but, of course, are not always) contrived, consciously or unconsciously (sometimes as a matter of professional convention), to produce certain desired results, such as certain desired policy implications. This point has been made about various economic doctrines, for example, the Coase theorem, the quantity theory, rational expectations, Say's law (and new classical economics), the Walrasian auctioneer, and so on. Models are not necessarily immaculate in either origin or use.

The four categories: *truth, validity, desirability* and *workability* can be usefully distinguished. I do not claim that these distinctions are always either clear or present in practice, only that there is something epistemologically important to be learned in drawing them. By *truth* I mean that a statement is descriptively or explanatorily accurate, that a statement is subject to the test of whether it is descriptively true or false. By *validity* I mean that a conclusion is, as a matter of logic, properly derived from its premises given the system of logic. (The premises, as a separate issue, may be true or false.) By *desirability* I mean whether or not something is good or bad, or ought or ought not to be pursued. Normative and prescriptive statements are two different matters, and the difference is material for present purposes: Something may be considered good but inferior to something else. By *workability* I mean that, possibly in accordance with some known, identified and understood criterion(ia), something works, in the sense either that it is operative and/or that it performs the intended function and/or produces an expected (perhaps also desired) effect.[4]

Models in economics give rise to results which can be designated and analyzed under the four headings of "truth," "validity," "desirability" and "workability." But, we must not mistake the substance of one conclusion for that of another. A conclusion as to validity is not the same as one as to truth. Nor is a conclusion as to truth the same as one as to desirability (notwithstanding the fact that conditions subject to a truth test can affect the desirability of a policy implication, say, relative to alternative policies). Nor is a conclusion as to workability the same as one as to desirability (though workability may affect judgments as to desirability). Nor, for that matter, is a conclusion as to desirability necessarily indicative of workability, or vice versa.

Consider several putative circumstances: The economy is necessarily and inexorably normative. Economic policy has necessary (even if only implicit) normative premises. People have desires for certain ideologies and/or certain values. Desirability is different from validity, truth, and workability. Ideology and values tend inevitably to intrude into analysis. And, *inter alia*, we have, as one value, a desire for discussion that is either value- and ideology-free or in which values and ideology are explicit. Because of these circumstances, tensions exist within economics and within the discourse of economic policy that should make us cautious about precipitously drawing policy implications and making policy recommendations.

One must also distinguish between abstract models and institutional details. The former inhabit the minds of economists and are necessary for empirical and other work. The latter constitutes the real world and how the variables and relationships adumbrated in the model operate can work out as well as reflect the operation of variables and relationships not included in the model. Models, for example, of the quantity theory, the corporation, competition, and the market may yield insight into their respective domains but are necessarily incomplete, as well as selective (with regard to the variables and relationships included therein). I shall subsequently discuss certain respects in which economists tend to be overzealous. One in which they tend to be underzealous is in enriching their assumption—although, it should be understood, no matter how realistic its assumptions, a model is still a model and not a complete representation of reality. There is inexorable fundamental unrealism by the very nature of a model. One must distinguish between our conceptual models, the real world, and the modes of effectuating connecting linkages between the conceptual models and real world.

Economists, especially economic theorists, seem to have become attracted to various forms of general equilibrium theory. The use of general equilibrium theory has largely (though not entirely) been limited to the identification of the conditions of equilibrium and/or of stable equilibrium and also of optimal solutions (about which more below). These concerns have generally obscured the most important facets of general equilibrium economics: That the variables themselves may change and that there may be a dual relationship between variables. Definitions of inputs and outputs are not givens but can change. Illustrations of duality include (a) that capital formation is a function of profits, and profits are a function of capital formation and (b) that consumption is a function of investment (through income), and investment is a function of consumption (through the marginal efficiency of capital). Economists—through the use of narrow, unidirectional models—are very prone to let partial equilibrium solutions serve as proxies for general equilibrium solutions; the former provide a comforting sense of determinacy and closure which the latter cannot.

The point under consideration has far-reaching connections. These include Ricardo's penchant for "strong cases," Marshall's identification of normal versus abnormal causes, the conventional treatment of "frictions" and "disturbing" causes and the equally conventional search for singular solutions. So-called strong cases, normal versus abnormal causes, frictions and disturbing causes are a function of one's conception of the normal which is always incomplete and always the point at issue (see below regarding the hermeneutic circle). Strong cases, etc., exist only in the conceptual confines of one's model and ignore variables and relationships excluded therefrom. Surely, distinctions have to be made, but taking the result of a model as totally representative of the reality to which it is deemed to apply is presumptuous and question-begging. Models are limited, and their strong cases and normal causes are model-specific. There is more to economic reality than is known to any particular model or family of models.[5]

My point about the general equilibrium or general interdependence nature of the economy has as a corollary the difference between great and ordinary truths. An ordinary truth involves a statement which is true and whose opposite is false. A great truth involves a statement which is true and whose opposite is also true.

Economists are both called upon to make and indeed generally have an affection for making policy recommendations or drawing policy implications from their analyses. The purpose of economics, for many economists, is to derive policy implications. But policy implications are tautological with the model and/or the particular normative premises which are added to a model. Economists also are called upon and often are eager to make predictions. For many economists, making predictions is another, perhaps the premier, purpose of economics. But it is one thing to elicit the implications of a model, which generally are tautological with what is built into the model. It is quite another thing to predict what will in fact happen in the future of the actual economy. Models can be used to predict consequences only within and on their own terms. They do not necessarily predict what will actually happen in the economy. The reason for this, in addition to the incompleteness of models, is radical indeterminacy. There is a difference between simple and profound ignorance. Simple ignorance pertains to what is knowable but is not presently known. Profound ignorance pertains to what is not knowable, especially the future which does not yet exist and will not exist until we have acted and made the future—sometimes on the basis of what arguably is error. The future will indeed be in part the result of our efforts to apprehend it. There is, therefore, quite a difference between predicting within the confines of a model and predicting the future of the actual economy.

It is extremely easy for two factors to enter economics: wishful thinking and ideology. In neither case does saying something is so make it so. This is particularly relevant in the case of those politicians and economists (economic politicians or political economists?) who desire a certain felicitous picture to be created in the public's mind as part of the process of creating and/or maintaining a certain climate of public opinion as a basis for psychopolitical mobilization and policy. Economic policy is a function of power, ideology, tradeoff determinations, specific goals, and so on. Most, if not all, statements, models, and theories in economics convey particular implications for or cast luster on particular policies. Each economic model or theory thus tends to have a particular or greater or lesser attractiveness for particular ideologies. Accordingly, there is, for example, a continuing contest over macroeconomic theories and models to define policy and to manipulate the political psychology used to produce economic policy. The quantity theory of money is attractive to some, for example, not simply because it focuses on the quantity of money as generative of inflation but because it focuses on inflation *per se* as the problem and, furthermore, because its focus on inflation is seen as instrumental to the control of government policy. This aspect of economic models and theories is a manifestation of the more general phenomenon of the political significance of knowledge.

One facet of the intrusion of wishful thinking and ideology into economics is the tendency produced thereby to define the world not as it "is" in some sense but on the basis of values, on the basis, that is, of how it should be, or defining "is" in terms of "ought." It is extremely difficult to separate the "is" and the "ought" elements in economics and easy to define the "is" in terms of "ought" values, despite the Humean injunction that one cannot derive an "ought" from an "is" alone; an explicit or implicit antecedent normative premise is always present. The same is true of selective subjective perceptions. Inasmuch as we are engaged willy nilly in the social reconstruction of reality, we should know what we are doing in these matters. At the very least, we will be less likely victims of saccharine manipulators.

One also should distinguish between economics as knowledge of Truth, of an independent and transcendental reality preexistent and preeminent to mankind, and economics as a system of belief. Several points here. First, assuming there is an independent and transcendent economic reality, there is serious question whether mankind can know it. Second, our perception and identification of economic reality may fundamentally be a projection of wishful thinking, an ideology or a world view. At the very least, a given reality is susceptible to contradictory perceptions. Third, economics to a very large degree is not hard knowledge of an independent and transcendent reality but a set of stories giving effect to various belief-systems. Fourth, all economic problems are value problems and are value problems which are not resolved by nature or by nature alone; if they were, there would be no need of economic policy. I am aware that there are those who believe in the real, independent existence of economic and other values, but I do not share that view—nor do I think that most discussions of issues of economic policy effectively presume that belief (rhetorical usages and pretense to the contrary). In any event, much economic analysis and policy making is not about what we may call "deep" reality but about benefit-cost comparisons and intra-opportunity set determinations. These comparisons often use prices, which are artifacts, episodic coefficients of choice having no transcendent independent status.

Further apropos of the conflict between philosophical realism and idealism, I argue that the two positions come to the same result for our purposes. Even if everyone were a philosophical realist and agreed that there was an independent and transcendental reality preexistent and preeminent to mankind, they would likely disagree as to its substantive content and portent for mankind. The result is an inexorable necessity to choose between alternative specifications of reality. This result is psychologically but not substantively different from the position of philosophical idealism, which ultimately reduces to a necessity to choose between different formulations of the ideal or of the ideational. The result is the same if one juxtaposes idealism, the belief that there exists one highest value or one best solution to a problem independent of and preeminent to man (Thomism), and practical realism (or pragmatism), the belief that the correct or most workable value or solution is that which comes through the actual decision making structure. Although the idealist denigrates the dependence (for the practical realist) of value or solution upon decision making structure (and the power play that enters therein) and rejects the choice aspect resident in practical realism, even if everyone were an idealist, their conceptions of the ideal likely would vary so that choice would still have to be made.

Selective perception is perhaps the most important characteristic of the construction and use of economic models. Nowhere is unspecified and unappreciated selective perception more dangerous than in the selective identification of freedom, control, continuity and change. Freedom can be perceived in various ways. Freedom is not solely the opposite of control: What freedom exists is due largely to the structure of control which generates that freedom. There is always a pattern of freedom and control; the key questions include: freedom for, from, and to what and whom. Similar complexities beset consideration of continuity and change: support for continuity of the status quo may be support for the mode of change which constitutes the status quo and not for some blanket notion of continuity *per se*.

There are enormously complex, subtle and kaleidoscopic processes in society working out solutions to the conflicts between freedom and control, and continuity and change, as well as other comparable tensions. These conflicts and tensions inevitably exist, and any economic analysis which fails to capture their richness and complexity, as well as the conflicts and tensions *per se*, will be doomed to be partial, presumptive and not at all dispositive of the issues to which it is addressed. Such an economic analysis will manifest implicit theorizing and ethicizing regarding freedom, control, continuity and change, and will resemble a morality play or ideological exercises much more than serious objective scholarly study. It will do so in part by giving effect to selective implicit premises as to whose interests are to count. An implication of this reasoning is, of course, that economists ought to go out of their way to recognize these conflicts and subtleties and also to study directly both the fundamental problems and the real world processes through which they are worked out. Thus far, I have emphasized the importance of selective perception in regard to freedom, control, continuity and change. Selective perception has an ubiquitous range which includes such other concepts as: coercion, injury, externalities, and government. Our most presumptive reasoning and implicit ethicizing involves selective perception less about what is "natural" *vis-à-vis* what is "artificial," and more about what is "private" and what is "public."

Economists tend to concentrate on the logic of choice from within existing opportunity sets. This tends to exclude consideration of the processes by which the overall structure of opportunity sets are determined, which are themselves matters of choice, however typically nondeliberative. Both choice within opportunity sets and choice as to the structure of opportunity sets are present in actual economies. Inasmuch as the total structure of opportunity sets governs whose interests will count, it is the total structure of opportunity sets which dictates and channels the consequences of choice within existing opportunity sets. In mainstream economics, considerations of power typically are obfuscated but nonetheless silently given effect. On the other hand, in certain radical expositions of economics, the results also are driven by implicit assumptions as to whose interests should and/or do count. There is too little objective nonideological analysis of power, wealth and income structures, of the total structure of opportunity sets and their microeconomic and macroeconomic consequences. Economists are prone to make policy recommendations without giving adequate thought to, and without making explicit their assumptions about, the processes giving the structure of opportunity sets. This has the tendency, among other things, to reinforce selectively the status quo hierarchic power structure. Underlying assumptions as to the scope and substance of analysis thus channels analysis and excludes certain very important economic processes.

Economists continue to be abused by their propensity to treat induction and deduction, or empiricism and rationalism, as mutually exclusive. One can, of course, identify their rationales as if they were mutually exclusive. But in practice economists always and indeed necessarily employ blends or combinations of both, although they are only rarely cognizant of both the nature and the substance of the combinations they use. Empirical "facts" are theory-laden, deduction is concept-dependent, and theory is experience- and fact-laden.

The point is particularly apropos of the nature of the national income, business and public utility accounting systems. These are contrived (I used the term advisedly) on the basis of subjective conceptual definitions and models and the numbers (prices, costs, benefits) which they produce and use are objective only within the subjective conceptualization on which rests the relevant accounting system. We tend to unquestioningly use the numbers produced by these systems as if they had some unequivocal and privileged representational status independent of our construction and use of them. They do not. These accounting systems are not objective; they are arbitrary in the sense that they are based on exercises of pure choice. That these choices were made long ago (which is not always the case) and by others does not negate their subjective nature.

Moreover, economists have used quantitative techniques too often without due regard to their epistemological and technical limits. Some of this has been done in order to reach certain substantive results, some to reach determinate results, and some to reach optimal solutions. But much of it is due to the failure to recognize the limits of deduction, the limits of induction, and the limits of particular econometric techniques.

Economists have not found an escape from the hermeneutic circle. Where we have to choose between theories or models, we almost always do so on the basis of normative, subjective or aesthetic considerations which constitute alternative formulations of the theories or models chosen. We generally cannot defend or choose theories or models on any grounds which do not already assume the gravamen of the theory or model in question. Economists have not found ultimate, meta-epistemological criteria. No wonder that there is a circularity or tautology between the premise(s) of a model and its policy implications. No wonder that there often is perception derived from (what Joseph Schumpeter called) social location, and thus a relativity and problematicity of belief contingent upon power structure and the psychology of power and class.

Economists only rarely try fully to identify the premises or preconceptions on which their theories and models rest. Only rarely do they try fully to identify the implicit antecedent normative premises which, in combination with the formal elements of their models, drive the policy implications or so-called optimal solutions. Only rarely do they fully identify the nature of and the limits to meaningfulness of their lines of reasoning.

Welfare economic reasoning, for example, is either necessarily formal and inconclusive or presumptive. It cannot reach implications for practical policy without antecedent assumptions as to whose interests count (as in, for example, the identification of which externality is to be made the subject of policy and not its reciprocal). Valuational and other premises tend to be present in economic analysis and are certainly brought to bear in their application to matters of policy. Indeed, such premises are necessary for determinate policy implications and recommendations.

The foregoing discussion addresses the place of values in the role of implicit antecedent normative premises. The role of implicit assumptions as to legal rights needs to be specified. It is through such assumptions that economists implicitly determine whose interests are to count, for example in such policy areas as externality, managerial authority, inflation versus employment, and welfare. In such theories as public choice and rent-seeking, analysis generates supposedly "correct" or "optimal" results laden with the patina of ostensibly scientific precision and determinacy. Whereas as a matter of fact the results are derived from implicit premises as to whose interest is to count, as to who has what rights. In the actual economy, of course, questions of rights are typically the point at issue—and it is this that much economic policy analysis begs.

There is a tendency among some writers in the field of law and economics to assert that rights themselves can be determined on the basis of costs and benefits. This obfuscates the fact that judgments as to whose interests are to count in the identification and measurement of costs and benefits are tantamount to assuming the very rights to be determined. This circularity with regard to legal rights is particularly evident in the view that courts should and do maximize wealth. The point is that courts determine the rights in terms of which market exchange and wealth achievement, if not maximization, take place.

Already implicit in the foregoing, many concepts and variables in economic analysis are formal and substantively empty. Their application in analysis, particularly with regard to any policy implication that may be drawn, requires further, selective specification. I have in mind here not only the concepts of freedom, coercion, change, and so on, but also "capital," "labor," "money supply," "unemployment," "voluntary," and "rational behavior." The substance of these concepts and variables are worked out in the daily life of economic actors in the actual economy. What constitutes "profit maximization" for a firm and "preference realization" for a consumer are things which must be and are worked out by actual economic actors. Economic analysis which reaches conclusions with regard to them is either formal and empty or made substantive through selective, limiting assumptions which substitute for the processes through which they are worked out in the actual economy. More is involved than that which can be reduced to assumptions generating neat curves on the blackboard.

There is a dual x:X problem in economics, one epistemological and the other linguistic. Let X represent the object of inquiry and x our knowledge of X. The key epistemological problem is whether x is representative of X. All work in deduction and, especially, induction (for example, statistics and econometrics) must somehow come to grips with this problem. The key linguistic problem is whether the language with which we specify X and x, respectively, has any meaningfulness with regard to X. Is language a derivative of the object of study or is it something which mankind superimposes upon it? Is language a tool, a system of belief, or something intimately derivative or expressive of "reality"? Our answers to these epistemological and linguistic problems, and to the question of realism versus idealism, affect the psychodynamic appeal but not necessarily either the truth status or workability of our analyses.

Mainstream economists, typically seek optimal solutions. Optimal solutions can be comprehended in terms of Pareto optimality or the solution to a problem of constrained maximization. Efficiency-optimality is always a means-end relationship. Optimal solutions are not unique, but the search for the optimal solution often tends to convey the impression that there are indeed unique optimal solutions (or optimal policy recommendations). Optimal solutions, however, are specific to the structure of power (and tastes, which are in part due to power), to the identification and assignment of rights governing whose interests are to count and whose not, and to the content of one's learning. Different distributions of entitlements or configurations of rights will yield different optimal solutions. Identification of an optimal solution gives effect to some (actual or presumed) set of rights, some prior determination as to whose interests are to count and whose not. "Optimal" solutions do not warrant a name so suggestive of uniqueness and other prescriptive baggage.

Economic analysis gives effect to either the status quo or some assumed distribution of rights (income and wealth), which enables certain interests and prevents other interests to be registered in the market. Interests which are not given the status of rights cannot register on the market, or only with severe disadvantage. Interests which are given the status of rights have only a problematic economic significance, depending upon their interaction in markets with all other rights and under changing circumstances. Environmental and ecological interests are typically not registered in markets except as incidental to rights (protected interests) having a quite different genesis. Interests get only incompletely valorized in markets; to take market valuations as definitive and conclusive to presumptive and gives effect to the existing distributions of rights, income and wealth. Prices are social and normative and do not exist in any sense independent of mankind.

One respect in which rights count is in governing whose interests are made a cost to whom. The concept of opportunity cost is positional:

Costs are identified and measured from the point of view of a decision maker. But the respective opportunity sets of various economic actors are directly governed in part by rights which protect one party's interest through making it a cost to someone else. Conversely, interests which are not protected as rights are not a cost to someone else. Costs are in part a function of the structure of power governing the total structure of opportunity sets. Use of the existing cost-price structure gives effect to and reinforces the underlying existing structure of rights.

Economists have been overzealous in seeking and reaching so called optimal solutions. In doing so, they have not been fully, if at all, aware of the enormity of the implicit selective normative exercise in which they have been engaged. Indeed, contrary to conventional belief, it is not true that Pareto optimality constitutes a minimal ethical position: It takes an implicit position on all ethical questions, especially those involving power structure.

Economists typically seek not only optimal solutions but also determinate results. The twin problems with this are that in doing so economists tend to foreclose the processes which work out results in the actual economy and substitute their preferences for those of actual economic actors. This is in part because economists generally have concentrated on the conditions of equilibrium rather than on the adjustment processes by which equilibrium putatively is achieved and in which actual economic activity takes place and results and solutions are worked out.[6]

Consider the representation of the economic process given by the conventional diagram in which the production possibility curve is juxtaposed to an actual social welfare function to produce at the point of tangency the socially optimal allocation. There are at least four processes at work underlying this diagram about which conventional practice typically makes restrictive assumptions in order to reach determinate solutions, assumptions about things which in practice must be worked out, so that in making these assumptions economists are both limiting and channeling their results. The four processes are those by which the values on the axes, the shape and location of the production possibility curve, individual preferences, and power structure are worked out.

The four processes are as follows: First, the process by which is determined which values (commodities or goals) are to be represented on the axes, the values between which choice has to be made.[7] When a politician states that "such-and-such is the issue in this election," he or she is in effect endeavoring both to get a particular value on the social agenda and to have it weighed heavily relative to a competing value(s).[8] The values with which we deal may or may not be given by objective reality, but they are worked out through markets, private and group choice, and politics. Economists can produce determinate results by making explicit or, more likely, implicit assumptions as to which values are on the relevant axes, whereas in reality these values have to be worked out.[9]

Second, the process by which is determined the shape and location of the production possibility curve, which governs the tradeoffs which have to be made. Economists have not studied this very much, though they understand that both shape and location are influenced by population size, quality of the work force, quantity and quality of natural resources, level of technology, and so on—factors which change and are themselves in some or many respects a matter of policy. Consider the production possibility curve relating price stability and employment levels. Whatever governs the empirical Phillips curve tradeoffs will help govern the slope and location of this production possibility curve. Among the factors governing the empirical Phillips curve evidently are such things as: inflationary expectations (and whatever governs them), the relationship between employment security and productivity, the relative power of managements and workers in arriving at wage rates, central bank money supply policy, and the pricing practices of businessmen. Economists can produce determinate results by making explicit or, more likely, implicit assumptions as to these governing factors, whereas in reality these have to be worked out.[10]

Third and fourth, inasmuch as the actual social welfare function (in contrast to one assumed by the economic analyst) is the product of individual preferences weighted by power structure, the processes by which first, individual preferences and, second, power structure are formed.[11] Economists have not studied either process very much, but in order to reach determinate solutions economists must and do make assumptions as to how these processes—and the values ensconced within them—work out. Individual preferences must be formed and reformed on the basis of experience and subjective perception of experience, encompassing both socializing and individuating processes. And the power structure is not given once and for all time; it too is formed and reformed, in part through processes endogenous to the economy narrowly defined and in part through broader processes.[12]

In all four regards, either the results are empty formalism or a matter of explicit or, more likely, implicit presumptions as to who has what preferences and how much they are to be weighted, that is, whose interests are to count—whereas in reality these have to be worked out.

These four processes are truly fundamental economic processes. The four processes obviously interact with each other. The main point is that the conduct of both partial and general equilibrium analyses, in order to reach determinate solutions, requires that the analyst make assumptions about the results of these four processes which assumptions generate the determinate solution, such that the determinate solution is tautological with the assumptions.[13] The processes of working things out are foreclosed.

Three points about that practice of economists. First, there is nothing intrinsically wrong with the practice, however mechanistic it may be. Second, the practice inevitably has its price, which consists of what the assumptions (and the conclusions tautological therewith) exclude, and the risk that ideological, cultural or class preconceptions will bias the choice of assumptions (that is, the desired conclusion will insidiously if unconsciously govern the choice of the congruent assumptions). Third, what is typically excluded are at least three things: (1) the *process* nature of the economy, (2) the ongoing, problematic[14] nature of the materials (including matters of putative knowledge) about which the assumptions are made, and (3) the institutional or power arrangements which form and operate through the market.

By concentrating on the market, economists have narrowed what is in actuality a much larger social valuational process, one which includes but extends beyond commodity prices to include all values and their identification, juxtaposition, selection, and reconsideration. In concentrating on the market and in making assumptions as to whose interests count, etcetera, economists have taken presumptive positions on the operation and results of this larger valuational process. Substantive implications and recommendations for policy can be reached on the basis of analysis otherwise formalist only on the basis of value premises. For most economic analysis these premises are made implicitly, and the actual larger valuational processes of society are not at all studied. It is nonetheless true but hardly appreciated by economists that economics is a participant in the total valuational process.

Notwithstanding the imposing limitations placed upon analysis by the quest for determinate, optimal, and equilibrium results, the great forte of economics, especially microeconomics, is its focus on marginal or incremental adjustments. But this too illustrates the general proposition that the meaning of everything—every model, every tool, every theory—resides in the combination of its strengths and its limitations. And the great limitation of incremental analysis is its inability to deal with wholes. This is best illustrated by the negligible capacity of microeconomics to cope with larger questions of environmental degradation and survival. Indeed, standard welfare economics assumes survival so that only marginal adjustments need be considered. At the very least, the limitation consists of the myopia which necessarily selects from all consequences.

The economy is not like the solar system. The economy is not given to man. It is an artifact, the product of a multiplicity of individual and collective actions. Accordingly, the economy is a normative phenomenon, a product of effective human construction and choice. The economy is made through our efforts to apprehend it, to know and to effectuate policy toward it. The supreme irony resident within economics is that we tend to adopt an official positivist methodology which presumes that the economy is independent and transcendental to man, as is in part the case with the physical and chemical world while at the same time we seek policy implications and recommendations—to make or to influence policy—which presume that the economy is not independent and transcendental to man and which have the effect of contributing to the (re)production of the economy. Indeed, it is by defining "is" in terms of ought that economists (and others) surreptitiously introduce the normative and the subjective into economics and thereby into (re)making the economy. This to many is after all the final object of all our work, "social engineering." It would be better if this particular process were out in the open.

Economic policy is important because it is one means through which the social construction of reality is effectuated. The normative nature of the economy means that economics necessarily has a normative nature. To have a normative nature means that values are inextricably involved. The presence of an overriding valuational process should not be obscured; both the importance of the valuational process and the identity and significance of the values entering therein, and constituting the meaning of decisions, should be made explicit. One cannot go from "is" propositions to "ought" conclusions on the basis of "is" propositions alone, nor can one go from science to policy without additional normative premises. These premises should be made explicit so that we know what we are doing. Each of us is a participant in the total decision making, and valuational, process. This situation does not behoove us to do nothing, or to pretend to do nothing or that nothing is being done. It behooves us to proceed with caution and humility, with diffidence and restraint.

Critique and Defense of the Argument

For all of these reasons and in all of these respects it seems to me that the true scientific and scholarly spirit requires considerable diffidence and restraint by economists. Economic analysis is sufficiently fragile, limited and problematic to warrant such diffidence. This conclusion should not be taken as negative about economics. Economics, for all its limits, is one of mankind's great possessions. Economics is rich and robust, indeed more so than its typical detractors and critics acknowledge. But the nature of its practice and its strength carries with it limitations. Diffidence, not hubris, is called for.

Both the general argument herein advanced in favor of diffidence and restraint and elements of the specific supporting case will be resisted by many economists. It will be argued, ultimately if not initially, that the very status of economics as a discipline will be adversely affected—indeed threatened—by giving credibility to the argument made here. Economists, it will be argued, derive their status from their social role as men and women of knowledge: to serve as experts in matters of economic affairs and policy, in part by providing economic predictions or forecasts, in part by bringing the weight of economic theory and analysis to bear on matters of policy and perhaps in part, as high priests, by making the case for the market or for other considerations and/or arrangements. If economists surrender their hard-won high ground, it will be left to politicians, journalists and television evangelists.

Invocation of the opportunity costs (to economists and to society) of diffidence by economists in these roles is impressive but not conclusive. It is also instructive of the selective perception and hubris ultimately derivative of a point of view or a social position. Evangelists and politicians have a similar self-perception.

Let us, however, assume that the above-mentioned social roles of economists are taken as desirable for both economists and society. Even given that assumption, it is not conclusive that economists should not be diffident along the lines and for the reasons which I have suggested. Economists who fail to be diffident render their position and credibility exposed. They assume risks of looking absurd, and, indeed, economists have too often looked absurd to others—and to other economists. That economists do not look more absurd to others may well be due to the facts that economists write largely for other economists and are often both inscrutable to and ignored by others.

Why have economists placed themselves in such an exposed position? It is because they have engaged in status emulation, a quest which, if one follows Adam Smith, may be deemed a great deception, although recognizing, quite realistically, that it is the way of the world. Economists desire determinate solutions because such will sanction their status as scientists. Economists desire optimal solutions because such will sanction their status as policy experts. Both desires are driven by status emulation and ambition; both desires produce or reinforce an intolerance for ambiguity, openness and pluralism in favor of a pretense of closure and finality. Both desires manifest status emulation and the marks of ceremonial adequacy associated therewith. In this we are after all, if Smith and Veblen are correct, only human. But as economists we ought to be cognizant of the costs of being human.

Economists perhaps ought to learn to be satisfied with less pretentious status and less demanding desires, perhaps to be on a par, as Keynes said, with dentists. Economists would serve both their science and democracy well if they identified the likely premises and consequences of alternative policy options, without attempting to give disciplinary sanction to one or another of them and without attempting to have economic ideology masquerade as economic science, value appearing as fact. Economists can serve as ends-means technicians, as utopian explorers, and as contributors to the formation of social consensus and thereby participate in evolving ends, but should do so with diffidence and restraint. Economics would arguably be better served if economists did what they could meaningfully do well and without pretension. Let a sense of modesty replace hubris. Let a sense of perspective, openness and multiplicity and a tolerance for ambiguity replace the lust to be authoritative. Let the exercise of professional expertise enlighten the choice process rather than serve, illegitimately, to mask both ideology and the surreptitious making of normative assumptions. Let economists confront the tension presently existing between their frequent affirmation of the optimality of market performance and their almost universal proclivity to make policy recommendations.

Notice that I am not saying that economists should be passive and silent. I am saying that economists ought to be self-conscious about both the limitations of their analysis and the nature of their ironic quest for the power of the expert. Economists should acquire the habit of specifying both the limits of and the values otherwise implicit in their analysis. And perhaps above all, we ought constantly to remember the irony resident in the conflict between our enormous drive to reach policy implications, which is the core of our drive for professional and personal power, and our general *laissez faire* noninterventionist stance. For there is more to the social reconstruction of the economy, and perforce more to the fundamentals of the economic role of government, than our theories encompass. Economics, including and perhaps especially neoclassical economics but also social economics, is a contributor not only to the objective description and analysis of the economy but to the social valuational process as well. Because the subjects on which we as economists work are important, it behooves us, following Marshall, to be careful rather than careless.

Notes

The author is indebted to John B. Davis, Steven G. Medema, and A. Allan Schmid for comments on an earlier draft of this address (Presidential Address to the Association for Social Economics, December 29, 1988).

1. The following statement is true even if values are the rationalization for what some brain modules do. The statement is not intended to imply mentalistic rationality.

2. Such obfuscation is instrumental on behalf of those with a "policy making" mentality as they attempt (consciously or unconsciously) to shunt aside those with and/or induced to have a "policy taking" view of the world.

3. Theories (hypotheses of explanation) have much the same limitations, but the present discussion is largely restricted to models.

4. For example, if one considers the syllogism:

All men are immortal.
Socrates is a man.
Therefore Socrates is immortal.

then, given the ordinary meaning of the term "immortal," one has a valid conclusion, albeit not a truthful, or true, one.

Another example: If one assumes that through a point, to a line, only one parallel line may be drawn, then one is able (in Euclidean geometry) to conclude that the sum of the angles of all triangles is equal to 180 degrees. If alternatively one assumes that through a point, more than one line may be drawn parallel to the initial line, then (in non-Euclidean geometry) one can conclude that the sum of the angles of all triangles can be equal to, less than, or greater than 180 degrees. Both conclusions are valid, even though they conflict. Both statements also are true, in the sense of descriptive accuracy: the former in regard to planes, the latter in regard to curved surfaces or space. The reason why Euclidean geometry for a long time sufficed for use on the surface of the spherical planet Earth is that the distances measured, in relation to the curvature of the surface of the plant, were relatively short. Non-Euclidean geometry is more useful in three dimensional space. Their respective workability is thus separable matter from both their validity and their truth status.

In neither of these cases (the mortality of Socrates and the angular degrees of triangles), moreover, does the issue of desirability arise. In economic affairs, however, given the normative nature of the economy and of economic policy, all four categories arise. A model chosen and instrumented for a particular purpose will give rise to certain policy implications generated by that purpose and channeled by the way in which the model is instrumented. Those policy implications have an aura of desirability because they follow from the model, but they are, as noted above, derived from the assumptions of the model which give rise to them.

5. In their quest for determinate solutions economists tend to pursue both a mechanistic and an over-intellectualized program. On the one hand, they treat economic variables as if they had an existence apart from the human beings who comprise the economy. On the other hand, they analyze the economy as if it were essentially a matter only of intellect. The former depersonalizes or dehumanizes the economy. The latter abstracts from the fact that the economy, in addition to having intellectual elements, is also a world of power and power play, uncertainty, selective perception, cognitive dissonance, love-hate, guilt, regret, other psychological states, the quest for advantage, wealth, power and status, and so on.

6. I must clarify what I mean by the term "working things out." I certainly do not mean anything either mystical, esoteric, or beyond specification for research and analysis. Consider the allocation of resources between the production of any two commodities. Producers form firms, organize production, assemble factors of production, engage in production, market their products, and perhaps sell some or all of their output. In the process, among other things, they must arrange relationships with factor suppliers. Consumers form life styles and preferences for types of commodities and demands for specific commodities both in isolation from and in conjunction with other commodities and other people. Producers and consumers meet in the market under varying structural and behavioral conditions. We would not say that any or all of the foregoing things, and the resulting phenomena of production and consumption, were either given or foreordained. They involve a general problem—production arrangements, for example—which are solved and resolved through time *via* the exploratory choices of individual agents and intersections between agents. It is in this sense that we would say that society, through the aggregated interactions of agents and their respective choices, works out the allocation of resources between commodities. Another way of saying this is that given scarcity, interdependence, the resulting conflicts and alternative allocations must be conducted/worked out/resolved in an on-going manner. Among the characteristics of this working out are, for example, learning by experience, the comparison and evaluation of values and their application to experience, the exercise of what John R. Commons called a negotiational psychology leading to complex and subtle forms of bargaining, and, *inter alia* determining and redetermining the working rules governing the interaction. Indeed, the rules governing how things are worked out are themselves worked out, which opens the door to the politico-legal process which is also inexorably involved as an economic alternative or supplement to buying and selling in the market. The key is that the results are the product of complex socioeconomic processes and are worked out through those processes.

7. In a diagram with more than two axes, say *n* axes, all values can be included so that no choice of which values to include is necessary. In the real world, however, there are limits to how many issues or how many values can be considered during any one period (which itself is a variable). There are only

"so many" (serious) questions, it seems, that a political process can deal with simultaneously. In this respect the economy is more robust.

8. Of course, it is also the case that the politician is trying to get (re)elected and thereby seeking to identify with values which he or she believes can be or are held by the voters (or sufficient of them for him to win election). Politicians do two things in this process which are instrumental to the discussion in the text: first, help form voter preferences; and second, serve as conduits or vehicles for whatever preferences voters come to act upon. Thus, politicians will try to reform voter preferences to be consistent with their, the politician's, own preferences or principals but also to "rise above" their own principles so as to better comport with the preferences of the voters (such as they cannot reform) so as to gain reelection (in the latter case the objective function of the politician obviously is not solely to advance his preferences or principles but to gain (re)election, period). As indicated in the text, these are all very complex processes. A principal characteristic of relevant reality is that neither the politicians nor the voters have well defined sets of values or preferences, and it is very difficult for them to be effectively communicated. It is also true that communication (information provision) is asymmetrical, though this is rarely studied.

9. The terminology of "working out" applies whether one believes that values exist objectively in reality and await discovery (that is, apply to the discovery process and are subject to selective perception) or that values are created by man (that is, apply to the creation process and are subject to selective perception).

10. The text specifies unemployment level on one axis, that is, as a value. In cases where ordinary commodities are represented on the axes, unemployment is an interior solution consequent to not reaching the highest possible social welfare function (level of output).

11. Notice that I am not dealing with an hypothetical social welfare function as designated by an analyst, even one who intends to represent the actual function extant at the time and place. I am only affirming that the combination of individuals with preferences for values (for example, for private and public goods) and a power structure which weights those preferences across individuals (that is, determines whose preferences count) *in effect* yields the actual social welfare function. The discussion is not intended to be a mechanistic representation of reality but a tool indicative of what is going on in society.

12. As a further indication of the complexity of these (and other) processes, consider the situation in which the power structure arguably does not change, but the beliefs of the (hegemonic or decisive) power holders change, thereby changing the decisional outcome. The more general problem arises when an outcome can be explicated in terms either of power, knowledge or

psychology factors, such that the analyst has to assess the relative weights of the three factors. There are, of course, also definitional and modeling problems, such as defining moral suasion (leading to a change of belief) as a form of power.

13. Tautological in the sense of restating or giving effect to the assumptions.

14. To clarify "problematic": Fundamental interdependence leaves all behavior and prediction subject to radical indeterminacy (the future cannot be known until we have made it by our actions) or at least stochastic.

15

THE RHETORIC OF DISAGREEMENT

ARJO KLAMER AND DEIRDRE MCCLOSKEY

Klamer and McCloskey are economists who live in Iowa City and talk together a good deal. They disagree a good deal, too—about the economy for example. McCloskey believes that competition runs it and that people are driven by self-interest. Klamer believes that power runs it and that people are driven by more than self-interest. They disagree also on what is to be done politically: McCloskey is a libertarian; Klamer is a social democrat.

And they disagree on how much economists disagree. McCloskey takes an American—even Midwestern—view that underneath it all our shared values can bring us together for barn raisings and economic analysis. Klamer takes a European—even Dutch—view that emphasizes diversity and conflict as social facts.

Their one point of agreement is their disagreement with the mechanical, scientistic notion of what economists do. They have noted the demise of positivism. Facts and logic, narrowly defined, are necessary but not sufficient for good economic science. The study of logical structure will not reveal all of what economists do.

Klamer and McCloskey agree on an alternative interpretation. They view economics as a rhetorical activity, in which economists deploy authorities, stories, and metaphors (models, for instance) to persuade each other (Klamer 1983b, 1988a; McCloskey 1985, 1988c, 1989c). To call economics "rhetorical" is not to attack the science. All writing with designs on its readers is rhetorical. A mathematical proof has a rhetoric, which is to say a strategy of persuasion (see Davis and Hersh 1987). "Rhetoric" means here the whole art of argument; it does not mean ornament or hot air alone. In Continental terms, Klamer and McCloskey think of economics as a discursive practice (they disagree on whether it should be plural—"practices"). Human argument has four elements: facts, logic, metaphors, and stories. They are not alternatives.

In most scientific argument they occur together and warrant rigorous study.

The rhetorical perspective points up a moral gap in the practice of economics. If logic and fact of the simplest sort do not suffice by themselves to produce good economics—and if God does not put in an appearance to settle the matter—by what principles can economists be guided? Klamer and McCloskey agree on the Maxim of Presumed Seriousness: that as serious scholars we must presume, until sound evidence contradicts it, that others are serious too. The official rhetoric of scholarship presupposes the Maxim of Presumed Seriousness. In linguistic terms, the Maxim is a "conversational implicature," which is to say, a rule for making sense of what another scholar says.

The Maxim has a consequence, the Principle of Intellectual Trade: considering that other scholars read different books and lead different lives it would be economically remarkable, a violation of economic principles, if nothing could be learned from trading with them. The Maxim and Principle are moral entry points into a conversation to which intellectuals and academics presumably have already committed themselves.

Just as differences in tastes or endowments are grounds for trade, disagreements about economics are grounds for serious conversation. Mutual respect prevents the conversation from degenerating into war. As Raymond Aron said, "Politics is dialectic when it unfolds between men who mutually acknowledge each other. It is war when it brings into opposition men who . . . wish to remain strangers to one another" (quoted in Alker 1988, 816).

McCloskey: You know, Arjo, disagreement in economics is exaggerated. We economists are all children of the blessed Adam.

Klamer: So you claimed in your book on rhetoric, and continue to claim in later work (McCloskey 1985, 1988e). But I can't entirely agree. For many purposes I see distinctive tribes within the community of economists (Klamer 1987). The intellectual trade among the tribes is limited.

McCloskey: I know what you mean—the tribes of Veblen and Thoreau, Kropotkin and Chayanov, Marx and Menger and Marshall hold themselves apart. But they share much: entry and exit; the accounting of general equilibrium; and at the very least a concern with how people earn their daily bread.

Klamer: You betray, Deirdre, the neoclassical's lack of interest in cultural and ideological differences. It undervalues the experience of people excluded from neoclassical discourse.

McCloskey: Wait a minute. We neoclassicals have no objection to the existence of other ways of thinking, such as the anthropological. But let the anthropologists do it.

Klamer: And then don't trade. Neoclassicals don't follow their own principle of intellectual trade.

McCloskey: Hmm.

Klamer: Neoclassical thinking is hegemonic in American academia, but even within the neoclassical camp there is massive miscommunication. James Tobin and Robert Lucas taken alone are both reasonable men, but they cannot talk reasonably with each other (see Klamer 1983, chaps. 2 and 5). Just try talking first with Harvard graduate students and then with Chicago graduate students.

McCloskey: I have, at some length.

Klamer: Well, so have I. You know then that it is like moving from one intellectual universe to another (see Colander and Klamer 1987; Klamer and Colander 1989). Such differences are not trivial.

McCloskey: I agree. (Though literally they *are* "trivial"—that is, concerned with the medieval *trivium* on which education is based: grammar, logic, and above all rhetoric.) The best way for a professor to raise a laugh at Harvard in the 1960s was to mention the name of Milton Friedman. The teacher didn't have to say anything about Milton; he just had to mention him. But it turned out that the best way to raise a laugh at Chicago in the 1960s and 1970s was to mention Ken Galbraith, or Joan Robinson; just mention.

Klamer: Of course: it's still the case in the 1980s, as I've seen. Gossip, laughter, and sneering fills the halls and classrooms, despite the rhetoric of respect on the printed page.

McCloskey: So I have slowly come to realize. It's a shame. But surely there is some basis for conversation among the tribes— genetic if nothing else: we *are* all progeny of Adam Smith.

Klamer: I wish there were a basis. But I don't see it. We are not witnessing a communitarian, barn-raising project in economics right now.

McCloskey: Well, all right, economics has a problem of communication.

Klamer: That sounds too easy.

McCloskey: Listen to what I'm saying. By "communication" I don't mean the drainpipe image that most people carry around in their heads.

Klamer: Sure, we agree on that. The old image posits a drainpipe
              between two minds through which communication takes
              place. The image makes conversation seem easy: *mere*
              communication, *just* semantics, *simply* a matter of style.
              Under such a theory we would all agree, or agree to dis-
              agree, if we "defined our terms."

McCloskey: That's right. The drainpipe image suggests that we have
              prepackaged ideas, hard little bundles created in isolation
              and transmitted to other people along the pipes. Keep the
              pipes cleaned out and all is well: the Roto-Rooter theory of
              communication.

Klamer: A small part of communication is taken for the whole, ig-
              noring such crucial matters as the standing of the speakers.

McCloskey: Yes. The theory of communication that you and I share is
              "rhetorical," which is to say that it recognizes that ideas
              change in the transmission. Communication is something
              that happens in a society between people, like the ideas
              forming in the minds of you and me as we speak. Or
              indeed like the creation of economic value in the agora, the
              marketplace.

Klamer: Sure again: *"Panu ge, Sokrates,"* as Plato would say, "All
              right, Socrates." In fact, there are deep similarities between
              speech and commerce, as we are discovering and as Adam
              Smith already knew: the "propensity to truck, barter, and
              exchange one thing for another," it seemed to him, was a
              "necessary consequence of the faculties of reason and
              speech" (1976, 1:17; cf. 1982, 336, an important connection
              between the two books). The old theories ignore the social
              character of communication even as they exercise it. Plato
              wrote in his dialogues—masterpieces of social drama—that
              mathematical theorems were remembered within an iso-
              lated soul from its previous life. Descartes talked in his
              masterfully persuasive confessions of all sure knowledge as
              coming from an individual's excoriating doubt, "shut up in
              a room heated by an enclosed stove where I had complete
              leisure to meditate on my own thoughts" (Descartes 1968,
              35).

McCloskey: Yup. Though practising a social rhetoric, Plato and
              Descartes advocated a Robinson Crusoe theory of knowl-
              edge, a theory of the lone person preparing packages in
              isolation for transmission to other isolated people. I just
              read a remark of William James that's pertinent to this:

The knower is not simply a mirror . . . passively reflecting an order that he comes upon and finds simply existing. The knower is an actor . . . He registers the truth which he helps to create. Mental interests . . . help make the truth which they declare (quoted in Myers 1986, 8).

Klamer: Yes. The master myth of modernism is the myth of the Object perceived by the Subject. Somehow we as individual Subjects are able to grasp the Objective—yet no one has been able to explain quite how, in twenty-five hundred years of trying.

McCloskey: The Objective/Subjective figure of speech has burrowed deep in our culture, and keeps intruding on conversations about rhetoric. The Objective is supposed to be what's really there; the Subjective is supposed to be what's in our minds. Unhappily, both are unknowable or, what amounts to the same thing for practical purposes, untellable. What we can know is what one might call the Conjective, which is to say, what we know together, by virtue of social discourse, scientific argument, shared language; even, if you wish, by virtue of the social relations of production.

Klamer: I do wish. But I like "conjective." It calls up a realm beyond what I have called the square and the circle. The square is the realm of logic narrowly defined, of strict, first-order predicate deduction; the circle is the calm of will and feelings, the subjective. Your "conjective" is the (social) soup in which the square and the circle float. "Conjective" also reminds one of "conversation," which we both like.

McCloskey: Good. The battle of square and circle, so characteristic of our recent culture, is seen to be lacking in point.

Klamer: On so much we agree. But I suspect your motives. Why do you bring up the social, cooperative, conjective character of scholarship? It reminds me of the rhetorical and social contexts in which economists speak. You need only recognize that there are many contexts and you will be driven to admit that diversity, opposition, and conflict are the salient facts. I suspect you of favoring the terms "conjective" and "conversation" because they evoke bourgeois civility. Like Jürgen Habermas you project the image of an ideal speech community; but unlike Habermas you seem to suggest we already live in it, or at least close by.

McCloskey: You insist on this European pessimism.

Klamer: And you on your American optimism. You see: we have found another cultural difference.

McCloskey: Touché.

Klamer: You must grant me that the *conversation* among economists sometimes becomes warlike. I have even seen you yourself get upset about some economic conversation. What do you think goes wrong?

McCloskey: Among economists as among others the conversation goes wrong in sneering. Habermas complains somewhere about the "strategy of mutually shrugging one's shoulders." Economists do a lot of shoulder shrugging; they have all been perpetrators and victims. Once during a conference I asked an economist at MIT to check one of two boxes: either offer a reasoned reply to my position on purchasing power parity, which he had sneered at, or go on sneering; with a smirk characteristic of the man he chose the box "go on sneering," much to the amusement of another economist nearby, who was courting his favor. Ha, ha. Very funny. But damaging to our joint purposes.

Klamer: We all have such stories, about what William James called "the smoking of cigarettes and the living on small sarcasms." He called it "the Harvard indifference."

McCloskey: Yes, though I knew many people at Harvard who chose never to sneer. Sneering is the obstacle to conversation in economics. The Chicagoans sneer at the Marxists, the Marxists sneer at the Neoclassicals, the Neoclassicals sneer at the Austrians, and the Austrians sneer at the Chicagoans. $C>M>N>A>C$.

Klamer: So much for academic conversation as a mechanism of rational choice.

McCloskey: You are too pessimistic. But I admit some grounds for pessimism. The main purpose of sneering is to protect the sneerer from having to learn anything new. The sneerer is an Expert, and as Harry Truman said, "An expert is someone who doesn't want to learn anything new, because then he wouldn't be an expert." Economists are proudly ignorant these days. If one can simply sneer at bourgeois economics (or Marxian economics or institutional economics or whatever), then one does not have to follow the Maxim of Presumed Seriousness. In her book, *Ordinary Vices* (Shklar 1984), the political theorist Judith

Shklar talks at length about snobbery, the trick of "making one's superiority hurt." The sneer is an assertion of rank. The economist sneers loftily at the sociologist, asserting rank and a fully finished education.

Klamer: Note the hierarchy that springs from the rhetoric.

McCloskey: Yeah: the topmost are the worst; or rather the second to topmost are the worst. The philosopher Clark Glymour, who exhibits no deep acquaintance with English professors, begins his book on *Theory and Evidence* as follows: "If it is true that there are but two kinds of people in the world—the logical positivists and the god-damned English professors—then I suppose I am a logical positivist" (1980, ix). Similarly, another eminent American analytic philosopher said proudly that he had never read a page of Hegel and furthermore (he added with a smile) proposed never to do so.

Klamer: Philosophers are not the only ones who do this. I know a leading macroeconomist who has never read Keynes and proposes never to do so. But he doesn't smile when he says it: his shallow philosophy of science, not laziness or malice, tells him that reading old books is beside the point. Anyway, what would happen if the sneering stopped?

McCloskey: The economists would do better, by forming a community with others interested in economic matters.

Klamer: Your newfound socialism of the intellect seems to me utopian. Sneering is more than an uncivil and unbecoming speech act, correctible through mere exchange. The sneering betrays deeper problems of knowledge and discourse.

McCloskey: Deeper in one sense. The deeper problems are philosophical. The sneering, I like to say, is supported by 3 x 5-card philosophies—"Go forth and Falsify," for example, or "Measure regardless" or "Depend on the *A Priori*." Without them, and without the accompanying passion, the disagreements would fade.

Klamer: The 3 x 5-card philosophies are vicious, I agree. They make people insist that they can settle their disputes by attending to the 3 x 5 card. Others fail to use the same card. Then the failure unleashes anger. Positivism, for example, makes the positivist believe that the only alternative to narrowly defined logic and fact is whim.

McCloskey: Yeah: the chocolate ice cream theory of morality. Moral choices are *mere* matters of opinion, like one's taste for chocolate ice cream.

Klamer: That's right. Scientific conversation is supposed to forbid such expressions of taste, since they are "mere," and supposedly undiscussable. To introduce them is to declare war. You and I would wish such people would recognize a realm beyond and including autistic logic—the conjective as you say, the social and rhetorical grounds for what we believe, between the square and the circle. But I doubt that such recognition would eliminate the sneering.

McCloskey: Sure it would. And does. How do you think schools form in economics? A group talks intensively to each other, *respectfully*. They allow each to influence the other. They stop sneering and start listening. They build something in the space between the circle and the square. I've seen it happen, in the bar of the Quad Club at Chicago, say, or at Iowa in the Project on Rhetoric of Inquiry. Such a community of scholars comes to have few disagreements, if the talking goes on long enough.

Klamer: There you are admiring "community" again. I certainly share your admiration for it! I do occasionally come across people setting aside their harsh feelings and discussing economics openly. I have even seen you talk at length with Marxists.

McCloskey: Don't tell anyone, will you? They'll take away my Chicago card.

Klamer: Hah! But such exchanges between radically opposed points of view are the exception. Ideology affects the exchange even among well-intentioned people.

McCloskey: What do you mean?

Klamer: Rhetoric can uncover the way ideology operates in discourse. Given the limits of strictly deductive reasoning, economists must always argue by means of metaphors, analogies, exemplars, authorities, and stories. You've made this clear yourself.

McCloskey: Yeah; the scientific tetrad: fact, logic, metaphor, and story. What of it?

Klamer: Ideology itself is couched in the metaphors and stories that economists use.

McCloskey: Hmm. Well, that's true enough. The Marxists see struggle everywhere, a story of *Sturm and Drang*.

Klamer: Yes. And you, like other neoclassical economists, think of human behavior in terms of individual calculation. Your

	basic metaphor is that of a Robinson Crusoe allocating scarce resources according to an optimizing algorithm.
McCloskey:	You mean the Samuelson program in modern economics?
Klamer:	Yes. Samuelson's master metaphor is that people come to life equipped with utility functions (which they know) and constraints (which they realize), then solve an engineering problem.
McCloskey:	Yeah: maximize under constraints. First-order conditions. Comparative statics. Methodological individualism. Sweet stuff.
Klamer:	Or "neat," another adjective that your comrades like to use, borrowed from the physicists. My point is that the choice of your metaphor and your story is ideological: it privileges one way of thinking about the world while excluding others. Thinking in terms of individualistic calculation can therefore be obnoxious. In many situations it can also be paralyzing.
McCloskey:	I don't see why. In some times and places the talk of individualism has been radically liberating.
Klamer:	True enough, but this is not 1776. Take one of our current projects, the writing of an elementary textbook for Macmillan. I grant you that each of us has his own reasons for collaborating. Call it self-interest if you wish, but our collaboration would break down if we were to specify equivalents in our exchanges too closely, calculating the optimum strategy, to the third digit. Such behavior would be obnoxious, and make the collaboration impossible.
McCloskey:	I agree. In fact, a quarter of every economics department behaves in just such a way, excessively loyal to their model. That's what makes administering an economics department so difficult, this loyalty to the selfish model of humans.
Klamer:	Sure. Real collaboration depends on trust and on negotiations more subtle than a game. It takes us back into the realm of the conjective. Or think of a worker who gets fired because the foreman does not like her color or sex. Your neoclassical metaphor and story will leave the worker without a language to legitimize outrage and to mobilize for political action. After all, the black woman is paid "what she's worth," (i.e., zilch to the white male employer).
McCloskey:	Wait a minute . . .
Klamer:	Accordingly, in spheres of both friendship and hostility the neoclassical rhetoric represents a dangerous or repressive

	ideology. In these cases people run up against the ideological walls of neoclassical discourse. Robert Heilbroner, by the way, made a similar point about your book in the *New York Review of Books* (reprinted in Klamer, McCloskey, and Solow 1988).
McCloskey:	I don't entirely agree. The language of markets and rational behavior would be a powerful weapon in the hands of the angry worker. Where businesses stick to profit maximization the market forces will eliminate discrimination.
Klamer:	That is a highly problematic argument.
McCloskey:	It may or may not be now; in the past it has often worked. But here's another argument against giving up the neoclassical model of a labor market. The alternative rhetorics of outrage and mobilization have their own down side, too. They lend power to the state, with its clubs and jails and staged rallies.
Klamer:	I doubt it has to. But apart from that, would you advise Bishop Tutu to preach the virtues of markets and self-interest?
McCloskey:	It would not be bad advice. Look at Japan, Korea, Hong Kong, and latterly Russia and China. Workers of all countries unite: demand capitalism.
Klamer:	Even if you were right and a free market system would punish those who discriminate, I don't think that neoclassical thinking provides much insight into what is currently happening in South Africa.
McCloskey:	I'm not so sure. Look at McCloskey, *The Applied Theory of Price* (1985). Second edition, page 496, problem 5.
Klamer:	The major problem with neoclassical economics is its methodological individualism. Amitai Etzioni has a nice image here (Etzioni 1988). He says that methodological individualism is like studying the behavior of a school of fish by taking one fish out of the school and watching what he does in a fish bowl by himself. It's the Robinson Crusoe story, a powerful one in economic literature. You take the businessperson out of the culture to study him, as indeed Defoe did, but you can't take the culture out of the businessperson (Crusoe was as bourgeois as they come, a regular Babbitt of his time). Likewise, you are not likely to take the racist culture out of white South Africans by unleashing market forces. We need to grasp the cultural and political context in which South Africans make their choices.

McCloskey: Your example puts me in mind again of the conjective versus the objective/subjective. But I still think methodological individualism is a sweet method of analysis, and gets us a long way. May I remind you that even some Marxists believe so, John Roemer and Jon Elster for example.

Klamer: Hmm. Their work complicates my argument. I agree that methodological individualism does not have a one-to-one relationship with a particular ideology. I have some problems with the Roemer-Elster approach—and so by the way do some of the contributors to *Rethinking Marxism* (see Norton 1988; Ruccio 1988; Amariglio, Callari, and Cullenberg 1989; Amariglio, Resnick, and Wolff 1989). But let me confine the case to the mechanistic metaphor that neoclassical language uses to think about the individual.

McCloskey: Go ahead. What's the problem?

Klamer: It's the second problem. The problem is the unexamined rhetoricity of "self-interest." In fact one's personal interest has to be argued, with oneself and others. Anyone Christmas shopping or looking for a new job or doing anything that is not habitual knows this.

McCloskey: I can agree with that. We are each of us committees.

Klamer: And "the firm's" interest has to be negotiated, too. A friend of ours in commercial publishing was contemplating moving to a job at a university press. His problem was that "bottom-line publishing" as he called it was in his eyes tougher, braver, more in the fight than university-press publishing. He hesitated long. It was not the calculation of advantage that was the hard problem; it was the arguing out of advantage, the social/cultural debate that raged within his utility function.

McCloskey: Well, sure. There's nothing in the neoclassical economics of Alfred Marshall that would deny such a line of argument. The rhetoric of negotiation in a Marshallian argument might be rather simpleminded (Axel Leijonhufvud compares the Marshallian industry to a bunch of wind-up mice), but it could be accommodated.

Klamer: Can the vagueness of our knowledge of the future be accommodated in the metaphor of a calculating machine? That's the third disability, after the rigid individualism and the unreflective character of the individual. The individual deals in huge, cloudy symbols, not in budget lines.

McCloskey: I agree neoclassical economics can't easily handle con-
            straints that only reveal themselves in the future, though
            we're trying. The point is in fact an old Austrian one,
            which has been rediscovered in the new classical macro-
            economics. The problem in economic life is not calculating
            what to do *after* knowing all that you need to know. The
            problem is coming to know. The Austrians see the
            economy with a metaphor of fog, the fog in which we
            maximize what the neoclassicals so confidently describe as
            "objective functions."

Klamer: I'm surprised you agree. Or are you just reporting on the
            Austrians.

McCloskey: No, I'm agreeing. Most of us wander in a fog of indecision.
            The bright sunlight in which the rational man strides
            forward is hard to credit. I can't see how an academic
            could argue otherwise. After all, he or she is employed to
            help others acquire the knowledge.

Klamer: Partial equilibrium analysis ignores the problem entirely.
            Game theory, in vogue now for the fourth time in its brief
            history, makes what it realizes are simpleminded assump-
            tions about the knowledge of players. Neoclassical analysis
            reduces the problem of knowledge to one of information.
            But having data is one thing, knowing what they mean
            quite another.

McCloskey: Search models have attempted to model learning—though
            admit that they don't go far in recognizing the depths of
            ignorance. But one can defend the notion that for large and
            unsubtle choices people make decisions that are rational as
            an approximation. I have argued so in economic history.

Klamer: Surely the general equilibrium and game-theoretical
            analysis is a lot of formal effort for little gain of social
            insight?

McCloskey: Yeah, I guess so. I can give you another, nonmathematical
            example, just to show that it's not the mathematics that's
            the problem. Since Hobbes we have been transfixed by the
            following abstract question: can a collection of violently
            selfish and unsocialized people form spontaneously a true
            community? I'd maintain that this is an existence theorem
            we can do without, as economists. Whether or not hypo-
            thetical sociopaths from Mars, lacking human culture,
            would form a community is of little interest if the actual
            problem facing us is forming communities out of French-

men or Americans. We need theorems about what happens when already socialized people face temptations to cheat or to kill.

Klamer: I'm surprised you go along with all this. Have you given up the Chicago School?

McCloskey: Certainly not: I've been a Chicago economist since the third year of graduate school at Harvard, having deconverted by stages from sophomore socialism. Surely you can see this in my economic history or my microeconomics textbook.

Klamer: Yes, I can. You talk about rational choice and the magic of markets. It's very neoclassical, very Chicago.

McCloskey: Only in a sense. By "neoclassical" you mean the mainstream model of Paul Samuelson and his students. That's one tribe of neoclassicals, and I admit the mainstream is how our students are trained. They are trained to think that economics is a matter of engineering math. (Not in my book, though.)

Klamer: But surely that's your own tribe, the Chicago School.

McCloskey: No. You stress differences but then overlook important differences within the neoclassical nation. I admit there has sprung up recently a *nouvelle* Chicago, the computer generated and time-series nourished Max Expected U, a younger brother to Samuelson's Max U. But my Chicago is "Good Old Chicago." Theodore Schultz is an example, an empirical economist who uses maximization lightly, as a mild presumption that people try to do what's good for them, mostly. Robert Fogel is another, the next recipient of the Nobel Prize, pursuing behavior through two centuries of primary sources. James Buchanan is another instance, a philosopher-economist, criticizing the metaphor that "the individual responds to a set of externally determined, exogenous variables": "its flaw lies in its conversion of individual choice behavior from a social-institutional context to a physical-computational one" (1979, 29).

Klamer: How about Friedman's methodology paper? That provided the standard justification for Max U.

McCloskey: Yes, it did. And you can find plenty of people in the Chicago tradition who fell for the line. But Friedman himself doesn't actually follow his methodology. He has a lot of Frank Knight in him.

Klamer: Yes. Frank Knight is a bit of a revelation to one who thinks of Chicago in 1980s terms. He took the problem of knowledge seriously. And in his writings you will look in vain for formal presentations of mechanical calculators.

McCloskey: Right: notice how reluctant Friedman has been to write down the maximizing model for his monetarism. I can assure you it's not because he didn't know the math: there's still a test in mathematical statistics that he invented in 1937. Knight was Buchanan's teacher, too. And there is the old-style National Bureau of Economic Research connection in the careers of Fogel (the prize student of Simon Kuznets), in Friedman himself, and in the other patient workers in the observatories. The Good Old Chicago School was skeptical of formalization and was devoted to collecting facts: Marshall himself exhibits these tendencies. Look at Milton's books with Anna Schwartz on the money supply. One could mention Ronald Coase, the inventor of law and economics, or A. C. Harberger, the inventor of modern cost/benefit analysis, or Merton Miller, the inventor of modern finance, or Gordon Tullock, the inventor of political economy, or Earl Hamilton, the inventor of cliometrics, or Margaret Reid, the inventor of household economics, or Greg Lewis, the inventor of analytic labor economics, or Leland Yeager, the inventor of modern international finance. They are conservatives (in a manner of speaking), but not such easy targets for sneering as are the devotees of Max Expected U.

Klamer: I must say you are right about Coase. Maybe I'd better have a look at some of the others.

McCloskey: Yes. The Good Old Chicago School is alive and well and living in economic history, law and economics, and other fields that do not view economics as a blackboard subject.

Klamer: I've done you an injustice by associating you with the neoclassical camp of Samuelson and Lucas.

McCloskey: Wait a minute. I admire Samuelson's contribution to economics, and Lucas's, too. It's their students and then their students and now their students who have wandered away from the Good Old truths. After all, Samuelson was an undergraduate at Chicago long ago, and Lucas shifted from the History Department at Berkeley to get his Ph.D. in economics from Chicago, under the old dispensation.

Klamer: Still, there's a sharp rhetorical difference between the Samuelson tradition and the one with which you associate yourself. While Samuelson et al. pursued a highly abstract theory of economic exchange, your brand of economics is more historical and calls for case studies. Their favorite metaphor is that of a mechanism while yours is organic. Samuelsonian economics values completeness and consistency whereas yours allows for the inadequacy of theory in recognition of human imperfections.

McCloskey: Maybe. I view the exact models as rough little instruments for measuring those "organic" beasts on the fly. I don't want to cut up the conversation so. Max U is a silly fellow sometimes, but sometimes he's just what we need for a problem. About Max Expected U I'm less sure, but even he must have a thing or two to say to us: the Principle of Intellectual Trade applies even to the work of those who would spurn it. The "historical" and "case-study" approach of the Good Old Chicago School, if that's quite how to describe it, should not be seen as a rejection of economic theory: it's not back to the German Historical School, with its naiveté about the relation between fact and theory.

Klamer: The difference in rhetoric, which you are acknowledging exists, is not merely a matter of preferring one metaphor over another. Even if we ignore its ideological implications, the mechanistic, Samuelsonian metaphor has argumentative consequences. It makes the formalistic style of reasoning seem natural: it makes it seem more scientific. This also explains the common failure of your Let's-forget-about-the-formalities-and-just-talk scenario. The rational expectations types sneer at such conversation, as "not serious." They consider the "informal" analysis as undeserving of the label Science. Conversation is pushed right outside the realm of the negotiable.

McCloskey: That's a little harsh, although I admit that their conversation does seem to revolve around what's happening in electrical engineering these days.

Klamer: I would argue that changing the discourse is not a matter of individual choice. Formalist discourse in economics is embedded in a larger, more comprehensive discourse. Its values and aspirations correspond to a modernism that has dominated music, physics, philosophy, visual arts, architecture, and mathematics since 1900 (Klamer 1988a, 1988b). Modernism, is responsible for the formalism, axiomatization, avant-garde-ism, and professionalism in all these fields. Samuelson and Lucas owe their persuasive-

	ness to a modernist environment. The Good Old Chicago School has been put in the shade because its organic way of reasoning did not suit the mood of the last thirty years.
McCloskey:	I suppose so. The same could be said of most Marxists as well. They too are modernists.
Klamer:	I agree, though there are Good Old Marxists, too. Resnick and Wolff (1987) and Amariglio (1988, 1989) argue this way. Marxists, they say, have bought into the modernistic ideals of universal truth and scientific laws. Have you read their stuff?
McCloskey:	Yes, a little, at conferences. Mainly I depend on vague memories of a Marxist youth. I pay professional attention to the historical studies of people like Bill Lazonick, Bernie Elbaum, Steve Marglin, and associates. What *are* the Rethinkers doing?
Klamer:	They do stuff very similar to our rhetorical work. They break open the rigid discourse of Marxism. They attack the essentialism and foundationalism in Marxist intellectual practice. You see how similar it is? We're attacking foundationalism, too.
McCloskey:	Yes, I do. Do they also get accused of being insanely "relativistic," and wanting to bring to earth a regime of "anything goes"?
Klamer:	Sure, of course: just the way the American pragmatists were attacked, and indeed the way the political anarchists you say you admire were attacked.
McCloskey:	Ah, yes: Godwin and Kropotkin!
Klamer:	The Rethinkers have some useful terms. For example, the concept of "overdetermination": any particular event is caused by many things.
McCloskey:	You mean the world is not economical in its chains of causation?
Klamer:	Indeed. And they use the notion of an "entry point" to a discourse. They use class as an entry point, the way neo-classicals use rational individuals. The entry point of course contributes to the determination—indeed, the over-determination—of the science.
McCloskey:	Hmm. You mean there's an "entry point" to neoclassical rhetoric, too?
Klamer:	Yes. Rhetorically one could identify it with the commonplaces assumed at the beginning of a speech.

McCloskey: Let me reduce it to neoclassical terms. I'd say that the entry point is like the choice of a set of prices with which to value national income, the index number. It picks a point of view.

Klamer: The Rethinkers would not like such reductionism.

McCloskey: I do admire what I've seen. What I most admire is the Rethinkers' openness to conversation. It never ceases to astonish me how a few people in academic life are actually interested in testing their arguments in conversation: that's why most people like the false rhetoric that frees them from having to persuade doubters, which they call "testing." My test is your fallacy, but in any case we don't have to meet each other on common ground.

Klamer: There's another rhetorical issue, with sociological consequences. The conversation of economics is defined to exclude people like the Rethinkers.

McCloskey: I know what you mean. The cry "that's not economics" means "I don't know what you are talking about and propose not to find out."

Klamer: Yes; and "I propose not to hire you, either."

McCloskey: A disgrace. Economists are willing to play hardball in the job market without remorse. They think again that it's made morally right by their model of the market. Anyway, we agree—we rhetoricians and Rethinkers—on what does not work: the platonic and cartesian programs of abstraction. Modernism is impractical, whether in flat-roofed boxes of buildings that leak and drop their window panes on passersby or in an economics designed on similar modernist principles.

Klamer: Right you are.

McCloskey: It doesn't work because the "human sciences" (in the useful French expression) cannot be *profitably* predictive. The ambition to construct an economic science modeled on electrical engineering, say, runs up against its own discovery: that people anticipate the future, and trump whatever cards the others play. In economics if we were so smart as to be able to predict the future of interest rates, for example, we would be rich. Economics contradicts its own ambitions. So too in linguistics, as economists can understand in terms of game theory or rational expectations:

[T]here is a fundamental way in which a full account of the communicative power of language can never be reduced to a set of conventions for the use of language. The reason is that wherever some convention or expectation about the use of language arises, there will also therewith arise the possibility of the non-conventional exploitation of that convention or expectation. It follows that a purely . . . rule-based account of natural language usage can never be complete (Levinson 1983, 112).

Klamer: That's a great quotation.

McCloskey: Yeah, I thought so too. It undercuts the modernist ambition to write down complete systems. Kurt Gödel and Alonzo Church showed that it doesn't work even for math. But what's beyond modernism in economics?

Klamer: And beyond modernism in art and architecture.

McCloskey: Well, what? My neoclassical principles do not permit me to claim to see the future.

Klamer: The alternative is not *post*modernism, which seems to me merely jokey and nihilistic, merely the last act in the decay of modernism. The alternative is "interpretive" economics, an economics (or art) that attempts to grasp the meanings of economic life.

McCloskey: I agree on the rejection of postmodernism as usually understood. We don't help ourselves much by handing over our lives to Parisian intellectuals. Anyway, they sneer at our attempts at French. And I agree with your call for an interpretive economics. It's what most economists do anyway, I'd argue.

Klamer: We need an economics for human beings, not for gods. Gods see through to the Truth; humans interpret. When Ronald Coase wanders around in law books looking for a way to understand externalities that makes sense, when Michael Burawoy participates on the shop floor looking for a way to see the struggle for control, when Bill Lazonick gets down to the old records of capitalism on the ground, when Bob Solow strains for a reasonable inter-pretation among the econometric models and journalistic rumors of the day—they're all doing *interpretive* eco-nomics, with a variety of purpose-built methods.

McCloskey: It's American.

Klamer: There you go again with your Midwestern chauvinism. Claude Levi-Strauss called it "bricolage," handimanship, making do with the tools one has and getting on with the job. Its opposite is the pursuit of universal laws and perfectly general systems, which would be useless if we found them, except to make us slaves.

McCloskey: I entirely agree. The modernists have Plato and Descartes and Bertrand Russell to admire. We have our own ancestors: Protagoras, Aristotle, Cicero, Quintilian, and then a stream of modern critics and maverick philosophers from James and Dewey to Kenneth Burke, Michael Polanyi, Stephen Toulmin, Alisdair MacIntyre, and Richard Rorty. Consider John Ruskin, for example, the nineteenth-century critic of architecture. The search for the Ideal, he noted, has been an incubus on classical and Renaissance (and now modernist) architecture. He attacked the domination by the Genius, seeking in his garret a universal system to impose on us all. See if it doesn't apply to modernism in economics. Of the Renaissance he wrote:

its main mistake . . . was the unwholesome demand for *perfection* at any cost . . . Men like Verrocchio and Ghiberti [try Marx or Samuelson] were not to be had every day . . . Their strength was great enough to enable them to join science with invention, method with emotion, finish with fire . . . Europe saw in them only the method and the finish. This was new to the minds of men, and they pursued it to the neglect of everything else. "This," they cried, "we must have in our work henceforward:" and they were obeyed. The lower workman secured method and finish, and lost, in exchange for them, his soul (1853, 228–29).

Klamer: Another good one. It certainly applies to modernism in economics.

McCloskey: I thought you'd like it. Your "interpretive economics" would be in Ruskin's terms "Gothic economics"—an end to searching for a grail of a unified field theory, an awakening from Descartes's Dream. As Ruskin said,

it requires a strong effort of common sense to shake ourselves quit of all that we have been taught for the last two . . . centuries, and wake to the perception of a truth . . . that great art . . . does *not* say the same thing over and over again . . . [T]he Gothic spirit . . . not only dared, but delighted in, the infringement of every servile principle (166–67).

Klamer: I should read that book. Anyhow you surprise me. By endorsing the interpretive approach, you've come some way from Good Old Chicago.

McCloskey: I think not. You just aren't sufficiently acquainted with Theodore Schultz and Milton Friedman and Robert Fogel, who all do Gothic and interpretive economics.

Klamer: I suspect that interpretive economics will take us to places that are different from the ones your favorites like to inhabit. For instance, it will call attention to the rhetorical dimensions of economic life itself. It will encourage us to explore the social/cultural/political contexts in which people make decisions. Consequently, interpretive economics may displace the individual decisionmaker as the central character. The work of Mary Douglas may be an indication, and of Albert Hirschman.

McCloskey: And other social scientists with a larger agenda than imitating electrical engineers. But that's for another day. We must quit: onward and upward.

Klamer: Yeah: time's up. Notice, though, that you've come round to arguing for a difference—between Max U and Good Old Chicago.

McCloskey: Well, there are *some* differences, naturally.

Klamer: And you've also argued for the softhearted values of community.

McCloskey: I tell you, you're definitely going to get my Chicago card taken away from me.

Klamer: If you subscribe to "interpretive" economics they will do more than that. Consorting with anthropologists is a serious offense in the Social Science Building.

McCloskey: Dammit: not among the Good Old Chicago School.

Klamer: Yeah. That's one major insight I've gotten from our dialogue—that all "neoclassical" economics is not Samuelson's *The Foundations* writ small.

McCloskey: Most American economists would recognize themselves to be "interpretive" if they tried it out. Anyway, I've learned a thing or two from our little conversation. Yes, there are intellectual differences, some of them bitter and unresolvable by this generation. I already knew there were social differences. Mainly, though, I've learned that interpretive economics is a way of exploring the conjective, beyond the square or the circle.

Klamer: Peace and tolerance. The Principle of Intellectual Exchange works once again.

McCloskey: Before you go, look here over at the blackboard. I've got a sweet diagram of an Edgeworth box that shows the mutual benefit from intellectual exchange. Now suppose, to start with, that both parties are self-interested . . .

References

Alker, H., Jr. 1988. "The Dialectical Logic of Thucydides' Melian Dialogue." *American Political Science Review* 82 (September): 805–20.

Amariglio, J. 1988. "The Body, Economic Discourse, and Power: An Economist's Introduction to Foucault." *History of Political Economy* 20: 583–613.

———. 1989. "Economics as a Postmodern Discourse." In *Economics as Discourse*, ed. W. Samuels. Boston: Kluwer Academic Publishers.

Amariglio, J.; Callari, A.; and Cullenberg, S. 1989. "Analytical Marxism: Critical Overview." *Review of Social Economy* (Winter).

Amariglio, J.; Resnick, S.; and Wolff, R. 1989. "Division and Difference in the 'Discipline' of Economics." Unpublished paper presented to the Seventh Annual meeting for the Group for Research into the Institutionalization and Professionalization of Literary Studies (GRIP), University of Minnesota, April.

Buchanan, J. 1979 "What Should Economists Do?" In *What Should Economists Do?* ed. J. Buchanan, 17–38. Indianapolis: Liberty Press. Reprinted from *Southern Economic Journal* 30 (January 1964): 213–22.

Cicero, M. T., 1942. *De Oratore*. Vol. 1. Trans. E. W. Sutton. Cambridge: Harvard University Press.

Colander, D. and Klamer, A. 1987. "The Making of an Economist." *Journal of Economic Perspectives* 1 (Fall): 95–112.

Davis, P. and Hersh, R. 1987. "Rhetoric and Mathematics." In *The Rhetoric of the Human Sciences*, ed. J. Nelson, A. Megill, and D. McCloskey, 53–68. Madison: University of Wisconsin Press.

Descartes, R. 1968. *Discourse on Method and the Meditations*. New York: Penguin Books.

Etzioni, A. 1988. *The Moral Dimension*. New York: The Free Press.

Fogel, R. 1964. *Railroads and American Economic Growth: Essays in Econometric History*. Baltimore: Johns Hopkins University Press.

Folbre, N. and Hartmann, H. 1988. "The Rhetoric of Self-interest: Ideology and Gender in Economic Theory." In *The Consequences of Economic Rhetoric,* ed. A. Klamer, D. McCloskey , and R. Solow, 184–203. Cambridge: Cambridge University Press.

Glymour, C. 1980. *Theory and Evidence.* Princeton: Princeton University Press.

Hirschman, A. 1970. *Exit, Voice and Loyalty.* Cambridge: Harvard University Press.

———. 1984. "Against Parsimony: Three Easy Ways of Complicating Some Categories of Economic Discourse." *American Economic Review* 74 (May): 89–96.

Klamer, A. 1983a. "Empirical Arguments in New Classical Economics." *Economie Appliquée* 36: 229–54.

———. 1983b. *Conversations with Economists: New Classical Economists and Opponents Speak Out on the Current Controversy in Macroeconomics.* Totawa, N.J. Rowman and Allanheld.

———. 1984. "Levels of Discourse in New Classical Economics." *History of Political Economy.* (Summer): 263–90.

———. 1987. "As if Economists and Their Subjects Were Rational." In *The Rhetoric of the Human Sciences,* ed. J. Nelson, A. Megill, and D. McCloskey, 163–83. Madison: University of Wisconsin Press.

———. 1988a. "Economics as Discourse." In *The Popperian Legacy in Economics,* ed. N. de Marchi, 259–78. Cambridge: Cambridge University Press.

———. 1988b. "Negotiating a New Conversation about Economics." In *The Consequences of Economic Rhetoric,* ed. A. Klamer, D. McCloskey , and R. Solow, 265–79. Cambridge: Cambridge University Press.

———. "The Advent of Modernism in Economics." Unpublished paper, Project on Rhetoric of Inquiry, University of Iowa.

Klamer, A. and Colander. D. 1989. *The Making of an Economist.* Boulder: Westview Press.

Klamer, A. and McCloskey, D. 1988. "Economics in the Human Conversation." In *The Consequences of Economic Rhetoric,* ed. A. Klamer, D. McCloskey, and R. Solow, 3–20. Cambridge: Cambridge University Press.

Klamer, A.; McCloskey, D.; and Solow, R., eds. 1988. *The Consequences of Economic Rhetoric.* Cambridge: Cambridge University Press.

Knight. F. 1940. "'What Is Truth' in Economics?" Review of T. Hutchinson's *The Significance and Basic Postulates of Economic Theory. Journal of Political*

Economy 48 (February): 1–32. Reprinted in Knight. 1963. *On the History and Method of Economics Selected Essays*. Chicago: University of Chicago Press.

Levinson, S. 1983. *Pragmatics*. Cambridge: Cambridge University Press.

McCloskey, D. 1985. *The Rhetoric of Economics*. Madison: University of Wisconsin Press.

———. 1985. *The Applied Theory of Price*. New York: Macmillan.

———. 1987a. "Counterfactuals." In *The New Palgrave: A Dictionary of Economic Thought and Doctrine*. London: Macmillan.

———. 1987b. "Continuity in Economic History." In *The New Palgrave*.

———. 1987c. "Rhetoric." In *The New Palgrave*.

———. 1988a. "The Rhetoric of Law and Economics." *Michigan Law Review* 86 (February): 752–67.

———. 1988b. "The Limits of Expertise: If You're So Smart, Why Ain't You Rich?" *The American Scholar* 57 (Summer 1988): 393–406.

———. 1988c. "The Storied Character of Economics." *Tijdschrift voor Geschiedenis* 101 (4): 643–54.

———. 1988d. "Thick and Thin Methodologies in the History of Economic Thought" In *The Popperian Legacy in Economics*, ed. N. de Marchi, 245–57. Cambridge: Cambridge University Press.

———. 1988e. "The Consequences of Rhetoric." In *The Consequences of Economic Rhetoric*, ed. A. Klamer, D. McCloskey , and R. Solow, 280–94. Cambridge: Cambridge University Press.

———. 1989a. "Formalism in Economics, Rhetorically Speaking." *Ricerche Economiche* (March).

———. 1989b. "Rhetoric as Morally Radical: Reply to Klamer, Stewart, and Gleicher." *Review of Radical Political Economics*, 87–91.

———. 1989c. "Storytelling in Economics." In *Narrative as an Instrument of Culture*, ed. C. Nash and M. Warner, London: Routledge; and in *Hermeneutics in Economics*, ed. D. Lavoie.

———. 1989d. "Why I Am No Longer a Positivist." *Review of Social Economy*.

———. 1989e. "Some Consequences of a Feminine Economics." Unpublished paper, Project on Rhetoric of Inquiry, University of Iowa.

Myers, G. 1986. *William James: His Life and Thought*. New Haven: Yale University Press.

Nelson, J.; Megill, A.; and McCloskey , D., eds. 1987. *The Rhetoric of the Human Sciences: Language and Argument in Scholarship and Public Affairs*. Madison: University of Wisconsin Press.

Norton, B. 1988. "The Power Axis: Bowles, Gordon, and Weisskopf's Theory of Postwar U.S. Accumulation." *Rethinking Marxism* 1 (Fall): 6–43.

Perelman, C. and Olbrechts-Tyteca, L. 1958. *The New Rhetoric: A Treatise on Argumentation*. Trans. J. Wilkinson and P. Weaver. Notre Dame: University of Notre Dame Press.

Polanyi, M. 1962. *Personal Knowledge: Towards a Post-critical Philosophy*. Chicago: University of Chicago Press.

Quintilian, Marcus F. 1920. *Institutio Oratoria*. Trans. H. E. Butler. Cambridge: Harvard University Press.

Resnick, S. and Wolff, R. 1987. *Knowledge and Class: A Marxian Critique of Political Economy*. Chicago: University of Chicago Press.

———. 1988. "Marxian Theory and the Rhetoric of Economics." In *The Consequences of Economic Rhetoric*, ed. A. Klamer, D. McCloskey , and R. Solow, 47–63. Cambridge: Cambridge University Press

Rorty R. 1979. *Philosophy and the Mirror of Nature*. Princeton: Princeton University Press.

———. 1982. *The Consequences of Pragmatism: Essays*. Minneapolis: University of Minnesota Press.

Ruccio, D. 1988. "The Merchant of Venice, or Marxism in the Mathematical Mode." *Rethinking Marxism* 1 (Winter): 36–68.

Ruskin, J. 1853. *The Stones of Venice*. Abridged by J. G. Links. NY: Farrar, Strauss & Giroux. Paperback ed. 1983. New York: Da Capo.

Shklar, J. 1984. *Ordinary Vices*. Cambridge: Harvard University Press.

Solow, R. 1981. "Does Economics Make Progress?" *Bulletin of the American Academy of Arts and Sciences* 36 (December).

Smith, A. 1976. *The Wealth of Nations* (Cannan Edition). Chicago: University of Chicago Press.

———. 1982. *The Theory of Moral Sentiments*. Ed. D. Raphael and A. Macfie. Indianapolis: Liberty Press. Reprint of Oxford ed. 1976.

Toulmin, S. 1958. *The Uses of Argument*. Cambridge: Cambridge University Press.

FURTHER READINGS IN THE ALTERNATIVE SCHOOLS OF THOUGHT: A BIBLIOGRAPHICAL ESSAY

DAVID L. PRYCHITKO

Austrian Economics

The literature on contemporary Austrian economics has exploded since the late 1970s. Many discovered Austrian economics through Israel M. Kirzner's *Competition and Entrepreneurship* (University of Chicago Press, 1973), which clearly detailed the traditional market-process approach, and the entrepreneurial role within it, against the foil of the perfectly competitive equilibrium theory. His more recent effort, *The Meaning of Market Process: Essays in the Development of Modern Austrian Economics* (Routledge, 1992), contains Kirzner's most advanced treatment of the equilibrating properties of the market process, a challenge to both neoclassicists and the radical subjectivists within the Austrian School. Murray N. Rothbard's two-volume set, *Man, Economy, and State: A Treatise on Economic Principles* (Nash Publishing, 1970), also serves as a useful introduction for students with some background in microeconomics, as it makes Austrian economics appear (rightly or wrongly) as a verbal variant of free market neoclassicism. Rothbard's two-volume set in the history of thought, *Economic Thought Before Adam Smith* and *Classical Economics* (Edward Elgar, 1996) splendidly traces Austrian themes in the development of economic doctrine.

The radically subjectivist wing of the Austrian school is exemplified by Ludwig M. Lachmann's *The Market as an Economic Process* (Basil Blackwell, 1986) and his *Expectations and the Meaning of Institutions: Essays in Economics by Ludwig Lachmann,* edited by Don Lavoie (Routledge, 1994), and also Gerald P. O'Driscoll's and Mario J. Rizzo's *The Economics of Time and Ignorance* (Routledge, 2nd ed., 1995). These books further explore the ideas associated with radical uncertainty, expectations and disequilibrium discussed in Lachmann's chapter in Part I. For those interested in the work of G. L. S. Shackle. from which Lachmann has drawn much inspiration, see his *Epistemics and Economics: A Critique of Economic Doctrines*, recently reprinted by Transaction Publishers (1992). A warning: this is a terribly dense work which may prove too difficult for the uninitiated. In this regard, James Buchanan's essay, "Natural and Artifactual Man," in his *What Should Economists Do?* (Liberty Press, 1979), serves as a good brief introduction to Shackle's concept of choice under radical uncertainty. Buchanan's *Cost and Choice: An Inquiry in Economic Theory* (University of Chicago Press, 1969) also provides a good discussion of cost theory from a radically subjectivist perspective. For a careful comparison (and defense) of the Austrian School's concept of market-generated knowledge against that of the mainstream's "economics of information" literature, see Esteben F. Thomsen, *Prices and Knowledge: A Market-Process Perspective* (Routledge, 1992).

On the other hand, Peter J. Boettke's *Elgar Companion to Austrian Economics* (Edward Elgar Publishing, 1994) provides a valuable encyclo-pedic account of Austrian theory and methodology with entries from nearly seventy economists. Bruce J. Caldwell and Stephen Boehm, eds., *Austrian Economics: Tensions and New Directions* (Kluwer Academic) offers a collection of essays and debates among the traditional and radical wings of the school, and serves as a useful introduction to the modern trends and concerns within the school, while Karen I. Vaughn's *Austrian Economics in America: The Migration of a Tradition* (Cambridge University Press, 1994) offers a solid and well-written history of the development of contemporary Austrian theory, from the 1880s to 1980s, and focuses in particular on the tension between traditional Austrianism and the growing influence of radical subjectivism in the Shackle-Lachmann vein. (Mario Rizzo also discusses the current Austrian controversy in his preface to the second edition of O'Driscoll and Rizzo's *The Economics of Time and Ignorance*.) Influential essays on market process economics stemming from Austrian, neoclassical, and other traditions have been collected in Peter J. Boettke and David L. Prychitko, eds., *Market Process Theories*, a volume in *The International Library of Critical Writings in Economics* (Edward Elgar, 1997).

Finally, the serious student must return to the classics within the school. A short list would include Carl Menger's *Principles of Economics* (1871; reprinted by New York University Press, 1981) and *Investigations into the Method of the Social Sciences with Special Reference to Economics* (1883; reprinted by New York University Press, 1985) for the early development of methodological individualism, subjectivism, and the notion of spontaneous order; rather than tackle Boehm-Bawerk's (discredited) capital theory, first see Frank A. Fetter's *Capital, Interest, and Rent: Essays in the Theory of Distribution*, edited by Murray N. Rothbard (Sheed Andrews and McMeel, 1977) for the contemporary Austrian pure time preference theory of interest; see Ludwig von Mises's *The Theory of Money and Credit* (1912; reprinted by Liberty Classics, 1980), *Socialism: An Economic and Sociological Analysis* (1932; reprinted by Liberty Classics, 1981); and his magnum opus, *Human Action: A Treatise on Economics* (Henry Regnery, 3rd ed., 1966), which best constructs and applies Mises's notion of "praxeology," and F. A. Hayek's *Individualism and Economic Order* (University of Chicago Press, 1980), which contains his classic articles from the 1930s and 1940s: "Economics and Knowledge," "The Use of Knowledge in Society," and "The Meaning of Competition." Hayek's attempted monetary theory, *Prices and Production* (1935; 2nd ed. reprinted by Augustus Kelley, 1967)—the work so much contested by Keynes and Sraffa—should also be read in conjunction with Mises' above-mentioned work on money. Also see Hayek's *The Counter-Revolution of Science: Studies on the Abuse of Reason* (1952; reprinted by Liberty Press, 1979) for a sophisticated defense of methodological subjectivism and the epistemological problems of economic theory. For a clarification of the oft-misunderstood Austrian position in the socialist calculation debate, see Don Lavoie's *Rivalry and Central Planning: The Socialist Calculation Debate Reconsidered* (Cambridge University Press, 1985).

Although Austrian economics is largely a "book culture," several journals have emerged to discuss Austrian theory and its free-market policy stance. These include *The Review of Austrian Economics* and *Advances in Austrian Economics* (both research annuals). The most important essays in the now-defunct journal *Market Process*, published during the 1980s at George Mason University, have been republished in Peter J. Boettke and David L. Prychitko, eds., *The Market Process: Essays in Contemporary Austrian Economics* (Edward Elgar, 1994). Also, Austrian writings are often found in *Review of Political Economy* and in journals that discuss the classical free-market vision (ranging in degrees of criticism), such as *The Journal of Libertarian Studies, The Cato Journal, Journal des Economistes et des Etudes Humaines,* and *Critical Review.*

Post Keynesian Economics

It is, of course, an understatement to suggest that the most important book in Post Keynesian economics is that by John Maynard Keynes himself—*The General Theory of Employment, Interest, and Money* (1936; reprinted by HBJ, 1964). The problem is, most self-labeled

"Keynesians" interpreted Keynes's treatise through the simple aggregate supply-aggregate demand (and later IS-LM) models, and most younger readers of the book continue to interpret it through the same or similar frameworks. Thus, Keynes's *General Theory* may not be the best introduction to Post Keynesianism. Instead, first see Hyman P. Minsky's careful yet readable alternative interpretation in his *John Maynard Keynes* (Columbia University Press, 1975). Perhaps then go to the original.

Alfred Eichner's *The Megacorp and Oligopoly: Micro Foundations of Macro Dynamics* (Cambridge University Press, 1976) and Paul Davidson's *Money and the Real World* (Macmillan, 2nd ed., 1978) play an important role in the contemporary literature. A more recent collection of Davidson's writings appears in his *Post Keynesian Macroeconomic Theory: A Foundation for Successful Economic Policies in the Twenty-First Century* (Edward Elgar, 1994). For a Kaleckian approach, see Malcolm Sawyer's *Macro-Economics in Question: The Keynesian-Monetarist Orthodoxies and the Kaleckian Alternative* (M. E. Sharpe, 1982). Marc Lavoie's *Foundations of Post-Keynesian Economic Analysis* (Edward Elgar, 1992) offers an intermediate-level textbook account of Post-Keynesian theory. Also see Philip Arestis, *The Post-Keynesian Approach to Economics: An Alternative Analysis of Economic Theory and Policy* (Edward Elgar, 1992). Minsky's *Can "It" Happen Again? Essays on Instability and Finance* (M. E. Sharpe, 1982) blends formal and institutional-empirical essays on the nature of endogenous instability among financial institutions, furthering the discussion of chapters 6 and 7 in his above-mentioned volume on Keynes.

Although by no means a text on Post Keynesianism, the essays in Robert J. Gordon's edited collection, *Milton Friedman's Monetary Framework: A Debate with His Critics* (University of Chicago Press, 1974), offers a wonderful juxtaposition between Monetarism and its rivals in the 1970s, and in particular interest is Davidson's chapter, "A Keynesian View of Friedman's Theoretical Framework for Monetary Analysis" and Friedman's (somewhat unfair) reply. Eichner's *A Guide to Post-Keynesian Economics* (M. E. Sharpe, 1979) has also served as a useful introductory reader to the diverse aspects of Post-Keynesian concerns. For Eichner's own methodological position, see his essay "Why Economics is Not Yet a Science," in his edited book with the same title (M. E. Sharpe, 1983).

For the historical evolution of Post-Keynesian theory, a short list includes the essays in Michael Kalecki's accessible *Selected Essays on the Dynamics of the Capitalist Economy, 1933–1970* (Cambridge University Press, 1971), Nicholas Kaldor's *Essays on Value and Distribution* (Free Press, 1960) (which contains his important *Review of Economic Studies* article, "Alternative Theories of Distribution"), Joan Robinson's *The Accumulation of Capital* (Macmillan, 1956), and Sidney Weintraub's *An*

Approach to the Theory of Income Distribution (Chilton, 1958). Post-Keynesians also share some common ground with the neo-Ricardian impulse of Piero Sraffa's *Production of Commodities by Means of Commodities* (Cambridge University Press, 1960) and Luigi Pasinetti's *Growth and Income Distribution* (Cambridge University Press, 1974). Here, too, a caveat is in order—these are difficult reads. Students might find an easier historical understanding of some of the general issues in Joan Robinson's *Economic Heresies: Some Old-Fashioned Questions in Economic Theory* (Basic Books, 1971); also see J. E. King's *Conversations with Post-Keynesians* (St. Martin's Press, 1994), which contains interviews with several prominent theorists in the school.

The leading journal in the field is the *Journal of Post Keynesian Economics*, although *Review of Political Economy*, *Cambridge Journal of Economics*, *Journal of Economic Issues*, and *Challenge* also publish articles in the tradition.

Institutional and Social Economics

The institutionalist literature is large and diverse. Classics in institutional economics include, in an admittedly short list, Thorstein Veblen's entertaining 1899 work *The Theory of the Leisure Class* (Transaction, 1992) and his 1919 collection *The Place of Science in Modern Civilization and Other Essays* (Transaction, 1990); (Note: Selections from Veblen's writings are easily accessible in Rick Tilman, ed., *A Veblen Treasury: From Leisure Class to War, Peace, and Capitalism* (M. E. Sharpe, 1993).); John R. Commons' *Legal Foundations of Capitalism* (1924; reprinted by Transaction, 1995) and his thick two volume 1934 treatise, *Institutional Economics: Its Place in Political Economy* (Transaction, 1990); Wesley C. Mitchell's 1937 *The Backward Art of Spending Money and Other Essays* (reprinted by Augustus Kelley), and C. E. Ayres's *Toward a Reasonable Society: The Values of Industrial Civilization* (University of Texas Press, 1961).

Wendell Gordon provides a traditional textbook approach in his *Institutional Economics: The Changing System* (University of Texas Press, 1980), which is accessible to students with some exposure to neoclassical economics. Gordon's book introduces students to the liberal wing of institutionalism. For those seeking instead a further discussion of the radical project, it is hard to beat William Dugger's edited collection, *Radical Institutionalism: Contemporary Voices* (Greenwood Press, 1989). Dugger's introductory chapter alone is worth the search. Also, James Ronald Stanfield's *Economics, Power and Culture: Essays in the Development of Radical Institutionalism* (St. Martin's, 1995) has recently appeared.

In his *Economics and Institutions: A Manifesto for a Modern Institutional Economics* (University of Pennsylvania Press, 1988), Geoffrey Hodgson further explores, in detail, institutionalism as a basis for a critique of the methodological-individualist pillar of both Austrian and New Institutionalist theory. The June 1995 issue of *Journal of Economic Issues* (vol. 39, no. 2) includes papers by Malcolm Rutherford, William Dugger, J. R. Stanfield, and others on Nobel Laureate Douglas North's New Institutionalism. Also see Rutherford's *Institutions in Economics: The Old and the New Institutionalism* (Cambridge University Press, 1994). (For a nice introduction and defense of the New Institutionalism, see Richard Langlois, ed., *Economics as a Process: Essays in the New Institutional Economics* (Cambridge University Press, 1986).)

The two-volume set by Geoffrey M. Hodgson, Warren J. Samuels, and Marc R. Tool, eds., *The Elgar Companion to Institutional and Evolutionary Economics* (Edward Elgar, 1994), offers an encyclopedic account of all major aspects of the literature, including the New Institutionalism; while a readable (and much more affordable) sampling of the concept of power in institutional economics, drawn from the leading institutionalist journal, *Journal of Economic Issues*, is collected in Marc R. Tool and Warren J. Samuels, eds., *The Economy as a System of Power* (Transaction, 2nd rev. ed., 1989). Samuels collects dozens of important articles from the "old" institutionalist tradition in his three-volume edited set, *Institutionalism* (Edward Elgar, 1988).

Mark Lutz's *Social Economics: Retrospect and Prospect* (Kluwer Academic, 1989) and the essays assembled in John B. Davis and Edward J. O'Boyle, eds., *The Social Economics of Human Material Need* (Southern Illinois University Press, 1994) provide the best single introductions to the social economics literature. The Association for Social Economics' journal, *Review of Social Economy*, offers a symposium on the historical evolution of Catholic Social Thought, and its role in founding the Association for Social Economics, in the Winter 1991 issue (vol. 49, no. 4), while the Winter 1993 issue (vol. 51, no. 4) offers a symposium on the diversity among contemporary social economists and the normative issues they will confront during the next century. The latter makes for an easily accessible introduction to most of the branches of social economics, including the feminist, Catholic, humanist, institutionalist, and radical. Fred Hirsch's *Social Limits to Growth* (Harvard University Press, 1976), Kenneth Boulding's *The Economics of Human Betterment* (SUNY Press, 1985), and Severyn T. Bruyn's *A Future for the American Economy: The Social Market* (Stanford University Press, 1991) represent efforts conducive to social economists' concerns. Friedrich von Wieser's *Social Economics* (1927; reprinted by Augustus Kelley, 1967) is an Austrian School classic, yet its impact in contemporary social economics is minimal.

Finally, the essays drawn from the *Journal of Economic Issues* and collected in Marc R. Tool's *An Institutionalist Guide to Economics and Public Policy* (M. E. Sharpe, 1984) provide a convenient sampling of policy perspectives and concerns.

Radical Political Economy

The foundations here begin, of course, with Karl Marx, although there's something to be said for J. C. Simonde de Sismondi's *New Principles of Political Economy*, translated by Richard Hyse (Transaction, 1990). Marx's *Economic and Philosophical Manuscripts of 1844* (International Publishers, 1944; Prometheus Press offers a paperback version together with *The Communist Manifesto*, 1988) is a good place to start. Better yet, John E. Elliott provides a wide sampling in his edited collection, *Marx and Engels on Economics, Politics and Society: Essential Readings with Editorial Commentary* (Goodyear, 1981). Robert Freedman provides a wonderful introductory overview of Marxism in general in his thin book, *The Marxist System: Economic, Political, and Social Perspectives* (Chatham House, 1990). Richard D. Wolff and Stephen A. Resnick offer a readable introduction to Marxist economic theory, juxtaposed against neoclassicism, in *Economics: Marxian versus Neoclassical* (Johns Hopkins University Press, 1987), which should be understandable to students with some previous exposure to microeconomic theory. *A Dictionary of Marxist Thought*, edited by Tom Bottomore (2nd ed., Blackwell, 1991) is an indispensable reference to Marxism's economics, philosophy, and history. Also see Philip Arestis and Malcolm C. Sawyer, eds., *The Elgar Companion to Radical Political Economy* (Edward Elgar, 1994), which also includes articles in the Post Keynesian and Institutionalist traditions. Serious students may try to tackle Leszek Kolakowski's three-volume set, *Main Currents of Marxism: Its Rise, Growth, and Dissolution* (Clarendon Press, 1978), which offers a magisterial history of the subject.

Classics in the European tradition include Eduard Bernstein's *Evolutionary Socialism: A Criticism and Affirmation* (1899; reprinted by Schocken Books, 1961) and Rosa Luxemburg's critical reply, *Reform or Revolution* (1898–1899; 2nd ed., reprinted by Pathfinder Press, 1973), Rudolf Hilferding's *Finance Capital: A Study of the Latest Phase of Capitalist Development* (1910; Routledge & Kegan Paul, 1985), V. I. Lenin's *The State and Revolution* (1917; International Publishers, 1943), and Nikolai Bukharin's criticism of the Austrian School in *Economic Theory of the Leisure Class* (1914; reprinted by Monthly Review Press, 1972). Also see Eugen Boehm-Bawerk's 1896 essay, *Karl Marx and the Close of His System* (reprinted by Augustus Kelley, 1973), which includes a response by Hilferding to Boehm-Bawerk's Austrian criticisms.

The American tradition is evidenced by Paul A. Baran and Paul M. Sweezy, *Monopoly Capital: An Essay on the American Economic and Social Order* (Monthly Review Press, 1966), Harry Braverman's *Labor and Monopoly Capital: The Degradation of Work in the Twentieth Century* (Monthly Review Press, 1975), and the joint work of Samuel Bowles and Herbert Gintis: *Schooling in Capitalist America: Educational Reform and the Contradictions of Economic Life* (Basic Books, 1976) and *Democracy and Capitalism: Property, Community and the Contradictions of Modern Social Life* (Basic Books, 1986). Also see John E. Roemer's *Free to Lose: An Introduction to Marxist Economic Philosophy* (Harvard University Press, 1988), which is something of a Marxist reply to Milton Friedman's *Free to Choose* (HBJ, 1979).

The case for decentralized, self-managed socialism is most developed in Branko Horvat's *The Political Economy of Socialism: A Marxist Social Theory* (M. E. Sharpe, 1982). The two-volume set, *Self-Governing Socialism: A Reader*, edited by Branko Horvat, Mihailo Markovic, and Rudi Supek (International Arts and Sciences Press, 1975) offers a wide selection of historical and contemporary essays. For an analytical model of such a system, see Michael Albert and Robin Hahnel, *The Political Economy of Participatory Economics* (Princeton University Press, 1991). The (largely neoclassical) self-management literature is thoroughly surveyed in John P. Bonin and Louis Putterman, *The Economics of Cooperation and the Labor-Managed Economy* (Harwood Academic, 1987), and the classic articles are collected in David L. Prychitko and Jaroslav Vanek, eds., *Producer Cooperatives and Labor-Managed Systems, vol. I: Theory* and *vol. II: Case Studies*, 62 in *The International Library of Critical Writings in Economics* (Edward Elgar, 1996).

The reawakened interest in market socialism comes to the fore in the well-written essays from the pages of *Dissent* magazine, collected in Frank Roosevelt and David Belkin, eds., *Why Market Socialism?: Voices from Dissent* (M. E. Sharpe, 1994). Also see Julian Le Grand and Saul Estrin, eds., *Market Socialism* (Clarendon Press, 1989), and Pranab K. Bardhan and John E. Roemer, eds., *Market Socialism: The Current Debate* (Oxford University Press, 1993). Alec Nove's *The Economics of Feasible Socialism* (George Allen & Unwin, 1983) helped rekindle the current interest. Finally, see Hilary Wainwright's *Arguments for a New Left: Answering the Free Market Right* (Blackwell, 1994) for a serious consideration of the Austrian criticism of socialist planning, and an attempted answer.

Journals in the tradition include *Monthly Review, Review of Radical Political Economics, Rethinking Marxism, Cambridge Journal of Economics, Research in Political Economy, Telos,* and *Praxis International.*

New Philosophical Considerations

Interest in the philosophy and methodology of economics has exploded since the 1980s, and cuts across all the alternative schools of thought. In addition to *History of Political Economy* and the annual *Research in the History of Economic Thought and Methodology*, both of which publish philosophical and methodological articles, two specialized journals have emerged, *Economics and Philosophy* and *Journal of Economic Methodology* (formerly *Methodus*). For general introductions to the subject, see the highly readable work of Bruce Caldwell, *Beyond Positivism: Economic Methodology in the Twentieth Century* (Routledge, 2nd ed., 1995) and John Pheby, *Methodology and Economics: A Critical Introduction* (M. E. Sharpe, 1991). The following are also worth the effort: Daniel Hausman, *The Inexact and Separate Science of Economics* (Cambridge University Press, 1992)) and Philip Mirowski's pragmatist-oriented, *Against Mechanism: Protecting Economics from Science* (Rowman and Littlefield, 1988). The latter offers a fine criticism of economists' enamoration with the method of the so-called hard sciences. Donald Polkinghorne's *Methodology for the Human Sciences: Systems of Inquiry* (SUNY Press, 1983) makes for a solid introduction to, and comparison of, the postpositivist methodologies of the social sciences in general.

Feminism in economics is the hot topic for the 1990s. Marianne A. Ferber and Julie A. Nelson edited the first book on the subject, *Beyond Economic Man: Feminist Theory and Economics* (University of Chicago Press, 1993). Also see Chris Beasley's entertaining (if not frustrating) work, *Sexual Economyths: Conceiving a Feminist Economics* (St. Martin's, 1994). The journal *Feminist Economics* has also recently been launched.

The loosely interpretive slant of Albert Hirschman's essay is further explored in the useful readers of Norma Haan, et al., eds., *Social Science as Moral Inquiry* (Columbia University Press, 1983) and Paul Rabinow and William Sullivan, eds., *Interpretive Social Science: A Reader* (University of California Press, 1979). Some economists have begun to explore hermeneutics as a potential interpretive methodology. See, for example, the diverse essays collected in Don Lavoie ed., *Economics and Hermeneutics* (Routledge, 1991). Perhaps the best introduction to hermeneutics is Richard J. Bernstein's *Beyond Objectivism and Relativism: Science, Hermeneutics, and Praxis* (University of Pennsylvania Press, 1983). Also refer back to Frank Knight's 1940 article, "'What Is Truth' in Economics?," reprinted in his *On the History and Method of Economics: Selected Essays* (University of Chicago Press, 1956), for an early defense of the interpretive approach to economic understanding.

For a discussion of the role of "paradigms" in the sciences (a term employed throughout many of the preceding chapters), see the pathbreaking work of Thomas Kuhn, *The Structure of Scientific Revolutions* (2nd enlarged ed., University of Chicago Press, 1970); start with the book's postscript. Readers of Kuhn may find the term used too loosely in the social sciences (see, e.g., Albert Hirschman's essay "The Search for Paradigms as a Hindrance to Understanding" in the above-mentioned Rabinow and Sullivan book). For discussion of the "hard core" of economic theory, see Spiro J. Latsis, ed., *Method and Appraisal in Economics* (Cambridge University Press, 1976). For postmodernism (another term with many meanings), see the rather different treatments in Richard Rorty, *Philosophy and the Mirror of Nature* (Princeton University Press, 1979) and Frederic Jameson's *Postmodernism, or the Cultural Logic of Late Capitalism* (Duke University Press, 1991). Postmodern aspects of economics have been discussed by Sheila C. Dow, "Are There Any Signs of Postmodernism with Economics?," *Methodus*, vol. 3, no. 1 (June 1991), David Ruccio, "Economics and Postmodernism," *Journal of Post Keynesian Economics*, vol. 13, no. 4 (Summer 1991), and Theodore A. Burczak, "The Postmodern Moments of F. A. Hayek's Economics," *Economics and Philosophy*, vol. 10 (1994). See Roy Bhaskar's *A Realist Theory of Science* (Humanities Press, 1978) for the realist position. For the pragmatist position that guides much of institutionalism, see John Dewey's *Essays on Pragmatism and Truth* (Southern Illinois University Press, 1977).

The positive-normative dichotomy was first clearly elaborated by John Neville Keynes (father of Maynard) (see his *Scope and Method of Political Economy* [4th ed. 1917; reprinted by Augustus Kelley, 1986]) and later became a guiding principle of neoclassical (and Austrian) economics with Lionel Robbins's *An Essay on the Nature and Significance of Economic Science* (2nd ed. 1935; reprinted by New York University Press, 1984) (some Austrians, however, have begun to question the value-free aspects of applied theory: see Mario J. Rizzo, "The Mirage of Efficiency," *Hofstra Law Review*, 8 (3) (Spring 1980) and Jack High "Is Economics Independent of Ethics?," *Reason Papers* 10 (Spring 1985)). On the role played by values and ideology in economics, it's still hard to beat Gunnar Myrdal's classic, *The Political Element in the Development of Economic Theory* (1954; reprinted by Transaction Publishers, 1990). But don't overlook Joseph Schumpeter's essay, "Science and Ideology," *American Economic Review*, vol. 39 (1949), reprinted in Daniel M. Hausman, ed., *The Philosophy of Economics: An Anthology* (Cambridge University Press, 1984). Schumpeter's notion of ideological "vision" versus scientific "analysis" finds renewed application in the recent work of Robert L. Heilbroner and William Milberg, *The Crisis of Vision in Modern Economic Thought* (Cambridge University Press, 1995). (For an early criticism of Heilbroner's position, see Peter J. Boettke, "Analysis and Vision in Economic Discourse," *Journal of the History of Economic Thought*, vol. 14 [Spring 1992].) Also see Homa Katouzian, *Ideology and Method in Economics* (New York University Press, 1980) and Conrad P. Waligorski's *The Political Theory of Conservative Economists* (University of Kansas Press, 1990). For a radical statement on science itself as ideology, see Paul Feyerabend's *Science in a Free Society* (NLB, 1978).

The best source for the rhetoric of economics comes from Donald McCloskey, who wrote the book, *The Rhetoric of Economics* (University of Wisconsin Press, 1985). Then refer to Arjo Klamer, Robert M. Solow, and D. N. McCloskey, eds., *The Consequences of Economic Rhetoric* (Cambridge University Press, 1988), and Warren Samuels, ed., *Economics as Discourse* (Kluwer Academic, 1990). Axel Leijonhufvud's "Life Among the Econ" (in his *Information and Coordination: Essays in Macroeconomic Theory* [Oxford University Press, 1981]) offers an entertaining and all-too-true "anthropological" discussion of the symbols, totems, and myths of that strange tribe known as the Econ. For a sense of how many leading neoclassical economists view their work against that of their opponents, see Arjo Klamer's *Conversations with Economists: New Classical Economists and Their Opponents Speak Out on the Current Controversy in Macroeconomics* (Rowman and Allanheld, 1984). For the perhaps tragic effect the formalist impulse has had on our current generation of students, see Arjo Klamer and David Colander, *The Making of an Economist* (Westview Press, 1990).

The Journal of Economic Methodology, vol. 1, no. 1 (June 1994) published a symposium on "Why Is There So Much Disagreement in Economics?" The participants disagreed. And finally, who said everybody agrees on the effects of a minimum wage? See the paper by David Card and Alan B. Krueger, titled "Minimum Wages and Employment: A Case Study of the Fast Food Industry in New Jersey and Pennsylvania," in the profession's leading journal, the *American Economic Review*, vol. 84, no. 4 (September 1994).

CONTRIBUTORS

Jack Amariglio	Department of Economics, Merrimack College
Paul Davidson	Department of Economics University of Tennessee, Knoxville,
William M. Dugger	Department of Economics, University of Tulsa
Alfred S. Eichner	formerly Department of Economics, Rutgers University
Roger W. Garrison	Department of Economics, Auburn University
Albert O. Hirschman	Institute for Advanced Study, Princeton
Geoffrey M. Hodgson	Judge Institute of Management Studies, University of Cambridge
Israel M. Kirzner	Department of Economics, New York University
Arjo Klamer	Art and Cultural Sciences, Erasmus University
J.A. Kregel	Department of Economic Science, University of Bologna
Ludwig M. Lachmann	formerly Professor Emeritus, Department of Economics, University of Witwatersrand
Tony Lawson	Faculty of Economics and Politics, University of Cambridge
Deirdre McCloskey	Departments of Economics and History, University of Iowa, and Erasmus University
David L. Prychitko	Department of Economics, Northern Michigan University
David F. Ruccio	Department of Economics, University of Notre Dame
Warren J. Samuels	Department of Economics, Michigan State University
Howard J. Sherman	Department of Economics, University of California, Riverside
William R. Waters	Department of Economics, DePaul University
Thomas E. Weisskopf	Department of Economics, University of Michigan, Ann Arbor
Frances R. Woolley	Department of Economics, Carleton University

INDEX

Index